Vorse receiving the UAW Social Justice Award, 1962. Left to right: Mary Heaton Vorse, Upton Sinclair, Eleanor Roosevelt, Walter Reuther. Photo: Archives of Labor and Urban Affairs, Wayne State University

# REBEL PEN

### The Writings of
## *Mary Heaton Vorse*

### *edited by Dee Garrison*

Monthly Review Press • New York

*HD*
*8072*
*.V755*
*1985*

"The Pink Fence" is reprinted by permission of
the McCall Publishing Company.


Copyright © 1985 Dee Garrison

*Library of Congress Cataloging in Publication Data*

Vorse, Mary Heaton, 1874–1966.
  Rebel pen.
  Includes index.
  1. Labor and laboring classes—United States—
1914–    —Addresses, essays, lectures.  2. Strikes
and lockouts—United States—Addresses, essays,
lectures.  3. Women—History—Addresses, essays,
lectures.  I. Garrison, Dee.  II. Title.
HD8072.V755  1985    331.4'0973    85-7130
ISBN 0-85345-669-0
ISBN 0-85345-670-4 (pbk.)

Monthly Review Press
155 West 23rd Street
New York, N.Y. 10011

Manufactured in the United States of America

10 9 8 7 6 5 4 3 2 1

# Contents

❧

# Introduction

*by Dee Garrison*

Four years before her death, in May 1962, Mary Heaton Vorse entered the twenty-fifth anniversary celebration of the Detroit-based United Auto Workers (UAW) on Walter Reuther's arm. The assemblage parted to make way—a swirl of applause, smiles, popping flashbulbs. Reuther presented her with the first UAW Social Justice Award, originally conceived to pay her recognition: "With admiration, affection and in thankful appreciation for your years of dedicated and unselfish devotion to the cause of labor and our common struggles to extend the frontiers of social justice. Through your years of writing you have been a continuing source of hope and inspiration to workers as they fought to win fuller and richer lives for their families."

Eleanor Roosevelt and Upton Sinclair were there to share her honor, all faces turned to hers, everyone applauding in a long, standing ovation. The photographs show a frail woman supported by others, wearing a new brocaded jacket, her large eyes predominant in an aged face lightened and softened by pleasure. She was eighty-eight—now the Grand Old Lady of labor, again the living symbol of a heroic era. The members of the cheering audience fused for that one moment, imposing upon her their deeply cherished, bigger-than-life memories of courage, struggle, meaning.

Mary Heaton Vorse could look back on fifty-four years of her life spent in active battle for egalitarian socialism, feminism, and world peace. It was a union of ideas which had been far too radical for most of her peers to consider. Many who knew her saw her life as hard and generally unrewarded strife, even while they marveled at her accomplishments and grit. Their vision was often determined by their misplaced pity that she had no male companion or material comfort to ease her last four decades. They could not believe that she deliberately followed that path. But Mary Vorse was content and held few regrets. Her tenacious insurgence was her rich bequest, to our present as much as to our history.

Labor journalist, foreign correspondent, union activist, Mary Vorse was also for many years one of the most popular women writers in the nation. For over three decades, she supported her three children and financed her political work through the freelance sale of short fiction

7

and articles to major magazines and journals. She wrote of women's lives, war and peace, and reported national and international politics, labor and radical movements throughout the world. Tens of millions of American readers were agitated and informed by her interpretation of world events, labor battles, and feminist demands. Her impassioned reporting pulled her audience to newer, more radical visions of democracy and justice. Above all, Vorse brought her readers better understanding of the growing power in the world of the socialist ideal—the force which so marked their time and challenged their past.

An innate rebel, Mary Heaton Vorse was a versatile and lively companion. Her intellect was balanced by energetic movement. There was hardly an important writer, radical, or reformer of her time whom she did not know personally. Her circles of close friends spanned the gap between literati and laborers, activists and aesthetes. She was welcomed as confidante by renowned literary figures and impoverished sharecroppers alike. She moved easily from Edmund Wilson and Mary Austin to Bill Haywood and Josephine Herbst, between Ernest Hemingway and Emma Goldman, from Frances Perkins to Mother Jones, from sophisticated literary salons and luncheons with senators to picket lines, feminist rallies, and Wobbly strategy sessions.

But Vorse's most significant achievement was her participation in virtually every American social movement which championed greater power for workers, racial minorities, and women; world peace; or economic democracy during her lifetime. Again and again, she sensed the moment and moved to the appropriate place where action would begin. She was present at major strikes and international hot spots, always in the vanguard of key political movements for change. Mary Vorse was a character dominated by the great social movements that operated under the surface of events. We are all to some extent such characters in a life only partly self-directed, moved by men and women we never knew or understood. But far more than most, Vorse's life rode the currents of unionization, of radical revolt, of feminism, and was tossed to and fro by all their defeats and advances.

By the 1920s Vorse had won a comfortable reputation and income from the sale of her light fiction. But in 1930, at age fifty-six, she purposely renounced material ease, determined thenceforth to concentrate her efforts on labor reporting. This resolve considerably strengthened her self-respect, but seriously depleted her income. By the 1950s Vorse had become financially dependent upon a meager income from rental of rooms in her beachtown home and the occasional charity from her friends.

When Mary Vorse died in 1966 at age ninety-two, she had published nothing in the past decade, and a mere two articles in the decade before. Her passing was only briefly noted by the mass-circulation media. Like a quick and guilty bow to an honored—but outdated and vaguely intimidating—past, *Time* ran her six-line obituary. The *New York Times* noted her exit under a two-column headline: MARY HEATON VORSE, A NOVELIST AND CHAMPION OF LABOR, DEAD, FIGURE AT MAJOR STRIKES OF '20's and '30's—REPORTED FROM EURUPE BEFORE WAR.

Essentially, however, Vorse's work did not survive her. With the advent of Big Labor, her literary reputation became nonexistent. With the beginning of the Cold War, her style of politics was forcibly quieted. With the ascendance of the Feminine Mystique, her generation of fighters lay largely forgotten.

But no matter. Mary Vorse perfectly understood the process of the momentary extinction of her work—for all her life and all her writing had centered upon the relationship between individual and society. Times were sure to change, she knew even in her last years, as she prepared her papers for deposit in Detroit's new library of labor history. She was confident that her experience had lessons to teach another generation. She fully expected to be studied and understood. Her life had carried exceptional impact. Her ideas would endure.

The lifestyle of Mary Vorse caught the attention of several of her male contemporaries. Curiously, each focused on her symbolic value as emblem for an age or an ideal, yet each drew a different meaning from her life. In 1918, when John Reed sat moldering in a Finnish prison, jotting notes for an autobiography, he wrote her name as representative of his education in prewar Greenwich Village. After the war, Malcolm Cowley, in *Exile's Return*, defined Mary Vorse as symbolic of the older set that graced the Village at its peak—"the oddly dressed remnants of an age that had just passed into history," as Gilbert Ostrander put it.

Intrigued by her valor, John Dos Passos, who knew Vorse well, took her life as counterpart for Mary French, one of the twelve main characters in his classic trilogy, *U.S.A.* Later, in his right-wing period, Dos Passos returned to Mary Vorse as model for his portrayal of Anne Comfort in his semiautobiographical novel, *Chosen Country*. Dos Passos admired Mary Vorse's devotion to purpose. Yet he found her essentially a tragic, although sympathetic, figure, her life made doubly vulnerable as a woman and as a radical. He used her to express his themes of democratic idealism corrupted by communism and of womanhood defeated by ancient circumstance.

Murray Kempton was another who fastened on Mary Vorse as symbol. In the mid-1950s, Kempton was sickened by the anti-American activity of Red-hunting congressmen and the neutrals, knaves, or cowards who gave them rein. In *Part of Our Time: Some Ruins and Monuments of the Thirties*, he wrote of the Communists and radicals of the

1930s, not so much in judgment as in explanation of their foibles and their strengths. Kempton found few admirable persons among them, and none so worthy as Mary Vorse. The American revolutionaries of the 1930s, he said (and he counted himself among them), were a dismally ignorant radical generation. He argued they knew little of Gandhi, Bill Haywood, or Rosa Luxemburg. According to Kempton, the radicals of the thirties thought themselves the agents of history, without consciousness of their own history.

> They seemed to think they had sprung full-blown; if they had models, they were European. They sang a folksong about Joe Hill, the IWW poet, but very few could tell you who Joe Hill was or how he lived and died . . . Mary Vorse was a living figure from Joe Hill's tradition. The scorned and ragged rebels of the first three decades of the century might logically have considered the thirties a time of redemption in which their survivors would be treated as triumphant saints. It does not appear to have been that way for Mary Vorse, who in any case would hardly have asked so much. She traveled her road and it is safe to assume that most of the girl comrades . . . had never even heard of her. . . . Mary Vorse lived on because she found her love young and neither forsook nor was forsaken. For Mary Vorse had joined the avenging army in 1913, because men and women were suffering for its triumph. (p. 217)

Unsung Mary Vorse "brought to her old age no need for survival," Kempton wrote. "She had been not *in* history, but *of* history. The chronicles which cover her life span had small room for her name. . . . She had known so many people so long ago, and she had buried most of them." (pp. 215–16)

Crystal and Max Eastman, Margaret Sanger, Clarence Darrow, Lincoln Steffens, Lillian Wald, Elizabeth Gurley Flynn, Carlo Tresca, Roger Baldwin, all had gathered in her Greenwich Village apartment so many years before. Bleeding young urban Wobblies had been bandaged in her New York brownstone. She had once loved a famous anarchist, who became a Communist and then left her for another woman. "For a while she was close to the Communists herself in the twenties," Kempton recalled, "but never in any easy, comfortable, ceremonial sense. Her chief labor for them had been publicity for their Passaic, New Jersey, textile strike in 1926. But that had just been one of so many others, Wobbly strikes, independent uprisings, AFL and CIO strikes, the quiet ones and the noisy ones."

Kempton's portrayal of Mary Vorse left her at a CIO convention in 1949, during a coal strike.

> She bore up under all the attentions for three days. Then the things of state were too much for her, and she went back to the coal mines, saying. . . . "There's an old fellow in Charleroi I knew long ago in the Wobblies. He always tells me what's going on. I'll have to tell Phil

[Murray]; he'll remember him. One of the old fellows, one of the very old ones."

And she was gone to the bus station, her legs a little stiff, her eyes a little rheumy, because she was, after all, seventy-five years old. To have pledged yourself and to have forsaken all others for forty years, to have understood that to love is to abandon sleep and comfort and the ease of age, and to follow, always to follow, the desperate road love sets out for you, such was the limit of the rebel girl's commitment. Mary Vorse sat in her bus as upon a burnished throne. (p. 232)

What has been the hold of Mary Vorse on so many observers? Her name is not popularly known even today, yet her books, short stories, and articles have been reprinted frequently, from the 1940s to the 1980s, most recently when her fiction was featured in *Ms*. Like a green tulip tip pressing through soil made warm by cyclic design, the memory of Mary Heaton Vorse recurrently emerges, as in the 1985 vignette of her life presented as part of the series "American Portraits" on CBS television. All those intrigued by her path hold in common their sense of her uncommon faith, of her dedication to a cause which they honor even if they doubt its victory. Kempton saw her story as pathos, as faith denied by history. Dos Passos, even more sadly, saw faith betrayed by an undeserving male and by the unworthy and uncaring human mass. These two authors contrast Vorse's humanism with the orthodox Communist's disdain for the individual in favor of some mightier, more distant triumph of "the masses." Kempton and Dos Passos share an entranced vision of Mary Vorse that lifts her well apart from their other dubious ladies. For a symbol is, after all, an epitome linked to mysticism and sacrament. There is mystery in a symbol, image for timelessness, slyly disquieting even to the symbolmakers themselves.

That such a legacy should almost vanish from historical consciousness gives credence to Murray Kempton's suggestion that each generation of radicals dismisses its predecessors as irrelevant. But this is only part ground for historical oversight. Male bias played its crucial role. Until very recently, women—if they surfaced at all in literary and political annals—survived best as useful support to male storytellers. Mary Vorse had no long-term attachment to any important male; she was not a figure closely associated with any political group. She was the most brilliant of journalists, but labor journalism, the field in which she made her name, effectively expired with the end of the great labor wars. And her serious fiction, with the exception of some short stories, falls short of genius. The silences and diminutions uniquely imposed upon women writers, from sources both external and internal, are other explanations for women's historical invisibility.

Mary Vorse would have been more honored if she had been more conventional. She fit nowhere into the shifting political groupings of the 1920s and after. She was not among those like Dos Passos or Edna St. Vincent Millay who were shattered by the execution of Sacco and Vanzetti. In Paris on the night of the deathwatch, she did not even attend the last ritual. She had long laid down the illusion that reasoned appeals alone could cancel capitalist-fueled repression of radicalism. Nor did she share the illusion of Communists, who drew new, hard assurance from the fate of the two men, and who even believed that the compromises of liberalism had helped to kill them.

Vorse learned the failure of the Communist promise through personal experience, while in Hungary in 1919, in Moscow in 1921, and at the textile strikes of the 1920s in Passaic and Gastonia. She learned far earlier than many of her socially engaged friends, and her popularity fell victim to her premature cognizance. More famous liberals and radicals lost their faith after the purge trials, or the 1934 Madison Square Garden brawl, or the Spanish Civil War, or the 1939 Communist flipflop. But it was the Bolshevik massacre of Russian peasants which began in the late 1920s that Vorse could neither accept nor forgive.

If she too early failed to accept the intricacies of "revolutionary necessity," she also stumbled at the point where liberals and democratic socialists turned right. She refused to publicly bait the Communist rank and file in the union trenches. She knew they often served justice with more constancy and courage than most. Vorse never confused the embattled labor activist, many of whom were women, with the Communist office functionary, or the carping bystander, most of whom were men. She cared little for abstraction. She judged people by what they did, not by what they said, by their action, not their theory. She always understood the distinction between the immense club of official power and the tiny barb of the radical few. She did not admire those inactive on the sidelines who felt compelled, with righteous fervor, to continue beating and beating the dead horse of American communism. More than that, she shamed those who did. Her usefulness to many political and literary figures lessened accordingly.

Not liberal, Red, or aroused anti-Communist, she eluded categorization. At a time when Communist officials knew her to be unreliable and unreasonable, the federal spy-hunters harassed her for over forty years. In 1944 the FBI placed her on the list of dangerous citizens to be immediately jailed on presidential order. To assure her rapid arrest, the agency maintained an up-to-date record of her location at least until 1956, when she was eighty-two years old. Mary Vorse was too big to fit into any momentarily popular slot.

In addition to her labor and newspaper work, Vorse published sixteen books and hundreds of short stories. Twice a widow, she wrote light romantic fiction for the women's magazines in order to support her family. After 1930 it was only when she quite literally ran out of money, and that was often, that she would hole up to dash off another "lollipop" to pay her way for a few more months. Financial necessity was the main cause of her having to write so swiftly, mimicking her own style with ease. Her public demanded nothing more. The work meant economic survival for her family. Vorse's popular fiction is a reliable guidebook to women's changing concerns over fifty years. Many of these stories rise above formula to provide stunning apparitions of female unity and discontent.

Mary Vorse's three serious novels are less impressive, chiefly because she could not bring herself to searching analysis of her own tragic experiences. Human frailty unexamined too often slid over into fictional characters without sufficient depth or nuance. Sealed corridors in her emotional life deprived her of certain sensibilities. As she admitted to her diary in 1926: "I go through death and despair. I look down the abyss. I go through a time when my hand no longer guides life, through a long recuperation [from morphine addiction; characteristically, she would not inspect the ruins, even in her diary], and not a word of it appears in my stories." Years of writing light romantic fiction took its price. It was easy to produce. It required no painful self-inspection and was infinitely more marketable. Vorse realized that her writing would have developed quite differently if she had been less rushed, if her work had met with more judicious criticism, if she had been less burdened as homemaker, mother, breadwinner.

Tillie Olsen, Joanna Russ, and others have detailed the daunting deterrents to women writers. They describe the fear of impropriety, the lack of female models or a female literary tradition, the inclusion of only extraordinary women authors in the literary canon, and the devaluation of women's experience and consequent attitudes, values, and judgments as less representative or less important than male experience. If a woman wrote frankly of women's lives or women's rage, she was usually censored, or, if published, judged "confessional" or an unhappy hysteric. If she compromised and wrote of kitchens and romance, her work was termed "minor." Foremost among these discouraging obstacles to women writers through the ages, the simple lack of time in which to write is surely the most common and the most heartbreaking handicap.

Few women writers suffered more desperately from lack of self-permission, space, quiet, and leisure to write than Mary Vorse. She put it simply: "When you are father and mother both you soon learn to choose. There are a great many things which it is pleasant to do and desirable to do which one may not do." To evade familial obligations in order to create and think became her obsession and her crushing self-

blame. In mid-life, for seven tortuous years, Vorse collapsed completely under the guilt. "I will do my writing at odd moments. Do it
now and then. Hide it. . . . I will arrange my work so the children will
be barely conscious of it," she once vowed during that long eclipse. We
all know the impossibility of being full-time writer, full-time housekeeper and mother, full-time breadwinner—to add labor activist and
reporter is to push beyond imagination. So Mary's family suffered, and
her house, and her writing, and her literary reputation. Yet she
fulfilled all roles, usually well, sometimes badly, often just barely.

Certainly Mary Vorse was not a typical woman in any obvious sense.
Still, her experiences parallel those of many women of her time. As
women's studies scholar Elaine Showalter has noted, there were important differences between the "modern women" of Mary's generation and the earlier generation of achieving women in the United
States. The earlier feminist group, born near the middle of the
nineteenth century, had recognized that for them, marriage and public
activity were mutually exclusive. These older feminists, suffragists,
and professionals had fought for the right of women to "free" themselves from domesticity and motherhood in order to become active in
the working world or in social reform movements. They accepted the
necessity of a choice between raising a family and forging a career.
Liberation for the earlier group of women had often included the
denial of a female sexual appetite. For many this became a source of
strength, drawn from their supposed spiritual superiority over men
and from their intense emotional bonding with other women.

By contrast, feminists of Vorse's age claimed the right to career,
marriage, *and* motherhood. Unlike their older models, they did not
want to purchase independence at the price of celibacy or childless-
ness. This newer generation of feminists painfully overcame the
puritanism of their childhood and freely acknowledged their sexual
needs. In the process, although they gained much, they also lost the
older reliance on a support system of homosocial bonding. Vorse and
her cohort also tended to blame themselves for their general failure to
successfully combine love and work, rather than directly accusing the
basic assumptions of a male-dominated society. Their struggles and
disappointed expectations set the basis for contemporary feminism,
which insists that role conflict is a political problem, not just a personal
one. Mary Vorse, like many of her generation of talented and ambitious
women, would suffer as many defeats as victories in her quest for
fulfillment.

But perhaps Mary Vorse's life expresses more about the ageless
experience of women than it does about women's lives in her own
time. Women have recognized over the centuries the conflict that
bonds and separates mother and daughter. We understand the

difficulty of finding a supportive and durable male relationship. We share the pain of rejected love. Her joy, pride, and agonizing despair as a mother sound a common chord. Her sensitive encounter with the problems of aging reverberates in personal knowledge. And as women we know well the angry emptiness of exclusion and alienation.

There is at least one reliable measure of Mary Vorse. Across the space of half a century, wherever men and women battled for a wider justice, she was apt to have been there.

Her wholehearted commitment to labor's cause came late in life. She was a thirty-eight-year-old mother of two and already a well-known author when she arrived in Lawrence, Massachusetts, to report the famed textile strike of 1912. There, her past and present merged to produce that sudden, soundless click of recognition that forever changed the map of her world.

At Lawrence, the unity created among workers in struggle, their dedication and courage, her realization of the terrible human cost of profit making—all these affected Vorse so profoundly that it altered the course of her life. "I leaped lightly to my fate one morning when I got up and went out to get an order to go to Lawrence," she wrote later. "I entered into a way of life I never yet have left. . . . Before Lawrence, I had known a good deal about labor, but I had not felt about it. I had not got angry. In Lawrence, I got angry. . . . Some curious synthesis had taken place between my life and that of the workers, some peculiar change that would never again permit me to look with indifference on the fact that riches for the few were made by the misery of the many."

Born into a wealthy New England family in 1874, Vorse attended several private schools and the high school in Amherst, Massachusetts, for a brief time, but the bulk of her education came through travel and home instruction. Like most girls of her station, Mary was educated for the purpose of making a financially advantageous match. She was expected to live a restricted life at home until released into the only slightly larger confines of marriage and motherhood, doomed to repeat her restless mother's frenetic attempt to deplete unused energy and intellect. Buoyed by the same rising current that carried the New Woman of the time, Mary early decided that one way out of the snare set for leisured women was through devotion to a career. Thus in 1893, at age nineteen, she persuaded her parents to enrol her in a Parisian art school.

But the victory was short-lived, and she was whisked home to Amherst after a slight stint in Paris. There she shrank anew from her mother's "petty cares of material existence" and instead held to "windy ideas of independence and career." The inevitable clash between Mary's needs and her mother's demands could no longer be avoided.

Mary's love of liberty was rooted in her rebellion against Ellen Heaton's idleness and dominance. Mary sought release to make of herself what she wanted. Yet her thwarted mother could not give her a blessing to be different. It was an ancient tale. Her love for her mother was blurred by contempt and guilt. Her mother's lack of choice became her injury to her daughter.

Mary's ultimate "desertion" of Ellen was a bitter scene. Twenty-two and determined, Mary induced her parents to send her to a New York art school, but only after she threatened that she would go with or without her mother's blessing. She had joined another host, she wrote, "a smaller force, the army of women all over the country," who are "out to hurt their mother, who have to, in order to work," the "strange army of all the girls who in my mother's time could have stayed at home and I wonder what necessity sent us all out?" She added, "More and more of us coming all the time, and more of us will come until the sum of us will change the customs of the world, and as we change the world, the world is going to change us." But Mary Vorse paid a dreadful price for her victory. Her mother's attitude toward her underwent a subtle, but permanent, change. Ellen turned away from her daughter, not in anger, but in dismissal. Ellen Heaton never forgave her daughter her elopement into adventure.

Still, despite four years of devotion to art, Mary could not blind herself to the unexceptionable quality of her work. She confronted her limited artistic talent with honesty and reached the joyless decision to seek work as an illustrator. The displacement of libido from dreams of artistic success to the practical reality of finding a job with a living wage apparently increased her awareness of men. Her parents and friends also were beginning to worry, as they frequently reminded her, that she might never marry and find her place.

In 1898, Mary wed Albert Vorse, a newspaperman and aspiring author. Bert was slight, mustached, and masterful. His fiction betrayed his fondness for women with soft, clinging hands who were both daring *and* submissive, willing to serve as backdrop for his dashing maleness. Bert believed himself a lover, a maverick, and a writer. He would enjoy real success at the first two endeavors.

The newlyweds settled in Greenwich Village, where artists and writers sought inexpensive studios and apartments near Washington Square. It was a grand thing to be young, to pioneer a new century, to be "the forerunners of a new world," as Bert and Mary dubbed themselves. Mary dared to wear only one petticoat and no corset at all. In the cellar of the Brevoort Hotel, Mary and her friends, following the example of George Sand, lit cigarettes in defiance of the house rules forbidding women to smoke. She and Bert mingled with the Bohemian coterie associated with the literary and drama critic James Huneker.

They lived an ideal of youth, gaiety, and sophistication, with a certain daring born of middle-class comfort.

In 1902, her first son, Heaton, was born. Soon after came the first indication that Bert was overstepping the bounds of monogamy. Mary was devastated by her discovery of his less than constant concern for her happiness. Finally, in defeat, even seeking and following her mother's advice, she accepted his philandering in the approved female fashion—with sacrificial passivity. She formed a theory that it was only Bert's failure to succeed as a writer that made him compensate with a "new personal success" now and then. She resolved to smother his dissatisfaction with himself by her own calm. She would ease *his* suffering through her maternal solicitude. She would be as endlessly sweet and tireless as a mother with a sick child. Tied to a marriage that frustrated her ambition and eroded her happiness, Mary's denial of self was real enough, an exercise in female survival.

In 1903, Bert and Mary reached a crucial decision. In order that Bert might quit his job and thus have the chance to develop his writing, they would move to Europe where living was cheaper. It was agreed that Mary would also write, but only temporarily, and only to augment their income. Two years later, Bert had published almost nothing, whereas Mary had sold almost everything she wrote. By 1907, her earnings supported the family, which now included her daughter, Mary Ellen. Between 1906 and 1911, Mary published three well-received books and over sixty articles and short stories in major women's magazines and general-interest journals.

The difference between Bert's and Mary's mode of literary production became too apparent for either's comfort. Meanwhile, Bert blamed her for neglect of home and family and for being too busy to provide him with the essentials of domestic service. Mary blamed him for his weakness of will. She focused her fury on all "men who are small enough to want to feel superior." Soaring sales of her work brought Mary a new sense of self-worth. From denial of unseemly ambition, she moved to open resentment of his inability to accept her strengths. Bert and Mary decided on separation in 1909. After eleven years of marriage, something more than her affection for Bert had ended. She was also free of her compulsion to please and pamper him. She transcended that self which practiced perfect goodness in perfect fraud.

On June 15, 1910, a phase of Mary's life ended abruptly. On that date, aboard a ship in the Atlantic, she received word that both Bert and her mother were dead.

On June 14, Bert died of a cerebral hemorrhage while on an unexplained visit to Staten Island. He was found unconscious in a hotel room in the morning—alone. Mary's mother, after hearing of Bert's death, died of a heart failure in Amherst the next day.

Even after the lapse of many years, Mary Vorse avoided all discussion of the effect on her of the deaths. It is likely, though, that she best spoke through her fiction, when she described the feelings of a widowed woman whose marriage had also cooled long before her unfaithful husband died. She wrote, "It wasn't grief I felt—it wasn't loss. In some ways it is worse to feel nothing than to feel pain."

After 1910, Vorse never wavered in her resolve to support her children through freelance writing. This was a momentous decision, for the cushion of her mother's fortune was lost to her. As a final reproof of her willful lifestyle, her mother left her not a penny of inheritance.

The next two years mark a critical point in Mary Vorse's life. Three intense emotional experiences of that period inspired her lasting commitment to radical politics. She outgrew the last vestiges of instinct and thought that characterized the often indulged daughter of a privileged family. Her participation in the 1911 women's pure milk crusade against infant mortality in New York City taught her that babies' lives could be bought. Her observation of the Triangle Shirt Company fire, where 146 workers died as a result of management disregard of safety precautions, shook her with the furious knowledge that political corruption, greed, and official neglect had killed the Triangle women. The explosive force which Lawrence proved to be was thus a logical development. When the Industrial Workers of the World came east to organize the workers at Lawrence, Mary had another first-hand chance to learn about class warfare—and she was ready to reorient her life.

Mary traveled to Lawrence with Joe O'Brien, a freelance reporter whom she married in 1912. Joe was a hard-drinking, high-spirited socialist and feminist. He won her heart with his sense of humor and *joie de vivre*. Most wonderful of all, Joe genuinely supported her need to write and achieve. Finally,,he was an eager new father to her two children and gladly shared household chores. Mary introduced Joe to her beloved Provincetown, Massachusetts, summer home, acquired in 1907. In 1914, her third child, Joel, would be born. Living seemed full, precious, and symmetrical.

In Greenwich Village, Mary and Joe were happily situated at the center of a social revolution. Beginning in 1912 and lasting until the 1917 entry of the United States into World War I, the Village was the heart of intellectual, artistic, and radical life in the United States. Mary Vorse was the core about which many of the Village cognoscenti gathered. As an editor of the *Masses* and a charter member of the Liberal Club, she functioned both as a conduit for the younger men and women entering the world of the *avant garde* and as a central participant in the ongoing revolt. Due to her influence, Provincetown became a kind of suburb for the New York intelligentsia. The famed Provincetown Players were born in 1915 on her fish wharf. In 1912 she helped to found that Village nursery of modern feminism, the remarkable Heterodoxy Club. Just as Lawrence shaped her social outlook, her experience at Heterodoxy and at the Women's International Suffrage Convention held at Budapest, in 1913, determined her feminist vision. Mary Vorse flourished in the intense excitement of Village life and forever remembered those too brief, fluid days as the most joyful of her experience.

During the abnormally cold winter of 1914, Vorse's New York house became the staging center for the IWW-led branch of the unemployed movement. What had begun for her at Lawrence was now hammered into shape, as her friends came in with their heads laid open by police clubs or disappeared into jail on trumped-up charges. But by the summer of 1914 Mary's most compelling concern was Joe's sudden illness. Although neither of them yet knew it, he had stomach cancer. Mary was offered a chance to serve as the Women's Suffrage Party of New York City delegate to the women's peace congress held at the Hague in 1915, and to report the war in Europe for several American magazines. Joe, seemingly much recovered, insisted that she go, while he stayed home to care for the children.

In her tour of the war zones, Vorse was driven to report the effect of war on the ordinary people in Europe, especially on women and children. She deliberately ignored the great diplomatic and military events of the time. Fresh from the women's peace congress, her understanding of women as victims and rescuers in wartime dominated her interests. In 1915, the preposterous slaughter of modern war was writ large on the Western Front, where men, like dreamwalkers, advanced and retreated, dying by the tens of thousands to gain, or lose, a few hundred yards of earth. In Germany and France Vorse saw troop trains filled with soldiers carrying flowers in their gunstocks and laughing and drinking from bottles, happy young men en route to the places where they would be killed. "There is that which makes man his own enemy and every woman's," she wrote in her diary then. "Man takes passionate joy in risking his own life while he takes the life of others. When women's understanding of this becomes conscious, it is called feminism."

On her return from Europe in 1915, she found that the scenes of war had so saddened and shocked her that she would never again feel comfortable at play with the literati. She felt alienated from everyone but Joe, emotionally isolated from her old friends, unable to communicate what she had seen: "An explosion more far-reaching than that of Lawrence. A reevaluation of all life." In quick anticipation of a mood which would become general, Mary sensed the coming crisis in American Progressivism. In the throes of the spring of 1917 demoralization and division which would be created by the entry of the United States into war and by the revolution in Russia, the Villagers would all choose their different paths—some to cooperation with the Wilson administration, others to artistic retreat, a few to revolutionary commitment.

To complete Mary's desolation, Joe died suddenly in November 1915. For the second time in five years, she had become a widowed mother.

In the spring of 1916, Vorse's only break from worry over family and finances was her work with the suffrage movement and in support of Margaret Sanger's crusade for birth control. That year, she went on to report the IWW-led mining strike on the Mesabi Range, where she served as a sort of co-leader to her close friend Elizabeth Gurley Flynn, and to cover the oil strike in Bayonne, New Jersey.

For the first time in her life, Vorse found she could not sell the light fiction which supported her family. She was convulsed as never before by her desire to escape daily responsibilities of childcare and household in order to write. It was now that her guilt-laden, desperate quest to retreat into lone peace began to assume the proportions of an obsession. It was chiefly her towering need for income that caused her to accept, with gratitude, a series of writing assignments from the Committee of Public Information—the American propaganda mill during the war. Vorse's contribution was three pamphlets written to convince the "captive" peoples of Yugoslavia, Czechoslovakia, and Poland that their best hope for the future lay in Woodrow Wilson's postwar utopia of democracy and self-determination. In early 1918 Mary still hoped that the presence of liberals in American government would enable the creation of an economic democracy. But she was quickly forced into a new political consciousness. The aftermath of war would teach her wrenching political lessons.

In response to widespread draft resistance, socialist protest, and labor militance during and after World War I, the federal and state governments and private vigilante groups used the cloak of patriotism to almost extinguish the organized left in the United States. By the time of the Armistice in November 1918, Mary had seen many of her most admired friends suffer arrest, trial, or jail. Her remaining faith in prewar and prowar liberalism disappeared.

Between 1919 and 1922, Mary Vorse lived apart from her children, whom she sent away to school or to live with relatives. Her fiction began to sell easily again. She reported postwar events in England, France, Italy, Austria, and Serbia for American magazines, the Red Cross, and the American Relief Administration (ARA). One of the few American reporters to visit Bela Kun's short-lived Communist Hungary, Mary's June 1919 visit was marked by her embroilment in political intrigue. She smuggled ARA documents out of Europe which showed the contribution of Herbert Hoover and ARA officials to the overthrow of Kun. On her return to the United States, she served as activist and publicist in the Great Steel Strike of 1919. Fearing she might be swept into the Red Scare nets, she persuaded Sidney Hillman, head of the Amalgamated Clothing Workers, to send her to the safety of the remote small towns in eastern Pennsylvania, where she went to work organizing shirtmakers. She later served as publicity agent for the union in the Amalgamated Lockout of 1920. Mary was one of the handful of American journalists first to tour the Russian famine area in 1921, several weeks before the male reporters from the great American dailies arrived. Hounded all the while by Red-hunting agents from the Department of Justice, she came home to report the 1922 United Mine Worker's strike and the campaign to free American political prisoners.

While in Paris in 1919, Vorse fell in love with egotistical and domineering Robert Minor, the famous American political cartoonist and anarchist. One year later Minor converted to communism. In early 1922 her affair with Minor ended disastrously, when four months pregnant with his child, she fell and suffered a miscarriage. While she was still in bed, he appeared in her room. He told her he was in love with a younger, more beautiful, more politically acceptable woman (who had no children and no career of her own and who would spend her honeymoon listening to Minor's instruction in Marxist theory). When Minor bid her an abrupt farewell, her despair was total. For she had suffered another tragedy even more devastating than the loss of her child or the rejection from Minor. As a result of her medical treatment after her miscarriage, she became addicted to morphine.

"I am imprisoned," she wrote in 1923. "I hold myself by free casting around to find a way out—the detail of the house is horrible and I crawl through as though expecting blows. I have the children about me and I function as mother, yet my life is intolerable to me. It offers me less at this moment than in all my life." Contrary goals and contradictory resolves brought her immense pain. Self-isolated by illness and dejection, she allowed herself only surface female friendships. And she permanently forsook love of all men, haunted for many years by longing for Robert Minor, whom she also hated.

In the 1920s, with the labor movement crushed, the feminist movement quieted, the reactionary Republican government empowered, Vorse returned home to be a mother. Her massive depression over her "failure" as a mother centered about the behavior problems of her defiant teenage daughter, Mary Ellen. For seven agonizing years, Vorse placed her work second to the presumed needs of her children. She felt she must pay whatever price necessary to compensate for the years spent away from them. Sunk in self-blame and, above all, guilt, she wallowed, shoved near the brink of death, found the courage to overcome her addiction, and, only partially understanding the whole experience, survived. When she finally surpassed debilitating self-sacrifice, she had learned little more than the necessity to leave her family.

Vorse returned to labor journalism as publicity director at the Passaic, New Jersey, textile strike of 1926. She fortuitously stepped into a power vacuum during the first weeks of the strike. The revolutionary publicity tactics she developed at Passaic would set the pattern for the successful techniques that marked the labor uprisings of the next decade. She was also a firstcomer to the southern textile wars, at Gastonia, North Carolina, in 1929, and in bloody Harlan County, Kentucky, in 1931, where her group, which included Edmund Wilson and Malcolm Cowley, was nearly killed before their expulsion from Kentucky by nightriders. The same prescience for what was about to become exciting and important took her to the unemployed marches in 1932, to the farmer's strikes in the Midwest, to the Scottsboro Boys' trial in 1933, to textile and mining strikes, and to the early New Deal offices in Washington, D.C., where, in her first and only salaried employment, she worked at the Indian Bureau under John Collier from 1935 to 1937. While in Washington, Vorse was associated with what would come to be called the "Ware group," a network of liberals and radicals later fated to receive wide attention for its connection to the Alger Hiss case.

With her uncanny ability to find her way to significant places at crucial moments, she was, of course, present at the pivotal struggle of the CIO at Chevrolet Plant Number Four in Flint, Michigan, on February 1, 1937, and went on to report CIO struggles across the nation. In 1937 her oldest son, a reporter for a labor press, was gravely wounded during a union skirmish in Indiana. A few weeks later, Vorse, at age sixty-three, was herself injured as she dived to escape ricocheting bullets from the guns of company guards during the Little Steel War in Youngstown, Ohio. Wearing a head bandage, she urged the strikers toward victory at a rally the next day. During the 1930s she also recorded the rise of Hitler, the demise of Labor in England and the scenes of Stalin's Soviet Union.

By the late 1930s Vorse was the acknowledged veteran of American labor journalism. The new career of labor reporter had been born in 1912 at the Lawrence textile strike, when, as never before, American readers had been provided generally accurate and comprehensive coverage of strike events in mainstream journals and the large dailies. The owner's brutality and the workers' living conditions had been well described at Lawrence, and the pressure of public opinion had been crucial to winning the strike. Not until the consolidation of the CIO victories, over three decades later, did the labor wars end, and with them the demand for labor journalism. Today, its survivors are channeled almost exclusively into the pages of union newspapers and the small radical press. But for forty years after Lawrence, the byline of Mary Heaton Vorse would represent the work of one of the earliest and most renowned of the new labor reporters.

The IWW leaders, and other beleaguered union organizers, were quick to recognize the supreme importance of publicity efforts by sympathetic and established reporters. Four years after the Lawrence strike, Bill Haywood would call on Vorse to serve in a similar fashion on the Mesabi Range. From that point on, Vorse was continually sought out by proponents of industrial unionism, from the IWW to the CIO, to provide the news coverage which could bridge the communication gap between union leadership and the general reading public. Her writing could compel interest and sympathy for the worker from an indifferent and even hostile audience. Vorse's measured, knowledgeable reports found easy entry into such middle-class journals as *Harper's, Scribner's, The Outlook,* and *The Independent,* outlets which were normally closed to writers too closely identified with left activists, and thus labeled as "propagandists" by the mainstream press. But Vorse also wrote for liberal intellectuals and reformers in such publications as *The Masses, The Nation,* and *The New Republic,* and for the workers themselves in her hundreds of dispatches for union newspapers, newsletters, and broadsides distributed by the labor press.

A consistent theme in her work is the need for industrial unionism. Year after year she exposed the failures and limitations of the AFL's goals and leadership. Her writing helped to convince many middle-class and working-class Americans of the wisdom of industrial labor organization.

Unlike many labor journalists, Vorse was often a participant in strike revolts. Her inside knowledge of union strategy and leadership, combined with her fervent commitment to accurate reporting, brought uncommon depth and passion to her work. Her middle-class readers, as well as her union friends, knew her version of events could be trusted. Always her writing was designed to make one feel, as well as think. For Vorse, a news story must include a re-creation of the human drama, as well as a recital of factual detail. Under her hand, the worker's determined faces, rough clothing, excited speeches, become visible and noisy. We feel the fear on the picket line as the armed goons or the awesome mounted police approach. We absorb the memory of the potted plant in a tin can on the miner's kitchen table, or the work-reddened hands of the miner's wife resting lightly on her son's shoulders, or the defiant strength of thousands of marching unionists. Cleanly shorn of maudlin sentiment, her reports are simple, direct, and often immensely moving—front-line dispatches from the war between the classes.

Yet Vorse's labor journalism was free of political dogma and strident rhetoric, in contrast, for example, to the crude *Daily Worker* style of harangues and exaggerations. Vorse followed a class analysis, to be sure, especially in her writing for the labor press, but the reality of class struggle was readily apparent to striking workers. At least before the New Deal years, unionists and their families hardly needed to be told that the owners, much of the economic elite, most public officials and religious figures, and the majority of the local police and judges, were allied against them in their struggle for a union. Vorse's basic appeal to every class of her readers was a call for common-sense application of traditional national ideals—liberty, equality, justice—all carefully placed within the ever-changing global context of the socialist movement.

But Vorse's most unique contribution to the labor journalism of her time is her consistent attention to the role played by women. Throughout her career, women and children interested her most. The worker's wife, the Serbian orphan, the starved children, the mean tenement home, the courage of girl pickets—these were the core of her material. Even today, the stirring epics of labor history are chiefly a tale of male leaders and activity. Through Vorse's eyes, we see a wider span, and are awarded tantalizing glimpses of the crucial contribution of women to labor advance. Amid the excitement of the 1937 CIO victory at Flint, tumultuous dramas lay close to every reporter's hand. But among the nationally known journalists present, only Vorse chose to write of the women "with babies and banners," her story of the Women's Emergency Brigade. Based on her articles, the modern award-winning film still inspires.

During World War II Vorse reported the lives of American women factory workers. She was apparently the oldest official American war correspondent (she was seventy), and served in Italy with the United Nations Relief and Rehabilitation Administration after the war.

Mary Vorse lived in semi-retirement at her home in Provincetown during the 1950s. But she continued to write—of Mafia union chiefs, textile workers, migratory labor, and civil rights work in the South. Her last big story to receive national attention was her 1952 exposé of crime in the waterfront unions, published in *Harper's* when she was seventy-eight.

In Mary's last years, during her eighties and nineties, the scope of her battleground shrunk to Cape Cod, her home base since before World War I. Fifty years later, she helped to organize a Provincetown protest against offshore dumping of nuclear waste. At age ninety-one, in 1965, she began her last campaign: she backed Provincetown's Episcopalian minister who would be one of the first to march against the Vietnam war.

From the Wobblies in Lawrence to the young protesters of the 1960s, incredibly, Mary Vorse was there.

Mary Heaton Vorse's life only slightly altered the system whereby the most privileged men dominate the earth. But she would have told us that a form of libertarian socialism and the end of war would inevitably come to rule. For she believed that human reason would someday prevail and that the few committed activists to lead the struggle would always emerge. She had, after all, sparked great change for the better in her own lifetime. And she knew that victory had come only through active resistance, individual sacrifice, and collective anger.

Anthropologist Ruth Benedict once wrote: "I long to speak out the inspiration that comes to me from the lives of strong women. They make of their lives a Great Adventure." Mary Vorse left us the record of her courage, her struggle, her strength, and her determination. That inheritance helps us to persevere with more clarity.

1. The Mary Heaton Vorse Papers are held at The Archives of Labor History and Urban Affairs, Walter Reuther Library, Wayne State University, Detroit, Michigan. The large collection contains manuscripts, diaries, letters, and clippings. A bibliography of her writings, compiled by Rusty Byrne, can be obtained from the Schlesinger Library, Radcliffe College, Cambridge, Massachusetts. Vorse's best-known books are *Men and Steel* (New York: Boni and Liveright, 1920), a study of the Great Steel Strike of 1919, *Footnote to Folly* (New York: Farrar and Rinehart, 1935), her autobiography covering the years from 1912 to 1922, and *Labor's New Millions* (New York: Modern Age, 1938), her story of the organization of the CIO.

# Labor's Struggles: 1912–22

# The Trouble at Lawrence

## Harper's Weekly, 1912

*Thirty-five miles north of Boston along the Merrimac River, a group of manufacturers founded Lawrence in 1845. Along with native New Englanders, miserably poor immigrants came to work in its textile mills— at first from Ireland and Germany, then in the 1890s, from southern and eastern Europe. By 1912 in Lawrence, twenty-five different nationalities spoke fifty different languages.*

*The immigrants provided an enormously profitable source of cheap labor for the mill owners. As profits and living costs rose, wages declined, for the employers had effectively crushed union organization in Lawrence before 1912. Indeed, the somnolent American Federation of Labor craft unions had shown little interest in organizing the impoverished "Dagos" and "Hunkies" in Lawrence.*

*Government statistics and congressional hearings show the result. Frequent slack periods in the textile industry drove the annual income for most workers below $400 a year, for an average working week of fifty-six hours. An additional increase in profits was made possible by the notorious bonus and grading system used in the Lawrence mills. Workers were humiliated and abused in other ways: foremen commonly demanded sexual favors from women employees in return for work; workers were forced to pay for cool water to drink and docked a full hour of pay for arriving a few minutes late. Outside the factory gates, one-third of the population resided on less than one-thirteenth of the city's land. The majority of mill workers subsisted on black bread, coffee, molasses or lard, and a cheap cut of stew meat once or twice a month. Ironically, the workers in the greatest wool center in the country could not afford to buy the overcoats they produced. The mills were also dangerous and inadequately ventilated. Lawrence had one of the highest death rates and infant mortality rates in the country. Respiratory infections killed almost 70 percent of the mill workers, whose average age at death was less than forty. One-third of the spinners died before they had worked ten years. Thirty-six out of every hundred of all men and women who worked in the mills died before they were twenty-five years of age.*

*The Lawrence strike of 1912 began when the state put into effect the new law forbidding women and children under eighteen years of age to work more than fifty-four hours a week. Rather than cut profits, the mills responded by cutting the hours for all workers, with no increase in wage rates. In January, 23,000 textile workers left the factories. With their families they composed 60 percent of the city's population.*

*Mill owners, politicians, small merchants, and religious leaders aligned themselves in opposition to worker demands. The city police, state militia, company guards, and Harvard student militia were moved into place to protect the sacred rights of property. Arrayed against these forces was a new labor organization founded in 1905, the Industrial Workers of the World. The IWW, or Wobblies, as its members were often called, represented a dramatic new departure in labor history—the creation of an anticapitalist, industrial union, with a vision of a workers' republic. The IWW forsook the rampant racism, nativism, and sexism of the American Federation of Labor and became the most open, militant labor organization in U.S. history. By March 1912 the Wobblies had enrolled 10,000 members in its Lawrence local.*

*The marvel of the Lawrence strike was that the IWW organized the "unorganizable," blending many ethnic groups into one smoothly functioning, high-spirited unit. The sight of thousands of disciplined workers walking in endless file through the mill district in the famous moving picket line and of daily parades of workers singing radical songs, tremendously alarmed the respectable elements and earned Lawrence its epic status in American labor history.*

*The workers remained nonviolent through the nine weeks of the strike, despite beatings, bayonetings, fines, and arrests. A clumsy plot to plant dynamite and blame it on the IWW failed when it became clear that the plan was instigated by a Lawrence businessman and the president of the American Woolen Company himself. The state's arrest in February of two IWW leaders for a murder for which they were obviously innocent, was equally bumbling, for the arrests fueled worker resistance. Public fury exploded when the Lawrence authorities attempted to prevent Margaret Sanger and her group from removing the workers' children from Lawrence and sending them out of the city to stay with friends and relations for the duration of the strike.*

*Publicity from an increasingly sympathetic press brought large strike relief contributions from trade unions, socialists, and ethnic groups across the country. When Vorse's report on Lawrence appeared in Harper's, the magazine lost the advertising business of the American Woolen Company. The publicity embarrassed the mill owners and led the governor of Massachusetts to notify the industrialists that he would soon withdraw the militia. Fearing that further public exposure might threaten the high woolen tariff, the owners capitulated in mid-March. The workers' victory was an important one: within a few months of the settlement, 245,000 textile workers in New England received wage increases.*

A few weeks ago a company of about forty children of the Lawrence strikers, bound for Philadelphia, were forcibly prevented from leaving Lawrence by the order of City Marshal John J. Sullivan. He was led to this act by the belief that some of those children were leaving town without the consent of their parents. Before this, several groups of children, to the total of nearly three hundred, had been sent out of town to the strike sympathizers in various cities, and public opinion against the departure of the children had been aroused. As Congressman Ames said: "The people here feel that the sending away of these children has hurt the fair name of Lawrence since it is a rich town and capable of caring for all its needy children without the help of outsiders."

The forcible detention of these children had an extraordinary response throughout the country. It was one of those things that cannot be done in America without stirring up public opinion from north to south and east to west. There had been earlier aggressive moves on the part of the authorities: . . . for instance, the railroading of twenty-three men to prison for one year each, during a single morning's police-court session, on the charge of inciting to riot; but in the minds of the country at large these things have been simply incidents. The abridgment of the right of people to move from one place to another freely was at once a matter of national importance. It had for its immediate sequel the sending of that touching little band of thirteen children of various nationalities to Washington to state their grievances and to testify as to what occurred at the railway station on that Saturday morning.

This was the culminating incident in a strike which has been an extraordinary one throughout, and which, throughout, has been diversified with incidents of an unusual kind.

It is an eloquent little commentary on the wage scale of Lawrence that the passing of the beneficent fifty-four-hour bill should have been the indirect cause of the strike. This bill limited the work of women and children in Massachusetts to that number of hours a week, and the mills of Lawrence could not run fifty-six hours for their men alone. Therefore they cut the hours to fifty-four as the laws demanded, and at the same time, cut the pay by 3.57 percent. It is also claimed that the mills speeded up the work. January 13th was the last payday before the strike, and a few days later the mills were no longer making cloth.

In the present-day labor situation, as every one knows, strikes are prearranged, and, on a certain given day, the people walk out; but the strike of the textile workers in Lawrence was the spontaneous expression of discontent of a people whose scant wages, averaging between $5 and $6 a week, were cut below the living point. They went out, over 25,000 of them, of all crafts, without organization and without strike demands. They had no leaders and they themselves were composed of all the peoples of the earth, and were of warring nations and warring creeds. In this extraordinary fashion did the strike begin.

At the same time the mill hands went out, the American Federation of Labor (AFL) had a membership, according to John P. Golden, president of the Textile Union of New England, of approximately 250, and the Industrial Workers of the World (IWW) a membership of about 280. The American Federation of Labor has not recognized the strike. Apparently this organization was annoyed that the strikers had not played according to the rules of Hoyle laid down by their organization. It was not their strike, neither was it the strike of the Industrial Workers of the World. The strike was merely the indignant expression of people who considered that their wages had been cut below the living point.

The IWW took immediate steps to bring some order out of the chaos in which the workers were plunged. William D. Haywood, Ettor, and Giovanitti began to organize all of the textile workers into one great industrial union. They enrolled the majority of the 25,000 strikers, men, women, and children, in the IWW. They formulated demands for a flat increase in wages of 15 percent, a fifty-four-hour week, double time for overtime, the abolition of the premium or speeding-up system, and no discrimination against those who were on strike. Arrayed against the strikers, along with the mill owners, the militia, and the police, were the officials of the Textile Union of New England and the Central Labor Union of Lawrence. The American Federation of Labor at Washington was also hostile, seeing in the ideal of labor solidarity that was being preached at Lawrence an attack on craft unionism. But it was a message which appealed strongly to the diverse mass of men and women who made up the strikers, and it held them. After Ettor's arrest the task of welding the alien groups into one fell upon the shoulders of Haywood, and the release of Ettor and Giovanitti was added to the demands.

As a contrast to the action against Ettor, it is interesting to cite this incident. John Ramay, a young Syrian of nineteen, went out on the morning of the 29th of January at six o'clock. He joined a crowd of strikers which the militia moved along. He was at the back of the crowd. At fifteen minutes past six he was brought into his mother's house with a bayonet wound in the back and he died at seven that night. The name of the militiaman who killed Ramay is unknown, nor has any action been taken against him. He was not held for murder nor complicity of murder as it was decided that he was within his rights.

Lawrence is in atmosphere a New England city. It has about 88,000 inhabitants, of which 60,000 are mill workers and their families. Thirty thousand of these people work in the mills, and it is said that over thirty-three dialects are spoken in this New England town and that of full American stock there are not more than 8,000 while 45,000 alone are of English-speaking nations.

The town sits in a basin surrounded by hills. Along one side of it runs the Merrimack River, wide and shining. If you approach Lawrence from South Lawrence you must pass through acre after acre of mill buildings and mill yards until you reach the wide waterway whose sides are factory-bordered, whose surface mirrors the monotonous pale-red brick of factory wall and factory chimney.

If you walk down Essex Street, the principal business street, and glance to your right and then to your left, you will receive an impression of always seeing at the end of the street on the one hand a little church steeple spring upward and on the other an imposing mill chimney. The ever-recurring little church steeples of Lawrence give one the impression of the children of a dying race; the big smokestacks are the young giants of a new, red-blooded generation.

From one end to the other of Lawrence run the mills, most of them situated on a piece of made land between the Merrimack and the canal. The mills *are* Lawrence; you cannot escape them; the smoke of them fills the sky. The great mills of Lawrence make the Lawrence skyline; they dominate and dwarf the churches. From Union Street to Broadway along the canal the mills stretch, a solid wall of brick and wide-paned glass, imposing by their vastness and almost beautiful, as anything is that without pretense is adapted absolutely to its own end. The mills seem like some strange fortress of industry, connected as they are by a series of bridges and separated by a canal from the town.

In the Syrian quarter, beautiful long-eyed Syrian women, their hair down their backs, sat Oriental fashion on meager cushions on the floor nursing pale babies in rooms where it was almost dark, although outside the day was bright and clear and snow sparkled on the ground. A typical family of this sort is that of a certain woman in an alley tenement of Oak Street. There were six in the family, which lived in three rooms. The halls were dirty and full of ashes and unremoved garbage. The family was supported by the work of children—a boy of sixteen and one-half years and a girl of seventeen, who earned between them $12.50 a week. The rent was $10 a month. It was this girl who cried, in the tone of one who would say—"Oh, that one would give me to drink of the water that flows! Oh, that only we had never come away from Damascus!" And one had a picture of these people who were so beautiful to look on in their own home, the sun at least about them. As a Syrian said apropos of the killing of Ramay, when Haywood cautioned his compatriots to moderation and patience, "If we have not much law in our country, at least we have satisfaction!"

It is in homes like these that one would find the posters of the Wood mills, representing long lines of the mills on the one hand and a happy band of workers with their full dinner pails proceeding to work on the other. These posters and the representations of agents caused many workers to come to this country.

It is only by chance that I have mentioned the Syrians; their case is of course that of all the other workers.

The Jewish strike delegate, an impressive man with a worn face, said he had a wife and eight children who were all too young to work in the mills. When he was asked how much he averaged he replied, "I'm ashamed to tell you!" They paid $2.25 a week for their tenement, and when he was asked if he took lodgers he replied in a matter-of-fact tone, "Why, of course, how else could I live?" Five of his children were among those who were being taken care of in New York and other cities.

The different nationalities keep together and have their own meeting places, from the substantial brick Turn Verein building of the Germans to the tiny Lithuanian church.

There are quarters of the town where you may not hear a word of English spoken. I have been in Italian towns where I have heard more American-English spoken on the streets by returned emigrants than I did in the narrow streets and alleys and Valley Street. The picture-show notices were in Italian; goats' cheese and salami hung up in the windows; women with shawls on their heads went in to buy meager stores of their day's marketing; and windows of the stores held colored posters which represented the glorious victories of the Italians over the Turks.

This is the town, so New England in setting and surroundings, so mixed in its nationalities—this town whose great mills are the latest expression of our tremendous industrial development—a development which has created a situation which no one as yet fully understands in all its complexity, with which our state government cannot cope, and which has caught in its tangled web the people who are the very creators of the situation itself.

The strike of Lawrence involves the questions of emigration and of the tariff, of the ability of a state with a fifty-four-hour law to compete with a state whose workers have two extra working hours: the effect on the country at large of a working community which habitually lives under conditions which do not make for healthy children.

Lawrence is a small town: there are 20,000 people there who, whatever else happens, can never again have the race hatreds and creed prejudices that they did before they had learned what working together may mean. They have learned, too, the value of organization and their one executive ability has been developed, for they have had to feed a great company of people and administer the use of the strike funds. Young girls have had executive positions. Men and women who have known nothing but work in the home and mill have developed a larger social consciousness. A strike like this makes people think. Almost every day for weeks people of every one of these nations have gone to their crowded meetings and listened to the speakers and have discussed these questions afterward, and in the morning the women have resumed their duty on the picket lines and the working together for what they believed was a common good.

# The Case of Adolf

## *The Outlook, 1914*

*During the winter of 1913–14, millions of Americans were out of work. In New York City, Frank Tannenbaum, then a twenty-one-year-old anarchist, later a distinguished scholar at Columbia University, led a novel form of protest: he directed thousands of unemployed men to various churches, where they demanded food and shelter for the night, in a nonviolent dramatization of the plight of the unemployed. After a visit from the jobless army, some churches offered food, shelter, or money.*

*But on the night of March 4, 1914, a Catholic church rector sent for the cops. Tannenbaum was arrested, along with 189 others, and charged with inciting to riot; he was sentenced to one year on Blackwell's Island. The arrests were followed by dozens of protests by jobless men and women, coordinated by a coalition of Wobblies, anarchists, and liberals.*

On the night of March 4, 1914, a crowd of several hundred men—men out of work, men ill clad, many of them without shirts under their tattered coats and without socks on their feet, with broken shoes and no overcoats—went to the Church of St. Alphonsus to demand food and shelter.

It was one of the nights of the blizzard, and a heavy snow was falling. The streets were piled high with snow—a very bad night indeed for any one to be out even for a little while, and a cruel night for homeless men. Before they went to the Church of St. Alphonsus this crowd had been standing in Rutgers Square for an hour and a half, with the snow falling on them, listening to their leaders declaring that, since society had no work for them, society owed them food and shelter until such time as society should again have work for them to do. It is probable that the philosophy of the thing was not apparent to many of the listeners. They had two poignant facts to face—facts that had nothing to do with abstractions: One was, they had no place to go that night to sleep; and the second, they had nothing to eat; and a problem just as poignant awaiting them on the morrow, and that was that they had no jobs or prospect of jobs to enable them to sleep and eat the next night or the next.

These men were of varying creeds and nationalities. They had come together because a group of young fellows, some of them members of the Industrial Workers of the World, some of them not, all of them themselves out of work, had been speaking at Rutgers Square on the subject of unemployment during a number of nights past, and had led them several times to churches which had either offered them food and shelter or had given them money so that they could find a place to sleep and get themselves something to eat.

Remember, this was during the most bitter week of an unusually cruel winter, and these men were homeless; they were only a tiny fraction of the homeless men—and homeless women, too—who formed the most unfortunate part of the unfortunate army of the unemployed. The more fortunate part of this army were the unemployed who had friends with whom they could stay for a night, the unemployed who still had a roof over their heads, the unemployed who lived partly on charity and partly on casual work picked up. How great this number was in New York City that night we do not know. It has been estimated to be from 300,000 and over to 100,000.

This group of men were naturally not concerned at that moment with solving the ultimate problems of unemployment—even if their leaders were. And what concerned them all, leaders and crowd alike, was where to sleep for that night.

Their leaders, therefore—Frank Tannenbaum, Charles Plunket, and Frank Strawn Hamilton—went to the rector of St. Alphonsus's Church, Father Schneider, and asked him if they might have shelter in his church. Father Schneider replied that by no means could he shelter them, for the Blessed Sacrament of the Body of our Lord was there exposed, and it would be sacrilege to allow men to sleep in the church at such a time.

The men had been told by Tannenbaum to wait outside the church until the rector's permission should have been asked, but in the meantime more than half the crowd had gone in. Tannenbaum was told by a police officer to go into the church and tell his men to go away. Of what happened in the church I will speak later. The result of their entry was that 190 men were arrested, including Tannenbaum.

Frank Tannenbaum was held on a felony charge of inciting to riot; his bail was fixed at $5,000, and later increased to $7,500. The bail of the other 190 men was fixed at $1,000 each. The prisoners were proportioned equally among four prisons—the Tombs, Jefferson Market, West Fifty-seventh Street, and West Fifty-third Street prisons.

In the Jefferson Market prison fifty men were herded together in one large pen; there were no sleeping accommodations in this pen. It has a stone floor and wooden benches around the wall. As many as ten men could sleep on these benches; the rest were compelled to sleep on the floor. For these fifty men there were eight blankets and no other covering. The first night of their incarceration they had no blankets, nor did they receive any food that night. For several days at least they had neither towels nor soap. They had to wash themselves in cold water at a running tap from which they also got their drinking water. The food was reported to be scant and of poor quality.

In the West Fifty-seventh Street prison the men were also confined together, herded in a pen under much the same conditions. The food there was so bad that the men went on a hunger strike and sent word to their keepers that they would not eat until they were given something fit to eat. Their stand had an immediate effect, for they were given some decent coffee and some nourishing stew.

In the other prisons men were crowded five or six in a cell. The sanitary conditions were vile and the food was bad. No effort was made to procure them the simplest comforts or decencies of life.

These prisoners were taken to the court at Mulberry Street and kept all day without food.

Bail had been procured for Tannenbaum and Plunket, but they refused bail while the rest of their comrades were in prison.

The news of the arrests was brought to the notice of the International Workers' Defense Conference, which is an organization called into being by what its members believe to be the many unjust sentences given to labor in its conflicts with capital. The conference has for its sole object the desire to see the courts working for justice, for labor in this country has too often been tried for its opinions and not for its actual acts of disorder. The Defense Conference therefore procured Justus Sheffield as counsel for the imprisoned men. He refused a "blanket" trial for the men—that is, he refused to let a joint sentence be passed upon all the men together, for there were men in that crowd some of whom did not speak English, some of whom had no knowledge of what was going on, and who only knew that they were homeless and shelterless, and here was a chance to sleep under cover.

There were other men who were in that church, also unemployed and also shelterless, who were there for the purpose of demonstration. Their motive was one beyond that of immediate food and shelter; they wished to bring to the ears of the careless city of New York a knowledge of the condition of the homeless unemployed men and women of this city.

It was manifestly unjust to give these men, who had a further ideal and reason for their conduct and who knew what they were doing, the same sentence that one would mete out to a foreigner of eighteen who merely followed the crowd in the hope of obtaining temporary relief for his misery. However much society, as represented by the newspapers, the courts, the churches, and all the comfortable people who read the newspapers and go to the churches, might feel that these leaders should be punished for their demonstration, not even the courts would feel that a man ignorant of the philosophy of the leader had equal "guilt" with the leaders themselves.

The first two men arraigned before Magistrate Campbell in the Mulberry Street Court were sentenced to thirty days each in the workhouse. A third man, who pleaded guilty and rejected the services of Mr. Sheffield, was let off with fifteen days. Isadore Wissotsky, a lad of eighteen years with the physique of a poorly nourished boy of sixteen, was sentenced to sixty days. He was one of the few actual members of the Industrial Workers of the World in the crowd.

I am a member of the International Workers' Defense Conference, and was therefore in the Mulberry Street Court witnessing the proceedings. Two or three days after the first victims were sentenced there was a public reaction against the wholesale prosecution of the unemployed. Assistant District Attorney Dickinson announced then that he would visit the prisons, talk with the men, and determine in that way which ones to prosecute. The result of his visit was that a large number of the men agreed to plead guilty. These were let off with suspended sentences. After that precedent it was manifestly impossible to deal with greater harshness with the men who refused to plead guilty, and they also were let off under suspended sentences, with the exception of three of the leaders, tried last, and given fifteen days each.

The toll, therefore, exacted by justice for the St. Alphonsus demonstration was: one boy sentenced to sixty days in the workhouse; four men for thirty days, three for fifteen; and Frank Tannenbaum, who was found guilty of unlawful assembly, was given the maximum sentence of one year in the penitentiary and a $500 fine, which means an additional year and a half in prison if the fine is not paid.

While I was in court I was asked to take the names and addresses of some of the groups of men as possible witnesses for the case of Tannenbaum. That is how I met Adolf. I asked him his name and address. He gave me his name, but shook his head as to his address; he did not understand me, as he spoke only German, so I repeated my question in German.

"I have no address," he said.

"Have you no friends where a letter might be sent?"

"No," he answered, "none at all."

Adolf was an upstanding, chunky, able-looking young fellow of, I should judge, twenty-eight or thirty. He came from Westphalia and was a skilled workman, a stonemason by trade, a good-tempered, able, courteous-spoken fellow.

"Why," I asked him, "did you plead guilty?"

He said: "I read in the German papers that those men who pleaded guilty would be let off, and that those who pleaded not guilty would be sent to prison. I pleaded guilty of having gone into a church that was not my own—I am a Lutheran. I do not know the laws in America on such things. What was it that the priest and those policemen testified?"

"They testified," I told him, "that you men were disorderly in the church, that you went in with your hats on, that you disturbed the worshipers by running up and down the aisles, and that there were cat-calls and 'booings' in the church."

"That's a lie!" he told me. "Oh, I wish I could speak English! I would like to have testified. Why should we, who came for shelter and to be fed, make disorder in a church? Myself and my three companions read in the German paper that homeless men were getting shelter in churches. We joined the crowd. Two of my companions are stonemasons like myself; the other is also in the building trade. For two nights we had gone to churches and had been kindly treated and given food and shelter. Why, then, should we make a disturbance in any church where we supposed we would be also kindly treated? It's unreasonable."

"They testified," I said, "that Father Kessler rose and asked you men to leave the church."

"I saw the *Geistliger* stand by a pillar saying something, and I asked one of my companions, who speaks English, what he said, but he could not hear him. The *Geistligers* in the other churches had always spoken to us also; we did not know this one was telling us to go. See, this is what happened:

"We walked into the church and took our seats as we had other times. One of my comrades, who is a South German and a Catholic, was praying. A flashlight went off in the gallery of the church, and we sprang, alarmed, to our feet, and others with us. At the same time policemen began hustling us about. It took us by surprise. We thought we were to be fed and sheltered as before.

"Then I turned around and saw men with hats on and cameras in their hands standing on the back seats. Then, as they began shoving us about, in our confusion there was some disorder. There were no cat-calls." On that point he was definite.

"The police frightened us. We did not know what was to happen. Then we filed out and found we were all arrested. I and my three German friends were all put in the same cell."

As we went up in the subway together he kept repeating to me:

"Why should we make disorder in a church when other churches treated us kindly?"

This man was honestly surprised by what I told him, and honestly indignant. He had been for six days in a cell with his companions. He had had no communication with any of the leaders and knew none of them; he had had no chance to discuss any favorable interpretation of the men's actions. All that he said to me had the weight of his own conviction behind it.

"How did you," I asked him, "a skilled workman, come to be so destitute?"

He pulled out of his pocket a cabinet-sized photograph of a handsome child about five years old.

"That is my little boy," he said; "he is with my mother and father in Germany. I have always sent home all my money to him and my old folks. When I lost my wife, I came out here and always sent my money back. A man by himself can always get along, I thought. I had steady work, always among Germans—that is why I speak so little English—for three years, and then from one day to another my work shut down.

"I took work on a farm near Philadelphia for several months; then again there was no more work for me. A friend of mine read that there was work in New York, so I and two others worked our way from Philadelphia, but the work we hoped to get was gone by the time we got here. And here I am. This is my baggage!"

He tapped the picture of the little boy, a well-dressed, prosperous-looking little German, a round, blond-looking baby, well set up, like his father.

"First I sold my clothes, even my overcoat. I got odd jobs for a quarter here and there. I stood in line whenever I saw an advertisement for work, but I never even got near the window. However early I was, there were others there before me. Of course it's against me not speaking English, but you know the hardest part of work is looking for it, especially when you have not slept in a decent place nor had anything much to get and when the weather's like this. Looking for work and not finding it is the hardest work I know."

There was no whine about his tone, no self-pity. He did not even say to me, "It's all in the day's work." He took his ups and downs with the cheerfulness of a perfectly courageous man, and a perfectly self-sufficient one who has a good trade behind him and who believes that eventually he must find work.

"I've been very lucky," he told me; "I've not caught cold, like my friend. All the time in prison he was coughing and had a fever. If a man keeps his health, he's all right."

There is just the point of it. If a man keeps his physical and spiritual health, he's all right. What happens to the man who never even "gets to the window" week after week, and the man who gets a cough like Adolf's friend, who goes out after six days in prison with a cough and a fever, with not a cent in his pocket and no address? Man after man of those 182 who were discharged had no address—not even the address of a friend who would receive a letter from him.

Adolf left my house with his head up and his shoulders squared, confident and good-tempered. But what of Adolf if, after another few weeks, he does not get "near a window"?

As he said, "looking for work is always the hardest work." It is so even in my sheltered profession. It is hard work even when you find work; but when you have no home, when you do not know where your next meal is coming from, when you have sold even your overcoat, and have no socks on your feet and no shirt under your coat, it is terrible, nerve-racking work, work that weakens a man's body and destroys his most valuable asset of all—his belief in himself.

It is very bad for a skilled workman like Adolf in the prime of his years, a man who looked as if he had a life of clean living and good conditions behind him. But when this fate falls upon an older man, or when it falls upon a man yet a mere boy, it is a process by which those derelicts of society called "bums" are made.

Down on Rutgers Square I saw the stuff of which bums are made. It was a young crowd that stood in the slush listening to the speakers, boys of eighteen and twenty; Frank Tannenbaum himself is twenty-one. The Committee of Ten who spoke and managed the affairs of these Rutgers Square meetings were all of them young, and the crowd to which they spoke were for the most part young too—nice boys, clean born as anybody's boy, boys ready to work if they had a chance.

In his speech before the jury Frank Tannenbaum said:

"The most religious sight I have ever seen was on that cold and stormy night when I had taken those half-starved men from the streets, placed them in a clean restaurant, and watched them laugh and joke over their food."

No one of us who had seen those boys and men eat could misunderstand what he meant when he said it was a religious sight. Every meal that those men received was helping to save their manhood. Every time they gathered together and came forth from the isolation of their desperate and desolate loneliness the hour was put off when they should lose faith in themselves and should be on the road to becoming bums.

It was said of these men that they did not want to work. The vicar of St. Paul's, Dr. Geer, said in his statement published in the *World* that of the men whom he sheltered in his church more than half left before breakfast was given them at seven o'clock, and many had gone to look for work as early as four o'clock. And if there were among that crowd those who did not want to work, the question puts itself to one, if one chooses to think about it at all, "Why didn't he wish to work?" Before a man wishes not to work some spiritual or physical catastrophe has overtaken him. At some time in the lives of all such men society has sinned against them. It seemed to me as I watched them, watched the attitude of the newspapers concerning this demonstration, and the attitude of the crowd that jeered them on their cold marches to their places of shelter, that I saw society in the act of sinning.

A thoughtful man asked me what the meaning of it all was. "Why," he wanted to know, "did the men go to the churches, and why did they assemble together?"

I replied that the leaders and the most thoughtful men in the group wished to get under the skin of society, to make this great and prosperous city realize what misery it harbored; to which he said: "Well, you may get under the skin of society the wrong way and cause repressive measures to be enacted."

That is the worst arraignment of society I have heard. It means that society does not wish to understand its own crying needs, that the most comfortable part of society is indignant at having its peace destroyed, that it does not wish to give those of its most needy members who have still courage to fight against adverse conditions the right to assemble and the right to show this need. It refuses to realize that these men were but the mouthpieces of the silent thousands who were suffering because society is so ill adjusted that there must forever be an army of unemployed who must be out of work at the first financial depression.

There were serious and conservative newspapers in this town that in their editorial columns advocated such repressive measures and called upon the police to answer the plea of the unemployed with the use of their clubs.

What are unemployed and homeless men in a city to do? The city cannot take care of all of them; it cannot shelter all of them. Far less can it find them jobs.

It is against the law to steal. Vagrancy is against the law, and yet vagrancy is the inevitable result when half-fledged and homeless boys must fruitlessly look for work day after day, or when men who for years have spent themselves in doing their share of the world's work must in middle age walk the streets in a vain search for work.

Suicide is against the law also, and surely slow starvation is suicide of the soul as well as the body. When Adolf followed Tannenbaum to the Church of St. Alphonsus, he was, in a way, "putting it up" to society; and the answer of society was, "Jail and suspended sentences," and the cry of the press was for the nightstick. These do not seem very adequate answers.

# The Mining Strike in Minnesota
## *The Outlook, 1916*

In 1890 a rich deposit of iron ore was discovered on the Mesabi Range,
an eighty-mile-long strip of low hills lying some seventy miles north-
west of Duluth, Minnesota. By 1901 most of the mines on the range
were owned by the country's first billion-dollar company, the mighty
U.S. Steel Corporation.

Unionism was kept alive on the Mesabi Range by the many socialist
Finns in the working force. In the summer of 1907, the Western Federation of Miners led a strike of over 10,000 men which was crushed by
U.S. Steel within a few months. The company brought in thousands of
strikebreakers from the Northeast, most of them fresh off the boat.
Ironically, it was the imported immigrant scabs of 1907 that supplied
much of the leadership for the much larger and more violent strike
against the mine owners which began in the summer of 1916.

A spontaneous outburst of fury over lowered wages brought a walkout at the St. James Mine in Aurora on June 2, 1916. Four hundred
men, with no labor organization to back them, voted to strike. The
strike spread rapidly, aided by a procession of miners, accompanied by
their wives rolling baby carriages, who walked the seventy-five miles of
roads along the range, urging others to join them. By the end of June,
two-thirds of the range miners—10,000 to 15,000 men—were out on
strike. The Mesabi walkout spread to the Vermilion Range to the south,
bringing out thousands more.

Unable to import large numbers of immigrant strikebreakers due to
war conditions, the steel company hired over 1,000 private police and
special deputies, generally thugs collected from the streets of Duluth
and St. Paul, to prevent picketing, harrass strikers, and arrest workers
on trumped up charges. Often drunk and brutally aggressive, the
owners' private army established a veritable range of terror.

The miners called on the IWW, who sent the largest number of their
top talent ever assigned to one strike; Elizabeth Gurley Flynn was
among them. A single strike committee was formed, organized into
different language groups on the model of Lawrence, and a financial
and publicity organization was established. In early July several top
IWW leaders were arrested and federal officials began deportation
proceedings on the range. The homes of strikers were entered fre-

*quently without warrants; the occupants were hurried to jail and given sentences for picketing. Giving up the fight as hopeless, many strikers left to find work in the harvest fields. For a few weeks, their wives and children took over the job of picketing. At first the deputies held back from attacking the families of the miners, but by early August they were beating women and children to the ground. By mid-September the strike was lost, although the miners did win, at enormous cost, a small wage increase and a minor reform of the hated contract system.*

*The publicity given to the strike by Mary Vorse and a few others helped to hasten the conclusion of an investigative report, requested by the State Labor Commissioner in Minnesota, which made clear that the mine guards hired by the company were chiefly to blame for the strike violence. Even so, the open shop was maintained by the employers, and the Mesabi miners remained unorganized until the CIO drive of the 1930s.*

One of the most sinister aspects of life in this country is the failure of the serious and thinking people to obtain prompt information about the various industrial struggles and to get at the causes which are at the root of our industrial unrest.

Since June 3 a strike has been waged on the Mesaba Range, Minnesota, whose largest single owner is the Oliver Iron Mining Company, an arm of the Steel Trust. This strike has affected the life not only of the twelve thousand miners employed on the Range, but of ten towns and villages from Aurora to Hibbing, a distance of sixty miles. The strike has been characterized by the prompt deputizing of a large force of gunmen, numbering, according to Sheriff J. R. Meining of Duluth, over a thousand; more, according to residents of the range towns.

And although this strike has aroused the bitterest feeling on both sides, although it has affected directly and indirectly thousands of people, although there have been three people killed, several wounded, and over two hundred arrested and six held for murder (Carlo Tresca and seven other organizers were held on the charge of being accessory before the fact), there has appeared in the public press only a brief paragraph or two—nothing that would give any picture of the magnitude of this struggle. According to George P. West of the Committee on Industrial Relations, "the city of Duluth, the county of St. Louis, and the State of Minnesota as represented by Governor Burnquist and other public officials have joined hands in a relentless effort to crush the strike of the iron-workers." He goes on to say: "With the support and good will of the United States Steel Corporation and affiliated interests in the State, Governor Burnquist, Sheriff John R. Meining, of Duluth, County Prosecutor Greene, and the Duluth Chief of Police are playing at ducks and drakes with the most sacred rights of the foreign workmen who mine the ore that goes down to the ships at Duluth for shipment to the Pittsburgh Mills." That this fierce and important struggle should have gone on so long without arousing comment is the direct fault of no one. It is not due to any consciously willful suppression of the news. It is due rather to the lack of communication between the workers and that thinking part of the community which forms the public opinion which asks that labor shall receive its fair hearing in the courts and in the press.

On the second of June, 1916, a small mine, the St. James, in Aurora, a town of 7,000 inhabitants, situated at the extreme east of the Range, struck. At that time and until several days later there were no organizers of any kind on the range.

The strike apparently had its origin in the losing of a beautiful hope. The miners on the Mesaba Range are paid in two different ways: the open-pit men by the day; some of the underground men who are not miners are also paid by the day, a system of payment known as "company count"; the underground miners are paid on a system of piecework known as the contract system. On February 1 the wages of the open-pit miners were raised; on May 1 there was another raise which brought the price of this class of labor up to $2.60.

The company alleges that the wages of those working under the contract system were raised proportionately. Apparently, the miners remained in ignorance of this raise, or it was in some way rendered inoperative, for they struck. In all the conversations that various investigators, including the federal mediators, have had with the miners, no miner seems to have known that his wages were raised. They proved how little they knew about it and how deeply they resented a series of injustices great and small which the contract system made possible by a spontaneous strike, which leaped down the Range as the forest fires which have devastated the great trees around the mines.

The demands made by the workers are as follows: $2.75 a day for open-pit mining; $3 a day for underground mining, dry work; $3.50 a day for underground mining, wet work; an eight-hour day; pay twice a month; abolition of the contract system.

The company asserts that only 28 percent of the underground workers—the real miners—are paid less than $3 a day, and that it would be unfair to the skillful miner to equalize the pay at his expense. The answer of the miners is that the contract system as practiced on the Mesaba Range makes wages so uncertain and leads to so much petty graft and unjust discrimination on the part of the shift bosses and captains that in the working out of the system they do not make $3 a day. So the paradoxical situation exists that, according to company figures, the miners are actually striking for a lower wage than the majority receive.

Under the contract system, the miner contracts to mine ore for a certain price a carload. The price of this carload may be, and is, varied at any time according to the conditions encountered. It is the mine captain who fixes the price. According to the miners, it has been the custom to sell the best places for prices varying from the virtue of the miners' wives and daughters to presents of drinks and cigars. So universal is this custom that any reference to the graft of the captain is received in any meeting of miners by laughter and applause.

There are at present in the hands of the federal investigators affidavits sworn to before a notary public concerning all these forms of graft, from insulting propositions made to the women of miners' families to affidavits that drinks or money were paid for the job.

The miners are supposed to work but eight hours; but, instead of their time being counted from the mouth of the mine until they are again above ground, their working time is reckoned only from the moment picks are in their hands.

A word concerning raffles, which, it is alleged, is a usual form of graft. The mine captains make out sometimes as many as a thousand tickets at fifty cents to a dollar on a nonexistent farm or a stove or a horse. These are offered for sale, and not a miner dares refuse.

Again, the miner has, in fact, to pay for powder, fuses, tools, spikes, but this account is never itemized. It does not appear upon his due bill, which states briefly what he is to receive for his month's work. He is paid monthly only, which means that the Mesaba Range is run on a credit system. If a miner is discharged or leaves before payday, he must wait until then for his money.

These are the injustices, large and small, as charged by the miners, which have led to the present difficulty. In the coal mines the system employed enables the miner to know day by day what he makes. An itemized account of his powder, fuses, and so forth is kept for him. The miner on the Mesaba Range never knows until the end of the month what he will receive. The system makes it possible for the unmarried man who can afford to bribe the captain to get the "soft places."

As soon as the strike occurred, every effort was made by the authorities to stop the strike through hired gunmen and through countless arrests. The miners have been extraordinarily patient in the presence of these hired deputies in their towns and villages. The Oliver Company, which holds perhaps a third of the mines, testifies to the orderliness of the strikers, who, however, have been given ninety days on the smallest charges. Deep injustice has been shown by the authorities in their treatment of disorders caused by strikers as compared with those caused by gunmen. During a clash of strikers and gun-men—a clash caused by the gunmen themselves—John Alar, a striker, was shot and killed. No arrests followed his death. On June 28 the home of a man in Biwabik named Masonowietch, who was suspected of running a "blind pig," was entered by Deputy Myron and three assistant deputies. The man was told roughly to come along. His wife started to get his shoes from an inner room, upon which she was clubbed by one of the deputies. The boarders sprang to her assistance. In the scuffle that ensued, Deputy Myron was killed, also a man outside the house named Lavalde. There were no guns among the strikers, and evidence goes to show that Myron was shot by one of his own assistants. At present Masonowietch and his wife and the three boarders lie in jail charged with murder. The woman has with her a seven-month-old baby.

At once Carlo Tresca, Joe Schmidt, Scarlett, and other Industrial Workers of the World organizers were arrested, and are held for murder in the first degree as accessories before the fact, it having been alleged that incendiary speeches made by them caused the killing of Deputy Myron. The country is familiar with the arresting of labor organizers on similar charges.

No arrests have been made for the murder of the bystander Lavalde. The mayors of the villages and the members of the American Federation of Labor place the blame for all disorders which have occurred on the presence of the gunmen, and on the system which makes it possible for gunmen to be hired by private corporations.

Up to this time the company has refused to have anything to do with the miners. It refuses to recognize that there is a strike or that the miners have grievances. It has maintained a rigorous course of aloofness since the gunmen were imported.

At present mediators Davies and Fairley, of the U.S. Department of Labor, are on the Range investigating the situation. It is to be hoped that their efforts to make the steel corporation consider the miners' grievances will be more successful than those of the miners' representatives and those of the mayors and businessmen of the municipalities, whose efforts at mediation have been met with blank silence.

# In Bayonne

## *The Blast, 1916*

*In 1915, Bayonne, New Jersey, erupted in one of the most militant labor conflicts ever to occur on the East Coast. Miserably low wages, intolerable working conditions, abusive foremen, arrogant company executives, and the workers' knowledge of Standard Oil's huge war profits ignited the immensely violent protest of the workers, most of them Poles and Hungarians. For two weeks in July the workers' attack on both the company plants and the scabs made the city into a battle camp. Worker-lit fires threatened the destruction of Standard Oil storage tanks and thousands of furious strikers filled the streets. Although Standard Oil refused to negotiate worker demands, the Bayonne workers won some concessions, partly because the governor of New Jersey refused to send in strikebreaker troops. But the wage increase went in disproportionate amount to the skilled workers, while the one-third of the workforce who were unskilled and mostly foreign born still received less than thirty cents an hour. When this unskilled group called for a new strike in October 1916, they did not win the support of most of the skilled and English-speaking workers.*

*Once again, the authorities of Bayonne and Standard Oil relied on police force to break the strike. The police confined the strikers into an area of several blocks lying east of the railroad tracks. Within this zone, the workers fought the police cordons and shot a scab. The police made a sweep of the isolated district, moving with riot guns in two ranks from east to west.*

*Mary Vorse's report was an eyewitness scoop which was printed in the* New York Globe *and the* Blast, *an anarchist paper published by Alexander Berkman in San Francisco. But the strike was almost over by the time Vorse arrived in Bayonne. The company refused to make any concessions and the entire labor force soon resumed work on the old terms.*

Chief of Police M. P. Reilly of Bayonne will tell you that Bayonne is quiet, and Director of Public Safety Wilson will say that the situation is well in hand. While I was listening to these reassuring statements, the group of people on the street corners grew larger; there was a little apprehension fluttering in the crowd. Every face was turned in one direction. Two motorcycle officers appeared. Around the corner came Captain Edward Griften in a pale gray suit, with a checked hat. He held a rifle tenderly in his arms. After him followed four detectives, also with rifles. Behind them marched thirty-six deputies, dressed in their new uniforms and swinging their new, pale yellow riot clubs. After them, more armed and uniformed detectives. Then came the patrol wagon, and in it were huddled the haggard, boyish-looking prisoners. After them were fifty deputized firemen.

The miserable little prisoners were being brought to judgment for carrying concealed weapons. After the firemen again came more detectives. One of them, Robert Russell, pointed his gun suggestively at the crowd and cried: "Get along there! Get along down the street!"

He ran up to the dark little huddled group at the corner and pointed the gun at them, at which the women shrank back, frightened. The procession swung along, and one began to realize why it was that quiet was regained in Bayonne.

Meantime the crowd at the street corner had been lined up in two rows by two officers, who searched them rapidly for concealed weapons.

"Sometimes," the commissioner of public safety explained, "they follow their friends up, and we don't want any more trouble."

So, after three days of warfare, Bayonne is quiet, but it is an unnatural quiet. For fear and suspense are in the air. Every one is afraid of every one else. The people outside of the strike district are terribly afraid of the strikers—how afraid is measured by the exclamation of a young woman of whom we asked the way to the strike district: "Oh!" she cried. "You mustn't go down there—you'll surely get shot."

Even the reporters, when you ask where the strike headquarters are, exclaim: "Keep as far away from there as you can. You'll get all the news you want at Police Headquarters, where you'll be sent."

So after a short time in Bayonne you realize the feeling of disquiet has deepened, and you realize that you are in a terrorized city, and that fear is in the very air that you breathe.

After the accounts of riot and bloodshed, after the warnings one has received concerning the violent character of the strikers, it was very strange to go through the silent, desolate streets. Life temporarily seems to have stopped. There seems to be some strange and mournful holiday—the saloons are closed, on each corner stands a dark group of strikers talking to one another in low tones. All up the street are more little groups of strikers. On the side streets women and children mingle with the men. On Broadway and Avenues E and F, the storm centers of the strike district, there are few women to be seen. And everywhere, wherever you go, you find the same atmosphere of fear and suspense.

The people are ready to scurry to their houses when the deputized police and detectives with shotguns and rifles march imposingly past. They run to their houses and there they hide. For men and women have been shot while standing in their windows. Anyone standing in a window is suspected of being a sniper, so the police shoot first, to keep from being shot themselves. But you cannot be long in Bayonne or talk much with men and women on the streets without feeling that the police have been very clever about shooting first. This deputized force of police includes not only the fire companies, but the city officials; inspectors of all kinds have been put into uniforms and have been called upon to perform the perilous duty of policing a town filled with 10,000 unorganized strikers.

It is no wonder that they too are afraid and that they turn uneasy faces toward the side streets as they pass them fearing stray shots from back alleys or housetops. Up to this time, however, only about fifteen persons have been arrested for carrying concealed weapons although all last night the town was patrolled and every passer-by searched and scores of homes have been invaded in the hunt for concealed weapons.

So, though the streets are quiet, every one is on the defensive: every one seems to be waiting apprehensively for something to happen. The strike district from the Hook to Avenue C is full of these groups of anxious people. Something strange is in the air. Calamity seems to threaten. The quiet is not the quiet of Sunday, but rather of a witch's Sabbath.

In three days the strike has been a bloody harvest; there have been three deaths and a hospital full of wounded. Several are said to be dying, the number of minor wounds is not known, but after each conflict with the police many men have been seen limping away.

Severe beatings of the strikers are usual. There have been, besides, thirty or forty arrests, the wrecking of saloons now by the police for the alleged breaking of the ordinance against selling drink, and now by the strikers.

Last night Mydosh's Hall, where the strikers were holding a meeting, was raided. Many arrests followed, seven men were said to have been wounded, and the hall was closed. The right of free speech and of assembly have been temporarily denied to the strikers. These extreme measures were considered necessary by the authorities for the preserving of order. The strikers' point of view is different.

The mournful little groups of huddled people seem glad to talk to you, especially the women, and their talk is about one thing—and that is shooting. In broken English one old Polish woman explained to us: "Why should they at the windows shoot? You must go and hide when you go to your house. You must not go near your window—No! The men will shoot—and maybe you die, like that Sophie Torach down the street. That Sophie Torach, she should get married this Saturday, but she stands at the window and the police walk by, and a bullet comes through her head—and she is dead!"

Wherever you go, in whatever group you find yourself, the story is repeated with a ghastly and unvarying monotony. One story is of a woman with a child in her arms who has been hit; in another street an old man has been hit; in another place yet, they'll tell how a neighbor dodged just in time to escape being struck, and they will point to a hole in the window. One sees many suggestive bullet holes as one walks up and down the strike district.

This strike came suddenly, but it is said that discontent had been growing for a long time and that the company has for a long time been expecting trouble. The strikers are asking for an increase of 30 percent for those who make under $2 and for 10 percent for those who make $3. They contend that they can't live as well now on what they make as they could a few years ago when wages were less. Other industries in Bayonne have shorter hours and pay higher wages. And the wives of these better paid workers have made the women of the Standard Oil employees discontented.

"We should like to dress our children just as well as those others do," they tell you.

The personality of George W. Hennessy, superintendent of Standard Oil, is said to have helped to create the general atmosphere of discontent by his methods. Since the walkout he is said to have refused to listen to any of the representatives of the strikers. And finally, the recent publication of the Standard Oil Company's profits for the year brought the crisis, and the men, unorganized and without leaders, struck.

As to why the conflict has been so bitter, there have been many contributory factors. It is asserted that the strikers have been blamed for the actions of toughs and gangsters. In fact, all of the disorderly element has seized upon this theme as an excuse to make trouble; and the strikers have been naturally blamed for everything that has occurred, and have suffered accordingly.

The strikers, while they are silent and subdued, are both resolute and bitter—bitter toward the police for what they consider unjustifiable severity. They repeat over and over again: "They had no right to shoot at our windows, they had no right to shoot at crowds where there were women."

They are bitter against the company that will not give them a fair hearing; and it is the opinion of the strikers' attorney, J. H. Dougherty, that had the strikers' representatives been received by Mr. Hennessy the trouble might have been averted. They are also bitter against the press, which they feel has not tried to find out their side, which has magnified their violence and overlooked the violence of the police. They have offered to cooperate with the director of public safety in keeping order and to patrol their own streets. And this offer has been refused and at present they cannot congregate to discuss their affairs.

# Steel

*The Call Magazine, 1919*

When U.S. Steel Corporation was born in 1901, the American steel industry was the marvel of the manufacturing world, producing more steel more cheaply than any competitor. The achievement of American steelmakers rested upon their paramount drive toward economy. Calculation of cost dominated every management decision. The greatest saving was made in the cost of labor. Some soft-hearted steel executives and stockholders within the steel industry might regret the consequent toll on the steelworkers, but few managers would think of diminishing the rate of profit.

The maximization of labor savings was made possible through the creation of a powerless labor force. After the famous labor defeat at Homestead, Pennsylvania, in 1892, the steelmakers eliminated unionization through well-financed blacklist and spy systems. In 1901 one-third of U.S. Steel's mills had union groups; by 1919 there was no union at all.

The American steel industry's enormous rate of profit was dependent upon the exploitation of the semi-skilled and unskilled workers—78 percent of the total labor force. Composed almost entirely of recent immigrants, this bottom two-thirds of the labor force existed on abysmally low wages. The accident rate of the unskilled workers was almost twice the average of the English-speaking workers. Local officials habitually cheated and jailed the lowest paid workers for minor offenses, raking off a portion of the fines imposed. Nativist sentiment and ethnic divisions divided them from the native workers. The AFL trade movement neglected them. Life in the Hunkyvilles of the steel district was dismal, harsh, and hopeless.

Labor stability was disrupted by the beginning of the war in Europe, which slowed immigration and brought a labor shortage to the United States. Most important, the federal government, in an abrupt departure from tradition, set up a price control system in 1917 and in 1918 established the National War Labor Board. The Board defended the right of labor to organize and put pressure on the steel companies to end the hated twelve-hour day.

Unrest among the workers, the unprecedented neutrality of the federal government, and the boost given to union spirit by the effects of *war, led some AFL officials to believe that the time had come to organize the steel industry. The impetus came from Chicago, where William Foster had successfully organized the packing-house workers in 1917. The next year, Foster established the National Committee for Organizing the Iron and Steel Workers and began organizing. Meanwhile, however, the war ended, and federal controls over capital were quickly released. Steel management again had a free hand.*

*When the steel strike began, Mary Vorse joined Foster's office staff as an unpaid publicist. She reported the intensification of company repression for the union press, mainstream journals such as the* Outlook, *and the socialist newspaper the* Call. *During the strike free speech and the right of assembly all but ceased to exist for the unionists in the crucial Pittsburgh district, as Vorse describes in the following selections. Large-scale deportations of strikers began, while 40,000 black strikebreakers were imported to the steel district as scabs. In the small steel towns of Pennsylvania, strikers and their families were terrorized by state and company police. Several workers were killed; hundreds were arrested. A heavily financed company propaganda blitz convinced most of the public that the steel strike was actually an attempt at communist revolution in the United States. Church and press were almost unanimous in their denunciations of the Red Menace.*

*The Great Steel Strike was thoroughly crushed by brute force, the companies' successful Red-baiting campaign and the only lukewarm support given to Foster by the AFL. In the last dreary weeks of the steel strike, before its official end on January 8, 1920, came the Red Scare raids of the Department of Justice. In the steel towns workers were spirited away by federal officials, their families told nothing of their fate. Some of the workers were deported, but most, having been held in prison for months without charge, eventually returned home.*

*The steel strike concluded without a single gain for the almost 350,000 strikers. Foster gravitated toward the Communist Party and Samuel Gompers of the AFL became even more vehement in his denunciation of "Bolshevism" in the labor movement. The "lean years" of labor in the 1920s had begun.*

The other day a man came into Foster's office. He had been on strike three weeks, and now he had about ninety cents left. He had some chickens, he had good neighbors, who had given him vegetables and things from their gardens. The man was a foreigner, a young married man, and what he had come for was not to ask for strike benefits. He wanted advice and the moral support of encouragement.

He wanted to know how he was going to get along. He came rather deprecatingly, smiling in an embarrassed sort of fashion over his difficulties. Then he went away, still with his smile, his only assets his friends, his ninety cents, and his indomitable will to stick it out.

The strike is based on people like this; people full of faith; people full of endurance; people full of sacrifice—thousands and thousands of them.

Thousands of them looking upward and forward to a better life for themselves and their children—for these people are striking for a right to be considered men. They are striking for the right of a little leisure. They want an end put to this dehumanizing double shift.

The other day in Braddock a mill superintendent stopped an old-timer on the street. "Aren't you working?" he asked.

"No. I am not working. I'm on strike; I'm taking a holiday. I am paying myself back those twenty Christmases I worked for the company," said the man.

That has been the situation with the mill workers. No Sundays, no Christmas. Work that took it out of a man so that he was old at forty. Work that left him so tired at the end of the day that he wasn't a human being anymore. And now these people are willing to sacrifice to change this sort of thing, for themselves, for their children, and for the workers of all time.

So when the history of this strike is written it is going to be a history of the faith and courage and endurance of men and women living in wretched slums, their windows looking on filthy courtyards—living in desolate mill towns in sheds around the great mills; living in bleak houses on steep hillsides where the roads turn to roaring torrents during each rain.

Allegheny County is a fair, sweet place. There are large, fat farms; oil bubbles underneath the earth, and all around are beautiful towns full of comfortable American homes. At each turn of the road the ravines and burnt hills make you a new picture. Smoke shuts out all of this when you get to the towns where the mill workers live. Their landsape is the rows and rows of great chimneys and the smoke pouring out of them. Their music is the din of the shop and the roar of the whistle.

They have no life, and now because they have asked for a few hours in which to live, every form of suppression and terror is being used against them.

Why has the strike not already been smothered out of existence? Only because of the dogged endurance of the workers, held together by the ordinary strike discipline. It goes on by its own momentum through the faith and courage of the rank and file.

There is no one who reads this who does not know how the morale of a strike is kept up. There is no one who has seen strikes where there were not meetings, entertainments, processions, the coming together of men working for a common purpose—there is nothing like this in the steel towns. It isn't allowed. If more than half a dozen strikers stop on the street to talk over their affairs they are arrested for "blocking traffic," "inciting to riot," and so forth.

No strike poster can be stuck up in a steel town—no leaflet passed on the street to tell the news. No meeting can be held without a permit of police. Many towns do not allow any meetings at all. In other towns where meetings are grudgingly allowed the halls are so little that they can hold only a very small fraction of the men on strike.

So a smothering silence shuts down over the men. Every day they get up to read lying reports in the papers. Every day they meet on the street mill employees who try to bribe them to go back. I know a young fellow who was discharged because he was getting men to join the union, though Mr. Gary states that men are never discharged for union activities. This man recently met the foreman of his shop, who offered him back his old job at an increased wage. He didn't go, for they are not going back because they have settled down to a long, grim fight, in spite of every force of the community against them, including uncertainty and suspense; in spite of all the rumors of strikebreakers and that their jobs are gone forever, in spite of the terror of the "Cossacks," the beatings, and the continual menace of arrest.

We must remember that in the steel towns people have been arrested wholesale because they have committed the crime of striking. There are charges such as obstructing traffic, unlawful assembly, and so on, which make it impossible to run a striker in without his having committed any real offense.

Suppression and oppression have been the father and mother of this strike and terror its godfather. But, when the company used terror, they forgot the old saying that the blood of the martyr is the seed of the church.

There hasn't been a home searched or an illegal arrest made that hasn't helped the strike. There hasn't been a club that has come down on a defenseless mill worker that hasn't sent men hurrying to get out their union cards.

Take the case of Clairton, for instance—this was the town where the union had got no foothold—the watchful authorities had kept the "agitators" out. ("Agitator" is the company's name for all members of

the American Federation of Labor [AFL] who try to get their fellow
workers to join a union.)

There were no halls in Clairton that could be rented. All permits
were denied and street meetings were broken up. That is to say, the
fundamental rights of Americans were sweepingly denied. There is no
right of free speech and free assembly in the steel towns. When the
people in Farrell want to go to a meeting they have to go over the Ohio
state line into America—and the other evening 4,000 of them walked
over to hear Foster speak.

There are plenty of steel towns not in America, and Clairton is one of
them.

After a time the organizer hired a vacant lot from one of the mill
workers. But a man in Clairton can't ask a few friends to a lawn party on
his own property—the Cossacks rode down the strikers and broke up
the meeting. The mill workers didn't know that it was un-American to
strike and they had put up an American flag—this the Cossacks tore
down and the flag was trampled under the horses' hoofs. This started
trouble, for there were some ex-servicemen there as there are in all
workingmen's crowds. The affidavits sent to the Senate abound in
statements like:

> The state troopers rushed on the lot and the people started to run away,
> but when said state troopers rushed to the platform and tore down our
> flag, the men became incensed and some ex-soldiers, seeing our flag
> being insulted and defiled, rushed at said troopers in defense of our flag
> and started the excitement and almost caused a riot, and loyal citizens
> were greatly incensed. There was no provocation for said interference
> and riding over women and children.
>
> (Signed) Mihon Terzich

Before this happened the organization made no headway in Clairton,
but the constabulary had made an irresistible argument—men rushed
away from the riot to get their union cards.

The state constabulary are a splendid-looking body of men in their
smart dark gray uniforms and helmets, but with their riot clubs, three
feet long, they are terror incarnate to the workers—they are in the
steel towns in many cases not because the town authorities asked
them, but at the request of the company. So brutal have they been that
one can explain their acts only on the theory that they were acting
under orders "to throw a scare into the workers" from the first, or else
that they were deliberately trying to incite riot. How else can one
account for the tearing down of the flag or the incident at Braddock?
There was a mission in Braddock in the Slovak church and the men
were coming out from instruction at about 9:00—the Cossacks rode
them down—not only that, but *they rode their horses up the narrow
church steps.* The men controlled themselves—they didn't attack the

Cossacks, and they did nothing in anger or reprisal when the Cossacks rode down a crowd of babies of the first grade who were going home from church.

No assembling in crowds is allowed in Braddock.

There is a narrow street in Braddock along which runs the Baltimore & Ohio Railway. A tall fence separates the street from the tracks and children play here, for nothing on wheels is allowed here by city ordinance. Since the strike one of the mill owners drove his car down this street, scattering the children in front of him. Behind him, for his protection, rode two of the steel gray troopers, but they weren't needed any more than they have been any time. The men are out to win the strike by peaceable means in spite of thugs, gunmen, and state constabulary.

The worst of the terror is over now. The people have been "pacified." They realize that they have no freedom—no right of free speech or assembly. There are communities where for a steelworker to belong to the AFL is to lay himself open to arrest and imprisonment.

The search for concealed weapons still affords a pretext for the constabulary to break into houses at night, smash open trunks and boxes with hatchets. Yesterday I went to the house of a Slovak woman who had called her husband when the Cossacks came rushing in, whereupon the trooper struck her across the face with his gloves.

These outrages, and more besides, were testified to before the Senate committee and, as the witnesses piled in, in ceaseless procession before the senators, the outstanding fact about them was their defenselessness. How small they seemed to lift their feeble hands against the giant of steel—the giant which can command not only the mills, but the courts, the police, and the press!

There was one thing more outstanding than their defenselessness, and that was their steadfastness as they are fighting one of the greatest battles of all history and fighting with no other weapon than their unshaken courage.

# Aliens

## *The Outlook, 1920*

As Father Kazinci and I walked through the Braddock alleys we bent our heads to the thin rain without speaking. I had been accompanying him on a round of parochial visits, and we did not talk because there seemed nothing adequate to say.

From the rampart of mills rolled up against clouds of smoke; this smoke mounts up night and day and never stops, coil on coil, cloud on cloud. It darkens the sky, obscures the sun. Its architectural patterns— white on black, black on gray, sulphur and black and gray—vary in stately fashion throughout all the hours. It is always there a symbol across the heavens of the never-ending toil going on within the mills.

Clustered about the foot of the mills live the workers. The houses are of two stories, and are mostly of brick. One set of houses faces the street, the other the court. The courts are bricked, and littered with piles of tin cans, piles of rubbish, bins of garbage, hillocks of refuse, refuse and litter, litter and refuse; and playing in the refuse and ashes and piles of cans, and with them, children.

I remember a certain bin of ashes and refuse. I had seen it in the fall, filled with ashes and putrefying vegetables and pieces of half-decayed old clothes. Now the tide of garbage and ashes had risen and over-flowed half-way across the street; children dug in the ashes and scaled the garbage-pile valiantly, one little boy beating like cymbals two tin cans.

They played here because there was nowhere else to play. There was nothing else to play with, so they played in the garbage-piles. They stamped their heels into the tin cans and skated across the frozen courtyard where the thin sooty rain froze upon the bricks.

Although school was not yet out, there was no end to the children. As Father Kazinci stopped to talk to a parishioner, they came flocking, greeting him with their treble "Good-day, Father," or, shyness coming between them and words, then with smiles. You could count them— bands of fifteen, eighteen, twenty.

Braddock was the cradle of the steel industry. Its mills existed before the great Homestead Mills. Carnegie Steel was born in Braddock. The mills grew, ramparting the Monongahela River, a frieze of mighty black chimneys belching forth their perpetual smoke, they spread to Rankin, to Homestead, to Duquesne.

It might be supposed that the chief product of Braddock and the other steel towns is steel.

This is not true.

Their principal product is children.

Swarms of children.

Hundreds and hundreds of children.

Generation after generation of children, born where no green thing grows, reared before the somber magnificence of the smoke which blankets the sky and obscures the sun. Generations of children playing in the refuse; hundreds upon hundreds whose only playgrounds are the forsaken bricked courtyards or the littered streets.

It was the spectacle of these children which made Father Kazinci and myself so silent in this round of parochial visits. House after house full of beautiful children, house after house where mothers had made attempts at beauty, where each poor adornment said, "I would not live here if I could live differently"; where the ornaments cried out, "I love beauty and color"; where the begonias growing in cans told of dreams of green fields and gardens.

All of Braddock is black; the soot of the mills has covered it. There is no spot in Braddock that is fair to see. There is no park, no open space; litter everywhere, a town of slack disorder, of scant self-respect. The people who have made money in the Braddock Mills live, most of them, in surrounding towns, away from the noise and clatter and dirt.

The steelworkers who can escape up to the hillsides; they go to North Braddock or to Wolftown; but many and many of them are condemned forever to the First Ward.

What condemns them to live in these slums is their children. The more children, the less chance of escape. This is an axiom. Here in these homes which we had just visited live the people of unfulfilled dreams. Here live the people whose hopes are constantly betrayed by every accident, the people without a margin.

Throughout the steel strike there was no group of people who stuck so firmly as did these Slovaks down in the Braddock slums. They would be striking yet; they were sorry to go back. The strike, to them, had meant opportunity; it had meant a road of escape; it had meant besides a court of appeal at last for grievances.

This is one of the things in the present condition of the steel industry which the workers find most difficult to bear. There is no way of presenting one's grievances. If you don't like your work, you can leave. This lusty, splendid industry, with its quantity production, is an autocracy.

It is as though principalities had ceased to exist as geographical areas, but exist now by industries. These principalities are young, and they have all the despotism of youth and power—of power that is built only on wealth and dominion, not on honor and glory. Power without responsibility. Power which can treat men's lives as commodities. Power which throttles among its subjects all efforts at self-government. Power, brutal, young, riotous, lusty, driven by the force of steam. A creative thing, made of fire and iron, and taking no account of the lives of the puny men shriveling before the blast furnace.

Smoke, fire, and iron and human lives are its substance. Gain and greed and the despair of many men are woven into the fabric of its lusty, unthinking despotism. Against this despotism the workers had revolted. They had been beaten. We had been visiting in this trail of the strike.

At last Father Kazinci spoke: "If you analyze what we have heard to-day, it means something like 'No advancement for the Slavs.' They cannot help giving them jobs, but they will give them as poor ones as they can. I wonder if John has his job." He looked toward a boy of twenty-one who was coming toward us.

"He was my most brilliant pupil. When he had to leave school, I wept. He comes from a most remarkable family. There are six boys; each one of them deserves a college education. I have to face no more bitter thing than to see one after another of my ambitious boys swallowed up by work. It's hard with all of them but with this boy it was nothing short of a crime; though he could not be kept down. When the strike came, he was on the road of advancement to chemist of the company."

We were face to face with him by now.

"How do you do, Father?"

"How are you, my boy? Did you get your old job back?"

"No, Father."

"Why not?"

"I don't know, Father; they wouldn't give it to me."

"Were you very active in the strike, my boy?"

"No, Father."

"You didn't stay around strike headquarters a lot?"

"No, Father; I was home."

"When you went for your job, what did they say to you?"

"They said, 'What's your name?' and when I told them they said: 'Nothing doing for you. We're not going to have nothing but Americans in the chemical department after this.'" He had spoken in a quiet, lackluster voice, and now bitterness broke out of him. "What makes an American?" he demanded. "Wasn't I born here? Weren't all of us born here? Ain't the boys like my brother Joe who volunteered as good

Americans, even if they have got 'ski' or 'ko' to their names—as good Americans as the fellows called White or Smith? I'll say they are! They said so too while the war was on. You remember the poster 'Americans all.' Say, Father, the man who made that picture ought to work in Carnegie Steel. He'd learn the difference between an American and a 'damn hunkey' quick enough!"

Again there was nothing to say. We had no answer for his bitterness. The thin rain fell on us. Some tow-headed children near had made a cheerful slide down the alley; an old woman, her head enveloped in a kerchief after the fashion of the peasants of Central Europe, toiled and slid along in her big shoes, carrying a load of wood. Almost every one in Allegheny County cooks by gas except the steelworkers of the slums. A silence as frozen as the rain held us. The boy broke the silence.

"What nationality do you suppose my little son is?" he asked. "He is only the third generation here. I guess he ain't got any country."

We walked on down the bleak alley, with its swarming tow-headed children who had found a plaything in the brittle surface of the icy pavement. At the end of the street towered the huge tanklike bulk of the mills, and over it rolled the heavy symphony of the smoke, menacing and magnificent; smoke that seemed to carry with it the promise of thunder and lightning.

"That boy's mother is a wonderful woman," said Father Kazinci. "She has eleven children, and each new one as it comes along she shows to me like a gift from God." We turned down a passageway which led down hill into a courtyard. The courtyard was lined around with smoke-blackened pens where the tenants kept hens and animals. The heaps of filth defacing the court were now covered with a thin purifying coating of ice. Five paces from the front door, on a slightly higher level, stood a privy common to several families. Near the door was a bench, on which sat a row of fowls, like everything else, shining with ice; while over the door projected three blackened boards—a shelter from the burning sun when the sweltering court became a brick oven, but now cutting out what little light there was. The brick house had been painted light blue, which gave it a cheerful air.

A smell of old grease, of drying clothes, rushed fiercely at us as we opened the basement door. A wide-bosomed woman who rocked a cradle greeted us. She was a strong woman, heavy, still comely, almost handsome, the mother of many sons. She broke into a torrent of greeting in her own tongue. Father Kazinci translated:

"She says, Father, you see me here in my bare feet and my rags. I have been here twenty-two years, and I live as you see. This is all I have—these rags, this cellar, my eleven children. Every night I bless God, who has kept them in good health. For twenty-two years, Father, I have worked from morning till night, and often late at night, but after all this work we have nothing to give them but this." She waved her hand about the room.

There were two small windows which did not open, a slit of a window behind where the front part of the house was higher than the courtyard, a stove, a table, four chairs, benches under the window, a cupboard with some dishes, while at one side of the room a staircase led upstairs, and on one side was a bright frieze of holy pictures. On the floor above the father and mother slept with the five younger children. In an attic room slept the four boys. Always there had been another baby. Before they could make a plan to escape from this cellar a new baby had come.

Peter and Lisa, the babies now in the room, had come the same year. John had had to leave school because other brilliant children were being born to the Savkos. Child after child, the pride of their teachers—the rising tide of aspiring young life had condemned those older to this filthy courtyard.

Lisa stood on the bench, her head silhouetted against the window. In her hand she held two flat pieces of gum; with these she made a cross against the window-pane, then a T, then an angle, then she put them carefully in her pinafore pocket. Then, tranquil, serious, absorbed, she looked at a book standing there, and so continued in her little world while her mother talked.

Father Kazinci translated: "Would I live here if I could get out? Would I live here, would I remain where the dirty water of the privy overflows and crawls over the court under the doorsill until it makes a pool on my kitchen floor? Is that a view for children to look at year after year, year after year? To keep them clean I must wash out in the yard. Look, missus, this is my apron!" She brought a stiff oilcloth apron, still frozen. "I wash out in the cold, so I won't splash water over my children, so they can have a dry place to play. Eleven souls to keep clean here in this Braddock means work."

She continued her story, illustrating it with wide and ample gestures:

"On Christmas we were all here, Johnny and his wife and the baby. Father, you see this little room and this small table, these few chairs? Fifteen souls. Some ate. I cleared away. Others sat down. The little girls sat on the stairs. Two boys used the black stove for a table. The children laughed and were happy because there was goose and stuffing, but my heart was heavy. Must the children eat from the floor like pigs even on this day of our blessed Lord? It was no comfort to me that he was born in a manger. For this one day I would have shortened my life if we could only all have sat down together. If only we might all of us, young and old, have celebrated Christmas by eating together at one table. I thought how beautiful if we could all have sat down together, each in his own chair, each with his own plate and knife and fork, on this one holiday. What happiness!"

Lisa put both arms around her mother, who gathered her up. Her arms had always been full of babies. You could have told that by the way she enfolded Lisa. She went on with her story. There was in it one green spot of delight.

Once, when Joe and John had been babies, she and her husband had $180 saved, and they had gone to Holyoke and visited a sister. They would have stayed, but there was no work for the father to do. That had been eighteen years before, but the memory of the wide Connecticut Valley and the sweet New England towns still gladdened this woman's heart.

The children began coming in from school. Tic, tac, toe, three little girls, Mary, Annie, Susie. They dragged a table out from underneath the big table and sat upon it, playing. Happiness lived in this meager room. It was a home made abidingly good by that undaunted, courageous mother. Here people were kind to one another. The little girls played together quietly with the harmony of children accustomed only to love.

Stevie came in, and George. The baby waked up, and his mother took him in her arms. The window was a luminous square of dark blue. She sat there, silhouetted against it, enormous, her head erect in the defense of her own. As the dusk deepened the children came to her, crowding themselves into her flanks. The three little girls stood on one side, Steven next, and then George.

She was talking: "Ah, my dears, that was a terrible time—yes, yes, that was the time! That was the time! Despair stared at me. Despair was stronger than God's hand. Despair walked at night beside me. They laid him off—they laid off our father! *We* were on strike just now, but it was the company that was striking *then!* I had Annie in my arms, another coming, seven mouths to feed! What can I do? I sat one day for six hours in the boss's office. 'I will stay on my knees here,' I thought, 'until he takes our father back. Even if it is a slack time, there is some work,' I thought, 'they must give him to do.'

"It was at that time I used to buy rags from the ragman—the rags the Americans had thrown away—and wash them clean and patch them and make clothes for the babies. What could I do?

"That was when my Johnnie went to work. He was thirteen. Ah, it broke my heart! He found himself work at night, so he could study at day. For a year he held the hot links of chains in a pincers from five o'clock at night until three in the morning, but the hot metal hurt his eyes. His eyes were always red, but he would not give up. You remember, Father, he did this for a year. He would fall asleep over his books, poor boy!

"Oh, my dear, misfortune has followed me from the day I left my own land. One misfortune after another. Now it is Stevie who must work."

"What do you do, Stevie?"

"I set up pins in the bowling alley from six till half-past eleven. I get five dollars."

"How could I help it, Father? It is always the same, so many mouths to fill." She looked at us with her extraordinary intensity and cried out: "Would to God I had never come! Would to God I had never seen this land! Would to God I had remained where, if we had no school, we might have had blue sky and green fields about us! What good does it do them—the few days of schooling? With them it is a thirst and a hunger for knowledge, and I must hunger and thirst with them and see them starve for the knowledge they cannot have. What is the meaning, Father? Why should things be so?"

She sat there in the dying light with her children around her, easing her overburdened heart by her talk. This was all she knew of America. The wide currents of our country had never touched her. Opportunity had proved illusion. There had been one glimpse into the country which we so love; for the rest she had lived within the iron autocracy of the steel town.

Yet she was the woman whose praise poets have sung down the ages—the unselfish mother. What could anyone have taught her in this country? Not a greater devotion, surely. Nor could she have learned to make a better home. Its enveloping goodness was as unescapable as light—an atmosphere in which those children throve. For them she fought a continual battle with the three fears which cloud the lives of all working people—the fear of unemployment, the fear of illness, and the fear of old age.

As I sat there and listened to this story of thwarted dreams I felt as if I had been trying to keep from crying for a long time. I was angry, and I was right to be angry. My country was being robbed before my eyes of its greatest wealth; it was being robbed of its ambitious children.

John Savko, whose brilliant mind clamors to be fed and who worked a year heating the links of chains rather than leave school; then Andy, Joe, Mike, and now Steve putting up pins in the alley at night.

Perhaps when Joe comes back from the Navy things will be better for this family so disinherited from things which we are proud to call American.

The door opened, and Johnny came in. Upstairs the father and Andy, the third son, were sleeping—both on the night shift. They were all gathered under one roof now, this family of aliens who had lived among us for twenty-three years in so precarious a fashion. John spoke. "Father," he said, "I found out the name of the American fellow who got my job." He spoke without irony. "It was O'Rourke."

# Fraycar's Fist

## Fraycar's Fist, 1924

Fraycar is dead and buried, but his memory lives. His fist and his anger
are symbols of the steelworker's irreconcilable revolt.

If you choose to be fanciful when you look at the everlasting smoke
that rolls up night and day from the tall chimneys of the mills, you may
imagine that it comes from the fires in the hearts of the men who work
in the mills.

I pieced together this story of Fraycar from many sources. Young
Pivač, who will never marry Rosie Fraycar because he is dying of
consumption, told me part of it. I learned some of it from Father
Kalish. I heard more from Greznac, standing in his empty saloon, and
there is the detail given me by the wife of the county detective. One by
one they built up Fraycar's life before my eyes until it seemed as
though I watched some menacing and heroic figure being molded by
an invisible hand. I see his rage dominating the strike—its heart—
since it was the emotion back of reason which made the strike possible.

I first heard of Fraycar on a raw, spiritless day in the last stretches of
the steel strike, of 1920, a time monotonous, dreary, desperate. The
strikers hanging on grimly—hunger stabbing the men—hope oozing
from the leaders—Valley Forge.

We were sitting around strike headquarters waiting for something to
happen, when news came over the phone that the state police had
broken up a striker's funeral over in Halkett, a nearby town. I heard
Dink Williams, the big organizer, telephoning:

"Broke up a funeral, did they—the sons o' guns! Whose? A Slavish
fella named Fraycar? No—never heard of him. Not active in the strike?
Then *why, why?* Rode 'em down, did they—lost their umbrellas—
musta looked rich to them Cossacks to see them umbrellas flying! So
long—see you when you get here."

Williams was a big, bald man; he limped and had only one eye and a
scar jagged a red road across the innocent-looking surface of his pink
scalp, which was covered lightly with a grizzled down. An old mine
worker.

"What made them Cossacks ride down a funeral for?" he wondered,
staring around at us.

"Corpse inciting to riot," suggested young Barstow, a flip young
newspaper man.

"You said a mouthful, young fella," Dink answered, cocking his one angry eye at Barstow. "Corpses've incited to riot before now, but not *this* fella—I wonder what for. I wonder—"

Williams sat with his game leg sprawled out in the dislocated way it had of looking as if it didn't belong to him.

"Havash was phoning. He says there's never been such a funeral. Says after the carriages there wasn't no end of it. When the Cossacks rode 'em down they went slipping an' splashing down the side streets and that there was wrecked umbrellas everywhere."

During the afternoon men came in dripping. Huge, silent men. They had not much to say. Yes, the mounted police broke up the funeral. The men had run.

"They said there were too many of us," was their explanation.

At that time, there being a strike, an ordinance was passed against processions; this funeral had become a procession, a demonstration.

These men did not seem surprised to have the funeral broken up. The "Cossacks," as they called them, were there, they all thought, to prevent, inhibit, invade other assemblages as harmless as funerals. Life is violent in the steel country. It has been violent since the Homestead days. There were men killed in Halkett in 1916.

I got the impression from the sparse trickle of talk of a very large funeral—a funeral as long as Main Street. During the afternoon Fraycar's funeral took form in my mind; it became something I myself had seen. A heavy picture, black on black, black with a massive background of smoke. Smoke uncoiling itself to the clouded sky, smoke of such density as to seem solid. This smoke was the background of a black hurly-burly of men in heavy shoes, slipping and sliding on slushy pavements.

I saw it as if I had been there—the piles of dirty snow, the oily smoke writhing upward to the menacing slate-colored sky. The wind wrenching umbrellas from hands. Black and white streets—mounds of tarnished snow—black streets shining with rain.

There was no clue among all these taciturn mourners why they had come in such numbers. But they had come from Monessen and Donora and Duquesne as easily as from South Pittsburgh—it seemed that every Slav and Pole and Rumanian had come to Fraycar's funeral. They came from Rankin stewing over the smoke of the mills and from Charleroi. Men had come who did not belong to Fraycar's church or his society.

One man said to another: "He told his last wishes in the end."

"He said his last wishes," the other agreed grimly. This speech seemed to have unloosed the men's tongues. Talk became louder.

The room began to smell of wet leather, of black dye, of men. There was a clash of guttural talk from a group in a corner. A big fellow shook his fist upward in a slow, menacing gesture. There was something solemn in this shaken fist, the symbol of revolt.

It was part of some story. A crash of laughter followed—disquieting laughter. Laughter more menacing than anger.

It seemed that Fraycar had died, one might say, of rage. With bare hands he had attacked a state trooper, and tried to pull him from his horse.

Out of the confusion of talk came the high note of a boy's voice:

"I seen him go for the Cossack! I seen him jump at him! They was chasin' every one back into their houses. Fraycar was comin' along.

" 'Get into the house,' said one of the Cossacks.

" 'This ain't my house,' Fraycar answered.

" 'Get into the house, you—!' the Cossack yells and lifts his club. Then Fraycar give a roar. I seen him spring with his hands crooked. I seen him fall back. He lay there crumpled up. First we thought he was shot, but he'd had a sort o' shock."

"His rage killed him," Dink Williams said into the silence that followed the boy's story.

That was my first picture of Fraycar—fury incarnate, leaping at a mounted trooper. Terror was what these police had meant to the strikers—these magnificent mounted troops with their riot clubs upraised. Anger had to come molten and fierce—anger had to be stronger than love of life to be stronger than that terror.

I heard this story again from the wife of the county detective. She had a nice home with a piano and Globe-Werneke bookcases and growing plants. There were pictures on the wall, and you could have found no prettier woman anywhere.

"I saw the Cossacks on horseback come riding along as if they was God. Every one comes out running and rubbering when they pass to see the show. When they got to the end of the street the troopers turned around and chased every one in. They chased women off their own porches and doorsteps. They tried to chase Fraycar, but he sprang at them."

You could not forget the man who was so blind with fury of outrage that he could attack an armed and mounted trooper. The thought of him followed me—something unexplained. There had to be a reason for the fury of his hate, which made him give his life in this act of violence.

The next I heard of Fraycar was in the union office of the steelworkers in Halkett. This town is a rampart of mills along the river. Near the mills are slums. Bricked streets, bricked courtyard—bricked courtyard—garbage. That is Halkett.

The Baltimore & Ohio Railway slashes insolently through the town as though it were master. But it is not master—the mastery is for the mills, which make steel ingots and pig iron from piles of red dust. The town mounts an abrupt hill as though to get away from the belching mills, and everyone who can lives on the hillside—away. The steel-workers—the condemned—live on the stinking, oozing bricked-over river bottom near the mills. The river is near but they do not glimpse it. Not far is country, but they see no green thing. No green thing can grow in Halkett—the smoke blackens all.

There was a crowd of men in the office—men of ten nationalities. They had come for the strike bulletin and stood crowded together. They were neither clever nor pushing; but they had strength and they had patience. They had no smartness or nimbleness of wit; but it is on such men that the strength of nations is built.

Pivač was talking about Fraycar. He talked in English because his listeners were of many races, though of but one occupation. They all made steel.

"Right off when I first come to this country I was comin' up Mill Street one night. I was a little drunk. The night was so bright you could see the smoke like day. Awful still. Then I heard some one cursin' in Slavish. I seen Fraycar standin' there cursin'. He seemed bigger than any one I ever see. God he cursed! He was cursin' the mills. Slag and slack, fire and steel, men and bosses. I stood there. I don't know what got me. I ran—I ran—"

A paroxysm of coughing interrupted Pivač. There was a murmur of talk among the men.

"I seen him like that—I seen him in Greznac's saloon."

Fraycar had seemed to young Pivač like a black blot of fury, raging there where the mill wall rises up sheer against a mean street. Above the wall are the great tanklike structures of the mills and the chimneys belching forth their perpetual smoke.

Men have been shot in this street. Every one knows that. Every one who goes to work knows that in 1916 there were machine guns at these gates.

During the strike many men died in the mill from molten metal. Men die easily making steel.

Fraycar cursed death, too, standing in the moonlight. He cursed the molten steel and the machines for killing. He cursed the men for being killed.

Pivač finished; this paroxysm of coughing dyed his dirty handkerchief red.

"After I ran away, I had to come back. Fraycar stood there. He lifted up his fist. He roared: *'I am stronger than you!'*"

There was silence. Then a man in the crowd repeated:

"I am stronger than you." *"I am stronger than you!"* They repeated in many languages. A light air of excitement swept through the room.

It was as though they had been drinking an exciting wine. Their dark eyes flashed. Every one was repeating Fraycar's words and Fraycar's gesture.

The rest of the story came to me from Father Kalish. I ran into him one day as I was slipping along Halkett's streets. There was a glaze of ice under foot. The mounds of snow were a dismal gray, but it had rained, and they were covered with a thin coating of ice—a day like that of Fraycar's funeral. The rain fell dense, insistent; a smoke cap brooded over the town. From the mill chimneys the smoke rose slowly coil on coil so thick it looked like something you could cut.

Father Kalish asked me to go with him, and we walked down Braddock Street together. This is a street which borders the B & O track. There is a sidewalk fenced off from the shining tracks and a row of sordid houses past which the trains run shrieking day and night.

Back of the houses are foul courtyards divided from other yards by untidy, blackened board fences. There are always piles of ashes mixed with tin cans, and children playing among them.

Before one of these houses Father Kalish stopped.

"Fraycar lived here," he said.

He knocked on the door, which was opened by a woman wide of flank, deep bosomed, a big bulk of a woman, heavy and strong with much childbearing. She might have come over yesterday from the old country. She had lived here a quarter of a century. She was a fair woman with eyes set wide apart.

A young girl was sitting bathing her feet—Rosie Fraycar. She got up and scuttled away. The girl was lovely, milk white, honey haired, her clear sea-green eyes set wide apart. Her two front teeth had a tiny space between them, which seemed like the last emphasis of her beauty. Flawless beauty is rare; and here it was in this gray street. Strange flower to bloom in this place—strange child to have been fathered by Fraycar. There was the distance of centuries of civilization between the girl and her mother. Rosie was lovely—too lovely, too perfect. You couldn't imagine her staying here.

"She's a comfort to you," said Father Kalish, nodding after the girl.

"She's a good girl," the mother agreed. She spoke without emphasis. She sat massive, remote, in her immaculate room with its frieze of holy pictures, which gave only the effect of a line of color, since they seemed to flow into one another. It was the cleanest place I had ever seen. The stove shone, and on each side there were five blue enamel pot covers arranged in a pattern. The curtains were freshly washed. There was an onyx clock and some begonias in painted tin cans.

Rosie came back, but it was her mother who held me. I never was near a woman who seemed less trivial. I had the sense that she had lived always within sight of the doors of birth and death. There is something shrunken in the natures of people who, like us, evade the thought of the unborn and who do not accept death.

I had, too, the sense that more was passing between Father Kalish and Mrs. Fraycar than appeared in the talk.

While he talked I looked around the room—a room neat as a church, a room of perfection, passionately clean in the midst of Braddock Street. I thought of Fraycar cursing in the moonlight, cursing before the implacable blank walls, the smoke rolling up over all the town— and this house with its cleanness, also a protest, a revolt as long as life, against Halkett, a mute rebellion against the stinking court and Braddock Street.

Suddenly Father Kalish asked:

"How long have you lived in this house? Twenty-four years?"

"Twenty-four years," she answered gravely.

They looked at one another—a long look. I knew what was passing in their minds. Here Fraycar had come as a young man. Here between the shrieking railway and the stinking court eleven children had been born.

We left; and walking through the filth of Halkett, Father Kalish told me the end of my story, and what it was that had brought the steel-workers streaming out behind Fraycar's funeral.

"I haven't been to that house," he said, "since the day Fraycar died. When they took him home he was unconscious for a day. Then I heard he had regained consciousness and I was already starting to him when his Joe came panting up my steps.

"'What's the matter, my boy?' I said. 'Is your father worse?'

"'He won't speak—he's come to, but he won't speak. He won't tell his last wishes.'

"Such a thing is a great calamity in a Slovak family. For with us when someone is going to die no one makes believe it's not so. When a Slovak man dies all the family sits around with him and he tells what he wants to be buried in and all about the funeral. It seems to help the family to have them leave last wishes. There is the feeling that you're doing something for the one you love even if they have gone. It's natural when you think of it, that a poor man should be interested in his funeral since that's the only time in all his life that he has had things nice. Our people, whatever they do, have splendid funerals. I preach against the extravagance of it in vain. They say to me, 'Father, if we have nothing when we're alive, anyway we can have a funeral when we die.'

"So no matter if you live in two rooms at Braddock Street all your life like Fraycar, with the smell of garbage in your nose all summer—day shift and night shift, ten hours day and fourteen night—they can't cheat you when you die. And now Fraycar was lying there and he wouldn't even speak of his funeral.

"'Why won't he speak?' I asked Joe.

"'It's because he's angry—it's because he can't remember.' But what he couldn't remember I couldn't get out of the boy, so I hurried along to the house.

"'How is he, Missus?' I asked Mrs. Fraycar.

"'He's dying with his face to the wall—he won't speak. I've gone in first with one pair of pants and then with the other. One pair he bought when he was a pallbearer to the saloonkeeper's father. These are new and the ones he should wear. But who knows? He may feel more at ease lying in the old Sunday ones, and how, if I choose the wrong ones, could I forgive myself?'

"She rocked to and fro as I sat there. It was a wet day outside and she had spread pieces of bagging over her handmade rugs, which she had woven, every one herself, out in the courtyard. Even over the door-step was some bagging to keep the house clean just like today.

"'It's hard to have your man dying with his eyes staring on a wall,' she went on, 'with never a word to let you know what his last wishes are, and a vein throbbing like a heart in his forehead. And it isn't his last wishes that's the worst. It's that he should be dying tormented by the anger that's been tormenting him all his life. For the matter with him is that he can't remember why he always cursed the mills when he was drunk.'

"There was a sound in the other room, and we all started up and stood in the doorway. The room was full of beds. Nothing but beds in the room. It's like that in all our homes. When you've got seven children at home in two rooms, how else do you make out? Steve was lying in the middle of the biggest bed. A terrible figure of a man, his shoulders wide as the doorway, and his hairy arms thrown out of the covers. A man like a giant, and his face purple as a plum against the white pillow.

"Steve opened his knotted arms and threw them out wide. His voice was thick as if there was blood in his throat.

"'Tell me,' he cried at us, 'what made me so mad when I got drunk? I knew when I pulled the Cossack from his horse, and now I don't. Maybe Greznac knows. I got drunk a thousand times in his saloon and run out cursing the mills.'

"Joe wiggled out as quick as an eel after Greznac, while we stood there ashamed that we couldn't help Fraycar.

"We went back and Mrs. Fraycar sat down in the heavy fashion of women who are carrying a grief.

"'I never found out why he got so angry,' she said. 'With all the children, I had more to do than to find out why our father cursed. It was his way, I thought. When he was drunk he was like a giant trying to break out of a cage. He would drink—Holy Virgin, how he would drink! And his anger would flow out. Often he talked about it with me.

"What did I mean by that?" he'd say. "Why was I angry? I know and yet I don't know. When I'm drunk I know why, and when I am sober I don't. I'm always angry inside. Mother, my anger don't go out any more than the blast furnace."'

"The door opened and the saloonkeeper and his mother came in. She was an old woman, as wrinkled as a fig, and her head tied up in a black cloth.

"'How is he?' they asked. 'Has he spoken?'

"Mrs. Fraycar shook her head.

"'Don't you grieve, my dearie,' said the old woman, 'don't grieve. Our father when he died did worse by speaking than if he had held his tongue. You know it's true yourself, John. You know your father did no good by speaking, for he was obstinate when he was alive, and he was obstinate when he was dying. Remember, Mary, he would have Sam Tomko as pallbearer instead of my Uncle Mike, and he a bachelor and old and with money in the bank. Little did our father care for his children as he lay dying. Sam Tomko he would have. Your own Steve came and reasoned with him, for Steve also was his pallbearer. "Leave me out," he said; "my feelings won't be hurt." Then our father cursed at me. "This is your doing, woman," he said. "Are my last wishes sacred or are they not?" What could I say? He had his will as was his right. So don't grieve, my dear—there's worse than hearing no last wishes.'

"Greznac went to the room where Steve was lying as we had left him, watching the door with his furious eyes. Steve asked in his thick voice:

"'What made me mad when I was drunk?'

"'When you were drunk,' said Greznac, 'it was as if smoke and the flames choked and burned you. You seemed more like a demon than a man when the anger took you and you ran out into the street. As well try to stop a furnace in blast.'

"'But why? Why?' Steve began. The vein on his forehead was swollen and seemed almost black in his purple face. The beating of it frightened us.

"'Men get drunk in saloons every night. What makes some laugh and some cry? Why do some want to kiss the bartender, and some go home and beat their wives? No one knows,' said Greznac. 'You got mad. One could see it bubbling and welling, until you would give a bellow and run out. This was a strange thing—no one laughed at you. When you left there was silence. You understand? The men would stop talking. The men at the bar drinking would stop with their glasses half raised to their lips. The young fellows would run out and watch you from a distance, and Mike Tomko, drunk as he was himself, would follow you until you went home.'

"This wasn't what Steve wanted to hear. It didn't help him. We all stood silent in the face of his anguish."

We had left the mean streets behind and mounted the hill. Father Kalish paused before the door of his rectory. I went in with him. We sat down in the living room overlooking the town and he went on:

"It does seem strange that none of us knew the reason for Steve Fraycar's anger. Every one knew this habit of his. We took it for granted as one takes things in life. We stood there stupidly. Celia, Fraycar's married daughter, came in from upstairs, where she lived. One baby clung to her skirts; another was in her arms. A cloak was wrapped around her big body after the uncomfortable way you try to hide such things in this country.

"Celia stood in the doorway, tears running down her face. All the children were proud of their father because of his anger, which had marked him out from among the other steelworkers. I had heard her say when she was little and the boys teased her: 'Leave me be, or my father will tear you to bits.'

"'Don't cry, Celia,' Fraycar said. 'Death's—nothing to cry for—death—birth—I go—a new one comes.'

"She sat down on the edge of the bed. The children stared at their grandfather. She had stopped crying, but she could not speak.

"'Celia,' said Steve, 'you look—as if you were born—among the slim birch trees where—I used to walk with your mother. There were—blue flowers there. It is a long ways—from here to there.' They were both silent while she held his hand. Presently he said: 'Celia, there's a long—way from you to me.'

"Mrs. Fraycar sat rocking to and fro, and I knew it wasn't for his last wishes that she grieved. I knew she felt, as I did, that for the sake of his soul, which was passing, he needed to know the reason for his anger.

"'If we send for Mike—' I said after a time. For it came to me that perhaps his old friend, Mike Tomko, the one who had always taken him home when he was drunk, could help his soul to search out what he needed to know. Then, as if in answer to our wish, he was there, wiping his feet outside the door, a man as big as Steve, an old man nearing fifty, with a chest like a cask. Fraycar turned his angry eyes on him.

"'They told you I'm dying, eh, Mike?'

"'We all have to go sometime,' Mike answered.

"And Fraycar said slowly: 'I have been—twenty-four years—in this house—eleven children—have been born in this room.'

"And I knew what was in the minds of both, for Tomko had gotten away from the courtyard where the little heat waves rose up in summer, and where the garbage accumulated all winter to rot in the spring, and he had a house on the hill all paid for but four hundred and fifty dollars. Twenty-four years Fraycar and his wife had lived here, always expecting to get free of Braddock Street to the hill overlooking the river.

"'Talk,' said Fraycar thickly. 'Talk of old times.'

"So Tomko began talking, in a soothing fashion.

"'Do you remember,' he said, 'when we first talked of coming to America? We were boys and we would go out for a walk down past the flour mill, where every one brought grain to be ground. Long lines of geese would waddle past us, ducks were swimming in the mill pond. Our lives—they were like the clear water running down the hill. We would talk of America. Sundays we went to church, all the boys and all the girls looking at each other. We used to lie on the side of the hill and talk about the girls and heroes, and how Big Marco wrestled. Budapest—how far that seemed. There was no steamcar nearer to our village than fifteen miles. What dreams we dreamed! Every one dreams those dreams who comes here. We saw our dreams come true. We worked early and late. America! It sounded like the call of a trumpet—a golden trumpet, it called to us sitting by our river or working in the brown earth. America! What it meant—what dreams!

"'I can see us sitting on the deck of the ship—each with his young wife. You said, "I shall save my money and go back and buy me a farm." I said, "I shall be an American, a citizen!" How our hearts beat when we came to the great harbor. What happened to our dreams—what happened to us? I wanted always to get away to green fields.'"

Father Kalish paused and looked out of his window over the mills. He began again:

"The room had gotten dark, and I noticed that tears were running down Mary Fraycar's face. There were tears, too, in Fraycar's eyes. And then I noticed that I, too, was crying, for Tomko was telling the story of all my people who come here to the mills—the story of their dreams turned to dust in their hearts.

"'Back and forth from the mills,' Tomko's voice went on, 'back and forth—a shuttle. They would not let us go. Those mills said, "You must live in my shadow. Your eyes shall never look on a green thing." Something choked me in those days—there is no air to breathe here. Look at the sun. You can look in its eye. It is more like the moon than the sun. Look at the twisting, writhing smoke keeping time to the wind blowing up and down the river. Back and forth from the mills—back and forth—a shuttle—a machine.'

"It was as though Tomko's thoughts came dripping from his mouth. He kept on talking while the boys, one after another, came in the room—Fraycar's five grown sons, four steelworkers. Tomko didn't see them, nor did Fraycar, who lay there still and formidable, the vein beating in his forehead.

"Suddenly Fraycar threw out his hand. '*I know now!*' he called. 'I know. It's *this!* These children—this room—our dreams. I know—I know. It's this— It's all of this—dreams. Twenty-four years ready to go!

"'When I was drunk I thought the machines were alive. I thought we were owned by the cranes—I thought we were slaves! I thought they kept us here. The mills sucked me in mornings—they spit me out nights. When I was drunk I thought the mills were eating me. I cursed at the machines that owned me. *It's not them—it's not the mills keeps us!* I have nothing—I die as I was born. I have only one thing. I leave you my anger.' He lifted up his great fist. '*I leave you this!*' he shouted."

The dark smoke rolled up slowly to the gray sky in front of Father Kalish's window. He walked to it and looked down gravely at Halkett.

"Hundreds of men have heard Fraycar's last message," he said. "Hundreds and hundreds saw that shaken fist."

# Organizing Shirts

## A Footnote to Folly, 1935

In November 1919 and early January 1920 the Department of Justice launched the notorious Palmer Raids, in the course of which virtually every major Communist or left-Socialist national leader was either arrested or forced into hiding. It was not until the late spring of 1920 that the illegalities of federal, state, and local Red-hunters were stemmed by a tardy protest from some outraged judges, reporters, government officials, and prominent liberals. By this time the disruption of the American organized radical movement was near complete.

With so many of her friends in jail or fleeing New York City, Mary Vorse feared that she too might be swept into the Red Scare nets. At this time, the Amalgamated Clothing Workers' Union was providing transportation for some of its best organizers, those who felt most vulnerable to Attorney General Palmer's reign of terror, to areas outside New York state. Vorse made use of her union friends and hastily acquired a job as an Amalgamated organizer—in the safely distant coal fields of rural Pennsylvania, where the Amalgamated was conducting a campaign in the heart of the anthracite district.

When the clothing trades were organized a decade before, some of the shirt manufacturers had escaped union wages by moving their factories to the little mining towns of Schuylkill County in eastern Pennsylvania. There was little other employment available to the miners' wives and daughters who were recruited to work in the shirt factories. The factory girls—many of them under fifteen years old—worked a six-day week and an eight- to nine-hour day for as little as $3.50 a week. The older women—widows or wives with large families or sick husbands—did piecework at home. They were paid an average of 10¢ per hour. The shirts they made sold for $3.00 to $4.00 apiece.

In the Schuylkill Valley, the Amalgamated had to fight the AFL as well as the employers. Factory owners who feared an Amalgamated victory frequently called in affiliates of the AFL, such as the United Textile Workers or the United Garment Workers, to raid the Amalgamated's organization. Employers and the town officials preferred to deal with the more conservative, and more easily corrupted, AFL unions which had demonstrated little real concern for the welfare of the female labor force.

When the steel strike was over I was offered a job organizing shirts in Schuylkill County, Pennsylvania, by the Amalgamated Clothing Workers.

This period has in it only memories of youth and gaiety. After the grim struggle and defeat of the steel strike, after the raids, organizing shirts was a relaxation—though everything happened to Ann Craton and myself: We were arrested, thrown out of halls, had our union taken away by the United Garment Workers (UGW). The Cossacks, the state troopers, were called out on our account—we were called "Bolsheviks" and wildcats by the bosses, and by the Amalgamated Clothing Workers a "Bolshevik organization" supported by mysterious Moscow gold. Our strikers got arrested "drumming scabs home"—yet in some way the ferocity of the other strike situations was lacking, and wherever we went the miners were with us as a comforting background. Even when the American Federation of Labor (AFL) fought us as a dual union, the sympathy of local labor was with us.

At that time the Amalgamated Clothing Workers had an organization in the men's clothing trade of about 200,000. It was, however, outside the AFL. In 1905 a convention of the United Garment Workers resulted in a split; the vast majority of the rank and file, having been tricked out of the United Garment Workers, formed the Amalgamated Clothing Workers under the leadership of Sidney Hillman. The United Garment Workers, the AFL organization, retained a membership of 5,000 only and of all men's clothing had control only over the overall industry.

In the five years of its existence the Amalgamated had become one of the strongest and most militant unions in America. It had developed boards of adjustment by which disputes between workers and employers could be settled without strikes or lockouts.

Each shop had a trade board composed of workers' and employers' representatives with an impartial chairman paid jointly by both sides.

The work of the Amalgamated did not stop with shop conditions, wages, hours, and adjustment boards. The organization maintained classes, helped the foreign worker to learn English; there were teachers in Chicago and New York in economics, science, and American history. In Rochester professors from the university lectured to the workers. The Amalgamated also had published weekly papers in several languages.

Nevertheless, it was rated a "dual union" by the American Federation of Labor.

In the winter of 1920 the Amalgamated Clothing Workers was conducting an organizational campaign in Pennsylvania, unionizing shirts. Of all the needle trades, shirts are the most underpaid and the most sweated. They were in 1919, and they still are. Our tactics were to lay our cards on the table. We appeared before the Central Labor Unions, calling attention to the fact that no UGW organizer had ever been seen in this district and asking for support, which we invariably got until word came from Washington that we were a "wildcat" organization.

Schuylkill County is the heart of the anthracite region. The Pennsylvania Dutch have given the towns their comfortable appearance; but every town has a mine for its heart, and every one of these towns has also one or more shirt factories.

When labor raised its head and organized the clothing trades, some enterprising shirtmakers had the bright idea of moving unostentatiously out of reach of the union. They moved to the mining districts and invited the miners' daughters within their gray doors. Until the Amalgamated started its organizing, these firms were undisturbed; they made shirts cheap and sold them dear.

Some of the factories looked like kindergartens. Here little girls of twelve and thirteen worked in defiance of the law. They worked from forty-eight to fifty hours a week, and for wages as low as $3.50. Most of the girls were working eight and nine hours a day for seven and eight dollars a week.

When the girls came pouring out of the factories, you could not tell the difference between them and the schoolgirls. Very few older women were among them. We soon found out the reason. The older women did homework. The sweatshop had moved out of the city to these pleasant Dutch towns.

Every evening you could see a boy coming out of the shop bent double under a load of shirts. These were distributed up and down the street. In some of those pleasant little houses with fruit trees behind them women were working with the same awful, unflagging haste of tenement sweatshop workers.

Into house after house, the great mounds of shirts went; in house after house, women were working until ten and eleven at night. There were widows, women with great families of children, women with sick husbands.

We sat in a house in Tremont, talking to one of the women working on a huge pile of shirts.

"I only do this in winter," she said. "In summer I have a big garden that keeps me busy, but what we make is so small that it hardly pays and I don't know what I'd do if I were dependent on it like some women I know. They have to work from morning to night to make out."

"How much can you make?" we asked.

"Well, if I work all the time," she said, "I can do five dozen shirts in two hours."

That is to say, by working as hard as she possibly could, this woman could make ten cents an hour. Compared with prewar prices, purchasing power of that ten cents was diminished one-half in 1920.

Ann Craton had already been organizing for some time when I was sent up to be her assistant. She was very small and very young to be responsible for the difficult organizing work. She looked hardly any older than the girls among whom we worked. The first day I got there, we went up to a town called Minersville where the night before the Amalgamated had given a dance.

Minersville is a sturdy, red-roofed town whose houses climb up and down steep hills with cheerful alacrity. Groups of red-cheeked youngsters were going skating, boys were sliding down hills of glare ice, boys sliding down in old dishpans, babies sliding down on bits of carpet, children sliding downhill on improvised toboggans. These boys and girls seemed to compose the entire population of Minersville.

Through every street we passed little girls ran out of the houses to speak to us, gay little girls, defiant little girls, girls flirting with the danger of losing their jobs.

Most of them were miners' daughters. They had cut their teeth on a union button and their lullabies had been the sound of their parents "drumming the scabs home" in the great anthracite strike of 1902.

"Oh, we know how to strike," they assured us. "You get a panful of rocks and nail the scabs with 'em and you wait outside the fac'try and drum 'em home!" You make a charivari; that is, you accompany home the scabs with whistles, catcalls, and booings and woofings and beatings on dishpans and the clash of pot covers. For so had anthracite conducted its strikes, and they were disappointed to learn that the Amalgamated was against "rocking" and "beating home scabs."

One of the girls who had been fired by the boss, Demski, joined us.

"He called me a Bolshewikis," she said. "'Don't get gay with me,' I told him, 'or I'll slap your face! I don't know what you mean but you don't mean nothing good.'" Demski had fired three girls and the widow. Everyone in Minersville called her "the widow" as a sort of tribute to the plucky fight she was putting up to support her four children. There were plenty of other widows in town, of course, because there was "miners' consumption" around there as well as in every other mining town and the flu had made widows enough the year before and the war had made more.

This widow had gone to work in the shirt factory. Then when the union came, she joined it.

"The other girls can join or not," she said. "I *got* to join. I got four children to support."

The same battle was being fought in small in Minersville as was being fought in the steel industry. The battle concerned itself with the right of the workers to organize for the purpose of bettering their conditions. Demski's methods were not unlike those that were used in the steel towns. Firing people was his classic answer to unionism in his shop. He was keeping time to the tune Gary played with such a great orchestra in the steel industry.

When he got the news that the girls were organizing, he bore down on them. "What's this I hear?" he screamed. "You vas Bolshewikis? You vas all making Bolshewisms in my factory? You vant you should be fired everybody, yes? Or that I move der factory so there won't be work for nobody?" When he found Ann Craton waiting in front of the factory to give out notices of a meeting, his anger overflowed.

"Vat do you make on me?" he yelled. "Do you make on me a Bolshewismus? You cannot make Bolshewismus in front of my factory."

"I have as much right in this street as you have," she replied calmly.

Demski's definition of Bolshevism was simple. "Bolshewikis" were those who disobeyed him, they were those who joined unions. Demski's head had got bald and his stomach round bossing girls. Treat 'em rough, work 'em hard, pay 'em little, had always worked until now.

Demski sounds like the funny papers, the fat bald boss screaming Bolshewikis! Bolshewikis! as soon as union labor shows its head. But he was not funny. He was a serious symptom. It was characteristic of the day that he should scream sedition at the first hint that there was organization on foot. If you can tar organized labor with the name "radical," it will be easier to crush. The same tactics are being employed today in the South where the Amalgamated is again organizing shirts.

After a long walk we got to the widow's house. It seemed to me I had never seen so many pretty girls together in one place. Their excited voices greeted us, all talking at once.

There was something essentially sound about their excitement. The ability to resent injustice promptly, the spirit of fair play was what had brought these girls here. They were citizens seeking their rights.

In the background stood the little widow, her hand on her boy's shoulder. The baby slept on a bed near the stove. Two lovely little Croatian girls sat side by side in the back of the room holding hands so tightly that their knuckles showed white.

Near me sat a little girl with dark eyes, her scarlet tam not redder than her cheeks. Her little skirts were halfway to her knees, her hair short.

"What made you join the union?" I asked her.

"I talked of it with Papa and Mama. Mama said I ought. She said it was a good thing. There was a union and all of us should go in. Papa said all the men's been wishing for years the girls had a union." Joining a union was no flighty adventure. It was something to be undertaken only after being put before the family forum and maturely advised upon.

We visited the union shop in West Philadelphia the next day. The room was long and light and everywhere were piles of light-colored shirts. Shirts of the best quality, shirts that sold for $3 and $4 apiece. Two little girls near the door were gravely examining them for bad work and sending the defective ones upstairs to be repaired. They were little girls, girls of eleven with broomstick legs, pink cheeks, and laughing eyes.

"How old are you?" I asked. They both chorused: "Fourteen!" Their eyes met. They giggled. Then laughter welled up. "Fourteen!" they gasped.

Upstairs the motors hummed and never stopped. A single boy was working in the midst of the girls. He was at a buttoning machine. He fed it with buttons, and then "buzz, buzz," the buttons were on, a hypnotizing process.

A lean girl in a long knitted sweater marked the places for buttons. She threw the shirt over a board shaped like a shirt front; a peg held the stud holes together. She marked the places for the buttons and then put on a new shirt with a jerky motion—jerk! One, two, three, four—jerk! One, two, three, four—jerk! There was no end to it. It went on all day. One of her shoulders was higher than the other, her shoulder blades stuck out, her freckled neck was like a pipestem. Jerk! One, two, three, four. We asked how old she was. "Fifteen," she answered without stopping. "How long have you worked here?" "Three years."

"They're Poles—they've got an awful big family," the little union secretary whispered. She was a shy, competent-looking girl, proud of her union, of the shorter hours, the higher wages. "She makes fifteen dollars, now."

"How much did you use to make?"

"Nine," said the girl without turning her head.

"That one is our little Maggie," she nodded at a little girl across the room. "You've heard of our Maggie. They're awful poor in her family, her mother's a widow. Her paw was killed in the mines. That's why the poor kids in that family have to go to work so young. It's breaking the law? Well, what can they do? They'd *starve!* They gotta work! She was most in rags as it was. So we girls collected a Christmas present, about forty dollars. We got her a dress and a lovely coat and shoes. You should have seen the poor kid. She cried!"

She knew we were talking about her. She came over to us shyly, a tiny girl. As we talked my arm slipped around her and she, not old enough to have outgrown the tricks of babyhood, slipped into my lap.

"How old are you, Maggie?"

"Fourteen," she said, blushing and burying her little face in my shoulder.

It was something that these little girls had six hours more rest a week. Six hours less of jerk! One, two, three, four. Six hours less of inspecting, of operating button machines. It meant a lot.

So did the difference in pay; every dollar these children brought home was instantly translated into terms of food and clothes.

After a meeting with Central Labor Union of Pottsville, which voted unanimously to give moral support to our campaign, we went to Tremont, which was off the railway, to organize. Tremont is an all-American town. That is to say, the people who lived there came from Europe so long ago that they had forgotten when and were proud of it. The black and gold roll of honor of soldiers in the war read like the signers of the Declaration of Independence. But for all its solid brick houses and its cheerful brick sidewalks, it had a dark spot, which disfigured all of Schuylkill County—and that was the sweated labor of women.

There were two factories.

We stopped in front of one of them and the windows were filled immediately with young faces, hands waved to us, a quiver had gone through the whole shop, the organizers were there. The great question of whether to join the union was being discussed in every house where a girl was working. The foreman at Fox's had stopped the power to tell the girls about it. The reports of what he had said varied. Some said that he had opposed it bitterly, other reports gave it that he had said that unions were a good thing, but why should the girls want to join the Amalgamated Clothing Workers of America, why shouldn't they have their own union? For to suggest a company union is as instinctive to an employer as to fire people for unionism.

Whatever they were going to decide, they were not indifferent; and we on our part were eager to know whether it would be as easy to organize American girls as it had been the Lithuanians and Poles and Slovaks of other towns, all American but with a different tradition.

One of the factories let out at 4:30 and the other at 5:00, so we could cover them both with literature. One of the shops was in a brick building sitting on top of a hill and overlooking suggestively the schoolhouse yard as though it were peering down to see how many little girls were getting ready to come and work in it. Here also, the girls who ran down the hill presently seemed no older than the girls who a few minutes before had come out of high school. In a moment a crowd of them surrounded us.

"Are you going to have a union here? When are you going to have a meeting?" "Are you really going to give a dance? When? In what hall? With what music?" In a moment we were friends with everyone. They were so full of spirit, they ran out so eagerly to meet the idea of a union. These miners' daughters did not need to have unionism explained to them, though not all the girls met us with such spirit.

Half an hour later when we went to the other factory most of the girls hurried past us, shaking their heads at our offers of literature. They ran along as though frightened by the bogeyman. But we felt sure they would join us in the end, for their fathers were with the union.

Tremont was off the railway and had no real hotel. We lived with an old couple who took in guests sometimes. Very soon we got acquainted with many of the miners' families. I remember sitting, one Sunday, in the house of a Scotch miner. He was an old man with silvery hair. He was reading his great Bible through gold-rimmed glasses. Never was there a better example of venerable piety. Tremont was Molly Maguire country. The Molly Maguires had been one of the early labor organizations of America, a secret society and very militant. To make talk I asked Mr. MacGregor: "What did the Molly Maguires do?"

He peered at me over the top of his gold glasses.

"Whut did they do? They killed their-r-r bosses and they done r-r-right!" he said and went on reading the Bible.

With that tradition behind us we soon had a strike on our hands. Soon one of the factories was divided against itself. The majority of the girls were out, but some of the best element obstinately stayed in. Things began to explode. There were two girls in the telephone office and one was with the union and one was against it. When the one that was for the union was on we'd learn what the bosses were going to do.

"Oh," she would recount, "they're going to arrest you! They're going to bring the state constabulary out on you!" Life was exciting and varied for two inexperienced organizers far from the base of supplies and from any advice.

It was a strange thing to feel the forces of the employers massed against me. I had so often described them. I knew all about them, but it was hard to believe they were going to turn out the state troopers against an inconspicuous, kindly person like myself.

There was one day, for instance, that Ann Craton and I called, for years, "the perfect day." It began at 6:30 with the picket line. We had our girls march far apart in a disciplined, soldierly fashion. We were very proud of our picket line, although it was disappointing for three girls who had dug under the snow for a pan of rocks. During the picketing, Ann Craton stopped one of the scabs who was trying to hurry by, and put her hand on her shoulder saying gently, "I wish you would let me explain a little to you."

It was for this she was arrested for assault and intimidation. If you so much as touch with a finger, it comes under the head of assault, which we were too green to know.

The picket line was no sooner over than our friendly telephone girl brought us word that twenty-five of our people and their parents had been arrested in the next town, where there was also a strike. They had, it seemed, drummed the scabs home with a terrific gusto, beating on kettles with iron spoons and clashing pokers. Men had been hastily deputized and the state police had been called for. Snow lay deep upon the ground. Trolleys couldn't run. We had somehow or other to get over to the town where our people were arrested, and someone had to stay behind to look out for the noonday picket line. Somehow we managed it all.

It was that afternoon that the state troopers appeared. We went down to meet them. They were two nice-looking young men and when we introduced ourselves they burst out laughing.

"Say, it can't be you *ladies* we was called out for. We was told that you was *labor organizers!*" Heaven knows what they thought labor organizers looked like, certainly not like us. That night we went to address the miners in their union hall in Tremont. There appeared upon the floor an organizer of the United Garment Workers to tell the miners we were an outlaw, wildcat organization. When we got through making our reply the miners were with us to a man. They said they didn't care whether we belonged to the AFL or not. A point of fact, Tremont had only then applied for its charter in the United Mine Workers, which was a very interesting sidelight on the organization of coal in the remote places. The perfect day was over. It seemed to us that nothing could have happened that had not happened.

We were not at the end of our trouble with the United Garment Workers, however. They had never organized in this district before but now they were disputing every step with us.

Organizers of the Amalgamated had organized the silk workers in Pottsville. Soon after our perfect day we were called up to Pottsville to speak at a union meeting. We found a curious atmosphere in the hall; we did not know what to make of it. Then one of our friends of the Central Labor Union appeared and explained that the United Textile Workers had taken our union away; they had frightened the young members by telling them we were a wildcat organization, that, indeed, we were part of the "Red terror" and were paid by Moscow gold.

The Amalgamated official demanded the floor while we waited outside the union hall. Ann Craton and Barbara De Porte sat close together. They were very little girls. They looked like two little birds on a branch of a tree huddled together to keep out of the way of cats.

In stamped the fire chief, Mr. Stevenson. He was not a tall man but his mustachios curled as ferociously as ever did those of the Kaiser. With him he brought an officer, one of those pleasant, small-town, homey policemen.

Mr. Stevenson threw himself in front of the door of the meeting in a heroic pose. One would have supposed the Red hordes were even then battering on doors of the Liederkranz Hall.

"Officer," he cried, "throw them out!" The officer looked at Ann Craton and Barbara De Porte. He looked at me, mild and meek. He looked at the young textile organizers sitting dejected in their corner.

"Throw out *them?*" he wondered. "Throw?" he asked in dismay, his eyes on the two tiny organizers who looked hardly old enough to have working papers.

"They aren't wanted here. They were asked to leave and they didn't. They aren't wanted here," said the fire chief.

"No one asked us to leave." We all called out together as people do in farces. "We didn't know they wanted us to go."

"Didn't no one tell you to go?" asked the fire chief.

"Ain't no one *asked* you to?" the officer inquired.

"Well, now they do," said steamroller Stevenson.

Of course, we shouldn't have gone. We had a right to be there and we should have made a fight. But we were so amazed at the turn of events and so green that go we did.

We went and got some coffee and talked it over and then stood with our friendly policeman in the snow on the corner and discussed the situation.

When he saw by the papers the next day that we had been "ejected" from the hall by him, he must have been as surprised as we.

We went to the editor of the paper, a young man. We wanted to know about his headlines which had said "wildcats ejected."

"It's a fight between two labor organizations, isn't it?" he said astutely. "Well, I treat you both fair. I use your copy when you send it in, and their copy, I use it too."

Only a short time before I had been a "distinguished authoress" and now I was a wildcat.

We soon had the satisfaction of worsting the United Garment Workers, who now began to organize—but the girls refused to join their organization, saying they wanted to be in "Miss Craton's Union."

# Ma and Mr. Davis
# The Story of Alexander Howat's Fighting District

*Survey, 1922*

*In April 1922 John L. Lewis, president of the United Mine Workers
(UMW), led the largest single coal mine strike in U.S. history. Lewis'
August strike settlement, which preserved existing wage rates but ordered UMW miners back to work before many strikers received union
recognition, was highly unpopular with many miners. Mutinies against
Lewis' leadership at once erupted among the UMW rank and file.
Alexander Howat, head of the UMW District 14 in Kansas, and a bitter
rival of Lewis', was greatly admired by many miners for his militancy
and courage.*

*Howat led the fight against the industrial control law passed in
Kansas during the postwar Red Scare, which effectively outlawed
strikes and mandated compulsory arbitration of labor disputes. Howat's subsequent endorsement of wildcat strikers brought him into frequent confrontation with Kansas officials, and with Lewis, during the
early 1920s. Lewis was forced to wage a fierce internal fight against
Howat and other opponents for control of the UMW, a battle which
Lewis did not win until 1928.*

Everyone who has been following the news knows what's happened in
Kansas. Republican Kansas mowed under the Republican candidate for
governor and elected a Democrat with what the newspapers call an
"overwhelming majority." Among the conflicting reasons which gave
Mr. Davis his victory was the patent one that a plank in his platform
called for the repeal of the Industrial Court Law.

In the four counties which made up District 14 of the United Mine
Workers—Alexander Howat's District—what a chopping off of political
heads there was of pro-Industrial Court officials!

I happened to be in District 14 just before the election and saw some
of the work that preceded the ousting of the supporters of the Industrial Court Law.

I went at once to Girard to see Alexander Howat, of whom no miner
speaks otherwise than Alec—you need only hear any miner speak his
name and it will tell you what Howat means to the coal diggers in his
district.

It's an hour's ride from Pittsburg to Girard by the Interurban. Sitting beside me was a white-haired jolly woman dressed in her "Sunday clothes." Real Sunday clothes, the lineal descendants of the heavy black silk of past generations. Her white hair was drawn straight back from her face and done in an ample knob behind. She evidently hadn't changed the way she put up her hair since she had pigtails. On top of her venerable head a madly fashionable hat balanced itself precariously. She had taken off her gloves and her big, brown hands with their swollen knuckles were eloquent of how she had spent her days. The lines on her face and the color of it told that she hadn't been too proud to do a hand's turn in the garden now and then. She had twinkling blue eyes and a mouth and chin that had never known weakness. I realized that I was sitting beside that unacknowledged ruler—Ma. Ma dressed up magnificently and leaving home on a weekday on some errand. I knew this errand must be one of weighty importance and that it could be neither a wedding nor a funeral.

She sat calm, relaxed, looking out of the window at cane fields from which flew flocks of impudent crows, at fields where the corn was already stacked, in the distance the tipple of the mine flanked by its smoking mountain of waste. Corn and coal—that's southern Kansas. I waited, for I had seen Ma's genial though appraising eye slide over me. To speed up the inevitable conversation, I asked a question.

"You're a stranger in these parts, I take it," said she, and then, as though overflowing with the chief immediate purpose of life, she informed me:

"I'm out campaignin' for Governor Davis. *Yes'm.* With all there's to do on the farm, I says to Pa: 'Autumn c'n wait, and pumpkins c'n wait, but 'lections *don't!* 'Lections don' wait no more'n feedin' critters. You feed the critters and I'll help 'lectioneerin' in this district. I want that law that put Alec Howat in jail repealed.'

"No, we didn't always have a farm. We haven't had the farm but 'bout fifteen years. Before that Pa dug coal. It was gettin' bad for his lungs and the boys was grown up by then. Says they, 'Pa, you get you a piece of land.'" She put her hand before her mouth and whispered loudly: "*I put the boys up to sayin' it.* Queer how obs'inate men c'n be, and how you have to take 'em. That's why women make better 'lectioneerers than men. Men's so *obs'inate.* You tell 'em a thing good for 'em, likes 's not, just for contrariness they'll go agin' you. So a woman who's got 'ny sense knows when it's best to go at the thing hammer and tongs and when you got to get what you want sort o' 'round about. How'm I goin' to conduct my canvass? Why, there's quite a few of us men and women got a section divided between us. There's men that just won't listen to any women. They're so scared o' women, they won't listen to 'em. Why, they'll just vote for the Industrial Court Law 'cause they hear that a woman is agin' it—they're that contrary. Childish, I call it. So scared o' women, that they're bound to do different than what they're told to do. You take Mrs. Hiram Allison. By bad luck, she's got five girls. Now her, when she wants somethin', do you suppose she can go to Hiram an' tell him square out? No, siree! She's got to go an' make out like that was just what she didn't want. The five girls and her ben talkin' of nothin' in this world for weeks except how they do hate strikes and how much the Industrial Court Law is doin' for the people. I don't have to bother about Hiram none. Three of the girls is of age. I don't have to bother a mite about the Allison family.

"Big meetin's is fine with big men talkin' to a crowd o' people—but what does the business in 'lections is house to house canvassin'. Goin' from house to house best of all when you get some one who knows the folks they're talkin' to.

"No, I never did any canvassin' before. There wasn't any Industrial Court Law to canvass against. But thinks I to myself when the committee come to me to talk things over, I know how to *visit*. I know the folks 'round here. I ought to, seein' I lived right around here pretty near forty years now."

She got out of the car at a small town between Pittsburg and Girard, her gorgeous new hat bobbing purposefully. Every firm step foreboding the downfall of the Republican governor.

I went on to the new sanitary jail in Girard where Howat and five other men are serving their terms for having fought the Industrial Court Law. He is the center of the political turnover in southern Kansas. Around him and the other men in jail the fight was being waged. That was why "Ma" had left home on a weekday and gone forth "visitin'."

There was no red tape in the jail in Girard. Alexander Howat, powerful, blond-headed, blue-eyed, was called out to meet me. Later, after I had talked with him awhile, I went up to meet the other men.

All six live together in a large room that takes up the whole top floor of the jail. I never saw men who had spent months in a jail's confinement who showed the effects of jail so little. There is a certain jail psychology to which even the strongest men usually succumb. There is something in Howat's fighting spirit that even jail could not touch. I felt that he and the rest of the men were still out in the world and that they were still fighting. I felt that concrete walls and iron bars had been powerless to shut them in. They had the air of men temporarily staying in a hotel instead of serving a prison sentence. Later I discovered that this fighting spirit of Howat's, which refuses even to recognize barred windows, has permeated his whole district.

It was late afternoon when I went back to Pittsburg. The streets were filled with a lively crowd. I have never seen a town like this

Kansas "city." It is the center of the mining district of southern Kansas, a town of 22,000 inhabitants. It has its Main Street, like other towns, lined with prosperous shops. If the dresses displayed are not the very latest style, they are very near it—they have good buyers in Pittsburg. Parked along both sides of Main Street is a never-ending line of "Lizzies" and cars of every make and vintage. Back of Main Street is row on row of comfortable, pleasant houses. Little houses, houses easy for a woman to do her work in.

It's the crowd on Main Street that marks the difference between Pittsburg and the other towns of the same size I know. Among the men that fill the street you hardly ever see a white-collared individual. The men that come in from the surrounding villages put on spandy clean overalls. At this season, they wear woolen shirts. It hits you between the eyes as a working-men's city. The few people you see with white collars are the professional men or the clerks in the stores. The crowd is made up of deep-chested miners, farmers who have come in to trade, of the striking shopmen—a crowd of workers. When school lets out for recess, on the boys' side there is a shifting running pattern of blue—the little boys all wear overalls to school.

For days I bumped over roads in an aged Ford from mining camp to mining camp. There was a ferment in the air and excitement that got into one's blood and made one feel as though one had come from a stuffy room to a place where salt air was blowing off the sea, something intangible and life-giving. It was the spirit of revolt expressing itself in the prosaic form of an election.

District 14 is split in factions this moment. On the one hand, the men who stayed on strike according to the unanimous decision of the District Convention which decided to fight the Industrial Court Law, and those who went back to work when ordered by the International. Hard feeling enough between these two sets of men, for the word "scab" bites deep in an industrial community and "scab" is what the Howat men have hurled at the men who went back on their own decision.

On one thing they are united and it is the repeal of this law which took from them their right to strike or even to discuss a strike. As one young man said to me: "If the operators in our mine should go back on their contract and two or three of us should be talking about striking together, we'd be liable to a jail sentence—that's a fine law for you!—in a 'free' country."

In one camp after another I found "Ma" at work, sometimes a wiry little woman with grown sons like Mrs. Rogers. Her living room is filled with growing plants. There are books on the shelves in Mrs. Rogers' home. On one side is a knitting machine for the making of socks. This is the way that she adds to the family income since she lost her job as school janitress because she marched in the Woman's March last December. We came to her house late one afternoon.

"If you'd come a few minutes sooner, you wouldn't have found me home. I've been out campaigning. I tell *you*, if the women in this district have their say, there won't be a sheriff today who arrested a woman last year when we marched!"

She was a little brown woman, swift in her movements as quicksilver with a little flush in her brown cheeks from the excitement of the day. Great fun Ma has had campaigning, visiting round, securing vote after vote. A sight to please the hearts of those who have believed in woman suffrage. Always I sensed something deeper than the changing of one candidate for another, one official for another—it was the fighting spirit, a subtle sense of power—which sped like an electric current from camp to camp, from one miner's cottage to another, linking men and women together. The immediate object, the repeal of the hated law and regaining of freedom to strike. At this moment a labor party is struggling to be born. The term "third party" is on every one's lips. I heard it talked about in southern Kansas. Springing into conversation spontaneously, you would hear Ma remarking, "We ought to have a party of our own."

It's hard for people who live comfortably to know what the right to strike means to working people. Women like Mrs. Rogers have seen the whole face of the countryside changed since they first lived here. There was a time when miners had to live in company houses, when they had to buy from company stores and when a striking miner could get no credit, when no man's job was secure if he wanted to be a union man.

At the cost of much sacrifice and hunger and want, they have seen all this change. Other causes were at work, no doubt, which changed a desolate collection of weatherbeaten shacks to little towns where houses were fit for human beings to live in, which raised wages so that the miners' wives could have a few of the conveniences of life that seem such a matter of course to comfortable people. The camps around Pittsburg are not the garden spots of the world even today, but they are paradise compared with some of the company-owned mining camps I know in Pennsylvania. But the long toilsome road that gave a comparative material comfort to the miners has done something far greater under Howat's masterful leadership.

People stopped being afraid.

No one could lose his job at the caprice of a foreman. This absence of fear is in the very air. When "Ma" living in some distant little camp tells you, "I'd like to give Governor Henry Allen an earful and maybe two," she means what she says.

The election was not the only thing women talked to me about in

District 14, nor was the story of the long difficult struggle the only tale that the old-timers will tell you.

The memory of the Woman's March of last December is woven like a brilliant thread through all the talk. In three days' time, with no previous organization, no working up of enthusiasm by the "outside agitator," thousands of women streamed together from all over the districts and went in a long procession from mine to mine and took the scabs out of the mines.

"We just went and told them that they were taking our sons' and our husbands' jobs. We explained it to them. They came out," woman after woman told me. This Woman's March is one of the most romantic pages in the history of American labor. No woman in District 14 will ever forget it, whether she marched or whether she didn't. From that march came that tingling sense of power which filled the air before election. That march is linked up with the reason why "Ma" left her home and went out electioneering.

As I went around from one mining camp to another, I found among the women a freedom of expression, courage of thought, that I have not found in any other industrial district. Nor does it come from the fact that people down here are of old pioneer stock. I found the same spirit among the French, Italian, and Austrian women.

Howat was in jail. He was in jail because of a law that took away from men their right to strike. In mining camp after mining camp I found women working as vigorously as my first acquaintance—Ma, in her new hat—against the party representing this law, upheld by that fearlessness which Howat has preached for twenty years; upheld by the sense of power they gained when they marched together, thousands of them.

# The Children's Crusade for Amnesty
## *The Nation, 1922*

*During World War I many persons were sentenced and jailed under the Espionage Act, solely for their expression of political dissent. One of them was Kate O'Hare, the "first lady" of American socialism. Released in 1920, she organized the "Children's Crusade" as a publicity tactic for the amnesty movement.*

Composed of thirty-five mothers, wives, and children of the political prisoners, the Children's Crusade for Amnesty left St. Louis in April 1922 for Washington, where the prisoners' families hoped to present their petition for amnesty to President Warren Harding. They were greeted at Terre Haute by Eugene Debs and treated to a bounteous reception and dinner. But at Indianapolis, where the American Legion opposed their entry, the city officials refused to let the children march or distribute handbills. Jane Addams met the group in Chicago. At Dayton, Cincinnati, and Toledo the crusaders were welcomed, fed, and housed by organizations ranging from conservative women's clubs to communist and anarchist groups. In Cleveland a mass meeting was arranged; clergymen, businessmen, and trade unionists spoke to 2,000 people demanding the release of all political prisoners.

Mary Vorse helped Elizabeth Gurley Flynn make the arrangements to greet the Crusaders on their stop in New York City, where they were received at the Fifth Avenue home of the wealthy liberal, Mrs. Willard Straight. The travel-worn women and children were allowed to parade from Grand Central Station up Madison Avenue, accompanied by reporters, photographers—and members of the New York bomb squad.

But when this brilliantly conceived and publicized procession reached Washington, the cheering stopped. Policemen barred the way into the White House. President Harding refused to see the petitioners.

A group of travel-worn working women and their children paraded from the Grand Central Station up Madison Avenue. The young girls stared straight ahead of them; babies stumbled with fatigue. Women, carrying children, sagged along wearily. They carry banners. The little boy who walks on ahead has a firm mouth and holds his head up. His banner reads A LITTLE CHILD SHALL LEAD THEM. There are other banners, which read A HUNDRED AND THIRTEEN MEN JAILED FOR THEIR OPINIONS; EUGENE DEBS IS FREE—WHY NOT MY DADDY? One banner inquires IS THE CONSTITUTION DEAD? One young girl carries a banner, MY MOTHER DIED OF GRIEF. One woman with a three-year-old baby holds a banner saying I NEVER SAW MY DADDY.

Reporters, movie men, and members of the bomb squad accompany the band of women and children. This is a new sort of a show. This is a *grief parade.* These are the wives and children of men serving sentences under the Espionage Act, the wives and children of political prisoners jailed for their opinions. Some of the men did not believe in killing, and some belong to labor organizations. Not one of them was accused of any crime. They are serving sentences from five to twenty years.

Their wives and children are on a crusade. They have come from Kansas cornfields and from the cotton farms of Oklahoma, from New England mill towns, from small places in the Southwest. They have been through many cities. They are on the way to Washington to see the president of the United States. They have come here showing their wounds and their humiliation. They have spread out before us their frugal, laborious days. With a terrible bravery they have displayed them so that you and I might see them and be moved—perhaps, and perhaps, help.

The little procession moves on solemnly. The banners are glittering mirrors held up to you and me—upholders of the Constitution, are you not? Proud of our country's tradition of freedom. Secure in our belief in the inalienable rights accorded to all men in America. You and I have waited for this quiet silent misery to come forth from its sacred reserve. We have waited, many of us—before we would even write a letter for amnesty—to see the poverty and grief of children displayed on the streets of our cities.

Look at the banners! They say: "Here is our civilization. Look at it. Our women and our children must parade sorrow on the streets to get justice. See these children. Look at their tired faces. This is part of America's show. Come, folks, look at the sorrow of the children. Men and women of America, look at these reticent mountain women. Look at these shrinking young girls staring straight ahead of them. Look at this home-keeping old mother and these sensitive boys. Look at the tired babies. And realize what desperation has sent them on this

crusade through your cities." These banners have another message for
the workers who look at them. It is: "The Constitution is a joke. There
are no inalienable rights for workers in America."

The little procession comes to an end. They reach the Amalgamated
Food Workers headquarters. Friends greet them. Chefs from great
restaurants have cooked them dinner and waiters have brought them
flowers, and gifts for the children. The strained faces of the children
relax. The tired women rest. There is one thing that they have gained
on this trip that nothing can take from them—the knowledge that they
have friends, for some of them have lived in a terrible isolation since
their husbands and fathers went to jail. A number of the crusaders are
women whose husbands belong to the Working Class Union. This
union of tenant farmers sprang up spontaneously in the Southwest.
The farmers were banded together, hoping through cooperative effort
to better their conditions. The union grew rapidly and promised to
become a power. The interests didn't like this. The war and the timely
Espionage Act furnished a pretext for a round-up. Over a hundred of
the most active were arrested. The rank and file were released, the
organizers and leaders given long sentences.

These women from mountain villages and their children come of a
breed which closes its mouth on grief. Their difficult lives do not allow
them such soft habits as the indulgence of tears. One thing they had:
They had their privacy. They had the habit of keeping their sorrows
inviolate. The proud instinct for seclusion is in the marrow of them.
They never came in conflict with the law. They settled their differences
between themselves. Understanding this, I want to say to them:

"I know you should have been left to bear the hardships of your lot
with your austere dignity. You should have been left to press the firm
lips of your determined mouths together in perpetual silence. The
decency of your reticence should never have been invaded. I know all
this. But the civilization in which we live has made the violation of
these sacred things necessary. That is why you left your home. That is
why you came on your crusade. That is why I must write, though to put
your story into printed words seems a further violation."

When I think of what we call the "American woman" again, it will be
of Mrs. Bryant—victorious in the face of poverty, illness, imprisonment. Her triumph is summed up in these words: I put my girls
through school.

Mrs. Bryant looks like a tall pine tree, battered by the storm. Like a
tree that has had little soil to grow on, but standing on a high place.
She has never bent or given to the blows which life has dealt her.

When Mr. Bryant was taken to jail, they were living in a tent in an oil
town. It was during the influenza epidemic and every one in the family
was sick in bed. The eldest daughter lay dying. George Bryant said:

"Don't feel bad, mother. Anyway, she won't have to see me go to jail."

As soon as Mrs. Bryant got out of bed, she made up her mind that the girls were going to go to school—father or no father, jail or no jail. She got a washtub, and she got a washboard, and she washed clothes, and those two girls went to school and they are graduating this year. Though I have never seen George Bryant, there is one thing I am sure of—that in his jail he is as unbent and as unbroken as that rock of a woman, his wife.

There was another thing that Mrs. Bryant determined to do. She determined to see her husband. Nickel by nickel and dime by dime, with sacrifices that soft people like us do not know about, she saved the price of a ticket to Leavenworth—$100. The bank where she kept the money failed. She has not seen her husband.

Somehow I imagine these two silent people have never lost touch. Through the walls of the prison their thoughts meet, for even a free country like ours has found no way yet to jail men's thoughts. As yet, we only go to jail for thinking.

There are many women like Mrs. Bryant in America.

The Benefield family live in a high mountain town, a small forgotten place. There are six children. Five are on the crusade. Some soft, kind-hearted woman asked Gene Benefield the sort of question you ask a chubby baby of six. "What do you play when you are home?"

He said: "I pick cotton and I chop cotton." That is all the Benefield children know about play since their father is in jail—they pick cotton and they chop cotton.

Last year the cotton crop failed. They worked from light until dark and what they made for all the year was $75. They are great, beautiful children, strong and bonny, but they do not smile. They live for themselves. You sense about them the isolation that a jail sentence brings to a family in a little community. They are close together as the fingers of a hand, closed against wounding intrusion like a fist.

Irene Danley carries the banner which reads MY MOTHER DIED OF A BROKEN HEART.

There isn't a neighbor around her place who wouldn't tell you that. There, in the Southwest, there is none of the backing that makes life easier for relatives of political prisoners in the cities. In the country places neighbors whisper and schoolchildren jeer at the children of a man in jail. So the mother of the Danley children could not stand the spiritual isolation that walls in the family of a convicted man as surely as the walls surround him and she died of it. Strong sixteen-year-old May Danley came on the crusade, leaving her plow standing in the field— the clay of the furrow still on her shoes. She is working as a farm laborer to support her sisters and brothers.

Mrs. William Hicks has tasted quite a few of the advantages of our democracy. Imagine a frail woman, not over five feet tall, who is always ailing. Her preacher husband has been a missionary in India. They were married on his way to America. They drifted to the Southwest. Mr. William Madison Hicks is a descendent of Elias Hicks, the founder of the Quaker Hicksites, and so a pacifist. He did not believe in killing, and this strange aversion caused the gorge of the brave people around him to rise and they dug up a letter which he had written in 1912 to a friend in England, foretelling the war and describing the effect of industry on the American workers. This convicted him.

A month after he was in jail, the baby Helen Keller was born. That made four babies under seven. Mrs. Hicks had to be cared for by the county. The judge took away the next older baby, and when in the courtroom she wept and begged for it he told her she could not have it because she was a county charge and the wife of a convict. So you see, Mrs. Hicks knows a good deal about the benefits of a democracy.

These are some of the stories that Kate O'Hare, their leader, told me as we sat together in the hall of the friendly Food Workers. The great majority of these women know little of the far-reaching conflict of the class struggle. The waiters made an ironic gift to the children—each child got a bank of the Statue of Liberty. But they saw no irony in this. They even sang "My Country 'Tis of Thee."

Kate O'Hare was herself imprisoned for two years in Jefferson City Penitentiary for her opinions. The plan for the crusade started in her office, when Mrs. Stanley Clark and Mrs. Reeder, travel-worn and weary, came in to tell her of their fruitless trip to Washington. Stanley Clark belongs to the Chicago Industrial Workers of the World (IWW) case—that remarkable legal process that will one day be a classic in our history. When the wide net was spread out for the IWW leaders a broad-minded choice was made. No fragile scruples were permitted to interfere with the magnificent course of justice. Dead men as well as living were indicted. They indicted murdered Frank Little. They indicted a man who had been smashed to death on a freight train a year before. They indicted men who had ceased for years to be members of the organization and they indicted men who had never been members. Among these was Stanley Clark, a lawyer, and, although a Socialist, ardently pro-war. His crime was that of collecting money for the families of the Bisbee deportees. Mrs. Clark went to Washington where she was told to get affidavits to support her statements. Through the states of Arizona and Texas Mrs. Clark gathered her testimony. She sent it to Washington. No one knows what has become of it. A wastebasket may have been its fate, or a pigeonhole.

It was hearing this story that made Kate O'Hare think of the crusade. She saw the tired, despairing women before her and she thought of all the women she knew in mill towns and on farms whose petitions have never been heard of, and she thought grimly "These women and children will be a petition that cannot be thrown into a wastebasket."

I cannot tell all their stories. Of the Reeders, who live in the shadow of Leavenworth jail; of Francis Miller, who inspected half of the cloth for the American Army, but is now serving his ten years because he is an IWW organizer; of gifted Ralph Chaplin, the poet, father of little Ivan, who has been given the savage sentence of twenty years for having once been editor of *Solidarity*. I do not forget them any more than I forget those other men in jail who have no women or children to march for them; Vincent St. John, for instance, who is serving ten years, although when the Espionage Act was passed he had not been a member of the IWW for years.

I will tell, though, the story of the only mother of a prisoner, Mrs. Hough. She is a little woman and she looks like the ideal picture of "Mother." She stayed at my house. We talked together homey talk— the common language of women. She told me about her children and I told her about mine and we got to know each other real well, and pretty soon she got telling me about Clyde and her story went like this:

"When the war came, Clyde came to me and said 'Mother, I've been studying over it all night and I made up my mind. I can't kill anyone. I'm not going to register.' Clyde was brought up in Wisconsin, where people do not believe in killing. This makes a difference to a boy. I said 'Clyde, you do what you think is right.' So he went and gave himself up to the jail. And my other son said 'Mother, I know how you feel about killing, but I've got to go.' I said 'Son, is this conscientious? If it is, go on.' And so, one son went to jail and the other went to France, both doing what they thought right. When Clyde was in jail the IWW case came up. Clyde, you know, had belonged to the IWW for a few months. The woodworkers union Clyde belonged to was an IWW organization. He was in jail when the Espionage Act was passed. The day he got out of jail they arrested him. Clyde thought it was an April fool joke—it was the first of April—and even when they took him to Chicago he did not think he was arrested; he thought he was a witness. He was never indicted and he was never tried—he couldn't have conspired, for, you see, he was in jail. Clyde never realized what was happening to him until they sentenced him to five years. He was so sure it wasn't anything that he even did not take his warm underclothes when he went to Chicago—I had to send them to him. I stood it all right for a long time, but then I got sick and got to thinking about Clyde in the night and I could not stand it and I took to crying. I cried and cried and could not stop crying for days, thinking of my Clyde. It was too much. One boy in France and the other in jail."

And as I listened to her talking, the same terrible sense of responsibility that had come over me at the sight of those children's banners came over me again: What have we been doing, the lovers of justice in this country, while Clyde Hough and the others stayed in jail?

The day in New York is over. They stand in a little group waiting in the Pennsylvania Station to make the next station of the cross. Curious people crowd around.

Look at their tired faces, ladies and gentlemen! Look at their scarred hands. Have a glimpse of Mrs. Hough's grief. Notice Mrs. Hicks, who never smiles. Take another look at Ivan Chaplin. He cries over the poem his father wrote him when he went to jail. It's an interesting sight, brimming over with human interest. A wonderful spectacle for a fine, free country.

There is a grim eastern legend that in the hands of the Angel of Justice is a cup, and when this cup is full with tears of children they overflow on the ground and from the place where the tears fall grows a magic tree—a gallows on which to hang the tyrant who caused the tears. This fable has the heart of truth. You may read your history to see if this is so. Ivan Chaplin and the Benefields and the Reeder children have helped to fill the cup here in America.

Maybe the last moment of their stay in New York was a prophecy. One of the children was late. She ran for the train. The door was closed. The Philadelphia Express was leaving.

"Open the gate," she cried. *"It's a Crusader!"* And the gate, that once closed opens for no one, rolled back, and the train stopped.

Perhaps the door of Leavenworth will fly back to the cry *"Open! The Crusaders are here!"*

*Labor's Struggles: 1926–34*

# The War in Passaic
## The Nation, 1926

Long abandoned by the American Federation of Labor, enraged by a 10 percent wage cut, 8,000 workers left the textile mills in Passaic, New Jersey, between January 25 and February 3, 1926. They were led by Albert Weisbord, a twenty-five-year-old Communist organizer who was a graduate of Harvard Law School. Because of its impact on public consciousness, the Passaic strike was the outstanding labor conflict of the Coolidge era. It also marked the first major strike in American history in which the workers accepted Communist leadership.

More than any other labor battle of the 1920s, the Passaic strike was destined to replay all the prewar themes of romance and drama symbolized by the Lawrence Strike. Like the cast of a giant morality play, the thousands of actors would take their place on the Passaic stage: haggard, courageous women workers; club-swinging policemen; venomous reactionaries; progressive politicians and clergy; sidestepping, obstructive officials; determined radical leaders; famous liberal strike supporters. Unlike the isolation of the Mesabi fight or the 1919 Steel Strike, the proximity of Passaic to New York City would bring the national press to attention and prevent official brutality from obtaining ultimate power.

On February 25 the Passaic commissioner of public safety forbade mass picketing—then a rare tactic used mostly by left-wing unions—on the grounds that it was a form of intimidation and also like a parade and thus could not proceed without a permit. On March 1, with New York reporters swarming everywhere, the workers' ingenious response to the ban was effected. Two thousand strikers ambled past the police. They walked in pairs, "just passing by," they explained, thus continuing the picket line while technically obeying police orders. The authorities, caught off guard, watched sullenly.

The next day, the workers—unarmed, orderly, and buoyant in spirit—again walked in line, two abreast, past the walls surrounding Botany Mill. The police hemmed in the workers, then attacked with tear gas and clubs, while firemen battered the workers with powerful streams of water from firehoses. Not only the retreating strikers were beaten, but bystanders as well.

On the following morning, scores of photographers and reporters, as

*well as hundreds of people sympathetic to the strikers, flocked to the
New Jersey town. The police again attacked, this time not only the local
citizens, but the visiting photographers and reporters too: they
smashed cameras, clubbed reporters' notes from their hands, and sin-
gled out members of the press for unrestrained kicking and beating.*

*Passaic was by now a national sensation. On March 4 the press
arrived in Passaic in bulletproof limousines and armored cars, while an
airplane hired by a New York newspaper circled low overhead. The
cooler heads in the power centers prevailed; the strikers were permitted to picket en masse. The New York newspapers never again so
flamed with righteous protest after the Passaic police began to give
reporters privileged treatment. Nevertheless, many newspapers became distinctly cool toward the New Jersey state and local authorities
and toward the mill owners in and near Passaic. A stupendous propaganda victory had been won for the workers—by the police.*

*Sympathy for the workers came from many quarters, as prominent
unionists, liberals, and leftists, many of them profoundly hostile to
Communist ideology, joined in support of the Passaic fight led by a
young Communist. Contributions of money and goods to the strikers
probably reached over $600,000 in all.*

*Conservatives, in counterattack, charged that the Communists, as
general advocates of violence, deliberately engineered the police riots.
By April, with the workers still standing firm, Red-baiting began in
earnest. The mill owners continued to build the impression that the
Communist leadership at Passaic was the only barrier to settling the
workers' demands. In mid-April, the arrest of the strike leaders on
flimsy grounds, the lawless behavior of marauding deputies, and the
imposition of New Jersey's riot act to prevent picketing, again ignited
liberal and left activists. But by August the strike had skidded to a halt.
Weisbord withdrew from further involvement in order to allow the
workers to enter the AFL's United Textile Workers, for the mill owners
had consistently refused to even talk to a Communist negotiator. Then,
to the vast surprise of many, the mill owners refused to deal with the
AFL union. Picket lines were again assaulted by local police and active
strikers were arrested on "bombing" charges.*

*After almost thirteen months, the great Passaic Textile Strike ended
with the 10 percent wage cut rescinded in most mills and union recognition granted in some cases. The United Textile Workers, which was
always lukewarm toward the unskilled, quickly lost the workers'
confidence. Meanwhile, the wrangling within the increasingly isolated
Communist Party reached even more fantastic levels, with Weisbord to
be officially expelled from the party in 1930.*

The strike of the textile workers in Passaic, New Jersey, was a strike of hunger. It is the direct result of a 10 percent slash in wages already far below a level of decent living. The pay of the textile workers is the lowest in American industry. They get from $12 to $22 a week. Heads of families work for $20, $17.50, and $15. It seems incredible that wages as low as these should have been cut by companies whose mills are among the richest in the country. But that is what happened. That is what has sent ten thousand textile workers streaming out of the mills. That is why after weeks of strike the picket line numbers thousands. That is why processions of workers march from Passaic to Garfield and Clifton singing. Never has a strike of such small numbers shown such mass picketing and such parades. Half the picket line is composed of young people. Mothers with children by the hand, older women and high-school boys and girls stream along, their heads thrown back, singing "Solidarity forever, the union makes us strong" to the tune of "John Brown's Body." The singing picket line has hope in it. Passaic crawling in its winter slush and snow watches its mill workers make a full-hearted protest against the intolerable conditions in the mills, against the inhuman and unbearable wage cut.

During the first weeks of the strike the numbers of strikers rolled up like a snowball. The Botany Mill came out first. One mill after another joined the strikers until nearly all the mills were involved. One day they formed a parade of twelve thousand to march from Passaic into Clifton. What a parade! Processions of baby carriages, bands of youngsters, older women, an old grandma of eighty-one. The undimmed, enthusiastic mill children, the youngsters in their teens.

This peaceful parade was set upon by the police as they tried to cross a bridge marching from one town to another. Clubbings of such brutal nature occurred that the daily press was filled with pictures of prostrate strikers and policemen with riot clubs in air. This clubbing did not dim their spirit. The big parade gave them a sense of power and solidarity. They had been striking against the wage cut—only that. Now they voiced demands: a 10 percent increase over the old wage scale, the return of money taken from them by the wage cut, time and a half for overtime, a forty-hour week, decent sanitary working conditions, no discrimination against union workers, and recognition of the union. Then came a further triumph, the Forstmann-Huffmann Mills with their four thousand workers joined the walkout.

The outside world began to notice the strike. Noted ministers, writers, representatives of labor organizations, supporters of civil liberties, streamed into Passaic. The town of Garfield invited the strikers to a meeting and the city council endorsed the strikers' demands completely, the only dissenting voices being those of the mayor and the chief of police.

At the beginning of the sixth week the mayor of Passaic menaced the strikers with a force of three hundred mounted policemen. This proved to be only a bugaboo. The picket line, two thousand strong, was practically unmolested, while the aged horses upon which a few policemen were mounted brought laughter from the crowd. Again the strikers formed a parade in the afternoon and marched into Garfield. Throughout all these demonstrations perfect order was preserved.

Then the authorities decided to break the peace. With tear bombs, mounted patrolmen, and a company of sixty-five foot police they tried to disperse a crowd of 2,000 strikers. They failed. The workers jeered and laughed at them. But finally, with the help of five fire companies battering the crowd with powerful streams of water, the guardians of order broke the ranks of the strikers, smashing them with clubs when they attempted to halt in their flight or to reform their ranks. The next day the police did better still. They charged a crowd of 3,000 strikers, bludgeoned many men, women, and children, and smashed with deliberate intent the persons and cameras of the news photographers and motion picture men present. That was their last victory. The strikers, armed with gas masks, helmets, and their unbending courage, defied the police successfully—and paraded in peace. Photographers took pictures through the slits in armored cars or from the safe vantage of a swooping airplane. The authorities were, temporarily at least, confounded. As a result of the disorders of the week Justice of the Peace Katz issued warrants for the arrest of Chief of Police Zober and two patrolmen charged with clubbing orderly and inoffensive men and women. To the date of writing warrants are still hovering over the heads of these guardians of the public peace; none of their fellow officers can be induced to serve them. Meantime the fight goes on and the picket line, an army of thousands, defies the police and greets the few remaining workers when the mill gates open.

The present Passaic strike is only a phase of the long fight of the textile workers for organization and a living wage. These million people who weave our cloth have always lived on the fringe of destitution. Employed by some of the richest corporations in America, their poverty is a byword. The conditions under which they live are a disgrace to this rich country. We are indicted, tried, and condemned by our textile workers. From time to time they remind us of this fact by a strike.

Fourteen years ago all of us who saw the strike in Lawrence were horrified at the conditions we found. Heads of families were working for $9, for $12. People lived in dwellings that were no better than rat holes. It was then that Vida Scudder, professor at Wellesley College, stated that the women of this country would refuse to wear cloth manufactured under such conditions if they knew the price in human life being paid for it.

Now after fourteen years we see people whose real wages are but little higher than those of Lawrence days. We see them living in tenements so ill-ventilated, in rooms so dark with walls that sweat so much moisture that the tenements of New York seem pleasant, airy places in comparison. Even in 1912 the laws of Massachusetts prevented some of the scandalous conditions of Passaic. Children under sixteen were not allowed to work in the mills. Passaic children of fourteen are permitted to work an eight-hour day. Night work for women was not permitted in Massachusetts. In Passaic we have the spectacle of hundreds upon hundreds of women, the most overburdened of all the population, the mothers of large families, forced by their husbands' low wages to work in the mills. These women, who may have six, seven, and eight children, go to work at night. They work for ten hours a night, five nights a week. They have no dinner hour. At midnight a recess of fifteen minutes is accorded them. They return home in the morning to get the children off to school and to do the housework. Most of them have children under school age as well and these they must attend to during the day—rest or no rest.

It is this night work in the mills that marks the difference between the bright-looking, eager girls and the dragged, hopeless, tired older faces which one sees, faces blurred by fatigue. The bearing of many children; the constant fight against poverty; the existence in overcrowded, unaired rooms; the long, grilling, inhuman hours of night work make these women's lives a nightmare of fatigue.

A law was passed by the legislature of New Jersey forbidding night work by women. A group of women mill workers appeared at Trenton and begged to have this law repealed. Of course they did. How can a family of nine people live on $20? Of course these women will clamor to be allowed to kill themselves with night work rather than forgo the pittance they make.

The recent wage cut was written in terms of life and death. The textile workers live so near the margin of destitution that 10 percent taken from them means undernourishment and disease and eventually death. The men and women in Passaic have met the conditions imposed on them with heroism and have tried for their children's sake to make good homes out of nothing. In the miserable dark rooms in which they live you will find bright hangings, touching bunches of gay paper flowers, often spotless cleanliness, always an attempt at beauty. Through their strike the textile workers have again questioned our civilization.

It would be impossible for any right-thinking man or woman to go into the homes of Passaic and talk to the women who work on the night shift without feeling that a personal responsibility had been laid upon him or her. When there is such want and suffering, when conditions of toil are so degrading, when the places that human beings live in are so indecent, it becomes the concern of the public at large to make its power felt and to see that this state of things is altered.

# Passaic Strike Journal
## Mary Heaton Vorse Papers, 1926

The police have now taken to chasing the children and knocking them down. On Wednesday, April 7, there occurred the most brutal police outrage that has yet darkened the pages of Passaic history. The picket line was proceeding peacefully to the Gere mills. School was not long out and marching ahead of the picket line were groups of schoolchildren, many of them the children of the women and men marching in the picket line. They walked along singing. It was like a picnic. No one was expecting any trouble. Suddenly the police drew a cordon across the street separating the picket leaders from the on-marching strikers. Then they charged them. Screams filled the air and curses. Children cried. Children were trampled under foot and jostled. Women fought for their children. Frantic mothers rushed for their little ones. The air was full of piercing screams of children who fled in horror from the charging police. And the clubs rose and fell, rose and fell on the backs of men and women and old people and children indiscriminately. The children had jeered the policemen. They shouted and laughed at the policemen and the policemen revenged themselves on the children. But the strikers' children of Passaic will remember this. Most of them are going to work in the mills. They will have no illusions about who their enemy is. They will know from the beginning that the police and the city councillors as well as the great senators are always going to be on the mill owners' side in a battle. They come up with clearer eyes than did their parents because they have had struggle forced upon them in their childhood. There will be very little that will have to be explained to the strikers' children in Passaic. No one will have to argue with them about a union. No one will have to talk to them about the necessity of the solidarity of the working people. They have had it proved to them as solidly as though it were a sum in arithmetic that the workers can depend only upon workers. Not for nothing did the policemen chase and frighten the children and beat them before their parents' eyes for peaceful picketing. These things will bear fruit.

The big women's meeting that was held one evening recently was like a big cross-section of the strike. A crowded hall, women of all ages, old women with shawls or kerchiefs over their heads, young girls, mothers with babies in their arms, you learn the very heart of the strike of Passaic at such a meeting.

There is strength in these women, and power. They are no passive audience who sit like jugs and have the words of the speakers poured into them. They take part in the meeting. There is a response and approval that makes it a live thing. You can see them thinking together and getting ready to act together.

The many weeks of strike have added something to them. They come out from the drudgery of the mill and home into the picket line and halls where they were fighting together, for the women knew what they were fighting for, their faces showed it. Animating these women is a calm determination to win the strike.

Weisbord appears, applause, more applause, applause that will not stop. There are hundreds of faces lighted up. Cheers from the young girls. At last he has a chance to speak. It is about the women after all.

Rows upon rows of women, the packed hall full of women who have welded themselves together in a fighting mass that means nothing short of strength.

This evening is only another step in the lessons on unionism that they have been learning from the strike, another expression of solidarity. A meeting like this could not have been held in a textile town a few years ago. Here are women of all races listening to speakers in English. Women have come out of their homes to meet together for a high purpose. The cry has been always before that you cannot organize the women.

# Class Justice Rules City of Rayon Strike

### Federated Press, 1929

*The Southern Appalachian Piedmont, where the nation's cotton indus-
try was concentrated, became a bloody union battleground in the
spring of 1929. The wave of strikes was a spontaneous protest against
low wages, long hours, and a work speedup. The revolt began in March
1929, near the small town of Elizabethton, Tennessee, where 5,000
workers, led by enraged women, rose to protest their fifty-six-hour
week and average weekly pay of $9.20. The rayon workers' strike was
met by a crushing injunction and then an agreement from management
to raise wages, an accord at once canceled by the owners as soon as the
strikers began to drift back to work. On April 4 twenty men, some of
them police and businessmen, including the local bank president,
drove a northern AFL man from town at gunpoint. Another mob beat
on a local unionist until his sister scared them away with rifle shots. On
April 15 the Tennessee governor sent in a military force which was paid
directly by management to suppress the strike. The mill workers re-
taliated by blowing up the town's main water line. Over 1,200 workers
were arrested. When the Tennessee strike ended in May, the workers
had won nothing except a promise, quickly broken, that they could
discuss their problems with the mill's new personnel director.*

*Vorse covered the strike as a stringer for the Federated Press, a
nonprofit daily news service organized in 1919 to provide labor and
national news from a labor viewpoint. At its peak in the 1930s,
Federated Press served over 200 major dailies and union newspapers.*

*Elizabethton, Tennessee.* The red courthouse looked like a stage set.
Militia with rifles and bayonets lounge around lofty pillars and up the
length of the flight of stairs. Six soldiers cross bayonets before you as
you try to enter.

Girl strikers sit on the steps kidding the soldiers. The square is
packed with strikers and strike sympathizers. From the courthouse
comes a burst of derisive singing.

Boys and girls lean from the courthouse windows and shout to
friends below. This is the morning haul of picketers. They are shut up
in the courtroom pending trial because the jails are already full. There

are guards all around the courthouse and around the mills. On top of both the mills are troops with machine guns with which to mow down 100 percent American strikers.

Are the hospitals of Stonerton full of wounded scabs? Are the local police walking around tied up in bandages and adhesive tape? Not at all. The only blood that has flowed has been that of strikers.

Why then the lavish display of armed force? Well, the striking rayon workers picket the entire county. They object to the importing of scabs from other counties. Boys and girls in cars and trucks patrol every load of strikebreakers coming into Carter county. They cover the roads to the mountains and those leading to Virginia and North Carolina. Five or six hundred picketers in cars are having a grand time.

The National Guard, which was called in when the rayon plants tried to open, arrest the picketers. A hundred boys and girls who have refused to give their names are being tried. To add to the forces of "law and order," fifty or more bright young businessmen have been armed and deputized. One of them . . . is being cross-questioned by the strikers' lawyer.

"Did she injure you, hit you, or inflict a wound upon you?" he asked.

"She swore at me and called me all kinds of son—you know what kind of a son she said I was."

"I can surmise," says the union attorney with dry emphasis. The courtroom of strikers roars with delight. The judge pounds with an empty pop bottle.

"This is not a show, but a court of law," he proclaims.

A young "looie," who looks like a stern-lipped movie actor, clamps up the aisle, followed by men at arms. Right face, left, soldiers are strung out before the court. The "looie" wears a little greenish tear-gas bomb at his belt. The courtroom full of farmers and strikers is like a scene in a comedy, with its guards and bayonets and tear bombs.

"I want to see the little girl who so intimidated you," says the strikers' lawyer. A small curly-haired girl in a red coat stands up smiling. The courtroom shouts with laughter again.

"Well," whispers a rangy mountaineer who has five sons on strike, "seems as if we had ten little girls in red coats mebee they'd get out their bombing planes and tanks."

It may come to that. Old Lady Tennesee has the hysterics. Four more companies of troops have been called for. Soon there will be two soldiers to every striker. The cavalry are expected.

"To tromp us," the strikers explain.

# Gastonia
## Harper's Magazine, 1929
❧

*The most famous of the 1929 southern textile strikes began on April 1 in Gastonia, North Carolina, a town of 30,000 which held the largest number of spindles in the state and in the South, and the third largest in the nation. Before the strike was ended, the name of Gastonia had been trumpeted throughout the world as a symbol of Communist struggle in a brutally hostile environment.*

*American Communists were then entering their ultra-revolutionary "third period," in which dual unions were established to challenge the moribund AFL. The Gastonia strikers were organized into the newly formed National Textile Workers and led by six relatively inexperienced, northern Communists, one man and five women.*

*The young Communist leaders in Gastonia were a hapless lot, isolated victims of both a hysterical community and a factionalized party. Actually, the Gastonia strike collapsed almost as soon as it began. With no relief or publicity organization worth its name in operation, most of the 1,800 strikers drifted away within three weeks, some back to the hills or to work in other mills. The strike leadership, so pitifully small in numbers and resources, was overwhelmed, while many of the striking women and children on the picket line were dealt gun blows, pricked with state trooper bayonets, and dumped in jail.*

*The Gastonia mob spirit triumphed in mid-April, when over one hundred masked men demolished the union headquarters. Attacks on strikers intensified and eviction of strikers' families from company houses began. Meanwhile, the frightened but courageous Communist organizers in Gastonia remained at their post, gamely directing the few recalcitrant strikers still left, who numbered perhaps eighty-five families by mid-April.*

*On June 7 the Gastonia mob again ran amuck. Fire was exchanged on the meadow where the workers expelled from company houses had set up a tent colony. When the police chief and three deputies entered the area without a warrant, four officers were wounded and the police chief was killed. A mob of 2,000 locals led by a Gastonian attorney destroyed the tent colony. Those strikers who could not flee were chased down and beaten or thrown in jail. The trial of fourteen strike leaders, who were charged with conspiracy leading to murder, ended*

*in a mistrial decision which set off three more weeks of almost unbro-
ken mob terror in September. Finally, in October, seven strike leaders
received sentences ranging from five to twenty years.*

*Vorse lived with the organizers for six weeks while she wrote* Strike!,
*her novel about Gastonia. She reported the second trial and was pres-
ent near the spot where Ella Mae Wiggins, a local strike leader, was
killed by a sniper in September.*

Spontaneous uprisings of the people are few. There is some patient
quality in man that makes him endure long past the point of actual
suffering. Especially is this true of man's economic state. It is appal-
lingly easy to get used to poverty; if one has been poor always one can
scarcely comprehend any other way of living.

When I first learned last winter that a wave of spontaneous strikes
was sweeping through the mill villages of the South I was skeptical. I
know how helpless and docile leaderless workers are. I remembered
the complaint of one good striker, Reilly, to Elizabeth Gurley Flynn,
"Gee! Gurley, me fut is bruk on me! I been assistin' at a spontaneous
uprisin' o' th' workers. Me an' Finnegan kicked them Hunkies in the
pants an' they spontaneously arose an' wint out of th' fact'ry!" Many
"spontaneous" uprisings have had such motivating causes—but not that
in Gastonia, North Carolina, or the other recent strikes in the
Carolinas and Tennessee.

It was not the number of people who had struck which made this
Southern revolt significant. It was the number and variety of communities involved. It was also the fact that those primitive and unorganized workers had struck without union or leaders. There was a
shouldering thrust as of a folk movement—of a great many mute,
patient people being driven by desperation to revolt. They had moved
in almost a score of communities separated by miles. Over the mountains in Tennessee the rayon workers had struck. Far away in Thomp-
son, Georgia, the workers had struck too; and through all the textile
towns they were quiveringly awake. One remembered the weavers'
revolt of the last century. There was a reverberation of strikes through
the textile South. People were talking strike everywhere. Everywhere
these "loyal and 100 percent American workers" were talking of organization.

In widely separated mill towns you will find the same reasons for
discontent. There are two of equal force—the introduction of the Be-
daud efficiency system, which the workers call the "stretch-out," and
the substantial cutting of wages, which has been almost universal during the past two or three years. Through the operation of the stretch-
out men and women often do double work while they receive less pay.

The mill hands who endured long hours and low pay as their lot broke down under the burden which was laid upon them. One after another I have heard them say, "We could not do it."

The effect of the stretch-out was explained to me most lucidly by a strike leader in Greenville, South Carolina, named Rochester. He is thirty-seven and has worked twenty-nine years in the mill. He began to work in the mill in 1900 when he was eight years old and did not make a penny his first month. Later he got seventeen cents a week. When he made a quarter a day he "thought he was running into money."

"It amounts to this," he said. "They cut my wages and increased my work. I used to tend forty-eight looms, while under the stretch-out I have to tend ninety looms, and I couldn't do it. Three years ago I was makin' over $19 a week. Now I make $17.70. I ain't a-braggin'. I'm an experienced weaver. I don't believe there's many can beat me. I make a hundred percent, the most any weaver can make." He hopes again to make $19, the highest reward to which he can aspire for a lifetime of unremitting work.

The average weekly wage scale in the great Loray Mill in Gastonia, North Carolina, is less, apparently owing to the parings and cuttings of workers' wages by the management. In 1927, $500,000 was saved on the payroll without cutting production. To make this possible two people had to do the work of three. Piecework prices were cut. This mighty saving was continued up to the moment of the strike.

The workers in the Loray Mill went out on strike on the same heaving surge of revolt which runs today through the Southern mill villages. Their strike was nonetheless a spontaneous demonstration even though a single organizer of the National Textile Workers' Union, Fred Beal, had been laying the foundation of a labor union in that mill. At the beginning of the strike whose tragic climax has been filling the newspapers of the country only a handful had as yet joined the union.

The Loray Mill is in West Gastonia. It is owned by the Manville-Jenckes Company, a Rhode Island concern. The mile of road which separates Gastonia from its suburb begins with ample houses surrounded by rose gardens. In West Gastonia the same street which began so pleasantly is lined with brick and wooden stores whose wares tell eloquently of how little people buy.

The great mill dominates the settlement. Behind it is the mill village, a flock of little houses all alike, perched each one on brick stilts. The big mill is like a huge hen with uncounted chicks around it, so obviously do the little houses belong to the mill from which a roar of turning wheels comes night and day. Night and day the men, women, and children from the little houses go into the mill. It is their whole life.

The strikers' lawyer, Tom P. Jimison, outlined for me the course which the strike took. On April 1, 1,700 of the 2,200 employees of the mill came out on strike. The immediate cause was the discovery of union activities and the discharge of union members. On April 2 the public street was roped off to prevent the strikers from approaching the mill. The workers pulled the rope from the hands of the police. The governor was then asked for troops.

During the first days of the strike there were large and orderly picket lines. These picket lines were broken up with increasing severity. Workers were beaten after their arrest and scores were thrown into jail. All the leaders were arrested at one time or another. Gastonia was in a ferment.

As soon as the strike was called, Vera Buch, Ellen Dawson, and George Pershing were sent down as organizers from the headquarters of the National Textile Workers' Union. This is an organization containing Communist elements, which was active in textile strikes in Passaic and New Bedford. The feeling in the town against the northern organizers ran high. Well-dressed people swore at them when they appeared on the streets of Gastonia. Threatening letters and telephone messages were frequent. Since then Mr. Jimison's life has been threatened for defending them in the murder trial.

The National Textile Workers' Union had rented a small shack on the main street of West Gastonia, which it used as strike headquarters. An empty store nearby had been hired as a relief depot, and to it the strikers went daily to get their food supplies. This relief store was supported by the Workers' International Relief, an organization which collects money from labor unions for workers on strike. I speak of these two buildings especially because it was against them, instead of against the strike leaders, that the threats of mob violence materialized. On the night of April 18 a mob of between 150 and 200 masked men descended upon the headquarters and with axes and other instruments almost literally chopped it down. They broke into the relief store, smashed the windows, and threw the supplies of food intended for women and children out into the road and destroyed them. The nine boys who, unarmed, were guarding the headquarters and store were arrested by national guardsmen. None of the raiders was arrested.

The militia was dismissed at the end of that week. A large number of extra deputies were then sworn in and armed with bayonets. On Monday, April 22, they charged the picket line with bayonets and blackjacks. A reporter was beaten unconscious. Women were beaten. Men and women, their clothing torn, were scratched with bayonets. Large numbers were arrested. The events of that Monday afternoon were a premeditated attempt to terrorize the workers from holding the picket line.

This was the general state of affairs when I arrived. A grand jury had already been called to investigate the mob outrage, which was very badly looked upon throughout the state. It failed to bring indictments or to throw any light on who was responsible for the trouble. Two of the nine guards made affidavit that they recognized members of the mill police among their assailants.

The first day I was in West Gastonia a striker, guiding me to the open lot where the "talking" was, pointed out the little lamentable wrecked building. Fred Beal was addressing a big crowd from a square platform. It was the first time I had seen an audience of purely American workers at such a meeting and I found the sight of them unexpectedly moving. I got an impression of a people unmistakably American yet of a different flavor from any I had ever known.

Fred Beal is wide-shouldered and heavily built; boyish, red-haired, sunburned, with very blue eyes set far apart. He has absolutely no pose, no "front" whatsoever. He is unassuming and seemingly uncon-scious that he is a big man hereabouts. He is one of the few young men who can stand the applause of crowds.

He was sweating when he got off the platform. He slumped down in depression beside me. The men didn't want to go on the picket line, he said, without their guns. When the militia had been succeeded by deputies with bayonets, the strikers had gaily said, "We'll get our guns, too!" This they had been restrained from doing by the young organizer from the North. The mountaineers were glum enough about this. Without their guns they felt emasculated, deprived of their manhood.

Beal felt deeply both his responsibility and his isolation in the South. For the moment he was the most conspicuous person in North Carolina. In the eyes of the well-to-do people and the mill owners, he was the "outside agitator," a menace which threatened the peace of the commonwealth. His shoulders, though broad, were not quite broad enough to carry the burden of so much hatred. But if he was the object of fear and hatred of thousands, he was also the spark of hope of thousands more. As Fred Beal walked through the crowd you could see the people loved him. The faces of the gaunt, earnest men and the meagerly clad women broke into smiles at the sight of him.

He and the other northern organizers were the focus of so much emotion that it was as if they were small incandescent points of radiance made visible by the burden of love and hatred they carried. There was an apprehensiveness among them that had nothing to do with fear. It was almost as if they, and Beal especially, had a prescience of what was coming. They all agreed that the terrible weight of public enmity oppressed them, this core of white-hot hate which the South visited upon them.

Around these young people were the gaunt mill workers, who are all of them American of the early English migrations. They come from the hills and from tenant farms in the valleys. It is largely upon the cheapness of their labor that the textile South has based its mighty development. Northern capital has poured in to take advantage of the "100 percent loyal American labor," following the advertisements which in the trade journals have read "Avoid labor troubles! Come South! Plenty of American cheap labor!"

The laws requiring children to go to school until they are fourteen have been in effect only a few years. It is not unusual to find mill workers in their late twenties who already have worked twenty years. Such people are, of necessity, illiterate. Yet there is a direct quality, a completeness about them. They do not belong to this century. Their point of view toward the clan, their kin, society, their bosses, is of the seventeenth or eighteenth century. The doubts of our time have escaped them. They are living in another day, when man occupied the center of the universe and communicated directly with his God. And when, moreover, he was the head of the family.

Poverty and lack show in their every line. The old women dress in dark, homemade calicoes as they did in the mountains. They show the effects of malnutrition. Pellagra is common among them and has increased during the last two years. Yet the men have dignity and the women have sweetness. They have not lost their mountain habit of hospitality.

The little girls are often exquisite—many of them blonde and blue-eyed and very English in appearance. At forty they are old women. The men are tall and spare and strong looking. One sometimes sees one of the Lincoln type—tall, rangy, and lantern-jawed. Among the women one frequently comes upon that delicate and lovely profile which has made southern women famous for beauty. The women of forty who look so worn still have heartbreaking moments of evanescent loveliness.

Like all people who read but little, they are great storytellers and they love a political argument. They are law-abiding and have the Jeffersonian jealousy of their constitutional rights. No policeman may enter a house without showing his warrant. They believe that a man should defend his rights as he defends his honor. Among these mill "hands" you will find names that are famous in southern history; they are many of them descendants of the men who turned the tide of battle at Kings Mountain, which is only a few miles from Gastonia.

I turned from my preoccupation with the strikers and the history of the strike to look at its setting. I spent some time acquainting myself with the look of the city and its surroundings. Nothing I had read prepared me for what I saw. The Industrial Revolution had here run its completed cycle in thirty years. I found myself in the presence of an industrial development which was so gigantic and had been encompassed in so brief a time that it had the terror of incalculable energy. There is in North Carolina a sense of ordered direction as though these multitudinous cotton mills had not sprung up for many varied reasons, but as though the whole industrial South was the plan of one. The transformation of North Carolina, within a period of thirty years, from a sleepy agricultural state still struggling with the problems of Reconstruction to one of the richest states in the Union is a miracle. The cities have appeared as if by magic.

North Carolina is so beautiful and so finished, there is such mastery in its great highways, that it seems as though it were the work of some superman—the result of a stupendous, organized plan.

It has beauty enough to make the fortune of a European country. In the springtime red, fertile plowed hillsides overwhelm the eyes with the flame of their color. There is no poet who has sung adequately of the gamut of reds which shout and sing in the Piedmont fields, and which in the evening light are washed with purple.

Among the red fields marches a mighty procession of ordered factories. And again one has the impression that the red earth has blossomed spontaneously and monstrously with red brick and plate glass; as if the God of Machines of the Industrial Revolution had said "Let there be factories" and there were factories.

Take the city of Gastonia, with its 22,000 inhabitants. It is situated in the southern part of North Carolina in that principality within states known as Piedmont. This is the high red-earth country which begins in Virginia and continues through the Carolinas. It encloses within its confines the richest portion of the textile industry and, therefore, the richest cities, of which Gastonia is one. Thirty years ago Gastonia was a hamlet on the crossroads. It gives the impression of having sprung out of the earth fully equipped. There is a new city hall, a new courthouse, a new county jail, all fine buildings. On an elevation stands a splendid new high school. There is a great orthopedic hospital, where miracles are performed on children and where nearly 90 percent of the work is done free. The only public building lacking is a library, and this lack, one feels sure, will soon be remedied by Gastonia's public-spirited citizens. There are new churches and new residences everywhere. The city is completely surrounded by fine new mills, of which I was told that the Loray in West Gastonia is the largest.

Few if any of these mills are over thirty years old. It is they which have supported the prosperity of the town and its well-to-do people. The mills created Gastonia, the city of spindles. It is handsome, prosperous, thriving. Here is the cotton-mill population culled from hill settlements and from farms supporting the handsome city. The picture one gets is as complete as an egg. Gastonia tells you its story, loud and clear, the very first day.

The order of these modern factories with their new machines is in strong contrast with the absurd disorder of mob violence: men with stockings pulled over their faces chopping down union headquarters and throwing workers' food into the street; militia called out against these workers; Americans chased by deputies with bayonets on American streets; all the old silly saws printed in the papers about the trouble being caused by outside agitators. How, the visitor asks himself, can a community be so orderly about industry and so disorderly about human life?

The answer was clear. Although other parts of the United States had already accepted the economic theory that short hours and high wages lead to prosperity, this splendid, vigorous, vital South had not yet attacked the human problem.

There was no communication, I found, between the mill people and the well-to-do people. When I asked Mr. Jimison if there could not be found at least a few women who would contribute to a milk fund for the babies—for this is one thing for which one can always get a committee in a northern community, even among people who disapprove violently of unions—he answered bitterly: "You don't understand. You, in the North, think of workers as human beings. The folks here think of them as hands!"

They can hardly think of them otherwise under the existing system of paternalism. Each factory is surrounded by a settlement of company houses. In East Gastonia, surrounding such factories as the Plymouth, are pleasant streets with rose- and vine-bowered cottages; elsewhere bare dwellings stand in naked and sun-dried earth. There are all grades of villages between the two extremes. The mill village will be bare or flowering according to the will of the factory owner. Within seven miles of Gastonia are to be found villages both better and worse than those within city limits. Cramerton is one of the mill towns where the last word in beneficient paternalism has been uttered. But whether the towns give information concerning a good or bad master, it is always a master of whom they speak.

There are towns in North Carolina which are not incorporated. This means that the very roads belong to the mill owner. He hires the police force, and if the schoolmaster or the minister does not please him he must go. In such towns paternalism becomes a despotic autocracy.

There are many mill owners throughout the South whose paternalism is infused with an ardent desire to do all that they can for the workers. There are few mills within corporate limits today which have not some form of welfare work. There are often women nurses and welfare workers attached to the factory. Some mills have ball fields, recreation grounds, community houses. Frequently day nurseries and rooms are provided where women may nurse their babies, the time they are absent being taken, of course, from their pay. The workers buy their food at the company store. They buy their coal, oil, and wood from the company. If they are ill a company doctor attends them. All this, of course, will be deducted from their pay.

Conscientious mill owners frankly consider their "hands" children, incapable of taking care of themselves. But whether their conditions are good or bad does not depend on the workers' joint effort to control hours, wages, and factory conditions. All depends upon the policy of the owners.

Company houses covered with roses still remain company houses. The workers cannot own them. Community activities do not raise the wage scale, which is so low that almost without exception children of fourteen go to the mill as a matter of course. Mothers of young children must work at night.

I heard of these things in terms of human lives. The strikers wanted to talk about themselves. Every day yielded stories like that of Mary Morris, who passed all the young years of her marriage in want because "when I was goin' to have a baby and got so I couldn't work, they'd fire my husband. Lots of mills won't have you unless there's two hands in the family working." Or of Daisy McDonald, who told me she has to support a husband and family of seven children on $12.90 a week.

"My husband lost his leg and has a tubercular bone. What do you think's left to feed my people on when I pay my weekly expenses? My home rent is $1.50, light 50 cents to 85 cents, furniture $1.00, insurance $1.25. What do you think was left the week I paid $2.20 for wood?"

"I used to work in the Myers Mill in South Gastonia, and they wouldn't take my husband unless I worked too, and I had a little baby."

James Ballentyne added another detail. It was a story of police brutality which recurred often in different forms. "I was leading the picket line and I was trying to get through a mob of deputies. They said, 'What do you think you're doing?' I said 'Leading a picket line if I can get through,' and I walked through. They jumped on me and hit me with clubs over the head and in the belly so I was spitting blood and hemorrhaging all night. It was two weeks ago, and I ain't well yet. I was all mashed up inside."

When I had seen some of the sights of Gastonia I went strike-sightseeing with a minister from Greensboro. We were going about strike headquarters getting the addresses of some of the people who had been chased with bayonets by the police, in order to verify to our satisfaction some of the well-nigh incredible stories poured into our ears by strikers and organizers, when Amy Schechter, the relief director, came up saying, "They're evicting people over in the ravine!" We drove to the place, a striker guiding us.

A woman I had noticed at headquarters, a Mrs. Winebarger, was standing in front of a lamentable little heap of household furnishings. Pots, pans, bedding, bureaus, were piled helter-skelter. What had been a home of a sort had in a moment become rubbish.

Three yellow-haired children sat solemnly on the heaped-up wreckage. The baby was asleep at a neighbor's. It waked up presently, and the little girl lugged it around. We went into the house, which like most houses in the neighborhood was built without a cellar and stood on little brick pillars. The lumber was of the cheapest. There were knotholes in the floor through which the wind poured. (This was not a company house but was owned by a private landlord.)

Mrs. Winebarger told us, "It rained in like a sieve. When it rained we had to keep moving our beds around to keep them dry." She had never had the electric lights turned on. "Where'd I get my five dollars for the deposit?" she asked angrily, for she was angry at her house, at the circumstances of her life, and she wanted to go back to the mountains whence she had come. "But it would cost an awful lot to get us back—fifteen dollars." Her husband had pellagra, and she was supporting him and her four children on what she made. She had a venomous feeling toward the house which had finally spewed her forth.

"Look at that chimney! It always smoked! We couldn't have no fire here! We couldn't keep warm. Once, I was buyin' a coal stove for my kitchen and I had $19 paid on it. Then I had to buy medicine for him and I couldn't make my payments and they tuk my stove away."

The furniture of the mill workers is almost inevitably bought on the installment plan. Mrs. Winebarger made $12.50 a week. She paid $1.50 a week for house rent, between fifty cents and a dollar for fuel and light, and more than a dollar a week for medicine. The house was a bungalow of four rooms. It had a fairly wide hall and small shallow fireplaces. Except for its flimsiness it was much better than the tenements of Passaic, New Jersey, or the overcrowded houses of Lawrence, Massachusetts, with their four courtyards.

We went next to the house of Mrs. Ada Howell, an old woman who had been beaten up on Monday, April 22, after the withdrawal of the militia.

Mrs. Howell sat in a rocking chair, her two eyes blackened, her face discolored. It gave one a sense of embarrassment and impotent anger to look at her. She told her story in a detached way. She was curiously without passion as she described something as unbelievable as a nightmare. She had been going to the store for supper on Monday, April 22. Policemen came down the street "chasing the strikers before them like rats." A policeman rushed at her with a bayonet.

"He cut my dress and he cut me too. Lawyer Jimison told me I should keep that dress without washing it so I could show it, but I didn't have enough dresses to lay those clothes away." Her idea was that the policeman had gone crazy.

"They acted like crazy men. They was drunk crazed," her son said.

"They had been a-drinkin'," she admitted, "an' they must'a been a-drinkin' to chase women and little kids with baynits. They chased 'em in and out the relief store like dogs huntin' rats.

"An' they hadn't no call to go in that relief store—the laws hadn't. You can't go in any place if you ain't any warrant.

"An' then the policeman came up an' hit me between the eyes with his fist. He hit me more'n twenty times, I reckon. I was all swelled up an' black an' blue."

I had seen photographs of her mutilated face. We didn't say anything. There didn't seem to be anything to say. I suppose when comfortable people read such stories they think, "This can't be true. Why, that just couldn't happen in our town. Such things *don't* happen." No wonder they feel this way.

We went on. Strike-sightseeing is a rather awful thing. There is obscenity in the fact that old women can be beaten for no reason when they are peacefully proceeding on their business; there is equal obscenity in the fact that a mother with four children to support has to work all night for $12.50 a week, and then be evicted because she cannot pay her rent. It does not seem reasonable that such things should happen here in this country, in 1929.

This was not the end of the sights Gastonia had to show that day. In the late afternoon I went out to watch the picket line. Perhaps a hundred men, women, and children walked two by two in orderly fashion. The procession was led by two boys and two gay girls of about fifteen, in overalls. The police whistles shrilled. Two or three automobiles containing police and deputies armed with bayonets speeded after the picketers. The picketers walked away from the mills. The deputies herded them with their bayonets.

I stood on a high bank, watching. A nice-looking woman was rushed to a waiting car by the police. She resisted. I saw a policeman twist the knot of her hair and twist her arms cruelly. She struggled. And still they twisted her arms. Women near me were crying. Murmurs of "Shame!" came from the crowd. One of the village women grasped my arm, trembling. Everyone was saying, "Why don't they do something?"

The arrested woman hadn't been in the picket line. Her little boy had been swept into the procession as it was rounded up by the police, and she had pulled him out. The reason she had struggled so against arrest was that she had a nursing baby. A few hours after her brutal mauling she was set at liberty. Why was she treated this way? There is no answer. Why was Mrs. Howell set upon when she was going to the store to get her evening's supper?

A few days after this a mill company began mass evictions. The fifty people evicted that first day lived in houses distributed through the different sections of the mill village.

"To show the others what's comin' to 'em," a mill official remarked grimly. One official stated frankly that it was intentional that union officials and the most active strikers should be the first to be thrown out.

Accordingly, the house of J. A. Valentine was one of those where the sheriff and deputies stopped first. Mrs. Valentine was sitting on a bench, a little girl in her arms. The child had been in bed when the mill doctor arrived to see if there was sickness in the house.

When the doctor was questioned about her, he answered: "She's convalescing from the smallpox. She's all right now; ain't any temperature. This ain't a smallpox-quarantine state. Compulsory vaccination and compulsory school age is enough without quarantine."

On the next street the deputies were at work taking out the possessions of fourteen people. It was Henry Tetherow's house.

Henry is the head of the family. He is seventeen, and looks fourteen. He and a sister support a family of nine. His father is too sick to work. With them lives the family of William Truitt, the secretary-treasurer of the local union of the National Textile Workers.

"This house has been a hotbed of union meetings," said the company doctor. "The company's been patient to let 'em stay here so long. Let 'em stay five weeks. What's the matter with the little girl in bed? Oh, she's got nothin' but runnin' ears. Might have 'em for weeks."

Men came out, bringing children's beds, a basket of pretty glasses, a tiny old-fashioned organ. A big doll was being evicted.

Henry, pale of face, very small, wandered at random among the swelling mountain of things. Mrs. Tetherow stood as if she would never move again.

At another house in the midst of the immense disorder of eviction a woman sat tranquilly writing a long letter to her husband. Not far from her, tucked into a fold of a featherbed, a little baby lay peacefully sleeping. She was a delicate and beautiful woman, and all her belongings were new and freshly painted.

Only one woman sat crying. The tears slid slowly down her cheeks. She had four small children and expected her new baby to be born any day. Around her were the shards of a home.

The work of eviction continued relentlessly day after day. The mill village became a gypsy encampment. People set up stoves and beds in the lots. The dwellers of 200 homes were evicted. Over a thousand people must have been homeless.

I went to visit other strike areas, and when I returned the Workers' International Relief, together with the National Textile Workers' Union, had erected a tent colony. Close by was a new union headquarters which the strikers had built with their own labor. The tent colony was picturesquely set among woods near a ravine. There was an air of general happiness and well-being among the strikers and organizers. There were rumors of great discontent among the workers at the mill. The strikers and the organizers talked hopefully of another walkout.

It was Decoration Day. A band of children with American flags was walking gaily off toward the picket line. They were led by little Sophia Melvin, who had come down recently from the North to teach organized play to the children. Old friends came up and greeted me. Everybody was brown; they looked as if they had gained weight since the early days of the strike. The women's faces were rested.

I was told that there had been prowlers around the tent colony and frequent threats that the new headquarters would be destroyed as the old one had been. Because of this the boundaries were patrolled at night by an armed guard. But this did not seem strange to me, coming as I did from Elizabethton, Tennessee. The place where I had stayed there had been guarded every night by boys peering out of the windows, their fingers on the triggers of their guns.

It did not seem possible that further trouble should occur. Least of all did the northern organizers expect it. Yet just a week later, during trouble at the tent colony, Chief of Police O. F. Aderholt was killed, and three other policemen and one striker wounded.

Two policemen, after a celebration in Mecklenburg County, chased a man into the Catawba River and playfully shot at him. Two hours later they were at the tent colony. It was 9:00. The guard refused to allow the police to enter without a warrant. Another policeman tried to disarm a guard. In the scuffle a gun went off and the shooting began. Each side claims the other fired first. In the next few days seventy persons were arrested. Sixteen people, including three women, were held without bail for first-degree murder, the unfailing penalty for which in North Carolina is the electric chair. The death penalty against the three women was later dropped. Seven others were held for conspiracy. Every northerner, man or woman, was arrested.

It is idle to think of Gastonia as a situation peculiar to itself. Edward McGrady, loyal representative of the American Federation of Labor, and Alfred Hoffman of the United Textile Workers were kidnapped in the principal hotel of Elizabethton, Tennessee. In Ware Shoals, South

Carolina, George L. Googe, vice-president of the South Carolina Federation of Labor, was threatened by a mob and left town under police protection.

There is no doubt in my mind and in the minds of many other people that had it not been for the northern organizers and their desire to avoid violence the workers would have shot in what they consider self-defense long ago. Not only would they have shot in Gastonia, but also they would have shot in Elizabethton and elsewhere. Everybody in the Carolinas and Tennessee has a gun. Peaceful citizens going on a long journey take revolvers with them as a matter of course. People think in terms of defending themselves. The trial now in progress will concern itself with the question whether the strikers shot in self-defense or not.

This trial began with a scene of grotesque unfairness, unprecedented in any American court. A life-sized manikin of Chief of Police O. F. Aderholt was rolled into the courtroom dressed in a bloodstained uniform. Conspicuous among the prosecution lawyers sat the widow and daughter of the chief of police. Confronted with this unexpected sight they burst into tears. Judge M. V. Barnhill, who throughout the trial was a paragon of impartiality, commanded the figure to be removed. The jury and the appalled audience, however, had filled their eyes with the ghastly effigy.

Three days later one of the jurors went violently insane—from the shock he had suffered at the spectacle of the "ghost," it was claimed. The trial had to be delayed. The defense had not been heard. The principal witnesses for the state had already been examined. Not one of the defendants had been connected with the shooting of the chief. The released jurors told the press that on the evidence before them they were for acquittal.

At this point of the story the mob reappears. Already on the Saturday before, union organizers going to a meeting in South Gastonia had been surrounded by a mob of 200, threatened with lynching, and beaten with blackjacks and bottles. The taxi had plowed its way through the crowd and they escaped with only minor injuries. Apparently as a result of the jurors' statement that they would release the prisoners, an "Anti-Red" demonstration was held in Gastonia on Monday, September 9, the night the trial came to its abrupt pause. A procession of one hundred cars went to strike headquarters, which was looted. The strike headquarters at Bessemer City, a small town seven miles from Gastonia, was raided.

The mob went next to a house in Gastonia where union organizers lived. A hundred men crowded into the house and kidnapped Ben Wells, an Englishman, and C. D. Saylor and C. M. Lell, local men. They were driven to a wood in a neighboring county where Wells was stripped and flogged. Two 'possum hunters heard his cries. The night riders heard the hunters approaching and thought it was the law and fled, leaving Wells unconscious to be rescued by his companions.

Meantime the major part of the mob had streamed over the twenty miles that separates Gastonia from Charlotte with cries of "Get Beal out of jail and lynch him!" "Let's clean up all the Communists!" "Let's get out Jimison and lynch him!" They went to a hotel where some of the communists and organizers lived and tore up the hotel register and broke fixtures. They proceeded next to the headquarters of the International Labor Defense, an organization which has been defending the accused men as well as those arrested on charges connected with the strike. The sympathizers and organizers in the office had been warned by telephone from Gastonia and escaped only one minute before the arrival of the mob. After breaking into the International Labor Defense office and finding no one there, the mob went to Tom P. Jimison's house, where they shouted and milled around and finally dispersed.

Two significant facts stand out in this night of terror. One is that no police protection was afforded. The other is that the mob was in nowise a rabble but proceeded along planned lines. It is considered by defense counsel part of the reign of terror which has been in effect throughout the strike and of which they consider the raid of June 7 an integral part. The better element in North Carolina has been deeply stirred by this lawlessness in which prominent mill people and members of the police took part. An investigation was promptly begun. Fourteen people were arrested including prominent mill men and police officers who were in the tent colony raid. Members of the Gastonia mob have asserted that they will not stop until they have cleaned out every union organizer in their part of the South.

The culmination to mob violence came on September 14. A truck load of union members were going to an attempted union meeting. The meeting was never held, armed mobs turning away all union members. The truck turned back to Bessemer City, whence it had come, and was followed by a number of cars containing members of the mob. A car swerved in front of the truck, apparently to stop it. The truck crashed it, and the car was upset. Immediately rifle fire was opened on the unarmed workers. A woman was shot through the chest and died instantly. She is a widow and leaves five young children. She was especially beloved among the strikers as the composer of the strike songs and ballads. When the chief of police was shot, sixteen people were indicted and tried for murder. It will be interesting to see if anyone will be tried for this murder.

Meantime, ever since the arrest of their leaders, the workers have been flowing into the union. This demand of the southern workers for better conditions, and a union to help them get it, is spreading. The South knows it.

Up to now, mob violence, police brutality, wholesale arrests of workers, ordinances against picketing, intimidation, and the calling out of the militia—in a word, repression—have been the only answer the South has made to this movement for economic equality among southern workers. History shows that repression has always failed. Not all the Inquisitions, not all the Black Hundreds, not all the various spy systems that humanity has devised have ever stopped an idea.

If the southern industrialists hold to their present policy they face a long and bloody war, bitter and costly. Sooner or later they will have to yield. Political equality cannot exist side by side with industrial feudalism.

# "Waitin' with the Dead"

## The New Republic, 1929

*While the young Gastonia defendants were waiting for their second trial to begin, another great textile strike occurred in Marion, North Carolina. Here, the low-paid female employees endured twelve-hour shifts, and worked their first thirty days without any pay at all. AFL organizers had been busy in Marion since July. But the anticommunist stance of the AFL's United Textile Workers was no barrier to the official terrorism practiced by local and state officials to break the strike. During a second walkout in early October, following management's violation of the no discrimination against former strikers agreement that had been reached, deputy sheriffs fired into the workers' picket line, killing six strikers and seriously wounding eighteen more. Later, the sheriff and his deputies were all acquitted from a charge of murder, and the AFL organizer was sent to jail.*

*Vorse's description of the funeral of the six slain workers is one of her most powerful pieces. Even the most comfortable, the most cynical, the most removed reader could hardly help but pause, for just a moment, to be moved, just an inch, to feeling, and perhaps to understanding.*

Lights shine in the mill village of East Marion. Folks are "waitin' with the Dead." Folks in cars are going on a strange round of visits. A steady trickle of visitors are going visiting—to the Brysons', to the Vickers', to the Jonas', to the young Randolph Hall's.

Death is giving a reception tonight in Marion.

Three men lie dead with gaping wounds in their backs. Some were shot so close to that doctors have testified that their clothing was burnt and their skin blackened. They were shot down by Sheriff Oscar Adkins and his deputies as they were dispersing from the picket lines in front of the Marion Manufacturing Company. A fourth, Luther Bryson, was blinded first with tear gas. Then he was shot. Two more have died since the night of the "visitin'." Two others are mortally wounded. Fifteen others received lesser wounds. This happened on October 2, when there had been a spontaneous walkout of workers because of the failure of the company to keep an agreement. People around here say quietly, "I'd hate to be in the sheriff's shoes."

With a party of strikers, I went "visitin' the dead." A striker drives us. We plunge in darkness down a sheer hill. We are at the Brysons'. The room is full of quiet visitors and watchers. People come in quietly and go out. Little is said. There are women sitting with their heads in their hands near the fire. The visitors pass quietly before the coffin. They are talking in low tones in another room. This is no ordinary funeral. This is no ordinary mourning. This is murder—mass murder in cold blood of many people. Their only fault was that they had gone on strike when an agreement entered into had been broken. For this they are lying dead, and the mill village is visiting.

"It's a sorry day," says someone. "We haven't seen the end of this," comes the answer. There are no threats of vengeance. There is an ominous quiet. Some one else says significantly: "Luther's got three brothers living." They are all there, three dark boys. We say good-bye to them, and to Luther's mother.

We wind dark corners and scale rutted perpendicular hills. Before the Vickers' the road is so steep we must block the wheels. There is a pile of homemade wreaths of dahlias on the porch. Inside in one room lies murdered Sam Vickers. They call him Old Man Vickers. He was only fifty-six. Men come and men go before him. They look at the quiet, murdered face, and recall how he ran four miles to join the union.

From the other room, the "warm room," comes the keening of Mrs. Vickers, terrible and monotonous. She has gone through the suspense dry-eyed, and has broken at last. The visitors come and the visitors go. A steady trickle of quiet fury. They will not forget your cry, Mrs. Vickers. Their eyes promise that you have not grieved in vain.

There are no tears at the Jonas house. There in the "warm room," people are asleep. Three young girls and a child in one bed. George Jonas' daughters, worn out with grief. The visitors murmur: "They beat him after he was shot and handcuffed. He was handcuffed when he came to the operating table."

Death has opened all the doors in old man Jonas' house. There are no proud reservations about his poverty tonight. Everyone can see how things were at Jonas'. They had nothing, for old man Jonas was infirm. The girls, still young, some of them children. If you want, you can see them crowded together, for a moment mercifully unconscious in sleep.

Hall's next. Hall was twenty-three. A handsome, magnificent boy, even in death. His record in the strike was that except for one night, during nine weeks of the strike, he picketed every night for twelve hours. He had had a twelve-hour day's work always, so he worked twelve hours for the union.

"He was running away, and the deputies chased him shooting," murmur the visitors.

They pass by the coffin gravely, looking at the dead boy one after another. There is a sound of wheels. More of the ceaseless line of friends has come. Everyone in the mill village is "waitin' with the dead" or "visitin'" tonight.

The day of the funeral, eyewitnesses were telling what happened in the hearing held before Judge Harding. The courtroom was packed with mill workers, friends, and relatives of the six dead men. Already Douglas Elles, correspondent for the Asheville *Times*, had testified that he had seen the sheriff and his people fire at the backs of the scattering mill workers, who, blinded with tear gas, were trying to escape.

"I saw Sheriff Oscar Adkins hold Sam Vickers with his left arm and fire a pistol point-blank into his body," J. B. Russell testified.

A vicious cross-examination by the mill lawyers could not shake his testimony.

"Didn't Minnish shoot Vickers, and didn't you pick up the gun which was used?"

"No, sir; *Adkins killed Vickers!* I was about eight feet away." Russell gave a dramatic illustration of how Vickers was killed. The people in the courtroom craned their necks forward. In the midst of complete silence, Russell pointed his finger at the officers who had fired into the unarmed crowd.

"Nary a shot was fired by the strikers. When Adkins released his hold of Vickers, the man fell back. The sheriff then began shooting at the fleeing strikers," Russell stated.

The fact that the workers were unarmed seems to be generally admitted. "Nobody'd be fool enough to pack a gun on a picket line. When you go out on picket duty, you may be arrested; so you jes' naturally don't pack a gun," the strikers will tell you as they gather around the courtroom door.

Walter Minnish testified next that the sheriff held and shot Sam Vickers. He rose to his feet and pointing his finger at the sheriff, he cried out with intense conviction: "There is the man who shot our people!"

The sheriff all through this testimony maintained a smiling front. Nothing is going to happen to an officer who has so nobly discharged his duty, his manner indicates. Nothing ever happens to sheriffs. He should worry. He merely smiles again as Lonnie Cole declares he heard the sheriff say: "Shoot 'em down, boys!"

Almost the whole of Saturday morning is taken up by the quiet, assured testimony of Allan L. Stewart. The lawyers for the defense bark at him, bully him, try to confuse him. This is not possible. Quietly, positively, he tells what he saw. He saw Adkins and his deputies standing at the mill gate. He saw the sheriff fire a tear-gas bomb. That was the signal for trouble; everything had been quiet. George Jonas—one of the murdered strikers—said: "Sheriff, don't throw that stuff in my eyes!" Jonas raised his arms and the stick he always carried because he was infirm, as though to protect his eyes. The sheriff "collared" Jonas and Alley Stepp squirted tear gas in his eyes. The sheriff had previously stated that Jonas had struck him with his stick before he ordered tear gas thrown.

"I was standing close by the sheriff," said Stewart, "Jonas never hit him. I saw what happened—I was standing right alongside. I saw the sheriff fire, and I saw Alley Stepp and Broad fire."

The gray caskets of the four murdered union men stand end on end in a long line. They are heaped with fall flowers—white dahlias and red. People who haven't gardens made paper-flower wreaths.

It is a long line of death. Here are Sam Vickers, fifty-six; George Jonas, sixty-seven; Luther Bryson, twenty-two; Randolph Hall, twenty-three. Up in the hospital, James Roberts is dead, too. He is eighteen.

The open coffins stand before the "speakin' stand," where for nine weeks the strikers came every day to hear the speakin'. Well, there will be a speakin' today too. Painted on the stand is UNITED TEXTILE WORKERS OF AMERICA, in high red letters. There are union flags. There is no American flag. It may be that an American flag seemed an irony to the strikers, with all the roads to the mill patrolled with soldiers—and their friends lying there dead, shot in the back by the sheriff whom they helped elect to office.

Behind the flower-heaped coffins, a line of fifty relatives and friends sit in chairs. Up the shaded hillside are a thousand people more, an audience of work-worn faces. Here are the "docile 100 percent American workers"—who are now paying the price of having dared to rebel against the stretch-out, a day of twelve hours and twenty minutes, and an average weekly wage of twelve dollars.

Flower girls have wide cotton bands with "Union Worker" on them. They gather near the speakin' stand and their thin voices ring out in "Nearer, my God, to Thee." A thin fine noise of weeping comes from the mourning women, a high keening of grief. They have been quiet for a long time.

The quiet weeping of the mourners becomes unrestrained. The hymn has to stop. The mourners are quieter now. The singing girls strike up a union song.

It was more of a demonstration than a funeral—a strange mixture of speakers, with the bearded evangelist preacher from the hills speaking on the same platform with George Gorman, vice-president of the United Textile Workers, and Jarvis John Peel, vice-president of the North Carolina Federation of Labor. A. J. Muste, of the Brookwood Labor College in Katonah, made the principal funeral oration.

"These men," he said, "were shot down like rats when they refused to submit, like whipped dogs, to a violation of the agreement by the mill owners. In all the stormy history of American labor, there has been no blacker outrage against the workers than this." He called on the American Federation of Labor to raise a fund of $1 million to organize the South.

Tom Tippett, also of Brookwood, who was in Marion most of the time during the strike, accused the mill owners of murder. More than any speaker, he reflected the feeling of the workers in the presence of their dead.

"Not in vain" is the thought left uppermost in the minds of the workers by the funeral services.

The services were over. The hymn singing had finished. The entire company of a thousand people filed slowly, slowly, one by one, before the dead. Every man and woman, every child, looked into the faces of the four murdered fellow workers. Amid the dead silence, Luther Bryson's tiny mother walked before the coffins. She paused at each one, to run her hand over the cool forehead. She bent over her son and kissed him, while Randolph Hall's young widow broke out into unrestrained weeping. She had sat for two days beside her dying husband without a tear. Now she cried aloud before the assembled workers of the mill village. People went slowly away in little groups.

"We haven't seen the end of this," men said gravely to one another.

# The Psychology of Demonstrations
## Mary Heaton Vorse Papers, 1932

During the depression winter of 1929–30 the American Communist Party organized many of the jobless into Unemployed Councils. In city after city the Communists led the unemployed in hunger marches and in protests against evictions. The demonstrators demanded adequate relief and passage of unemployed insurance legislation. In 1930 and 1931, serious clashes between police and demonstrators occurred in Washington, D.C., Boston, Seattle, Detroit, and New York City, and the Unemployed Council movement mushroomed.

The Communists called for a National Hunger March that was to start from various parts of the country and converge on Washington, D.C., on December 4, 1932. The capital city prepared for the event as though for war: 4,000 federal troops stood by to meet the "national emergency" proclaimed by the local press; 1,700 police and Capitol guards manned the streets, power plants, bridges, dairies, and other strategic points. City firemen were called in to augment the police, all issued vomit gas, tear gas, guns, and gas masks. American Legion Commanders in adjacent states sent excited alerts to their citizen-protectors, while salesmen peddled riot insurance to alarmed residents. Meanwhile, 400 Klansmen, observed by 1,500 spectators, burned their crosses in Arlington County, Virginia, and vowed their defense of the American Way. All this was created by the approach of some 2,400 unarmed marchers, one-third of them women.

The exhausted marchers were ushered into the city under armed guard and hemmed into a small area on New York Avenue, blocked at both ends by police ranks five deep. Communist leaders circulated through the crowd, urging discipline and peaceful order, while the D.C. police taunted and provoked the marchers. On December 6, led by 300 police, and surrounded by police, the unemployed demonstrators were allowed to march to an appointed distance from the capital, as they sang the "International" and "Hinky-Dinky Parlez-Vous," before their peaceful exit from Washington the next day.

Mary Vorse reported the Hunger March with her young Catholic friend, Dorothy Day. For Day, the event was a significant turning point in her life. Tremendously moved by the sight of the hunger marchers, Day slipped away from Vorse to visit the national shrine at the Catho-

*lic University, where she prayed for direction as to how she could best use her talents to aid her fellow workers. Five months later, Day established the* Catholic Worker, *and thus launched the Catholic Worker Movement.*

Every few days in the paper there are headlines: "Police disperse unemployment demonstrations"; "Unemployed marchers routed by police clubs"; "Gas ready for hunger marchers." There are also with equal frequency headlines which state: "Two thousand farmers in Iowa, or Nebraska, or North Dakota prevent mortgage sale"; or "Ten thousand miners' wives march to petition Governor of Illinois"; or "Farmers plan statewide march on Nebraska capital."

The country is cobwebbed with processions of men and women, all demonstrating. Processions of farmers, processions of unemployed going to the city halls of the cities to petition the mayors. Still larger processions threading their way to state capitals and finally demonstrations of farmers and unemployed ending up at the Capitol in Washington (or as near there as they could get) to petition Congress.

A formidable lot of marches on city halls and statehouses have occurred this past couple of years. An enormous number of meetings have been held. It is interesting to observe that the most spectacular marches—demonstrations—have been staged by unemployed groups or by farmers. One exception to this is the march of the miners in Illinois when a procession two miles long went into Franklin County and were met with state troops and tear gas, their cars overturned, many people wounded, and several people killed.

Why are the people marching? What is the basis of demonstration? What do they think they are going to accomplish? No demonstrations occur without papers asking these questions clamorously.

As I write, the Farmer Holiday Association is holding a national convention in Des Moines, Iowa. This convention is in the nature of a demonstration. If the farmers do not get aid from the government by the thirteenth of May they say they will pull a nationwide strike. The farmers' strike will also be in the nature of a demonstration.

A significant definition of the nature of demonstrations was given me by a peasant woman at a mass meeting in Bologna. She was a very beautiful old woman, and for the sake of hearing her speak, I asked her what this demonstration was about.

"Signora," she answered, "all demonstrations are about the same thing. They are about the Three Fears; The Fear of losing one's job, the Fear of sickness, the Fear of old age—"

She thought all demonstrations were about hunger. She was wrong. There are also demonstrations about injustice. There are demonstrations of joy—say as for the end of the war—for the fall of despotism. When the Russian Revolution occurred, the people demonstrated.

The people got out on the street and marched. They sang as they marched. Someone made a moving picture of this—cameras shot the marching throngs. I saw this picture, for it was brought to this country and never exhibited except privately. It had no high light and no plot—only thousands of feet of film of marching, singing people. Sometimes someone stood above the others and made a speech and the rest were all the people marching.

The most significant of joys in our times was the demonstration at Armistice, when all over the world men downed tools and went out in the street to rejoice that their brothers were no longer being killed. No one who saw the workers thundering down in their big trucks will forget that million-throated roar. No one who saw all the people emptied out of office buildings, filling the streets with joy, can ever cease to remember forever the impression of the people's power.

There are demonstrations which have to do with injustice. The protest meetings held all over the world for Mooney, for Sacco and Vanzetti, for the Scottsboro boys, are among such demonstrations. Strikes are a mixture of protest against hunger and injustice.

The first general strike I ever saw was in Venice in 1904. Two miners had been killed in Brescia by police during a strike. A general strike over the principal cities of Italy had been ordered for two days by the Confederatione Generale Del Lavore—the Italian American Federation of Labor. Venice was closed tight as a drum. All work stopped. Not a sandola or gondola moved upon the canals. The Grand Canal, perhaps for the first time in history, was empty of boats but for the police control. The hotel employees left in a body while the proprietor's family made shift to serve food to guests. All shops were closed and all wine shops. Shutters were up universally. Families were allowed to buy strictly necessary food. Venice was like a city of the dead. The lights in all the streets and the Piazzeta were turned off. But because the electric light company was under contract to furnish the city a certain number of kilowatts a year, the lights burned all over the city by day. There was a procession of all the guilds down the Merceria, the whole conducted with absolute quiet and that absolute discipline which is the very core of a successful demonstration. No unusual police precautions were taken although the whole working population of Venice was parading or watching the parade. No arrests were made, except of a few sprigs of the nobility who created a nuisance on the Piazzetta singing the "Marche Reale" in an obstreperous way. These prerunners of the Fascisti were promptly arrested and briefly shut up. Otherwise, this protest against injustice, this demonstration of solidarity, went off without incident.

This demonstration advertised to the rulers and employers that the workers in Italy protested against the unjust shooting of their fellow workers. Thousands on thousands of workers in Venice tied up the city to make this protest. Workers lay down on the railway tracks before the engines. No trains moved in or out. The loading and unloading of greater steamers on the Zallere stopped. No food barges entered Venice during the appointed time.

Demonstrations hold a common denominator. They are the most primitive form of advertising. Demonstrations about injustice or hunger or oppression advertise to the rulers the suffering of a people. The more orderly, the more impressive, a demonstration, the more it fulfills its purpose. Its purpose is to advertise the people's unbearable wrongs to the rulers and those in power. Demonstrations are designed to make those in power feel as uncomfortable as possible; they are designed to make the well-to-do think furiously.

For instance, the girls in white with their provocative banners marching in front of the White House concentrated people's attention on the fact that women in this country wanted the vote. It made the police seem ridiculous to march off quiet and well-born women to jail. Those neat young ladies dressed in white got suffrage more talked about, got it advertised more, than did all the reasonable arguments. A demonstration which makes the rulers ridiculous is perhaps as effective as any demonstration in this world.

All demonstrations imply "Mene, mene, tekel upharsin." They say, "You are rich and therefore powerful, we are very numerous and therefore potentially powerful. If we unite, our weakness and your power may cease."

Even absolute despotism allowed this form of advertising, admitted the petitioning of a ruler through the medium of a great number of people. Demonstrations are permitted to go off without disturbance in such secure countries as England. The people come, present their petition, then go away without benefit of police clubs. When in 1931 a girl was arrested in Glasgow during an unemployment demonstration, and burst into tears, the fact of her arrest was so unusual that every paper in England made a human interest story of it. During the past years, 30,000 unemployed people marched on London to protest the cutting of the dole. The casualties were negligible, though they marched up to the very steps of the House of Parliament. Until the East End hooligans of London began to make trouble the demonstration remained a pure demonstration. It partially accomplished its end, as a larger sum was voted for the dole.

It is a strong state which understands the purpose of a demonstration and is not seized with terror when a people come to present its wrongs to its ruler; it is a weak and uncertain state which meets a demonstration with police violence. A demonstration expresses an emotion; it may carry a threat, but it is not a revolutionary attempt. In its very essence, it is peaceful.

When in 1905, in Russia, peacefully petitioning Mujiks led by Father Gapon were mowed down in front of the Winter Palace in St. Petersburg, a cry went out through the civilized world. The shooting down of these people who had come to petition the tsar was an act of weakness and fear. The tsarist regime was a shell, Razputin was only around the corner. The revolution of 1917 already cast a long shadow, yet this shooting reechoed around the world. It advertised to the world the wrongs of the people of Russia. A demonstration which ends in the shedding of innocent blood by the nervous or terrified guardians of the law is probably the most successful of all demonstrations. When unfortunate unarmed petitioning people are shot down even the very callous listen to their complaints.

In this country we seem to feel convinced that every time people march, every time they petition, they are about to break out into revolution, and that every march of the miners, of the unemployed, is but a rehearsal to riot.

The week of the opening of Congress, three thousand hunger marchers, a rump gathering of bonus marchers, and a conventional group of farmers—more revolutionary than either—converged on Washington. It was a week which makes one proud of one's country. I defy any capital in Europe to teeter on the edge of massacre for two days and then relapse into Gilbert and Sullivan.

Washington will forever be identified in my mind with the massive blue backs of policemen. There were phalanxes of policemen. There were cordons of policemen. Policemen, nervous and distraught, obviously awaiting the revolution. All of them were so jumpy, so staccato, that one wished someone would come along with a pail of bromides the way they do down at the Tombs after a narcotic squad has been busy, and ladle out a soothing drink for each of the poor hag-ridden fellows.

For days all the city of Washington was in a dither of apprehension. The Hunger Marchers were coming!

The Hunger Marchers threw ahead of them a long distorted shadow.

Everybody in Washington was aquiver as though anarchy and assassination were abroad; as though, actually, bloody revolution were stalking down the highways. This apprehension flowed from the presidential mansion through all the arteries of the government, down to the children on the streets who, when the Hunger Marchers were finally imprisoned up beyond the railroad tracks, said, "Woo! They can't let them in! They can't let folks like those Hunger Marchers into Washington!"

The skirling of the press and the heating of the tomtoms of disaster which they kept up a week beforehand had whipped the city up to a state of hysteria. It is a very queer thing to see a great capital having the jumps, and a stirring spectacle to behold hundreds of policemen all with the jitters.

The entire police force was put in the field. The firemen were deputized as police. Cavalry and the marines were held in reserve. State police cars patrolled the highways leading into Washington by the dozen. Postal and telephone companies cooperated with the police and kept them informed of every footfall of the marchers. Department of Justice men were star-scattered on the asphalt. Meantime these preservers of the peace were armed with sawed-off machine guns, clubs, hose lengths, and indeed what have you of a lethal nature, besides $10,000 worth of gas.

"The matter with that riot to the Ford Factory," a police officer confided, "was they didn't have enough gas. Now we got plenty; four trucks. We got tear gas, and if that don't settle 'em, we got nauseating gas."

Thus Washington waited to receive the Hunger Marchers. Directly they arrived they cooped them up on a spectacular site. Highway Number One has been cut through it. The cut is twenty feet high, of yellow ochre streaked with red. An embankment of thirty feet covered with cinders falls to railway tracks over which trains are always chuffing. On this road the picturesque array of marchers was penned up. They were not allowed to have any water until 10:00 at night. There were, of course, no sanitary arrangements. I saw them in the morning engaged in such homely occupations as shaving or sleeping, chatting, eating, singing in front of the leviathan trucks with their banners and slogans.

A cordon of police was thrown around the Capitol. Ambulances stood at one side, presumably to gather up the dead and wounded after the massacre. The populace assembled in great numbers to witness the tragedy. The policemen were gruff and noncommittal as to why they were so numerous. Busy police heads in sidecars buzzed up, sirens shrieking. No one except those who had cards was admitted into the Capitol buildings. Everybody with bundles was looked upon with suspicion. One could see the army plane soaring overhead, one knew that numberless troops could be called on a moment's notice.

Meanwhile the Hunger Marchers, who were surrounded by police, machine guns, newspaper reporters, and tear gas, as an island is with the sea, were free from care and unperturbed. They were doing exactly what they had come for. They were demonstrating. That was the purpose of the Hunger March. The Hunger Marchers had demonstrated unemployment and hunger with songs and slogans and by their presence. They considered that they were speaking for 12 million unemployed people.

Every added policeman, every tear-gas bomb was a symptom that this demonstration was succeeding admirably.

The tension grew. The permit to parade was denied. Quarantine was threatened. The police bullied and harried individuals. Rumors spread through the papers that the marchers would rush the police.

Then one afternoon the marchers started in parade formation. Four abreast they came down the half mile of their encampment past the huge trucks, carrying their banners, led by their exciting band, which wears Russian uniforms. They marched on and on and on, up to the barrier which penned them in. The police were ready with gas and machine guns. Not ten feet divided the two camps. And exactly as they reached the barrier, Herbert Benjamin and Anna Burlak, the leaders, gave the order "right face," and wheeled the whole column back on itself.

They had told the police they were going to have a dress parade and the police hadn't believed them. The laugh was on the police.

When they made their right turn the police booed them. The police cried out, "Yeah! You bastards, you're yellow!" The police standing with tear gas and machine guns taunted the marchers for not rushing them. They had discipline and restraint in the face of provocation. The police were ill-behaved, undisciplined, and provocative. I do not think they were this on their own initiative. I do not mean by this that I think they were ordered to call the hungry mobs "bastards and sons-of-bitches" by those higher up, but I do believe there was a general policy of provoking the Hunger Marchers into violence so that they could be cleared out of Washington with club, gas, hose, and bullet. I claim that there was a definite effort on the part of the police to provoke the marchers into reprisals so that that which had been a demonstration should degenerate into a mob, and then a riot, and then a rout. It was not the fault of the police that no opportunity of massacre occurred.

They marched and counter-marched, a long line, very colorful. There was something triumphant about them, in spite of their draggled clothes. They stopped being individuals and for a moment became massed power. Still the police would not believe that they were not contemplating a rush. I heard them saying among themselves, "They're just warming up. They're waiting for dark to rush us."

Dusk came. The panorama of Washington grew faint. The monument became a ghostly exclamation point and the Capitol incandescent. Still they marched and sang and shouted to the menacing "boom-boom-boom" of their drum.

But nothing happened at all except that at midnight the tardy permission to parade was given.

Next day, led by 300 police, surrounded by police, lines of police marching with them on either side, lines of police bringing up the rear, they marched to the appointed distance from the Capitol, singing:

> The police are having a helluva time,
> Parlez-vous,
> The police are having a helluva time,
> Having to march with the Hunger Line,
> Hinkey dinkey, parlez-vous.

The petition was presented to the vice-president and to the vice-president elect.

What would have happened if the police and not too many of them had received the Hunger Marchers as they entered Washington, and had let them go to the empty nearby market which the leaders had engaged as their quarters? This market would have been as easy to guard as was the spectacular hillside encampment.

Nothing would have happened, of course! Demonstrations are not riots.

I, personally, have never seen a disturbance in any of the unemployed doings that was not caused first by the police themselves. There are probably some exceptions to this rule, though I have not happened to see them.

In 1914 the unemployed demonstrated in New York. It was the winter when they entered churches to ask for shelter. Meetings in Union Square were frequently broken up by police; police clubs battered heads or women. I, and the other reporters covering these meetings, knew the orderly and peaceful manner in which the International Workers of the World (IWW) leaders drilled the men.

Lincoln Steffens finally went to Police Commissioner Woods before a big meeting in Union Square and suggested that he police the meeting only sufficiently for traffic. He explained to Woods that the object of the meetings and demonstrations was not riot and revolution, but to advertise to the public and to the government the fact of unemployment. It is an elementary psychological truism that the more uncomfortable people are made about a certain set of circumstances, the more likely are the circumstances to get attention. That was why the unemployed were going into churches. They had conscious leaders who knew the purpose and psychology of demonstrations.

Commissioner Woods agreed to Steffens' request. Companies of reserve police were hidden in lofts surrounding Union Square. They were never called on, of course; they were not needed any more than the vast and ludicrous forces in Washington were needed for an unemployment demonstration happening almost twenty years later.

Meantime, a less spectacular and more revolutionary march was being made on Washington. The farmers were marching in. There were 250 of them, and they came from twenty-six states, from Montana to Florida. There was every kind of farmer; stump farmers from Minnesota, sugar maple farmers from New Hampshire, black sharecroppers from the southern states, wheat farmers, corn and hog farmers.

They were dressed in creased and rumpled Sunday best, for they had been traveling days in trucks. They wore corduroys and leggings. They wore pull-down caps and old fur caps, and a few had on overalls. They were extraordinarily literate. They talked excellent uncolloquial English. Washington welcomed them, not realizing that they carried more high explosives in their blue jeans than any Hunger Marcher ever did. The Hunger Marchers were only demonstrating. They were saying, "We want unemployment insurance, and fifty dollars to see us through the winter." But if the farmers got all their demands, the credit system would cease. They have faced this, and they don't care. What good is the credit system to the evicted? They ask such things as $500 million relief, moratorium on taxes and all farm indebtedness, cancellation of food and farm loans, and no more evictions. They have pledged themselves to "protect our fellow farmers from suffering, and their families from social distintegration by our united action, if our duly elected national representatives and Senators fail as did the local county and State authorities."

This farmers' march on Washington was part of the farmers' nationwide demonstration, which had been going on since the past September. For years the farmers had been in a bad way. They've known all about depression for the last thirteen years. Times had been hard enough; now they were losing their farms in vast numbers. The farmers organized, the farmers tried all sorts of political means to better their conditions. They had their lobbies in Washington; nothing was done for them. Their condition tobogganed downhill to the utter disaster of bankruptcy and eviction. Such legislation as was enacted to help the farmers proved a boomerang, and it was often worse than no help at all.

The farmer is notoriously conservative. He belongs, according to his location, to one of the two big parties; he is a churchgoer and, with few exceptions, a conservative in every sense of the word. Having tried every possible means at his command and finding nothing of any avail, the farmers startled this country by demonstrating—by going on a farmers' holiday. Their demonstration was close to the border of direct action. Picketing the roadways of the big conventions, the farmers' parade for the two candidates for the presidency; these were demonstrations. The march on Washington, the march on the state capitol; these were advertisements to the nation. This warning to the nation:

"We want help, and we want it now." The numerous gatherings which stopped the mortgage sales through a dozen states, the demonstrations which said to the nation "No more evictions." The farmers had learned that it does not pay to be polite, that as long as you suffer in silence, you will be allowed to suffer. As soon as the farmers demonstrated things began to happen. Several states granted moratoriums, several of the largest insurance companies which were mortgage holders granted moratoriums as well.

Legislation for the farmer is being rushed through Congress. If the farmers had not demonstrated, it is safe to say that they would still be being evicted in great numbers.

The unemployed demonstrations have had their victories. In Chicago, the Unemployed Councils and Workers Committee on Unemployment (Socialist) held a monster parade which stopped a 50 percent relief cut and sent the secretary of the Illinois Emergency Committee on Unemployment hurrying to Washington where he borrowed $6,300,000.

Mayor Cermak, when he appeared before the Illinois legislature in January 1931 to ask for $20 million relief appropriation, spoke of this money as insurance. He referred to the action of the Unemployed Councils. It is doubtful if without their pressure he would have asked for this appropriation.

It is claimed that every important unemployment demonstration has been followed by victory either in increased relief appropriation or in stopping relief cuts. The so-called St. Louis riot when the police fired on an unemployment demonstration saw 13,000 men put back on the payroll.

These victories occur in spite of police violence. Why is it not possible for us to understand the nature of demonstrations? While there are abuses, this primitive form of advertisement will be used. The people will continue to use their primitive right so as to dramatize their wrongs and to demand redress. We see the grotesque show of force as in Washington. Why must tear gas, clubs, and bullets be the answer to the announcement that we are unemployed—we are hungry. We want food and jobs.

# Pineville Journal

## Mary Heaton Vorse Papers, 1932

*The tale of "Bloody Harlan County," Kentucky, in the 1930s is today an American epic of labor history, memorialized by one of the most enduring of protest songs, "Which Side Are You On?" In 1931 the Harlan coal miners, who composed two-thirds of the county's population, existed in feudal-like peonage, their lives bound by the lords who owned the coal fields. With electoral revolt closed to them—due to bought votes, stuffed ballot boxes, and fraudulent election returns— the workers fought back through the institution of unionism. When a 10 percent wage cut was announced in February, 1931 the miners went on strike, led by the United Mine Workers. In May, at the famous battle of Evarts, where a thousand shots were exchanged in the course of about thirty minutes, several deputies and miners were killed. The appearance of the National Guard halted picketing, while grand jury indictments and mass arrests eliminated the union leadership. Bitterly defeated in their fight for a union, all but about a thousand miners had reentered the mines at reduced wages by the summer of 1931.*

*The Communists' newly formed union, the National Miner's Union (NMU), entered Harlan to enlist the workers who refused to sign yellow-dog contracts. Because the NMU recruited unemployed workers who could exert no economic pressure upon the coal operators, the Communists were in fact leading what was more a demonstration than a strike. The Harlan mine owners at once made communism, not unionism, the issue. The entire apparatus of county force was turned against the NMU and the hapless blacklisted miners.*

*In November 1931 the National Committee for the Defense of Political Prisoners (NCDPP), an affiliate of the Communist Party, sent a delegation to Harlan County to investigate the conditions of the miners. The report of the delegation, which included novelists Theodore Dreiser and John Dos Passos, brought national publicity to the plight of the Harlan miners.*

*Again sponsored by the NCDPP, a second delegation, which included Mary Vorse and the writers Waldo Frank, Edmund Wilson, and Malcolm Cowley, journeyed to Pineville, Kentucky, in February 1932, to deliver food to the miners. En route, the delegation learned that a young NMU organizer who had left Pineville that morning to meet*

*their caravan had been shot by two deputies, and that one of the trucks
carrying clothing to the miners had been stopped by a mob and overturned.*

*Vorse and the other members of the delegation were met by a host of
armed and sullen men. The town officials allowed the delegation to
deliver their food from a location outside the city limits, although the
last 200 pounds of salt pork was stolen at gunpoint by one of the local
sheriff's men. Later that evening, Vorse and her group were taken from
their hotel rooms and marched under armed guard to the courthouse.
They were first charged with disorderly conduct, and then told that the
charges had been dropped. They were next placed, two by two, into
waiting cars and driven to the state line. Each car carried two armed
deputies. Two members of the delegation, both Jewish, had been sav-
agely beaten by the nightriders before they were released into Tennessee.*

Charles Rumford Walker had been following the miners of Kentucky
closely. He had organized a group to go down the year before and had
made recordings of the numerous stories, which had resulted in a book
called *Harlan Miners Speak.*

It was in the early spring of 1932 that I got a telegram from Charles
Walker to join a party going down to take food to the miners in Pineville, Kentucky.

"There, I knew it!" said Sue, my daughter-in-law. "Now you'll get
shot or lynched or something."

As we drove over the winding road leading from Knoxville into
Kentucky, the other cars strung out ahead of us like beads on a string.
It was a lovely day. Everyone was in good spirits. The big truck full of
food lumbered on behind us.

I had a guilty feeling that I alone among all the sixteen of us knew
that we were heading for trouble. I knew that when southerners make
a threat they mean it.

The mayor of Pineville had telegraphed down to Charlie Walker that
he did not want any of our ilk coming up to Bell County and interfering
with the miners. Charlie Walker had appealed to the governor for
police protection, and he had explained that our mission was just to
distribute some food to the miners. We had received no reply.

When I had warned our little company of pilgrims to bring no literature of any kind along, and to leave personal papers behind because
our baggage might be searched, I was met with somewhat patronizing
assurances that men give to a hysterical woman. However, I couldn't
get them to leave their papers behind, and no one was more surprised
than they when subsequently all their baggage was searched. One of

the men had his shoes wrapped in the *Daily Worker,* which was giving the best accounts of the Pineville strike—probably the only paper giving an account of the Pineville strike, too.

We wound around the mountain, through beautiful country, over the boundary from Kentucky to where there was a wide plateau so we could admire the view, and a sign which read: "Over this road came Daniel Boone in search of liberty." Then after a time we came to Pineville.

The place looked as if it were in a state of siege. Militiamen were everywhere. On top of the town hall there was a nest of machine guns. It looked as if the public square—the square in the middle of the town—was milling with miners. There was an explosive feeling in the air that gave you an uneasy feeling that anything might happen.

Waldo Frank, Quincy Howe, Malcolm Cowley, and Edmund Wilson had already arrived and were having a conference with the mayor and the board of trade I think it was. We joined them.

The mayor was a spidery little man. The men were all gathered around a long table. They were big, rangey, nice-looking men of Scotch-Irish descent whose ancestors came to this mountain country a hundred years ago, and I couldn't help thinking how much I would have liked them under different circumstances.

As we came in, the mayor was reading the city ordinances for our benefit. There was someone in the corridor who was coaching him from time to time—he would dart out of the room and come back with a new ukase of what we could not do: "Any gathering together with the miners within the city limits I shall call 'congregating with a view to disturbing the peace,' and it will be my duty and pleasure to arrest you."

Here someone gave him a nod from outside in the corridor and he darted out.

"Yes," he said, "I want to amplify my statement."

He said, "If two or three of you gather together I will consider that 'congregating' too, and arrest you." Here he darted out again.

"And having any of the miners in your room—that I shall consider 'congregating' too."

Waldo Frank was our spokesman. He tried to explain with great reasonableness what our mission was—it was a matter of free speech and free assembly, he said. We had understood that the miners were being kept from having food distributions, and this concerned the whole country.

In this little town of Pineville, perched on a mountain, Waldo Frank might just as well have been talking in Chaldean. Why anyone up in New York should have been concerned about how miners fared in Kentucky just didn't make sense, and just wasn't so.

Finally, we were told that we could distribute our food outside the town limits. But all "speech-i-fying" and any disturbance was forbidden.

I did not know until the following year how right I had been about our climbing up the mountain to Pineville. In Moscow, in 1933, I met Bernard Smith, who then was working, I think, on the *Moscow Daily News*. He was one of the Communists who were in jail in Pineville at that time, and he told me the story.

The jail was full of the most disreputable characters. In fact there was scarcely anyone there except those convicted of bootlegging or murder, although there was still quite a little feuding in the hills and shooting a Revenue-er was considered public-spirited.

The Communists became very popular for two reasons: Smith started a class in local history, and the part played in the Revolution by people of Kentucky and Tennessee; and there was another member who killed rats by throwing a shoe at them with amazing accuracy. Both of these things endeared them to the general public at the jail. Very soon the Communists were approached by a local lawyer: "You call your friends off from coming up," he said, "and we will treat you good."

The group replied: "They are not our friends; we don't know any of them."

"Oh, come," said the lawyer, "if they ain't Com-mu-nists who are they? Or who else would come up this mountain? They are coming up this mountain because you are here. Maybe they are coming up to rescue you with guns. How do we know?"

"Nonsense," said Smith, the spokesman. "I tell you we don't know any of them."

Which was entirely true, except for Corinne Michaelson, an old Thomas socialist, and a liberal turned Communist.

"We will see you get some consideration," coaxed the lawyer, "just keep them away. They'll give Bell County, and Pineville, and Kentucky even a bad name, having all you folks coming up the mountain."

Nothing they could say would convince them that we were anything but emissaries of the Communist Party.

Upon that, the board of trade met to see what they would do with us. They quickly split into a right and a left wing. The right wing was all for drastic measures: "Let's just lynch 'em, and be done with it. That'll stop 'em coming up the mountain."

"No," said the left wing. "Let's not lynch 'em. There's most twenty of 'em. How do we know some of them don't have southern kin—in the Legislature even—let's just throw 'em in jail—arrest them—as soon as they come in. Throw 'em in jail, put chains on them, and feed them on bread and water. That way we don't get into trouble."

These two points of view were argued heartily, when one side was ahead, the other cut in; the board of trade was pretty evenly split; now one side was ahead, now the other side. The Communists listened with great concern. They couldn't get word to us what was about to happen. They didn't know whether we were going to be murdered or thrown into jail and loaded with chains.

But here the voice of pity and mercy arose in the form of a Baptist clergyman:

"Friends," he said, "don't let's lynch these misguided folks; don't let's load 'em with chains and throw 'em in jail. Let's just get a nice orderly posse of night riders, and ride 'em right out of the state. That won't bring any trouble to any of us. It won't bring us any bad publicity."

Luckily for us, the "party of peace and mercy" prevailed on the day we came to Pineville.

# How Scottsboro Happened

## The New Republic, 1933

In March 1931 a fight broke out between two groups of young male hobos riding a freight train between Chattanooga and Memphis. Several white boys were forced from the slowly moving cars by the group of black adolescents. The ousted white youths complained to a station master who got word to a county sheriff. A few miles farther down the line, the train was stopped by a white force of armed locals who took nine black boys off the cars to the nearest jail in Scottsboro, Alabama. The oldest of the Scottsboro Boys, as they were forever known, was twenty years old. Two were thirteen. Two miserably poor white girls, Victoria Price and Ruby Bates, were also taken off the train. The terrified black boys learned the next day that the girls claimed they had been raped aboard the train by the jailed black youngsters. Both physicians who examined the girls after the alleged attack found no evidence of motile semen or any other physical sign to support the girls' rape story. But within fifteen days, with no reliable evidence presented by the prosecution, one thirteen-year-old black boy was sentenced to life and the rest to death.

In November 1932 the Supreme Court of the United States reversed the lower verdict on the grounds of inadequate counsel. The second trial, which Mary Vorse reported, began in Decatur in March, 1933. Despite Ruby Bates' confession that she and Victoria Price had not been raped, the first black defendant was found guilty. The judge reversed this verdict, claiming that the evidence did not warrant a conviction. In 1935 the U.S. Supreme Court reversed the convictions of two of the Scottsboro Boys on the grounds that blacks had been systematically excluded from the grand jury which indicted the black youths. That year a black man sat on an Alabama jury and all nine of the Scottsboro Boys were indicted for rape once again.

The final trial of the Scottsboro Boys, held in 1936, led to the dismissal of charges against five of the black defendants, sentences of 75 to 99 years to two others, and a death sentence (commuted to life in 1938) for another, Clarence Norris. It was 1976 before Norris received an official pardon from Governor George Wallace.

Out of the contradictory testimony of the trial, the Scottsboro story finally emerged. It unwound itself slowly, tortuously. As witnesses for the prosecution and the defense succeeded one another, they revealed what took place on the southbound freight between Chattanooga and Huntsville, and how they happened to be riding on it, and how they lived at home and in the hobo jungles. It was a murky story of degradation and horror that rivals anything written by Faulkner.

The Scottsboro case is not simply one of race hatred. It arose from the life that was followed by both accusers and accused, girls and boys, white and black. If it was intolerance and race prejudice which convicted Haywood Patterson, it was poverty and ignorance which wrongfully accused him.

Victoria Price was spawned by the unspeakable conditions of Huntsville. These medium-sized mill towns breed a sordid viciousness which makes gangsters seem as benign as Robin Hood and the East Side a cultural paradise. As you leave Huntsville you pass through a muddle of mean shacks on brick posts standing in garbage-littered yards. They are dreary and without hope. No one has planted a bit of garden anywhere.

Victoria Price grew up here, worked in the mill for long hours at miserable wages, and here was arrested for vagrancy, for violation of the Volstead Act, and served a sentence in the workhouse on a charge of adultery. Here she developed the callousness which made it possible for her to accuse nine innocent boys. In jail in Scottsboro she quarreled with the boy who remained on the train, Orval Gilley, alias Carolina Slim, and with Lester Carter, the Knoxville Kid, because they refused to testify with her. Orval Gilley said he would "burn in torment" if he testified against innocent boys, but Victoria, the product of the mean mill-town streets, said she "didn't care if every nigger in Alabama was stuck in jail forever."

The chief actors in the trial besides Haywood Patterson, the trial's dark core, were the three hobo children: Victoria Price of the hard face; Ruby Bates, the surprise witness who recanted her former testimony and insisted that she had accused the boys in the first place because "Victoria had told her to"; and Lester Carter, the girls' companion in the "jungle."

On both Ruby Bates and Lester Carter the jury smelled the North where they had been. Carter offended them by his gestures, by the fact that he said "Negro" showing "subversive northern influences." Ruby Bates was dressed in a neat, cheap gray dress and a little gray hat; Lester Carter had on a cheap suit of clothes. Their clothes probably threw their testimony out of court for the jury. The jury, as well as most people in the courtroom, believed these clothes were "bought with Jew money from New York."

Ruby Bates, Victoria Price, and Lester Carter among them gave a picture of the depths of our society. They told how the hobo children live, of their innocent depravity, of their promiscuous and public lovemaking.

Lester Carter, just off the chain gang for pilfering laundry, was taken to Victoria Price's house by Jack Tiller, the "boyfriend" for whom she had been serving time in the workhouse. Carter was staying at the Tillers'. There would be words between Tiller and his wife, and Tiller would go over to Victoria's. It is interesting to note that Tiller was in the witness room during trial, but was never put on the stand.

In the Prices' front room there was a bed; behind that was a kitchen room, and a shed, and a yard behind that. Victoria's mother and Carter talked together. Tiller and Victoria sat on the bed. Later they went out. The next night Victoria introduced Ruby Bates to Lester Carter, and the four of them went off to a hobo jungle. "We all sat down near a bendin' lake of water where they was honeysuckles and a little ditch. I hung my hat up on a little limb—" And here in each other's presence they all made love.

"Did you see Jack Tiller and Victoria Price?" Lester Carter was asked.

"Sure. They would scoot down on top of us. They was on higher ground." All four of them were laughing at this promiscuous lovemaking. It began to rain, so they went to a boxcar in the railroad yards. Here they spent the night together and made plans to go West and "hustle the towns." The girls both had on overalls, Victoria's worn over her three dresses; both had coats, probably their entire wardrobe. The girls were already what Judge Horton had called them in his charge to the jury: "women of the underworld," whose amusements were their promiscuous love affairs, whose playgrounds were hobo swamps and the unfailing freight cars.

Why not? What was to stop them? What did Huntsville or Alabama or the United States offer a girl for virtue and probity and industry? A mean shack, many children for whom there would not be enough food or clothing or the smaller decencies of life, for whom at best there would be long hours in the mill—and, as now, not even the certainty of work.

With hunger, dirt, sordidness, the reward of virtue, why not try the open road, the excitement of new places? One could always be sure of a boyfriend, a Chattanooga Chicken or a Knoxville Kid or a Carolina Slim, to be a companion in the jungle and to go out "a-bummin'" for food. More fun for the girls to "hustle the towns" than to stay in Huntsville in a dirty shack, alternating long hours in the mill with no work at all. Ruby Bates's mother had had nine children. What had Ruby ever seen in life that rewarded virtue with anything but work and insecurity?

In the cozy boxcar they went on with their exciting plans. Jack Tiller said he had better not go with the girls on account of the Mann Act and the conviction already on record between him and Victoria. He could join them later. So the two girls and the Knoxville Kid went on to Chattanooga together, bumming their way.

Victoria Price had said on the witness stand that when they got to Chattanooga they went to "Callie Broochie's" boarding house, "a two-story white house on Seventh Street," and had looked for work. In reality they had stayed all night in the hobo jungle, where they picked up Orval Gilley, alias Carolina Slim, another of the great band of wandering children, another of those for whom this civilization had no place. Here the boys made a "little shelter from boughs" for the girls and went off to "stem" for food. Nellie Booth's chili cart gave them some, and "tin cans in which to heat coffee." Many different witnesses saw them there in the hobo swamp in the morning. The quartet boarded the freight car which was to make so much dark history. They found five other white boys on the train. Scattered the length of the freight car were Negro boys.

Among these were four very young boys, Negroes from Chattanooga, Andy and Roy Wright, Haywood Patterson, and another boy of fourteen. One of the Wright boys was thirteen. These little Negro-boy hoboes stayed by themselves on an oil-tank car. White tramps came past and "tromped their hands."

"Look out, white boy," Haywood Patterson warned. "Yo'll make me fall off!"

"That'd be *too* bad!" said the white boy. "There'd be one nigger less!" Then the white boys got off the train as it was going slow, and "chunked" the Negro boys with rocks.

There is one precious superiority which every white person has in the South. No matter how low he has fallen, how degraded he may be, he still can feel above the "niggers." It was this feeling of superiority that started the fight between the white hobo boys and the black hoboes on the train between Chattanooga and Huntsville.

It started because seven white-boy bums were above riding even on the same train with Negroes. The Negroes decided to rush the white boys. The four very young Negroes were asked to come along by the older boys. The dozen Negroes on the train fought the seven white boys, and put them off the train.

The only decent moment in the whole story was the dragging back of Orval Gilley—Carolina Slim—by one of the Negro boys, apparently Haywood Patterson. He had pulled the white boy Gilley back on the train by his belt, perhaps saving his life. When asked on the witness stand if he had committed the crime, Haywood Patterson cried in a loud voice—

"Do yo' think I'd 'a pulled a white boy back to be a witness if I'd ben a-fixin' to rape any white woman?"

Gilley then climbed in the gondola with the girls, a "churt car" full of finely crushed rock for mending the road bed. It was in this car that the conductor later found Victoria's snuff box. The four young Negro boys from Chattanooga went back to their former places and sat facing each other. The white boys who had been put off the train complained to the authorities at Stevenson, who telephoned ahead.

At Paint Rock a posse of seventy-five men arrested the nine Negroes in different places on the train. The girls in overalls, fearing a vagrancy charge, then accused the Negro boys of assault.

Ruby Bates, Victoria Price, and their companions, Orval Gilley and Lester Carter, were all taken to the jail together. The rest of the story is known.

Observe that this quartet of young people has no standards, no training, no chance of advancement; that there is for them not even the promise of low-paid steady employment. They have one thing only— the trains going somewhere, the boxcars for homes, the jungles for parks. They pilfer laundry, clothes, as a matter of course. They bum their food, the girls "pick up a little change hustling the towns," and it's all a lot better than the crowded shacks at home and the uncertain work in the mills.

Apparently Victoria had come in and out of Chattanooga often. Lewis, a Negro who lived near the jungle, the one whose "sick wheezin' hawg" wandered in and out of the story, testified that Victoria had often begged food "off his old woman." Victoria Price and Ruby Bates are no isolated phenomenon. The Children's Bureau reports 200,000 children under twenty-one wandering through the land. These two girls are part of a great army of adventurous, venal girls who like this way of life.

For it is a way of life, something that from the bottom is rotting out our society. Boys and girls are squeezed out of the possibility of making a living, they are given nothing else; but there are the shining rails and trains moving somewhere, so the road claims them. The girls semi-prostitutes, the boys sometimes living on the girls, and all of them stealing and bumming to end up with a joyous night in a boxcar.

The fireman on the freight train was asked what he thought when he saw the girls on the train. He answered "he didn't think a thing of it, he saw so many white girls nowadays a-bummin' on trains." Victoria Price is only one of thousands who put overalls on over all the clothes they own and hit the road; only one of thousands, one who has had all kindness and decency ground out of her in her youth.

# Women's March

## *The New Republic, 1933*

*With the advent of the New Deal government, the Communist-led unemployment demonstrations were greeted by federal officials with considerably more sympathy and consideration than under the Republicans. New Deal agencies such as the Civil Works Administration gave hope to millions of unemployed that the new government was moving to meet the people's needs. As participation by the unemployed in Communist-led demonstrations declined, the party shifted its unemployment activity from noisy confrontation to lobbying within Congress. Their focus was the Worker's Unemployment Insurance Bill, introduced in Congress in early 1934, which called for direct payments to the unemployed, the funds to be raised by an income tax and administered by workers' councils. The Worker's Unemployment Insurance Bill was eventually voted down by a House committee in 1935. FDR's plan depended upon the states to devise unemployment insurance laws, with payments to be financed by a payroll tax, rather than drawn from general revenue funds.*

Recently 10,000 miners' wives marched to the state house in Springfield, Illinois, to present demands of the Women's Auxiliary of the Progressive Miners to the governor.

"Their statement was tersely written," says the *Progressive Miner*. "It rang with the tone of resentment against the impoverishment of the workers dependent upon coal for an existence."

These were the coal-digger women's demands:

1. Restoration of civil liberties in the coal fields.
2. Increased and more equitable distribution of state aid.
3. Unemployment insurance paid by industry and state.
4. Defeat of the state sales tax.

These women, presenting their demands to their chief executive, has been organized only a brief time and had little chance for preparation. One week an announcement appeared in the *Progressive Miner,* their official paper, that on a certain day the march would occur. It was predicted by Agnes Wieck, president of the Women's Auxiliary, that 5,000 women would march. Instead, 10,000 women responded. In perfect order, each dressed in white, a white band around her head,

they assembled. They came marching from every corner of the state
with their banners and their music. They came in rattletrap Fords, in
trucks, on trolleys. They came from the Midlands, which has borne the
brunt of the fight against the Peabody Company and John Lewis's
strikebreakers—the part of the country where militia and gunmen
have been terrorizing the miners for the better part of a year.

These fighting women who had lived so long under terror saw with
joy the banners of the women from all over the state. They came from
fifty-one different communities. They marched eight abreast, and five
coal-digger bands led them in their hour march from the state arsenal
to the capitol. Watching the white-clad women streaming past with
their banners and music was a great congregation of miners. They were
looking on a new sight, the miners' women taking up the men's fight
and protesting against the four years of hunger, want, and the use of
the armed forces of the state to aid in breaking the rank-and-file union.

Mother McKeever, the ninety-three-year-old veteran, led the Toney
delegation—Mother McKeever who, in her spirited letter of protest to
Bishop Brown, so well described the terror:

> I have witnessed more strikes than anyone through the coalfields, but
> such an outrageous strike I never witnessed as this one.
>
> How would you like a drunken deputy to flash his light in your bed-
> room window three or four times a night, fire off his big gun at two or
> three o'clock in the morning to scare you to death? That is the conduct
> that I have witnessed in my home. I have tried every possible way to do
> what is right and I think I have done so. They have even took my state aid
> off me which I received $1.30 a week. They have done everything that
> could be done with rascality in this neighborhood. They have thrown tear
> bombs in the streets, on the sidewalks when we would be walking, we
> were ordered off the streets like a dog. I have been a taxpayer for over
> thirty years and am a law-abiding citizen. . . .
>
> Father, we have got no justice in Taylorville Court House, nor we can't
> expect none from them clockers.
>
> Father, I made lots of sacrifices to pay to the cathedral in Springfield
> which I thought part of my duty to do so I'm sorry to say that I have heard
> such results.
>
> > Mother McKeever.

As they approached the capitol the women broke ranks and surged
like a sea of white through the open space before the building and up
the steps. The bands played; banners punctuated the crowd. Agnes Burns
Wieck stood near the parapet bordering the statue of Lincoln, raised
her fist and cried in a loud voice "Solidarity." The delegation of women
then presented their demands to the governor, making their way past
the police, the plainclothes men, and the inevitable tear-gas bombs.

This extraordinary demonstration of women with its splendid solidarity had back of it long hunger, unemployment, undernourished children who had no adequate clothes to wear to school. Fear of eviction, terror of gunmen, helped to organize these women.

The Women's Auxiliary of the Progressive Miners of America has for its slogan, "Fight Hunger!" It was organized almost simultaneously with the new union. It held its first enthusiastic convention in Gillespie in November, with hundreds of delegates attending. Throughout the coalfields it has worked untiringly at relief and has, singlehanded, fed thousands of unemployed miners' families and clothed thousands of children. The Women's Auxiliary has fought shoulder to shoulder with the men. They are not without victims. One woman standing in her own home was shot and killed by gunmen. The vitality of the Women's Auxiliary reflects the vitality of the young rank-and-file union in its revolt against corrupt officialdom.

There has long been stirring in the coalfields a revolt against the United Mine Workers (UMW) leadership. Time after time leaders have betrayed the workers. The history of past years has been one of shameless disintegration of the most militant and one of the best-organized unions of the United States. In Ohio and parts of West Virginia a new union has been formed. In the South, in Kentucky and in part of Tennessee, when the UMW deserted the Harlan miners, the National Miners' Union stepped in. Last year, when John Lewis and John Walker substituted a $5 wage scale for the $6.10 wage scale, there was the Progressive Miners' revolt. A rank-and-file referendum was held, and it was alleged by the miners that their ballots were stolen by UMW officials. A strike was declared. There was a huge procession of miners into Franklin County to bring out their brother miners. It is ancient history how their cars were turned over, the miners gassed, beaten, and wounded, the whole demonstration broken up through the treachery of the police and the use of gunmen. All doubts had vanished at last about the wisdom of forming a new union. The UMW has never formed a new local without a baptism of blood. The old miners, who had suffered and been blacklisted and evicted for the sake of unionism, could not bear to desert their old union. They continued to say, "We must reform our union, and get rid of our corrupt politicians." They had not realized how closely the leaders were allied with the operators, which meant that they had at their disposal the state machinery and the armed force of the state.

The new union is a rank-and-file organization. Instead of the huge salaries and expense accounts given the old organizers, the organizers receive $18 a week, a miner's wage. The president and officers must be changed every four years. There are so many checks and balances designed to keep power in the hands of the coal diggers themselves that a convention moves cumbrously. The miners have had enough of railroading a thing through by steamroller methods. Although John Lewis predicted their downfall when they, too, had to give up the old wage scale and when they made settlements under $5—a really major defeat—the union has steadily grown. Mine after mine has gone over to the Progressive Miners. And operator after operator has settled with the new union. In November 17,000 miners were working under agreements with the Progressive Miners. The large Peabody interests, in the Midlands, and some mines in Franklin County are the principal ones that have held out.

The brief history of the Progressive Miners is already bloodstained. They have had to fight not only gunmen, the sheriffs, the militia, but also the armed thugs and strikebreakers of John Lewis, who has done everything a strong and unscrupulous man could do to put down the new union—the dual union abhorred by the American Federation of Labor.

The Progressive Miners claim they are not a dual union, that they are *the* union, and that they have 90 percent of the rank and file. A short time ago came the news of another victim, it is claimed, of John Lewis' gunmen. There are other deaths and there are shootings, beatings, gassings, jailings without end, and always terror such as Mother McKeever described. The union, nevertheless, has kept on and flowered into the magnificent march of the women.

# Textile Trouble

## *The New Republic, 1934*

❧

*The thunder of mass revolt shook the nation in 1934. Four major strikes and over 1,800 smaller ones involved almost 1.5 million workers.*

*The largest of these, the national cotton-textile strike, which brought out 376,000 workers from Alabama to Maine, ended in a bitter labor defeat. Called by the AFL-affiliate, the United Textile Workers, the national strike began in September. Employers responded in the usual fashion—armed guards, spies, eviction of strikers' families from company-owned houses, attacks upon union leaders, jailings of organizers, and pressure upon state authorities to call out the National Guard. Repression was especially vicious in the South, where mill owners, governors, militia, and company guards crushed the strike almost at once. In the North, the governor of Rhode Island, convinced that a Communist uprising was imminent, sent in the National Guard. On September 20 the FDR-supported Board of Inquiry into the textile strike issued its finding against union recognition, and suggested that wages, housing, and working conditions receive attention from future government "studies."*

The streets are still dark, the big oblong of the mills is gray and silent. From a distance comes a faint noise of the sea. There are already men standing in threes and fours on street corners. It is New Bedford the morning after Labor Day, the day set for the big textile strike—"The first strike of its kind in the history of the labor movement of America," as the organizers have been telling the workers in the mass meetings throughout the nation.

This strike is in the nature of a showdown. It was fathered by the speedup and stretchout and mothered by evasions of the code, by the disregard of Section 7a. People can no longer live on what they are getting: They can no longer exist under the conditions under which they work. Too many skilled workers have been discharged and reemployed as "learners"—one means of avoiding the minimum-wage clause. Too many workers have been forced to do three people's work in one day. In the past five years less and less of every dollar earned by the mills has gone to the worker.

It is a time of anxiety. Are "they" going to come out? Will there be a break for the mills? I'm striking and you're striking, but are the others? Our mill is striking but what about the other mills? And if we tie up New Bedford, what about the rest of the towns in New England and what about Manchester and Lowell and Lawrence? What about Passaic and Paterson?—These are the things the workers are thinking as they watch the crowd on the street become larger, as the streets get bright. The small groups have flowed into each other; the streets are filled. The Hathaway mill stares empty-windowed at the mounting crowd. On the mill side there is no one. A guard at the gate, a few policemen, very few, no imposing display of armed force—as yet. On the side away from the mill, every language in the world is spoken: French, Portuguese, and Italian predominate. Everybody is good-tempered, even jolly.

*No one has gone in.* There is no picket line. There does not need to be. All the workers are out on the street opposite the mill. There are no scabs against whom to picket the mill. These mills in the South End are out 100 percent. Organization is no new thing to the New Bedford workers. They have gone through many a struggle. In 1928, the big good-natured Portuguese women who look like full-blown peonies snatched clubs from policemen's lifted hands and hit back. The black-eyed little French Canadians fought like wildcats. We wonder if the North Side is holding as well and hurry over there. The two manufacturing sections of New Bedford are far apart. We drive past sleeping, old-fashioned houses, past the business section. Down the steep street near the Wamsutta mills the workers are gathered. Here one sees an old-fashioned type of worker. Middle-aged prissy Americans, they hold themselves apart from the foreign worker but they are out here striking in the street for all that. Some people tell you four people have gone in. Others say they have counted seven, a handful. It's the same in the Nashewena mills—it's the same in twenty-five mills in New Bedford. A 100 percent strike—only the three great tire-fabric mills have not come out, Firestone, Goodrich, and Fisk.

People begin to drift away slowly. Everyone is relieved, everyone seems happy. It seems more like a fiesta than a strike. There is just time to eat something before the mass meeting in the park. Yesterday William Beatty had made a fighting speech. He refused in a round-about way the unity proposals of the National Textile Workers' Union, the left-wing, Communist-dominated union which before the National Recovery Act was strong in New Bedford. This union has already formed a merger in Paterson. The local United Textile Workers' leaders will not hear of it.

Today's meeting is short. There are three messages from the orga-nizer Sylva; one a new one. "Don't think of yourselves as New Bedford workers—your fight is the fight of all the textile workers of America. It is as wide as the land." The next is "Trust our president. He will see we get justice." Yes, the steelworkers were told that and the automobile workers—one knows the result and a heavy feeling of defeat comes over me as I look at the hopeful people in their holiday mood. Dressed as for church instead of for work. The third message is concrete: "We're out 100 percent except the tire fabrics. We've got to get them out. Everybody go over to Fisk and Goodrich and picket; *now*."

The meeting breaks up. We go over and now they come in groups. Men and girls, old and young, hundreds and hundreds of them stream-ing over to the great factories, and filling the streets in front. Mr. Beatty and Mr. Sylva lead a small picket line on the mill side. On the opposite side the gay crowd calls to the workers who throng to the windows. There are few police.

The papers come out with screaming headlines starting a Red witch-hunt. They say the left-wing textile leader, Ann Burlak, is in hiding. But we have seen Ann Burlak quietly attending the meeting. Ann Burlak, secretary of the National Textile Workers' Union, will be ar-rested. What for? Oh, anything will do.

We read the papers on our way to Pawtucket and Fall River. The papers say that yesterday, Labor Day, in the big mass meeting the independent unions in Fall River voted not to come out. The As-sociated Press reports Pawtucket working as usual. But in Fall River the dreary, the workers are buzzing excitedly in the street. The mills are tied up. The United Textile Workers have struck 100 percent and they have the loom fixers. So the mills are tied up, perhaps over 60 percent.

The Pepperell mills are being picketed by a gay band of young girls. There are silent mills in Fall River from whose windows stovepipes protrude as in Moscow in 1921. There is where fly-by-night sweatshops operated. Other mills have been torn down. Piles of gray stones lie about.

In Pawtucket a lively meeting is going on. The union hall is full of weavers and spinners. The place hums with life. A national organizer, Elizabeth Nord, is making a comprehensive talk. She is slender, young, full of fighting spirit. Later she tells me thousands are out. The Associated Press story has been contradicted. She calls for pickets for a mill out of town where they make Fruit of the Loom. The real story will be the coming out of those mills not already on strike. In the South they have called out the militia. The tone of the evening papers is more sensational.

Back in New Bedford we hear there is trouble near the tire factories.

A large crowd has gathered in an open square nearby. It is after ten.
Mr. Beatty has stopped picketing. Fifteen thousand people have been
down around the tire-fabric mills this evening. The police have been
reinforced by the khaki-clad motorcycle cops, who hoot their sirens as
they tear past, by members of the liquor squad, by the traffic police.
For the first time there is tenseness. Thousands of workers are in the
open space, near the mills. They are pale under the high arc lights.
The day which began quietly has been one of mounting excitement. It
is as if one could see and feel the massed will of the workers who are
out directed toward the workers who have not yet come out.

The young socialist editor of the local labor paper mounts a gray
outcropping of rock and makes a speech about everyone's being on
tomorrow's picket line. A Negro near us calls out, "How about the
night-shift? What about a picket line now!" They form a picket line, the
editor in front. The crowd swarms forward behind him. At the street
by the mill they are stopped. The police bar the way to the mill, the
crowd pushes on under the pressure of those behind. Stones are
hurled—the chief orders the workers back. The crowd breaks. Motorcycle police and police wagons herd the crowd down the street, but
their action might well be a lesson to the police of other cities. There
have been no beatings and no arrests.

Wednesday morning mass picketing was barred in front of Fisk and
Goodyear on the South Side and on the North Side in front of Firestone.

Wednesday noon one picket alone walks up and down, up and down,
in front of the Goodyear plant. It is none other than Mr. William
Beatty. Up and down he walks on his endless patrol. No workers are
allowed within the police lines. The New York correspondents are
sharply questioned. There is a squib in the paper about a car with a
New York license supposed to contain "outside agitators" and "literature." It contained its owner, Mr. Waldo Frank. The morning papers
also contain statements from the managers of the three factories that
they expect no trouble. Not a chance in the world of these contented
workers striking. We walk along by the mill. A group of a dozen men
are leaning on a wall facing the mill. "Staying out?" we ask.

"Yeah, we're twisters from Fisk. We're staying out," they grin. We
drive blocks around the enormous mill, then down one side where
there are only a scattered handful of police. We see the street lined
with an excited crowd.

Girls are pouring out of the back entrance of the Fisk factory. The
crowd is applauding.

"Are you coming out?" we ask.

"Sure thing," they chorus.

"Many of you?" "We're 'most all out." "Yes, only the boss men left."
The word goes from mouth to mouth.

"Fisk has struck! Fisk has struck—the fabric workers are out!"

The word has gone out over the wire to Washington, "Fisk is out."
The tire-fabric factories are all closed. The first victory.

# Perkins, This Way!

## The New Republic, 1934

*After almost a decade of internal strife, the Progressive Mine Workers of America (PMW) was organized in September 1932, as a rival organization in opposition to the dictatorial control of the United Mine Workers (UMW) by John L. Lewis. The PMW billed itself as a defender of rank-and-file union democracy. Warfare between the PMW and the UMW was exceedingly bitter and violent during the mid-thirties. In 1933 Lewis sent his former foe, John Brophy, to investigate the strength of the PMW and to determine the prospects for ending the shooting war between the two unions. Brophy reported to Lewis that the PMW's organization of a women's auxiliary was one of the most important factors supporting its high spirit. Nevertheless, Lewis continued to oppose the demand usually voiced at UMW annual conventions by rank-and-file miners for the creation of a women's auxiliary within the UMW. A thoroughly traditional sexist, Lewis was appalled by the militant action of women who, in his opinion, belonged at home, cooking the meals and tending the children.*

"This way for Perkins! Perkins, this way!" someone yelled. The women delegates of the Unemployment Convention formed into line.

"Walk two by two," the voice instructed. "Walk several feet apart. Keep up a good pace." The file of women, forty perhaps, started on their way to visit the secretary of labor [Frances Perkins]to tell her their stories and to make their demands.

It took them a long time to get there. Traffic stopped them. Police stopped them. Their guide, a Washington man, was for no reason hurled on the car tracks by a policeman. Why? One of those obscure acts of violence without object or meaning which constantly punctuate the labor movement. They were to find Secretary Perkins away and Miss Abbott, of the Children's Bureau, away too, and substituting for them, Assistant Secretary Batelle and Miss Lenroot.

Other groups had started at the same time. Some to see the president; to see Mr. Hopkins of the Civil Works Administration; to see their representatives and senators. A large delegation from AFL unions was waiting on pink-faced Mr. Green, whose lower lip always looks as if it were about to quiver.

These groups are the picked representatives of the 900 unemployed delegates who have been meeting for the past two days in the Colored Masonic Temple—they represent some 3 million workers. They are letting the country know in no uncertain terms that they want unemployment insurance, cash relief, no discrimination in relief and jobs, no discrimination against Negro workers; that they protest the Civilian Conservation Corps (CCC) camps and the militarization of thousands of young men.

The women's demands, presented by their spokesperson, Juliette Poyntz, are: jobs through the CWA for all unemployed women without discrimination as to race, nationality, or marital condition; adequate cash relief in absence of jobs for all women workers without discrimination; no discrimination against Negro women workers in wages, employment, working conditions, or distribution of jobs or relief; shelter for all unemployed women, providing decent and permanent living quarters under management of their own committees; for the Workers' Unemployment and Social Insurance Bill; wage increases and equal pay for equal work for women workers; against wage cuts and starvation wages; for workers' rights—the right to organize, demonstrate, strike, and picket; against the high cost of living, high prices, and inflation; against evictions; for establishment of public crèches and nursery schools for infants and young children with free feeding, clothing, and care; free meals for children in school, free medical care and clothing; and free medical and maternity care for working women.

This is a fighting program and these are fighting women. The women all over the country are fighting for more to eat for their children. They are fighting to get clothes for their children and to ensure them warmth and a roof over their heads—and really fighting—with hands if need be.

Now here stands the delegation in Miss Perkins's office—schoolteachers and laundry workers, steel workers' and miners' wives. Women who represent the homeless single women, the most lamentable of all the depression victims. Negro and white women from unemployment committees—they stand waiting in good order. Two or three begin to talk at once. A fine-looking Negro woman objects.

"Sho' sisters, we kin all sing together, but we cain't all talk together!"

Many of these women have told me their stories. There is Matilda Lee, who represents 23,000 miners' wives, the Women's Auxiliary of the Progressive Miners, and is state auditor of the Women's State Committee. Her comely face is tanned. She has very broad shoulders and snapping blue eyes and her blond hair is swept back from her forehead.

"Can you use my name? Of course you can." She has been in the thick of the fight of the Progressive Miners. She has also been in the thick of the Unemployed Councils' struggles. Her story is one of alarms at night with thugs intimidating the women. Of men shot down by thugs. Of scabs protected by militia. All through Illinois the women have organized auxiliaries. They have been remarkable in self-help, in getting relief, applying to the farmers for their surplus food, in putting pressure on the authorities.

"There's nothing will make them move but more pressure. You don't get anything without organization," says Mrs. Lee.

This has been painfully taught to hundreds and thousands of women throughout the land. Their textbooks have been empty larders, children's shoeless feet, cold houses, fear of eviction. North, South, East, and West, they have learned to band together. Look at Mrs. Dorio. She comes from around Scranton; she is pretty, educated, and gentle in appearance. One can imagine her at another time living pleasantly. Life today has separated her from her husband. Their jobs folded up. She had to go home to live and she became a militant fighter because of the sights which passed before her eyes.

"You have to go into the workers' homes to realize how things are in the mines and of course everything is mines around where we are. About 60 percent are out of work and no one's working full time. The union didn't help any more. The United Mine Workers laid down on the job, so they formed the United Anthracite Miners."

Several organizations work together. The Small Home-Owners' League, which resists foreclosures and evictions. The Unemployed Councils and others. Nine hundred women from six towns organized and marched on the Scranton City Hall to protest relief cuts. The police clubbed and arrested them, but they won.

"Before we organized we couldn't get shoes for the children. They'd say there wasn't any shoes. When we went together, we got twenty-two pairs of shoes. Why, I know a family where there were five boys who couldn't go to school because they hadn't shoes. They hadn't anything. We protest against discrimination. I know a family who owned a cow and still were getting four quarts of milk for relief. They sold that milk along with theirs to other families with little sick children who couldn't get a drop free. We stopped that, too."

All the demands of the workers, small and large, Mrs. Dorio looks after. It fills her life. She has become a crusading fighter.

How long will Miss O'Hara look so genteel? She is one of the best-dressed women here, with her neat black coat, her close-fitting black hat on her gray hair, a soft gray scarf around her neck, and gray pearl beads. She used to be a pastry cook. But she is one of the homeless single women. The city has no place for them but the municipal lodging home. There is a whole city of such women in New York.

"I've never been in what some of them call flophouses, dear; no, not at all," she says. What next? Will she pawn her coat, shift from one flophouse to the next until her carefully guarded gentility is gone and only an old broken bum remains? What's the answer?

There are girls here who have slept in subways rather than go to the municipal lodgings. Girls here with bitter words about Camp TERA. There is no public relief for single girls. They are sent to the YWCA, to the Salvation Army, for their precarious existence.

How Helen Baker found her courage I can't tell. She is a modest, retiring little woman from one of the southern states. She works in a cotton mill. "I'm a widow by desertion," she'll tell you. Such widows are common on the mill hills. A man can't stand it any more and quits. She has five children, "but my oldest boy, he's seventeen, is strollin' the world. I can't tell where he is." Sometimes when she is lucky she makes $7.40 for sixty hours' work. Once she made $12. This was fabulous.

She is bringing to the secretary the story of the discrimination in relief against Negro workers; how of 6,000 CWA jobs in a county only a handful of Negroes have received work. She is protesting the Herndon case, the young Negro of twenty who got ten years for "insurrection," for taking part in a demonstration. "They locked him up because he ast 'em for brade," she tells the assistant secretary.

She walked, the only white woman, in a protest funeral. There were 200 Negroes protesting the shooting of Glover Davis, a blind Negro. I can imagine no more courageous act for a southern working woman.

"He was a settin' on his bed an' they come in an' shot him. They said they didn't mean to, they was lookin' for someone else." So she walked in the protest funeral. There were six white men—"the laws claimed them, but they didn't get me." She belongs to an Unemployed Council that "scrambles around and fights for the Negroes." I asked her how she got to feel as she did, and she told me she read the *Daily Worker* and it said things she'd always been feeling. So here she was bringing the Herndon story and the case of the Negro fellow workers to Washington—as heroic as she was unconscious of any heroism.

The remarkable unemployment convention which has just come to an end was lusty and young. It had indignation and laughter. Here was a cross-section of the workers of America. Homely people, pungent and forceful of speech, a notable gathering. Tall oil drillers from Texas. A big delegation of Pennsylvania miners. Metal miners from Minnesota. Marine-transport workers, farmers, longshoremen, neat young men from offices, a few professional men. Architects and draftsmen.

Miners' wives, steelworkers' wives. Fleet young office workers. Ample Negro women. Ready all of them to tell their stories, ready for a hearty laugh, bound together by a common experience and a common purpose.

There were very few reporters from local papers and the stories they printed were insignificant and trivial. There was nothing at all in the papers about the fact that the working women of America have gotten fighting mad.

*Labor's Struggles: 1936–59*

# Organizing the Steel Workers

## The New Republic, 1936

❧

*The long debate between the proponents of industrial unionism and of craft unionism came to a head in 1935, when John L. Lewis sparked the formation of the Committee of Industrial Organization (CIO). Established to organize the unorganized, especially in the mass-production fields, the CIO member unions were suspended as dual organizations by the AFL in 1936.*

*Lewis believed that the organization of steel, the nation's basic industry, was vital to the success of the CIO in other industries. He at once established a Steel Workers' Organizing Committee (SWOC) and provided it with an initial treasury of $½ million drawn from the funds of his United Mine Workers. The CIO steel drive was officially launched in June 1936. Contrary to Lewis' expectations, however, the pivotal struggle of the CIO occurred not in the steel industry, but at the United Auto Workers' sit-down strike in Flint, Michigan, in February 1937. Less than two months after the key victory at Flint, U.S. Steel quietly and secretly came to terms with John L. Lewis and the CIO. The U.S. Steel agreement, announced in March 1937 with sensational effect, accorded bargaining rights to SWOC, raised wages and reduced the work week to forty hours. Hundreds of other steel companies soon did the same. In order to avoid a violent, expensive, and unpopular confrontation with labor, Big Steel, long the chief bastion of the open shop, capitulated to the unionization of its labor force in 1937 without even a fight.*

The meeting in Memorial Park of Tarentum, Pennsylvania, is the first mass meeting on the Allegheny River in the organizational campaign of steelworkers. It is a lovely little park, stretching narrow along the wide river, the abrupt green hills mounting the opposite shore. People have come slowly, somewhat tentatively; now they begin to wake up and become a real audience.

Smiley Shatac is speaking: he has just led a short, victorious strike. Haltingly, briefly, in broken English he is saying that the 660 victorious workers of the Hubbard Steel Company are organized 95 percent.

Smiley Shatac has dark red hair and strong features. He has vitality and easy strength.

"I just talk to one—I talk to another. All of 'em say, 'Smiley, we join.'"

There is a delegation of the victorious workers here. They stand smiling, waiting to be introduced. Suddenly, by the enthusiasm of applause, the audience is fused into something living. It isn't just that the Hubbard employees have braved the threat of the lockout and have come out on top, or that these workers who make electrical equipment have won a 5 percent increase, a forty-four-hour week, recognition of the shop committee, two ten-minute rest periods for the women workers, and better sanitary conditions throughout the shop. More than this, at the signing of their agreement, they did not rush back into the mill—they decided to stay out two days more and to march back two by two from Croatian Hall. There is a fine quality about them as they stand there—not insolent but with the ease of security. They have communicated this security to the hesitating, uncertain audience.

The Congress of Industrial Organizations (CIO) and the Steel Workers' Organizing Committee (SWOC) are at work. Something entirely new has entered the labor movement. This same organizing committee has behind it the massed power of the 1,225,000 workers of the twelve great unions of industrial organization that form the CIO.

The workers (mostly young) in the Hubbard plant wanted to organize. They came to the CIO. They were no longer a little, cut-off group of inexperienced workers. They became part of the great drive in the labor movement. Labor leaders have dreamed, for years, of such a vital joining together of forces. Now it is an accomplished fact.

Down in Portsmouth, Ohio, the 7,000 workers of Wheeling Steel won their strike the middle of July. Two weeks ago the workers of RCA in Camden, New Jersey, settled after a spasm of terror that jailed several hundred of their workers, including the CIO organizer, Powers Hapgood. The organization work done at Hubbard Steel is the first victory in the Pittsburgh area. So in this meeting at Tarentum, never for a moment can one forget the large forces involved. This meeting is a small part of a great movement headed by John L. Lewis.

John L. Lewis—his name rings through the meeting. It almost seems John L. Lewis is present. John L. Lewis, president of the United Mine Workers of America, is back of the steelworkers. They applaud when his name is mentioned. They do not forget there are a million and a quarter workers back of them. There is an awful power and might in steel, but there is an awful power and might in the age-old drive for freedom. The last time the urge for organization pulsed through the steel mills, it was led by the rank-and-file committee. This time, instead of standing alone, isolated, repudiated even by their own International, the workers know that the might of the CIO and the power of John L. Lewis are behind them.

The local organizer, Paul Fuller, speaks: he was organizer in the South during the great organizational drive of the textile workers. Earlier, at the union headquarters, we had talked with him. He believes that if you can organize southern textile workers (and they have been organized) you can organize steelworkers.

The biggest steel mill around here is that of the Allegheny Steel Company in Brackenridge, a couple miles down the Allegheny River. All around it is organized industry. Glass is organized; the United Mine Workers are organized; other industries are organized. Aren't the steel operators more set against organization than the textile operators, haven't they a greater power, we asked him. "No," he answered, "no one could be more ruthless, no one more determined, no one more murderous than the southern textile-mill operators."

Up to now organization has progressed in the Allegheny Valley as in the rest of the steel towns—quietly. There has been house-to-house visiting; there have been secret meetings in the woods; inside the mills workers who have signed up talk with other workers. The quiet, steady drive goes on throughout the mill towns. It is not spectacular but it goes on steadily. Only a few days separated the secret meeting in the woods from the open meeting.

Pat Fagan talks: he is an organizer of the United Mine Workers of America, District 5. If you can organize West Virginia, he tells them, you can organize steel. Briefly he rehearses the bloody story of West Virginia. "The banner of the United Mine Workers flies over every tipple in West Virginia," says Pat Fagan. They applaud—many of the audience have been mine workers as well as steelworkers.

Glen W. McCabe speaks: he is president of the Federation of Flat Glass Workers. In himself he is a proof of how times are changing— formerly a craft-union man and a Republican; today, by force of events and the necessities of labor, he is an industrial unionist and a Roosevelt man. He tells about a victory of yesterday. Three years ago glass was practically unorganized—today it is 98 percent organized in an industrial union.

The history of labor is present here at this meeting. The story of its evolution is here. Here are the men who fought through impossibly difficult situations and who have organized when no organization seemed possible. They are here to tell the steelworkers, "It won't be easy; many of you may lose your jobs; it may be dangerous, but *it can be done.*"

Hope and courage have been awakened. The faces of four Negroes near me, so stolid when they came, have brightened. It is a fine-looking audience, healthy, young, and self-respecting. It seems incredible that terror will be visited upon them for following their need to organize. But terror and intimidation are already present. Up and down the Allegheny Valley, up and down the Monongahela, the Ohio, the Mahoning, wherever the great steel mills are belching forth fire and smoke, workers are being intimidated. There are threats of lockouts, there are threats of moving the plants—in one great plant the workers have been called in two by two and told not to join the union; around the Homestead area, where the memories of the lost battles of labor hang over the town, there has been a drive to make the workers believe that joining the union means an immediate strike. The workers want no strike. This drive is for organization.

In Aliquippa, the situation got so tense that two state troopers have been called for. They sit around, large and handsome, and no one can get them to say they are here to protect the workers. They say that they are here to keep law and order, but this time it will be truly law and order. They won't be riding down the congested steel-town streets, their three-foot riot clubs raised high, driving the workers into their houses. They won't break up funerals and ride into a crowd of parochial-school children as they did in 1919. The governor of Pennsylvania is for organized labor and the lieutenant-governor is a former member of the United Mine Workers of America. This will be one terror that will be lacking.

There are other kinds of "law and order." Aliquippa is the stronghold of the Jones and Laughlin plant. The company employs 9,000 men. From the coal piles, like small mountains, from which they make their own coke, along past the great furnaces, the mills seem never ending. On the front page of the Aliquippa paper, in the lower-right-hand corner, appears a suggestive little framed advertisement of two columns. It reads simply: "Please enroll me as a member of the Citizens Committee of Five Hundred." Below this is room for a name and address.

It is Mr. J. A. C. Ruffner who is sponsoring the Committee of Five Hundred. Mr. Ruffner is a prominent man of affairs and a public-spirited citizen. He is chairman of the Republican committee, part owner of the paper, director of the bank, partner in a flourishing real-estate business, and he will tell anyone who wishes to inquire that the function of the Committee of Five Hundred is "to take over when law and order breaks down." It develops that his idea of law and order breaking down is, for example, workers picketing. Then if the police can't stop it, law and order have to be preserved. Some reports say that when he was asked if he thought it was a good thing to preserve law and order as was done in Ambridge two years ago when workers were shot down, he replied heartily, "That's the finest thing that was ever done in this valley."

The Steel Workers' Organizing Committee is housed on the thirty-sixth floor of the Grant Building in Pittsburgh. From it, you look down upon what is known as the Golden Triangle where the Allegheny and Monongahela join to form the Ohio River. There is no spot where one may so fully realize the might and power of the steel industry. From every side, down every river, rise the black chimneys. At night the skies are stained saffron with the blast of the furnaces and by day the smoke rolls up in great convoluted clouds. Phillip Murray, vice-president of the United Mine Workers of America, is at the head of the committee; Clinton Golden, late of the Labor Relations Board of Pittsburgh, is district organizer; Lee Pressman is legal adviser.

What has been accomplished by the SWOC up to date could be learned at the first conference, attended by over 100 organizers last week. This was a conference of the northeastern district. For the sake of convenience the steel area is divided into three districts—the northeastern, which takes in all the Pittsburgh area including the Bethlehem Steel in Johnstown; the western and Great Lakes area, Chicago and Lake districts; and the southern area. There are more than 2,500 volunteer organizers on the job, besides nearly 200 paid organizers. Despite the vigilance of the steel operators and perpetual espionage, more than fifty mills in the northeastern region have been penetrated by volunteer and paid organizers. The high point of the meeting was the appearance of a dozen representatives of company unions from as many mills who pledged their support in the drive to unionize the steel industry.

Already there has been a complete swing over of the company union in the South Chicago works of the Carnegie-Illinois Steel Corporation, where 3,000 members voted as a body to join the Amalgamated Association of Iron, Steel, and Tin Workers. Thus the workers replied to the assertion of the operators that the men were satisfied with company unions. These company unions are of course one of the most important factors in this campaign, and should they turn in numbers, as in the South Chicago workers, they might easily prove a Frankenstein's monster to the employers who created them. McKeesport organizers report talks with more than 5,000 steelworkers. Similar reports come from the Bethlehem-Coatesville district. William Mitch reports from the South an independent union in the Sloss-Sheffield plant, comprising about a third of the workmen, wanting to join with the Amalgamated. Extreme caution of course has to be exercised in the South. There, the movement has to be all but underground.

Here, meetings can be held where no meetings were possible in 1919. In Aliquippa the first meetings since the death of the National

Recovery Act (NRA) have been held. In Braddock that fine fighting priest, Father Kazinci, addressed the steelworkers in the playground not far away from his new church. Company-union men talked, as did the pro-labor burgess of West Homestead, Richard Lowry.

Here, people are too busy to think much about the possible impending expulsion of the Congress of Industrial Organizations (CIO) from the American Federation of Labor. Organizing goes on quietly from house to house, comes out in the open at meetings and picnics. The first phase—education and contact—is over and the second phase—organization and giving charters—is here.

The organizing committee is at work. The CIO is on the job.

# Women Stand By Their Men
## Eye Opener, 1937

When CIO organizers began moving into Detroit, Michigan, in December 1935 they found many auto workers more than ready for industrial unionization. By July 1936 the progressive faction within the United Auto Workers (UAW) had moved the union out of the AFL and into the CIO. The organizers' prime target was General Motors (GM), then the largest manufacturing corporation in the country. In labor espionage GM was in a class by itself, spending, for example, almost $1 million for labor spies alone between January 1934 and July 1936. The report of the Senate's La Follette Committee, which during 1937 exposed corporate espionage and union-busting tactics, stated that GM's espionage apparatus resembled a "far-flung industrial Cheka."

A series of wildcat strikes in late 1936 pushed the UAW leaders toward a strike for which they did not feel ready. On December 30, when GM attempted to move dies from a body plant in Flint, Michigan, employees sat down at two GM body plants in Flint—Fisher One and Fisher Two. The most crucial CIO battle of the 1930s had begun.

On January 11, 1937, in below zero weather, GM turned off the heat in Fisher Two. Flint police surrounded the plant entrance and forbade strike supporters from taking food to the sitdowners inside. That night a pitched battle between police and workers raged for three hours, ending in a smashing victory for the UAW. This "Battle of the Running Bulls" led Michigan's Governor Frank Murphy, just elected in the New Deal landslide, to send the National Guard into Flint, but he refused to use the Guard as strikebreakers. The state troops, many of them sympathetic to the strikers, and led by an experienced officer who had once been an auto worker, restored order around the plants, where the sitdown continued.

A few days after the "Battle of the Running Bulls," Genora Johnson, a twenty-three-year-old mother of two and the wife of a strike leader, organized the Women's Emergency Brigade, to function as a unit of the Women's Auxiliary at Flint. While the Women's Auxiliary supported the sitdown in various ways, including participation in picket duty, the Emergency Brigade was made up of women who were ready to place themselves between the strikers and any attacking police, company guards, militia, or vigilantes.

175

*On February 1, 1937, union headquarters announced that unionists were needed at once at Chevrolet Plant Nine in Flint, where a sitdown attempt was in progress. About 300 men, accompanied by about 50 members of the Emergency Brigade, quickly left for Chevrolet Nine. As they arrived, followed by reporters and newsreel crews, fighting between company guards and strikers had already begun. Behind the plant windows, shadowy figures could be seen battling in eerie silence. The Emergency Brigade slowly marched toward the building, concealing clubs made of wood under the long coats they wore over their dresses. They swung their clubs and broke the windows to let in fresh air to the tear-gassed workers inside. The women ran from one window to another, smashing the panes of glass, while another group of women fought off the policemen who were trying to stop them.*

*The fighting was soon over. As the unionists emerged injured and defeated, the crowd learned that the UAW leadership had created this diversion at Chevrolet Nine as a way of drawing the company police away from Chevrolet Four, the real target of the sitdowners. As the story spread, reporters and observers ran the few hundred yards to Chevrolet Four, where all Chevrolet engines were produced.*

*Genora Johnson was one of the few union leaders who knew the real objective of the sitdowners. Following her instructions, she strung a lean line of her most trusted and militant Emergency Brigade members across the entrance to Chevrolet Four. When the city police sought to pass through the gap, the women locked arms and refused to move. For a precious few minutes, the Emergency Brigade held the police back, for the officers were reluctant to attack unarmed women. Johnson and her crew, desperately stalling for time, attempted to reason with the police and to ask them why they were taking the side of the company against the workers. The time gained was important: shortly after the women slowed the police entry, the union gained complete control of Chevrolet Four, thus completely stopping the production of Chevrolet automobiles. During the next few hours, assisted by thousands of unionists from Detroit and Toledo, the sitdowners barricaded the entrance to Chevrolet Four with heavy metals moved into place by cranes. Meanwhile the Emergency Brigade members who had retreated from Chevrolet Nine appeared in front of Chevrolet Four, marching single file down Chevrolet Avenue and carrying an American flag. The Emergency Brigade set up a revolving picket line outside Chevrolet Four. Over and over they sang, "We Shall Not Be Moved."*

*The next day, a local judge issued an injunction ordering the evacuation of the sitdowners in Fisher One and Fisher Two. The sitdowners refused to obey, and UAW leaders urged their locals to send as many men as possible to the strike area. By dawn on February 3, the roads leading into Flint were clogged with hundreds of autos filled with people responding to the call. A crowd of 7,000 spectators and 3,000 pickets gathered around Fisher One. It included about 700 members of women's auxiliaries from the surrounding area, all wearing their green or red tams. The authorities did not attempt an enforcement of the injunction. A week later, on February 11, GM executives, under pressure from federal officials, determined union leaders, and Governor Murphy, agreed to sign GM's first agreement with a union. The Flint strike settlement was a prodigious victory for the UAW, the CIO, and for industrial unionism.*

*Flint, Michigan.* Soon after 2:00 the Red Caps began to assemble in Pengelly Hall to get ready for the parade. A permit to parade had been granted by the city commission over reluctant City Manager Barringer's head, whose name is booed whenever it is mentioned by the strikers.

The hall downstairs was full of red-capped women with EB (Emergency Brigade) on their arms. There was a large contingent of women with green tams and green armbands. They were members of the Detroit Women's Auxiliary, before whom members of the Flint EB spoke in Detroit. Already a thriving brigade has been formed there. In Toledo a brigade is being organized that will wear blue tams. Brigades are springing up wherever cars are being made.

"Before we are through, there will be Emergency Brigades in steel, in rubber—wherever there are women's auxiliaries," a woman said.

The procession forms. Carrying their banners, they march through the business section. The procession has been gotten up almost at a moment's notice, but Flint, Detroit, Lansing, Toledo, and other towns are represented.

Five hundred women are making history, since this is the first EB parade that has even been held. The march around the business district was only the beginning. Soon the women were in cars on their way to the picket line around Fisher One.

Here they take part in one of the most amazing demonstrations this country has ever seen. Veterans in the labor movement insisted they had never seen anything like it. Six deep the pickets marched around and around the factory. The picket line enfolded the great plant. Thousands of people on the picket line. Thousands of strike sympathizers looking on. Thousands of singing men and women guarding the sitdown strikers from the threat of violent eviction after the injunction has been granted.

Ten thousand people in all must have assembled here, and a note of color was added by the hundreds of bright red and green hats. Not a policeman was in sight. The traffic was patroled by the strikers themselves. Late in the afternoon the central strike committee at the request of the sheriff sent word to the crowd to disperse. The picketers broke up the crowd without disorder. Not one unfortunate incident marred the afternoon. The immense crowd was handled by the workers themselves. It is an example of how workers manage things when police do not interfere.

After dinner at the union kitchen the women adjourned to the meeting in Pengelly Hall.

What a meeting!

The hall was already packed by half past six although the meeting was scheduled for eight and remained crowded until long after midnight. The women ran their own meeting, and the most significant speeches were made by women from various towns, because here you saw a real women's movement in the making. Saw it forming before your eyes. Something creative and vital, stirring through the working women of the country.

A woman from Detroit gets up: "Our auxiliary is growing by leaps and bounds," she said. "We are expanding in all sorts of ways. The children come in from five to six in the evening for singing. We put on amateur shows about strike incidents. For instance, a woman came in who hated unions. She came looking for her husband. Of course her husband was on the picket line. Oh, she was plenty mad. One of the ladies said to her, 'We are awfully shorthanded here in the kitchen. Don't you want to help?' 'Now I'm here I might as well,' and now she is one of the most prominent members of our auxiliary. We made a little play out of that."

The importance of such a thing can't be overestimated. This making of a play out of a strike incident of the workers themselves is the beginning of a new form of workers' theater.

The auxiliary has, besides, tap-dancing classes, visiting committees, and since there was a barber shop in the union hall, the ladies thought they might as well have a beauty parlor—"though you wouldn't think we had one to look at us today, but we've been marching around the picket line all day."

Another woman speaks: "I'm not a very good speaker, but I'm a very good sitter. I sat twenty-four days in the Bohn Aluminum plant. Since we won our strike things have gone fine."

The home and the union are becoming fused. In several places the women are starting nurseries in the union hall. The young girls cooperate in taking care of the babies. A new era is coming to the women in the automobile industry.

# Soldiers Everywhere in Flint; Unionists Hold the Fort

### Federated Press, 1937

*Flint, Michigan.* The sprawling city of Flint is like a French town in wartime. There are more than 4,000 troops quartered here, soldiers are everywhere—now a convoy of trucks clatters down the street, now there is a company on the march, in every drugstore, hotel lobby, and restaurant there are men in uniform.

General headquarters is in the Genese County Building on the fourth floor. There Colonel Lewis holds the fort. Here are maps of every plant and of the surrounding country. The press room on the first floor is where military passes are given out. There is always a crowd of people trying to get military passes to get through the lines, flung closely around Chevrolet and Fisher Body No. 2. Over three hundred newspaper reporters, camera and sound men have been given passes.

The Chevrolet works cover eighty acres so there is a big hole taken out of the heart of the city. Many people live within the barricaded area. Children whose schools are only a few blocks away now have to go a long way around in buses or cars. Red lanterns warn that there is no thoroughfare.

We went through the lines late one night. Snow was falling. A guard scrutinized our cards suspiciously. We walked down toward Chevrolet No. 4. Again we were challenged. This happened four times in a five-minute walk.

There is a fringe of heads at the windows of Fisher No. 2. It is nearly midnight but they are still cheering and singing "Hold the Fort." The streets are dotted with fires in salamanders. It is bitter cold. There is a fire in front of Chevrolet No. 4, the scene of the latest sit-down.

The sitters are watching behind the door at the top of the steps. A wire gate with barbed wire guards the entrance. The gate has never been opened since the sit-down. People who wish to leave the plant must go over the fence. A man jumps over. The guard challenges him. He holds in his hand a permit to leave.

"Got to have a permit from the strike leader to get out of here," the guard explains to us. Strikers come down to talk to us—they call to the guard: "How you coming for wood, buddies? Want we should pass you out some?"

"Thanks, we'll be getting some more soon."

No bad feeling here. Why should there be? Most of the rank and file of the National Guard have worked in an automobile factory at one time or another. When you listen to them talking in drugstores or around town you can hear them commending the governor, who refused to let them in for any "dirty work."

We walked back up the snow street. The soldiers' fires are winking in the snow. The boys in Fisher No. 2 are singing "Hold the Fort."

# The Emergency Brigade at Flint

*The New Republic, 1937*

About the time that the pressure of the crowd waiting to get into the injunction hearing was tearing off the hinges of the courtroom door, word came to union headquarters that there was fighting in the Chevrolet plant.

Anyone experienced in strike atmosphere could have told at the mass meeting on Sunday night that there was something in the air. The meeting, which was addressed by Father J. W. R. Maguire and Mrs. Cornelia Bryce Pinchot, was no ordinary mass meeting. It was an assembly of men and women who are on the march. It was almost impossible to get through the good-natured crowd. Every seat was taken. Workers were packed close against the wall. They thronged the stairway while Father Maguire was talking to the overflow.

One felt that this special meeting was the molten core of this historic automobile strike. Here was a strike whose outcome might influence the labor movement for many years. Its success or its failure did not concern automobiles alone. It took in its sweep steel, coal, rubber, electrical workers. The fate of the whole labor movement was bound up in it. It had emerged from the frame of unionism and had become a contest now between industrial leaders, like the duPonts, Morgans, Sloans, and a president and administration favorable to organized labor. Here in this hall was the burning center of this momentous strike. Failing immediate settlement, action of some sort was inevitable.

The action came. All that week the Chevrolet workers had been holding meetings about the discharge of workers for union activities. Now there was a sit-down in the Chevrolet plant. Plant Manager Lenz would not meet the union to iron out the trouble. First he agreed to do this, then he withdrew. This is one striker's story of what happened:

"A hundred of us started walking through the plant calling a sit-down. The company police and thugs sprang up from nowhere. They kept them shut up in the employment office and sprung them loose on us. In a moment there was fighting everywhere. Fighters were rolling on the floor. They had clubs and we were unarmed. They started shooting off tear gas. I saw one fellow hit on the head and when he swung backwards he cut his head on the machinery. He started to

stagger out. Two of the thugs knocked him down again. I let go on a
couple of thugs. You kind of go crazy when you see thugs beating up
men you know."

There were about eighteen casualties in all. Two of them had to be
taken to the hospital. Most of them came up to the room in the
Pengelly Building, where there is a nurse, a striker's wife, in attendance all the time. The room was soon full of bleeding men, the table
heaped high with crimson gauze. None of the casualties happened
outside the plant. All the injuries occurred inside, showing who made
the trouble. Union headquarters say they have definite proof that there
are 500 thugs from a strike-breaking detective agency in St. Louis
scattered in the plant. At the present moment the majority have barricaded themselves in Plant No. 8 of Chevrolet.

The Women's Emergency Brigade had come back from their first
march past the plant. One of the women I knew was wiping her eyes,
which were smarting with tear gas. Around her clung the acrid smell of
gas. "They were fighting inside and outside the factory," she said. "The
fighting would have been much worse if it hadn't been for us. We
walked right along with our flag at our head. The gas floated right out
toward us. But we have been gassed and we went right on."

Someone speaking admiringly of the Women's Brigade said, "Gee,
those women can sure break windows fast!" But they didn't want to
break them. "We had to break windows, I tell you, to get air to the
boys who were being gassed inside. We don't want violence. We just
want to protect our husbands and we are going to." These women were
veterans of the battle for Fisher No. 2, known in Flint as "Bulls Run"
because the police ran away. I have seen women do yeoman service in
strikes. I have seen some pretty good women's auxiliaries in my time,
but I have never before seen such splendid organization or such determination as there is in the women's auxiliary of Flint.

Who are these women? They are strikers' wives and mothers, normally homebodies. Ma and the girls in fact. They are most of them
mature women, the majority married, ranging in age from young
mothers to grandmothers. In the auxiliary room there are always some
children playing around. A big crowd comes after school to find out
what Ma's doing, more come in after movies, and there's always a baby
or two.

I should judge the majority of the brigade have been to high school,
and all are neatly and carefully dressed. There isn't a flaming-eyed Joan
of Arc among them. One and all are normal, sensible women who are
doing this because they have come to the mature conclusion it must be
done if they and their children are to have a decent life. So they are
behind their husbands as long as there is need, with the same matter-
of-fact capability—and inevitablity—with which they get the children
off to school.

Today their job was "protecting their men." I went down to the Chevrolet plant with two of them. The workers had now captured Plant No. 4. The street was full of people; there were about twenty police behind the bridge and the high plant gate. The police were quiet and unprovocative so the crowd of pickers was good-natured. The sound truck was directing operations as usual.

The use of the sound truck is new to me in strike procedure and it is hard to know how a strike was ever conducted without it. As we came down past the policemen a great voice, calm and benignant, proclaimed that everything was in hand, the plant was under control. Next the great disembodied voice, really the voice of auburn-haired young Roy Reuther, urged the men in the plant to barricade themselves from tear gas. Every now and then the voice came, "Protection squad. Attention! Guard your sound car. Protection squad, attention!"

Then the voice addressed the workers who crowded the windows of the lower levels. At the top of the steep flight of steps were other workers, lunch buckets under their arms, waving at the pickets in the street, and still more workers fringed the roof. The sound truck inquired if they were union men. They shouted, "Yes." The crowd cheered.

The measured, soothing voice of the sound truck boomed: "Word has come to us that there are men in the crowd anxious to join the union. Go to the last car, you will find the cards ready to sign. If you have no money for dues with you you can come to Pengelly Hall later." The sound car strikes up "Solidarity," the men at the top of the steps, on top of the plant, in the street, all sing. A woman's voice next. She tells the crowd that the women have gone to the auxiliary hall to wipe their eyes clear of the tear gas and will soon be back. "We don't want any violence, we don't want any trouble. We are going to do everything we can to keep from trouble, but we are going to protect our husbands."

The Chevrolet plant covers eighty acres and has twelve departments. Plant No. 4 is the key plant, because it makes the motors. Without Plant No. 4 Chevrolet cannot make cars. This plant is set in a hollow, below a little hill about five hundred feet long. Down this hill presently came a procession, preceded by an American flag. The women's bright red caps showed dramatically in the dark crowd. They were singing "Hold the Fort."

There was something moving to all the crowd to see the women return after having been gassed. A cheer went up; the crowd joined in the song. The line of bright-capped women spread themselves out in front of the high barbed-wire-protected gate. Some of the men who had jumped over the gate went back, amid the cheers of the crowd.

I went to the top of the little hill where a string of men were coming out of the back of the building.

"Are you going home?" I asked.

"Home? Hell, no! Half of us are sitting down inside, and half of us are coming out to picket from the street."

"How many of you are for the sit-down?"

"Ninety percent," a group of them chorused.

It is getting dark, the crowd has grown denser. A black fringe of pickets and spectators is silhouetted against the brilliant green lights of the plant windows. "Protection squad! Guard your sound car!" the voice warns solemnly. I go with members of the women's auxiliary to Flint No. 2 to get salamanders and material for a shack for the night picket line. The women are going to stay all night.

There is plenty of excitement in union headquarters a mile and a half away, a meeting is being held. You can hear the cheers as you push up the crowded stairway. Presently some of the Women's Emergency Brigade come in to warm up; the night is bitter. "The Guard has been called out," they report. "We met the soldiers going down as we came back." Why has the National Guard been brought out? I have been in scores of crowds where trouble hung on the edge of a knife. This crowd in front of Chevrolet No. 4 was not so terrifying as a Christmas crowd. After the first fighting was over there was not even the semblance of trouble.

I was at a union meeting at the Cadillac-Fleetwood Hall in Detroit, where a pale organizer started his speech with emotion, saying, "Your hardsweated wages are being used to pay hired thugs and gunmen!" This was Organizer Mayo, who, with three other organizers, had been surrounded by a mob in a hotel in Bay City. They appealed for police protection, which must have been meager, since the organizers were kidnapped in Saginaw. Mayo escaped and made his way to Detroit. The other organizers were sideswiped by the thugs' car on the outskirts of Flint and are still in the hospital, one in critical condition.

It is not only in Flint that one gets the impression of a vital movement. In all the union meetings I have attended there is this sense of direction of workers knowing what they are doing and where they are going. Here at this meeting in Detroit were reports from the picket captains; the welfare committee, which had been in Lansing and had succeeded in cutting red tape for strikers under relief; the "chiselers'" committee, which goes to various merchants to get donations of food; the recreation committee; and the strategy board, which is always in contact with the central strategy board of the union in Detroit. There is also a women's auxiliary, which cooks the food, goes on picket duty, and so forth.

The vitality of this movement shows itself by the many spontaneous cultural movements that are springing up on all sides. Inside Fisher Body Nos. 1 and 2 the sitters are going to classes run by the union.

Since last Monday the plants have been turned into workers' educational institutions. Classes conducted by Merlin D. Bishop include parliamentary procedure, public speaking, and collective bargaining. The workers are writing their own plays. There are two groups of strikers who want to put on incidents of the strike in a living newspaper. Classes in journalism and workers' writing classes have been started with a graduate student from the University of Michigan journalism school as an instructor. This is a strike, Model 1937.

# American Scene
## Mary Heaton Vorse Papers, 1937

*Anderson, Indiana, was as complete a company town as could be found in 1937. About 11,000 of its 14,000 wage earners were employed in General Motors' Guide Lamp and Delco-Remy divisions. In early January, several hundred Anderson businessmen organized the Citizen's League for Industrial Security—a thinly disguised strikebreaking organization—and began to whip up opposition to local United Auto Workers (UAW) organizers. The first serious violence came on January 25, when a mob of about 1,000, led by GM foremen, company guards, and "loyal" employees, beat up some unionists, demolished the UAW headquarters, and drove off union pickets at the Guide Lamp plant. The Anderson police made no attempt to stop the violence.*

*On February 11, after the great UAW victory at Flint, the UAW local in Anderson held a celebration meeting at the Crystal Theater. A mob estimated to be as large as 1,500 surrounded the theater and threatened the unionists inside. Again the Anderson police made no serious effort to disperse the mob, although they did prevent it from entering the building. While the unionists in the Crystal Theater were under the all-night siege, a group of about fifty UAW members and reporters left Flint in the early hours of February 12 to go to the aid of the trapped Anderson unionists.*

*Among those who left for Anderson was Mary Vorse's son, Heaton, then a stringer for the Federated Press, the labor news service. (In 1981 Heaton Vorse would appear as one of the twelve "witnesses" presented in Warren Beatty's movie, Reds. ) During the afternoon of February 12, Heaton Vorse and seven others were wounded at a confrontation in Anderson between unionists and a local tavern keeper. At this point, the Anderson mayor requested Governor Clifford Townsend to send in the National Guard and the town was placed under martial law. Heaton Vorse and fifteen other union organizers were indicted on trespassing and riot charges, but the accused were never brought to trial.*

It was snowing when I got to Anderson—a blizzard of dry snow. You could see the shape of the wind in the white eddies on the black streets.

Heaton was lying wounded in the hospital. I had been in Flint, and had packed and been ready to go to Anderson before I heard about it. While the rejoicing for the settlement of the General Motors strike was going on in Flint a mob had attacked the union victory meeting in Anderson. The center of interest had moved there.

When the newspaper called me up and said my son was shot, I said indignantly, "Oh no, he isn't. He never gets shot."

I resisted the idea of his being hurt. I would not believe it. Just as later I rejected any idea of death. How it had happened, I did not know. All I knew was that a delegation of Flint boys had gone to Anderson to protest the mobbing of their union brothers and that Heaton had gone along to cover for Federated Press.

Now he was shot. A man named Emory Shipley, a tavernkeeper, had shot him. All the hours on the train, I kept thinking of Heaton and Shipley, approaching each other all their lives to meet at this point of intersection.

It was very late when I got there, almost 2:00. I called up the hospital. A soothing voice answered that "he was resting quietly." They always said that. I went early to union headquarters. Mrs. Rose and the baby had just gotten in. She was the young wife of the other seriously wounded man. Martial law had been declared. There were soldiers in the street. Young soldiers stood guard in the corridor. The union headquarters up a narrow flight of stairs was cold and damp. A fire was being made in the big coal stove. There was a smell of wet clothes. Snow had been tramped in. People had the appalled air of disaster.

We drove to St. John's Hospital. Mrs. Rose had been driving all night from Flint. She kept murmuring, "Thought we'd never get here." She had not heard until late in the afternoon. That was one queer thing about it all. The news never got out. The story of what happened was never published in any paper. In the center of America, thirty miles from Indianapolis, in a good-sized town, your boy can be shot, nearly killed, and arrested for doing precisely nothing, and the story won't even get into the papers.

The police gave out the story of Shipley, the tavernkeeper, and that was the story the papers used. Shipley posed for his picture, with his gun, and bragged that if he only had a machine gun, he would have done even better. As it was, he nearly killed two boys and wounded seven others. Pretty good.

The Mother Superior met us in the hall. She took me aside and whispered: "Your boy is going to be all right, my dear, but the other boy—." She shook her head.

I walked through the light corridors that were to hold my life for a month. The holy statues, the sisters in their white habits and their big fluted coifs, gave it an air of kindliness that was heartening. I have always had a hatred of hospitals, of their institutionalized stupidity. But this hospital was full of kindness. I hurried along with a feeling of complete unreality, as if I were in a dream and that I would soon wake up.

And there lay Heaton—his eyes sunken, his face pale, saying in a politely surprised tone, "How did you get here?" And in the same ward on a bed opposite, propped up, lay young Rose, with his red hair, his face an awful pale green. Out in the corridor sat a state trooper, guarding the boys. They had been arrested for being shot. In all, eighteen boys were arrested. Then I learned the story that was never published in any paper. Heaton wrote it himself later in a letter to his wife.

Dear Sue:—All was quiet in Anderson. Too quiet. The vigilantes had evidently been tipped off. Went up into union hall. A big sign, "Thank you, Flint" hung in the assembly room. Units from Detroit, Toledo, and even Cleveland started to drift in. Since it was obvious that there would be no trouble, plans were being formed for a big labor parade.

Many of the Flint contingent, myself included, found their way to the barroom downstairs. No one drank heavily. An Anderson boy called me to his table and introduced me to his pretty wife and sister. Other Flint and Anderson boys joined us from time to time. It was all gay and social.

I was called upstairs to do my turn on the door. Union halls here aren't free to the world. You have to have satisfactory credentials to enter, as a guard against stools, finks, etc. Anderson's hall had four on duty that evening, Anderson, Flint, Toledo, Cleveland. A steady stream of men were flowing in and out. It kept us busy checking. As the moments passed, the tension eased.

A sudden commotion at the foot of the stairs. A young fellow somewhat bruised about the face is hustled up the stairs. I understand that he has been beaten up by vigilantes at the "Gold Band Tavern." There are other union men out there who are in danger.

"Flint upstairs!" I check the boys through and follow the last one into a conference room. There is some question as to where the place is, but off we go. Our car was the first out. We discovered the tavern to be a shanty in shanty town, varying only from the other scattered ugly boxes in that it had a glass front. Another carload drew up. We walked toward the tavern. At which point, the bartender drew a shotgun from beneath the bar and fired through the window. I ducked in time to miss the shot, but the flying glass burned my forehead.

At this point I decided that I didn't want any, and started moving. The decision was fairly unanimous. The bartender fired twice more through the broken window and then came out the door. Another man scooted out of a side door and took up an observation post about ten yards away. He shouted directions to the bartender. It seemed so well planned.

As I ran I saw that the barkeeper had cornered three boys who had taken refuge behind a parked sedan. He hounded them, ducking back and forth till he got one of them—in the back—Rose (the other badly wounded boy, now in the hospital with me). I heard the man on observation shout, "Get that one running!" I got it. The newspapers carried that he was protecting his property.

Men can be so amazingly gentle. The kindliness and care given me by the boys who carried me to the hospital made the nurse and doctor in charge seem almost brutal. All of them are under arrest for their kindness.

Heaton Vorse.

Now they were all in jail, these men who had been so gentle. They were arrested by the civil authorities. Directly after their arrest, martial law was declared. They were held incommunicado; the rights of counsel and of habeas corpus were denied them although the right of habeas corpus is guaranteed by the Constitution except in times of war. Roy Post, the only boy who actually went inside the tavern, was kept in solitary and was so severely beaten by the police as they put him through the third degree that his ribs were cracked.

Heaton and I talked all that day about what had happened and I got a clear picture of them walking across the dark street and Shipley outlined against the light of the tavern, silhouetted brightly, shooting at the dark shapes of the running boys.

What happened before the boys were shot I learned later. Union boys were looking for a nonunion boy. One of them was beaten up in the Gold Band Tavern by anti-union men, while Shipley held the other men against the wall with his gun. The boys got away and one of them reported to union headquarters. When Shipley saw a crowd approaching he must have thought the union boys were coming to clean him up and shot. At first it seemed to be a frame-up.

But it was not. It was all chance. A point of intersection. He had been a machine gunner, a factory worker. Now he was a tavernkeeper and for all his forty-odd years he had been coming step by step toward the point of intersection with Heaton. And all Heaton's years had been bringing him to this crossroad where Emory Shipley would shoot him. And he would almost die; almost he would lose his leg, almost but not quite, because of another point of intersection which made Dr. Drake his doctor instead of someone else.

Later, details about Shipley drifted to me through the hospital corridors. The visiting barkeep still a little rosy from the night before told me, "They'll never arrest Shipley. Why he's too much protected. He's paid too much to the police, him and his family. First there's his sister's sportin' house. Then there's his brother who's still bootleggin'—"

"How about the other brother? The one with the poolroom?" asked the patient with a broken leg.

"Yeah, how about him?" the bartender answered brightly. "They're all protected. They can't get him in this living world."

But this was later when all the life of Anderson seeped into me through the hospital corridors. Among the stories were the details of what must have been a night of sheer terror, the mob crowded around the hall throwing stones and breaking windows. Shots were fired into the hall.

Men, women, and children were crowded into the little hall and they stayed there until morning because they did not dare to go home. The police cleared the streets around the theater of the mob but they only dispersed to the armory and other points nearby. Union men leaving the hall were beaten. The police offered to take the union heads into what might be termed "protective custody." They refused to leave.

Victor Reuther, the young strike leader, said he lived ten years that night. He never knew when hysteria might break out in the theater or when the mob might attack from the outside, and when someone would shoot. Children cried, parents shivered throughout the long night of terror.

It was during this night that Flint and Detroit were telephoned: "Send union sympathizers to protect our headquarters."

A parade was planned protesting against the civil liberties of the union being interfered with by the mob. The most responsible men were chosen to go. They were warned against any provocative action. They were told never to take the offensive.

Why the men from Flint, Toledo, and Cleveland were in Anderson was never understood by people in Anderson. When I asked acquaintances why they thought the Flint boys were here they answered, "Well, they came to make trouble," or "They came to beat up nonunion men," or "They came to make people join the union." There was nothing in any paper which connected the cavalcades of out-of-town people with the disturbance at the Crystal Theater.

The out-of-town boys who had trickled in during the afternoon had worn white bands on their arms to distinguish one another. The appearance of these men with white arm bands had set the town in a panic. It was still in a panic. It was as if the violence of the mob hung in the air in solution. Everybody was expecting something more to happen. If the citizens of the little town had been invaded by an army they could not have been more appalled.

It was as if everyone was waiting for an air raid. It was a queer experience to come into this town full of military after the great joyful demonstration in Flint.

What had happened that day in Flint was something no one who saw it could ever possibly forget. It was one of those great expressions of the human spirit that one may experience only once or twice in a whole lifetime. Since Armistice I have never witnessed anything like its intensity or its dramatic beauty. A mighty emotion shook the working people of that town. A released, joyful people flowed through Flint's commonplace streets.

The unbelievable had happened. General Motors had bargained with the union. The long days of suspended violence were over. Joy was in the air. Here was the antithesis of a mob.

No one in that crowd remained isolated. People's small personalities were lost in this great hallelujah. The wave of this emotion was so far reaching, so vast that it upheld a boy like Heaton near death, almost mortally wounded, so he forgot himself completely while he tried to record what he had seen, what he had felt.

To look at it was pure beauty. The crowd, the moving flags, the great camera lights fell into a composition that was like something a master showman had planned. I had looked from a window of Fisher 2 awestruck with beauty. An unforgettable moment was the one when the cordon of soldiers strung across the empty street had stepped aside and the joyful crowd had surged forward to be met by the men from Chevy 4. It was so beautiful that tears sprang to my eyes as they do at the sound of great music.

That night at the great victory meeting we heard they were mobbing the Anderson workers.

The mob had reached out, and the pattern of Heaton's life and of my life was changed. My life was lived within the walls of the hospital and bounded by the military. Through the hospital the life of Anderson seeped into me. I was getting to know it with an intimacy that no investigation could possibly have given me. Underlying everything there was a good Hoosier quality. There was something American and endearing, something hearty and warm, a neighborliness that had stretched over from the old days. More and more people asking me, "How is your boy today? How is he, is he better?" People in the restaurants, in the hotel, even on the streets, coming up and saying, "Aren't you the lady whose boy was shot? How is he?"

There is no single distinguishing feature in all Anderson. There are the great orderly mills and a multitude of smaller manufacturing plants. There are acres and acres of small mean houses and still more acres of comfortable undistinguished homes. In the center of the town is the courthouse, which looks like one of the stone block houses Heaton and I used to build when he was little. There is a river but it is sort of out of the way. Everything has been built a while ago.

A great deal has happened to this country in fifteen years. Communities have waked up to beauty. The garden movement has spread throughout the land. Towns and cities have revolted from the drab

nightmare of Main Street. But not Anderson. I would go back and forth
to the hospital and the essence of this town would envelop me. To the
hospital came a cross-section of the town. To the hospital came the
town's disasters. Through the casual talk one learned that here this was
a town of small vices. One learned such details as that there were a
great many crooked poker games in Anderson and a great deal of
drinking. It had the vices that all towns have where the vitality of the
young people has no place to go.

As I look back on Anderson I see a town with shabby, toothless old
men chatting comfortably on street corners. An intimate town prodigal
of incidental kindness. Even the prosecutor was kind. Saturday night is
payday—a festival, everyone on the streets, crowds of young people,
pretty girls, mothers of families, kids, all out to shop if only a dime for
the "five and ten."

I will never forget the demonstration when they won the basketball
game, a town gone wild. There was something here that was good that
one got to know about. Three good strains laid the foundation of the
people of Anderson. The early settlers of a Scotch-Irish stock came up
from Kentucky; there was also a New England strain and a sprinkling of
the old Germans of 1848, the revolutionary refugees. Some of the older
people as I began meeting them would say, "We used to have the most
interesting society here for a little town. People sent their children
East to school. Everybody went to Europe at some time or other."

They spoke with a nostalgia about this time. It was the Indiana of
James Whitcomb Riley they were talking about; the Indiana that bred
so many distinguished writers a generation ago; the Indiana of anti-
slavery days, solidly Republican, indignantly abolitionist.

Anderson was the county seat, proud of its homes, proud of its
culture, which it compared to Crawfordsville. Proud of its own tradition that in the early days when some men in liquor killed some inoffensive Indians camping by a stream, Anderson brought them to justice, and convicted them. And this was a time when shooting up a few
Indians was a commonplace.

Then came the gas and oil boom that transformed the sleepy county
seat with its tradition of New England culture into a bustling town.
They became so rich that the people will tell you the street lamps
burned all day—they didn't care. And Anderson grew and changed in a
comparatively short time from a country town of 6,000, the shopping
district for a rich farming country, into a manufacturing town of 20,000.

But the old neighborliness persisted. The abolitionist spirit, the
James Whitcomb Riley spirit was still alive. In the days before the war
Anderson was a union town. There was a considerable Socialist vote.
Debs spoke here. People took "The Appeal to Reason." And there was

a big group of Young People's Socialist Leaguers (YPSLs)—500 of
them. "Though half the time they only joined to go to dances."

Alexandria today, only eight miles away, is a union town, supported
by a union-sympathizing community. When the Aladdin Lamp strike
was won, the union had left on its hands a hundred pounds of chickens
and turkeys contributed by the farmers for strike relief.

What changed Anderson over into a union-baiting town that could
breed a mob and turn it upon the union headquarters? What happens
under a dictatorship? What happened in Germany happened in a small
way in Anderson. Dictatorships smother thought. Life stops some way.
People don't think. Graft thrives; vice thrives.

Right after the world war General Motors moved in. It doubled the
population of Anderson within a brief time. It dominated the financial
life of the town and instead of relying on Hoosier labor, it imported
labor from the hills of Kentucky, Tennessee, and Missouri.

It dominated the social life of the town also. In the country club and
the churches General Motors people ruled. The old families who remember with nostalgia the time when Anderson was a town of culture
resent, though mutely, the rule of General Motors. The feeling toward
General Motors among many of the older people could be summed up
by what one woman said to me. Speaking of the advantages General
Motors had brought to the town, I said: "After all, it came bearing
gifts."

She said grimly—she had been giving me a picture of the earlier
Hoosier Anderson whose ghosts still lingered so nostalgically—"Yes, it
came bearing gifts in one hand and a curse in the other."

This sense of the conflicting currents in Anderson came to me
through the hospital corridors, through casual conversations. For I was
not trying to find out about Anderson, I was absorbed only in Heaton.
His legs had been so mangled by gunshot wounds that it was necessary
to operate for blood clots the second day after I got there. All through
the day his mind wandered.

When Mrs. Rose and I came back after luncheon—by this time
young Rose was out of danger—the state trooper barred our way and
said that it was the colonel's orders that no one was to be allowed to
visit the wounded boys. So that afternoon was spent in trying to get
hold of the colonel. I had the sense of a blind, stupid, blundering
machine being between me and Heaton lying there suffering in the
ward. I sat waiting for word from the colonel.

Across the hall old Bill, who was dying of a gangrenous foot, was
bellowing. Mr. Brown with a broken leg, who had been gassed in the
war and had bad lungs, was coughing his sepulchral cough. "Pop"
snored.

Finally I got Colonel Whitcomb, who immediately sent up a lieutenant to tell the guard that we were to be admitted. So it was almost closing time before I could get in to see Heaton. The nice young lieutenant waited in the corridor. The big cop stood at the foot of the bed, inside the curtain, talking.

After this I seemed to be always going to the military. I was always having to get permission to get in the hospital. I went to ask why he was arrested. To find out why his mail was being detained and opened by the police. Probably because the *Indianapolis Star* had reported he was a Communist. The reporter said the police who questioned Heaton that first night might have said that. We got very friendly with the kind officer, Mr. Noble, who when he found out we were Episcopalians introduced me to Father Harris. When I told him the newspaper man had said that it was he who told him Heaton was a Communist, he was very indignant.

"I never said such a thing. I said he was a labor columnist. He told me he wrote a column for a labor paper now and then."

Columnist—Communist. They are so alike you need only change an *l* for a *m*. Yet that mistake of a letter has colored the whole case. When Governor Murphy made inquiries about the case an Anderson friend wrote him:

> I might say, however, that the facts as represented by Mrs. Mary Heaton Vorse are just about as erroneous as you could make them. As a matter of fact the son is classified as a Communist and writes for a Communistic paper. The man's place where these fellows were shot was closed and they broke the door down and knocked the window lights out before he ever fired a shot. It happened to be that he was an old machine-gunner in the A. E. F. and very active in the Legion, and is considered a very good citizen.

Meantime, even through my own absorption I could feel the town having the jitters. A reporter gets trained to sense the imponderables and to venture assertions about things which are invisible.

You could feel fear and violence in the air. Many people on the street corners, talking, talking, talking. Words as you went past: "They got a right to have the union if they want." "The way they treated them union men was the most radical thing I ever see." A well-dressed man talking to a crowd of workmen: "We know what we can do. We don't need no military to tell us. We are going to clear them out of here, military or no military." The mob speaking.

Soldiers on the streets. A small union meeting permitted to the Women's Auxiliary, and the smell of wet clothes and melted snow up in the crowded little union hall. On Saturday night I was in the drugstore and there were explosions outside that made me say to the girl at the counter, "Don't they clean their spark plugs ever in this town?"

"Oh, that's not spark plugs. That's the kids setting off firecrackers. They won the baseball game."

But that sound that anyone could tell was not gunfire made panic in Anderson. In a moment the military had arrived and the young guards clanked importantly down the street. The street was cleared. A cordon was flung across the street. Investigations were made. Colonel Whitcomb told me, "Everybody left their porch lights on the first week I was here as if they expected their houses to be entered. If there was a backfire anywhere, I would get twenty-five telephone calls. The wildest rumors ran about the place of mob attacks on both sides."

By Wednesday, Rose was up, talking hopefully about going back home. On Thursday when I went to the hospital Rose was gone—four burly troopers had tramped in and taken him to jail. Four days ago he had been dying. I was late that day and Heaton had been waiting for me. His face had sunken a great deal. We looked at each other. He voiced what I was thinking.

"I don't want to go to jail and get gangrene in this open wound."

His right leg was swollen beyond all recognition. His foot did not look like a foot. He had been conscious during his operation and looked at his mangled leg and it had done him no good.

This was about the only time that he had been worried about himself. He had been so filled with the spectacle of Flint rejoicing that he had no time to think about himself. It was the only time that I, too, felt panic. There was that senseless machine, the military, that, once started, went on its way like a tank and the ordinary safeguards to liberty did not count. If Rose, who had been worse wounded, could go to jail, it seemed quite possible that Heaton might.

I hurried over to Indianapolis to see the governor. I could not see him, but got in touch with him through friends. I wired friends in Washington. I wired senators I knew. I did everything to ensure Heaton's staying in the hospital. Later, I went to the military.

"Why," I wanted to know, "should Heaton be arrested at all?" He had gotten out of a car—had been fired at on a public highway. He was a reporter. They replied that he had been too much integrated with the auto workers for a reporter, and moreover he knew they were going on what was an "unlawful errand."

I asked them if rescuing friends was unlawful, and if when they were in the American Expeditionary Force and heard their friends were being beaten up in a cafe in France, would they have waited for the police. They laughed. They were kind and jolly, even when they insisted he shouldn't have been there. This was taking the law into your own hands, they said. The police should have been called in. What I couldn't make them believe was that the union had been trying to get the police to give them protection. They had appealed to the chief of police. They had appealed to the mayor, to the governor of the state.

The police had stood by while the union members were beaten up and their headquarters wrecked.

When the mob had rioted on state property in the very city hall—the police had stood around and made exactly no arrests. Failure of police protection was what had brought the boys from Flint to Anderson. But this I couldn't make the officers see.

During these days the picture of how the mob had been formed I pieced together in my mind. I got broken pieces of what had happened in the union hall, and more pieces in the hospital corridors.

Outside the factory the mob took the name "The Citizens' League for Industrial Security." Mr. Homer P. Lambert, a prominent businessman, was elected president. He comes from a wealthy and respectable family, hard to associate with mob violence. He made an eloquent speech over the radio which refused to give any time to the union. In this speech he pointed out the benefits which had come to Anderson through General Motors. He painted a dismal picture of what would happen if General Motors was forced to move from Anderson because of labor troubles.

People saw Anderson a ghost city. Delco-Remy and Guide-Lamp, who between them employ 12,000 people—gone. At Mr. Lambert's dismal prophecy, a shiver went through the community. The local papers took up the hue and cry. The usual "Red" bogey was waggled.

Meantime in the factory the mob was being formed. The company union of so-called loyal workers was called together and the most trusted among them were given red tickets and word sent through the factory, "Be sure and be there." This happened before each mobbing. Before each outbreak, workers by the dozen would come to report at union headquarters that something was going on. They had seen the tickets going out. They had seen the workers conferring with the foreman. *The mob was fomented by the company in the plant and on company time.* I don't think there is anyone in Anderson who will dispute this.

It was in the hospital visiting my son that I heard about the meeting in the Grand Hotel. They were always talking about the union and things that had happened. One of the visitors said, "That was a real reasonable mob, after all. I was in that meeting at the Grand Hotel when it was being planned up. They told them to 'go slow.' 'Fellows,' they said, 'use eggs, don't carry guns. Don't hurt no property, except the union's. Look out and don't break the restaurant windows, nor the plate glass window in the barber shop.

'And if you are going to give them agitators a little love-tap fer a lesson, be keerful, don't send them to the hospital.' Now you see, it was a real reasonable mob. They pertected private property, all but the union's."

"Were you a part of the mob?" I asked him.

"Well, no," he said. "I didn't do no mobbing. I just stood around. There wasn't more'n fifty or seventy-five people chose to do the mobbin'."

So, according to the plan, the mob went to the courthouse and packed the union meeting which was to be held there. They threw eggs. They followed Kramer, the organizer, to the Stilwell Hotel and beat him up in the lobby. The police stood by benevolently.

Led by an assistant production manager of one of the plants, a large mob armed with clubs proceeded to the union headquarters.

The mob was hooting and screaming, "Clear the yellow sons of . . . out of here." They called for the women and children to come down from the union hall, that they did not want to hurt them. Police stood by calmly throughout. A lane was cleared and the union organizers came down and the police took them to the jail to protect them—in protective custody as they say in Germany.

The mob surged into the union headquarters and wrecked the place, broke the typewriters, and threw the records out of the window. These records, containing the names of the union members, were picked up by the General Motors people, who have them to this day. This seizing of the records was all part of a prearranged plan, which was made to look as though it were an outburst of an outraged citizenry.

I have talked to a great many people, both union men and nonunion, who all testified that the officials of the company and the police stood by enjoying the mob. I have the names of a dozen such officials.

One day I wrote down the summary of what happened in Anderson. It goes this way.

On January 25, union workers were mobbed and egged in the courthouse; union headquarters was raided; union property was destroyed; records were thrown out of the window of the union headquarters; the picket shack was burned; union men and organizers were beaten up. The police stood by and made no arrests.

On January 28, Delco-Remy allowed workers time off to mob organizers coming in by train. No arrests were made. On February 12, the union meeting at the Crystal Theater, held for the discussion of terms of settlement, was surrounded by a mob. Union men were beaten, windows broken, shots were fired in the hall. *No arrests were made.*

February 13, union men were called to go to Gold Band Tavern to protect union men being beaten there. Nine union men were wounded, two seriously, by the tavernkeeper, Emory Shipley, who was never arrested.

*Fourteen union men including wounded arrested.*

While I was learning this, Heaton was growing worse. He was burning up with fever. No one told me his temperature was rising. I did not need to be told. No one told me until the day of his second operation that his leg was infected—they did not need to tell me. He was operated on the day the boys got out of jail.

They bailed them out finally on Saturday, a week and two nights after they had been arrested. We waited for them to come out of the firehouse, the street being guarded by sharpshooters to prevent a jail delivery. There had been a ridiculous rumor that the United Mine Workers were going to march on the jail with the auto workers to get the men out, so the streets were barred to traffic, and everyone who went by was held up by the military. The little sharpshooters stood shivering on the snowy street, their eyes on the dirty white brick jail.

Finally, off went the big fat sheriff up to the hospital with Heaton's bond, and now Mr. Noble, the friendly policeman, would not have to sit all night in the hospital anymore.

You see, it was all mixed up; kindness and decency and friendship, and the flagrant breaking of the National Labor Relations Act and the mob, whose hand had reached out and brought Heaton from Flint and on whose account he was now dying in St. John's hospital.

For he was dying.

The doctor said in guarded hospital phraseology that Heaton wasn't reacting as he should to the operation. In other words, they meant they would have to take off his leg and he was not strong enough to stand it.

I could feel his heart fluttering. I could feel the burning of his skin. He looked like death. He smelled like death. The smell made me think of the boys I had seen dying in the hospitals in France.

Now here was the strange thing. I could look at his shrunken body— he could not have weighed more than 100 pounds. I could see death in his sunken face. Yet neither Heaton nor I ever admitted the possibility of death.

That night when I went home to the hotel, I never felt so alone. I wanted to talk with someone—with anyone. I met the young Reuthers on the street and tried to communicate my loneliness to them, but they were in a hurry, and they were in love, and it never got to them.

When I left the hospital at night, I always had the feeling that my health and strength were communicated to him. For ministering to him this way was my life. All the other things, the mob and the military, and the things that I learned about the town, all the crowded things that kept coming to me unasked—none of them meant anything to me.

The reality was guarding Heaton, as though when I were sitting there beside him I was actually defying death. I would go home nights, after the hospital made its visitors leave, and would sit up as though I were still beside him. All night I would sit with him, quietly and confidently, until the morning nurses came on about half-past five, then I could go to sleep.

So that night when I left him with death on his face, I went to my room at the hotel and sat up with him, with that confidence and quiet that means prayer.

Very late in the night a serene happiness filled me. I knew then that everything was going to be all right. I sat with him until the morning nurses came on. Next morning the doctor told me that Heaton had taken an amazing and unexpected turn for the better—that there would not have to be a consultation.

After that night, Heaton never had a relapse. Now out on bail, he could have visitors. I would come in to find friends from the union saying, "My son's finger shore did twitch for his trigger when he saw that ornery skonk, Shipley, but I sez, 'Son, he's Heaton's!' We're savin' him fur you, Boy, savin' him fur you!" For the southern mountain people felt it was Heaton's privilege to deal with Shipley.

He had become a hero. He had come from the outside with sympathy and he had been shot and arrested in their struggle, and so he was a symbol to them. This accident had made him their martyr.

When the boys came out of jail and had a dinner given them by the union, they made me come and sit in Heaton's chair and they wrote him a round-robin letter.

Workers would come up to me in the union hall and say, "Been talkin' it over with m' wife—we want you should come and stay to our place, both o' you, long's you want, when he gets out of th' hospital." Or, "When he gets out you don't need to worry none. You got a home with us till he's well enough to work."

Workers know how hard the convalescent times are. We were not strangers any more and they wanted to share their little with us. We were enveloped with a warm atmosphere of kindness. But they wanted to do more than that. They wanted to do something to celebrate when "he came out."

"If he could wait till third pay day before he came out, so's we could get a little even, we'd like to take him back to Flint in a motorcade."

"We sure would like to give him a motorcade home."

"We want to do somethin' for him now he's livin' like we would've if he'd died. We sure woulda give him one grand funeral if he'd a died!"

"We'd a had a funeral here, then we'd a took him to Flint for another funeral!"

"We'd a had auto workers from everywhere in Flint, from Detroit, and Lansing, and Cleveland even. He'd a had five thousand workers behind him!"

"*Five* thousand, pshaw! He'd a had *ten!*" They had it all planned, that magnificent funeral. But they were not even to have their motorcade. "He got out" before the third pay day.

Always I had to tell them at union meetings how he was getting on. The first night, when he was so bad, the union opened its new hall.

The time when Homer Martin spoke, when Heaton had made the first definite change for the better, that night you could not get through the crowd. They had been browbeaten, told their leaders were Communists and Reds, and the union had been split. But this meeting with youthful, dynamic Homer Martin speaking fused them together and gave them confidence again.

Colonel Whitcomb had been invited to attend. He sat on the platform and said a few words to the effect that he was honored to be at a union meeting and they cheered him warmly.

As I sat there looking into that packed audience—while the former Baptist minister, Homer Martin, told them how he was led to be a union man, why he had to leave the ministry to organize workers, I noted the friendly attitude of the crowd to the military.

Why, I thought, this is the very heart of America. This confusion, this damming up the news, the Red scare, the wistful older people who look backward at their cultural past, the Saturday night crowds when, even in mid-winter everyone literally is on the streets and there is a lively sense of carnival in the air, the roaring, jubilant crowds of young people after a basketball game—a wild young enthusiasm which has no place to go, the misunderstandings, the shooting. All the things that had happened, good and bad together. Here was America.

# The Steel Strike
## *The New Republic, 1937*

A group of independent steel companies known as Little Steel was U.S. Steel's biggest competitor. Led by Tom Girdler, head of Republic Steel, and determined to stop the CIO drive in steel, the Little Steel group refused to deal with the Steel Workers' Organizing Committee (SWOC) in the spring and summer of 1937. "Girdlerism" soon became synonymous with the most violent form of union-busting.

Little Steel prepared for all-out war, spending almost $50,000 on munitions alone during May and June 1937, and expanding its espionage and police units. The Little Steel companies spent thousands of dollars to organize vigilante and citizen's committees, and to finance a back-to-work movement. Girdler also hired a New York public relations firm to handle the Red smear propaganda campaign against the steel organizers.

Girdler precipitated the Little Steel strike on May 26, 1937, at a time when he knew that SWOC was ill-prepared for conflict. The most shocking act of violence in the Little Steel war occurred four days later at the "Memorial Day Massacre" outside the Republic Steel mill in South Chicago, where Chicago police shot into the backs of peaceful union marchers, killing ten and wounding thirty.

Youngstown, Ohio, was the heart of the strike against Little Steel. On June 19 company guards fired tear gas at women pickets near the Stop 5 entrance to the Republic mill. When unionists ran to aid the women, company snipers and city deputies shot into the crowd of excited strikers. Two workers were killed, and forty-two others, including Mary Vorse, were injured. Fearing greater violence if the steel executives attempted to reopen the mills, Governor Martin L. Davey declared martial law and sent the National Guard into Youngstown.

Girdler also refused to cooperate with the federal mediators. Most of the disheartened unionists had returned to work by July 1937, and their defeat stalled the momentum of the CIO organizing drive. It was 1942 before the Little Steel companies agreed to sign a union contract.

The first week of the steel strike sees both sides marshaling all their forces. Already the strike has spread to involve coal and iron ore, railroads, governors of states, the La Follette Civil Liberties Committee, the National Labor Relations Board. Eighty-three thousand men are idle in five states and a dozen towns and cities. At present only Youngstown Sheet and Tube, Inland, and Republic Steel are affected. Bethlehem and National will enter the picture later. In all, 175,000 workers may be involved. It is on the integrity of these workers that the outcome will depend in the long run—workers like those in the parade of about 2,500 people which masses near union headquarters in Campbell, formerly East Youngstown, and marches to Struthers over the bridge.

Many women are marching. Youngstown Sheet and Tube is paying its workers today—the last pay day for a long time, they are warned. The Sheet and Tube workers have made this an excuse for a protest parade. Before the parade got under way the organizer in charge dispatched workers to picket the Dollar Bank Building, where the "back-to-work" movement is in full swing. The company union has been transformed into a so-called independent union. The Republic "independent" union and the Youngstown Sheet and Tube "independent" union have opened offices, by an odd coincidence, next door to each other. A dark trickle of Negro boys goes sheepishly past the pickets who carry signs—JOIN THE CIO—YOU CAN'T MAKE STEEL IN A BANK. There are defiant white boys. No older men go in while I watch. Groups of men watch the pickets. Other buildings have men and women in front of them. The Dollar Bank has only watchful men. Deputies too are there, most of them ex-soldiers. One of the independent-union officials is asked, "It must have taken some organization to get this gang?" "Oh, yes," he replies brightly, "we had 160 men out visiting the houses." One wonders who paid these visitors.

A strategy meeting of the Steel Workers' Organizing Committee (SWOC) organizers is taking place. They are here from Canton, Warren, Niles, Cleveland, the whole Mahoning Valley, to compare notes on the first week of strike, to map plans and strike activities for the future. There have been no strike bulletins. These will now be published and the sound truck will broadcast strike news. Mass meetings are planned throughout the area, with such speakers as Homer Martin, Dalrymple, president of the rubber workers, and Philip Murray.

Two investigators for the La Follette Committee have arrived, to study the charges of the union that the plants are arsenals filled with machine guns and tear gas, that 50 percent of the personnel now in the plant are strikebreakers.

This seems to have been admitted by Tom W. Girdler, who made three-inch newspaper headlines when he proclaimed proudly: "*Sure*

*We've Got Guns.*" This admission coming after the Memorial Day massacre is a little more than the workers can stand. In all the outdoor meetings in the Youngstown area workers stand with bared heads in memory of those killed. Steelworkers will never forget that because Tom W. Girdler, president of Republic Steel, found a way of getting around the Wagner Act, seven men lie dead and nearly 100 are wounded.

"They are Girdler's victims and the responsibility of their death should be placed at his door as definitely as if he had killed them with his own hands," Philip Murray told us.

So the Youngstown picture must have for a background the fact that on Memorial Day a procession of over a thousand union men and sympathizers marching from a union meeting toward the Republic Steel plant in South Chicago were attacked by a force of two hundred police armed with tear gas and guns. When the tear gas cleared away, there were four dead and others dying. The ground was littered with wounded men and women. The details as they pile up show a picture of cold-blooded brutality that has no recent parallel.

Eyewitnesses report that police dragged wounded workers by the feet "as though they were dead dogs." Pictures confirm this. Pictures give irrefutable testimony that instead of "fighting for their lives" as Police Chief Horner asserts, the police pursued and clubbed strikers fleeing with their wives and children.

At a press conference Philip Murray brings out the fact that these deaths and shootings occurred not because the union and management disagree on terms of settlement but because the independent steel companies have suddenly discovered that nothing is said in the Wagner Act about signing an agreement—three little words were lacking in the act.

Youngstown is the heart of the strike. Thirty-three thousand workers are affected in the Youngstown Sheet and Tube and Republic, which runs like a river of chimneys and tracks for miles through the center of the town. The 2,400 workers in Niles and the 6,000 workers in Warren, a few miles distant, are also included in this area.

Youngstown Sheet and Tube and Republic in Youngstown are closed down. There is no attempt to run the plants. Only Carnegie Illinois's triumphant blast goes saffron against the sky, a constant reminder to idle Youngstown workers that 157 separate companies have signed union agreements covering 380,000 men.

John Mayo, who was a victim of the Bay City mobbing, is chief organizer for the Youngstown district; under him are organizers for each mill. Youngstown Sheet and Tube is organized independently from Republic, and Brier Hill Sheet and Tube at the opposite end of town from Struthers and Campbell has its own organization. The strike is young and the activities still resolve themselves into picket line and commissary. No time could be obtained on the radio, so each of the six strike groups remains comparatively isolated from the others. Though no women's organizations have yet been set up, there is a drive to take part in the struggle by the women themselves. They go on the picket line, they work in the kitchen. At Brier Hill gate I saw several women come to get out scabbing husbands. As one husband appeared, a woman's hand shot out in a sound slap. "Sign here," she snapped, shoving a union card under his nose. He signed and she walked off with him triumphantly.

The working community is being fused into a fighting whole. Its core is the picket line, whose organization is one of the best I have ever seen. The union in Youngstown claimed a large majority when the strike was called. Since then over a thousand are said to have joined in both Youngstown Sheet and Tube and Republic. The union membership was built up solidly after nearly a year of organizing. It was necessary to organize quietly; John Stevenson said that for months he spent six out of every eight hours in house-to-house visiting. Last summer there were few open meetings, but there was a surprising number of "beer parties" on farms of former steelworkers, often miles from Youngstown. Finally the union was strong enough to have open mass meetings. The union in Sheet and Tube rested on two blocks of picked men of 500 each, called the organizing committee. The members of the organizing committee now largely form the flying squadron.

Six weeks ago it became evident that the independents would force a strike, and a systematic organization of pickets began. By the time the strike came, disorderly and uncertain elements had been weeded out. The picket lines during the day are small groups of people at all gates, at strategic points, on railway embankments all along the miles of boundary of a big steel mill.

"It may not look like so much, but I can get 500 men out in a half hour, 1,000 in an hour, at any point," John Mayo tells you. A system of communications has been evolved by which key men communicate rapidly with those in their jurisdiction. "We had 1,500 on the picket line the other night in no time, when we had the all-night meeting with the mayor and sheriff and chief of police." This meeting was held after the Chicago shooting and was for the purpose of devising means to prevent a repetition of the bloodshed here.

No one can go on the picket line unregistered. Pickets are asked which gates they want to patrol and which "turn" they want. There are four turns of six hours each. The pickets are divided into blocks of five with a leader for each group—parties of friends are encouraged to be together. There are one picket head and four division captains, one for each turn. Forty-two flying-squadron cars are attached to each turn.

They patrol the picket line and transport organizers and pickets to any point.

Warren is the hot spot of the strike. This is where observers look for trouble. No such careful piece of organization has been done as in Youngstown. Company airplanes fly over the mills, where the management claims that 2,000 out of the 6,000 workers have remained inside. Men out in the swamp are said to snipe at the planes, which land passengers and food. The food falls with a terrific thud, often outside the plant. Over a gatepost outside the Niles plant, smashed cans of beans are nailed, with the sign "Scabs' Breakfast."

The union reports that all the tough characters and gunmen have been concentrated in the Warren mill in preparation for battle. As though to prove the truth of this, the scabs have made four sorties, attacking the picket lines with nuts, bolts, and gas pipes.

The circumference of the big Warren plants is about eight miles. All along this distance groups of men sit in the shade, play horseshoes, or camp on the railway. The strike dominates the community. All approaches to the mill are barred. Only if you are accompanied by an organizer can you pass the numerous picket camps. In this area you realize that the two sides are drawn up in battle array.

Recently a strikebreaking technique has been perfected—the Mohawk Plan, invented by Remington Rand—which has become the strikebreaking employers' manual. First you create an atmosphere of terror. You form a citizens' committee. You call for more police, you start a back-to-work movement. It is all vividly described by the National Labor Relations Board in the Remington Rand decision.

These moves are all punctually being carried out in the Mahoning Valley. The mob is in process of being formed, though the burning of the fiery cross before the mill gates, threatened the other night, did not materialize. Failing all else the employers have already indicated their readiness to shoot it out, as steel has always done since 1892.

For to the independents this is no ordinary strike; it is a strike they will use every means to win, for they are fighting not only the CIO but also U.S. Steel. This strike marks the emergence of the independents as rivals to U.S. Steel for domination of the Steel Institute. Weir can already cut prices under U.S. Steel. Now, if this bloc can beat the CIO, they will take the leadership and will punish Myron Taylor and his organization, by whom they feel they were let down. More is at stake than defeating the CIO or even conquering the leadership of the Steel Institute. Here are being fought out the administration's policies regarding organized labor. These are under assault by the independents.

This winter has seen American labor and American employers make greater gains in settling their difficulties in a reasonable way than ever before. The independents propose to scrap these gains. But this is neither 1892 nor 1919. The union has countered with a surprise announcement that the strike will be spread to iron ore and coal. A vigorous organizing program has been outlined by the Mine, Mill and Smelter Workers and extra CIO organizers are already on the Youngstown Sheet and Tube and Republic Steel properties in the Calumet area in Michigan and the Mesaba Range in Minnesota. Congressman John Bernard is to be chief marshal of the ore miners' drive. There is to be a conference of United Mine Workers of America (UMWA) presidents to discuss the possible action in coal also.

The Labor Relations Board and the La Follette Committee are on the job, and instead of twenty-four apathetic craft unions there are twenty internationals of young, vigorous workers behind the steel strike determined to win.

While a peace move is on foot with Philip Murray and Governor Davey conferring in Columbus, nothing much is hoped from it. If a prolonged strike is to be averted, a strike that will follow steel's old pattern, a return to repression and bloodshed, plus the modern technique of the use of mob violence, the federal government will probably have to take a hand.

# Two Dead in Youngstown, Ten in Chicago
## Federated Press, 1937

*FP Correspondent, Herself Injured, Tells Story of Youngstown.*
*The following eyewitness story of the June 19 Youngstown massacre*
*was written by Mary Heaton Vorse, Federated Press correspondent*
*and noted novelist, shortly after she was wounded by gunfire from*
*deputized vigilantes gone berserk. Though six stitches were taken in*
*her forehead, Mrs. Vorse was addressing a huge Youngstown strike*
*rally the next day.*

Youngstown, Ohio. "We got tired on the picket line," she said. "Our feet hurt. So the men got chairs for some of the older ladies from Bavlasky's Cafe."

But it happened that the chairs went over a few inches on Republic property. That's what started the riot in Youngstown June 19 from which two strikers died, twenty-seven were wounded, and hundreds gassed.

A strike call went out to 1,800 union truck drivers in protest. In the wake of the massacre, Republic and Youngstown Sheet and Tube concentrated their police and vigilantes in Youngstown and announced they would reopen the morning of June 22.

Make a picture of the picket line. Women's day in Youngstown, the first women's day workers here have known. Women with paper bands on their arms reading "Women's Brigade." These are solid-looking, older women. There's a young mother with a four-month-old baby in her arms. Maybe thirty women in front of the Republic gate at 5:00, and by 8:30 they've gotten tired, so a few women are sitting in chairs.

Here the picket-heckler, Captain Richmond, swings into action. He's always at the pickets, trying to fray their nerves to provoke them. The police tell the women to move off company ground. As they start, the cops hustle them with: "Get along, get going!" Someone says: "We're moving as fast as we can." Someone says: "We've got a right to be here."

"I'll show you how to move along," says Richmond. At that he fires a gun three times in the air. A signal. Police fire tear gas point-blank at the woman with the baby in her arms; at the others with children by the hand. You don't bring little children where you expect trouble.

Men are gathering across the street for a meeting. They start toward the police, but Bob Burke, Republic organizer and former Columbia University student, gets the men to the meeting place behind Bavlasky's Cafe. He tries to keep them calm.

But there's a shot and a cry for help. The men stream out to defend the women. Sheriff Ralph Elser sends out carload after carload of deputies. Hundreds of people are gassed, but the strikers don't break. Then 200 grenades are fired before 9:00.

"The men ate the gas," one woman told me. The women ate it too. The strikers who had retreated pushed back the police 400 yards. At midnight more deputies rolled out of the police station while the crowd booed.

"What's happened?" I asked Sheriff Elser.

"These CIO murderers are surprising my men from the hills. One of my men is shot in the leg."

A striker is dead, a dozen wounded, a policeman is shot in the leg.

"Here I was keeping the status quo, and they start this, and they're asking Tom Girdler to sign with murderers," raves the sheriff. "They've asked for war. They'll get it! I'll deputize another hundred tonight." There's no end of deputies. Mayor Lionel Evans has deputies, so has the sheriff, and there's a vigilante committee coming out in the open. With Scotty O'Hara, Steel Workers' Organizing Committee organizer of the Homestead district, I go late up to Poland Avenue. The lights are out. Clusters of excited people on the dark streets. We pass the pickets, pass the open hydrant. An armored car of deputies roars past. The fourth I've seen. The small crowd boos. Further on we hear the popping of gas guns. We are perhaps two blocks away. We run into a gas pocket and my eyes stream. The street ahead of us is empty but for a few shadowy figures. No crowd.

Another armored truck in which are twenty deputies roars up. It stops near us. There are flashes. Shots ring out. They are shooting down defenseless workers before our eyes. We turn to run out of bullet range. A man falls at my feet. Another falls in my path. I see Scotty on the ground, and I fall too. One man near me groans. The other is silent. Bullets spatter. Scotty picks me up. I'm wounded too, blood drips from my face. People are picking up the other wounded.

Up at the hospital where I go to get my head sewed up, the wounded are arriving by carloads. A little boy. A woman who lies with her eyes still closed. A man. Three more women.

Youngstown, Chicago, what's the difference? Two dead here. Ten dead there. Twenty-seven wounded here, a hundred there.

And Tom Girdler has shot us all.

# The Tories Attack Through Steel

*The New Republic,* 1937

Jim Eperjesi is dead. They buried him today. A thousand workers' cars followed this Hungarian steelworker to the cemetery. It was the second steelworker's funeral that day. I never saw Jim Eperjesi, but, also wounded, I fell beside him, as he lay fatally shot, and I heard his groans.

The men killed in Youngstown were as needlessly murdered, the fifty wounded were as needlessly injured, as were the Chicago steelworkers three weeks ago. The press and that section of Congress that has cried out in horror at Governor Earle for closing the mills to prevent bloodshed in Pennsylvania, and is so eloquent about the right to work, has been silent about a worker's right to remain alive, and quick to cry that the police shot in self-defense. Jim Eperjesi, the fifty-seven-year-old steelworker, was not shot in self-defense. He was fired on, point-blank, by deputies standing in a truck. I know because I was there. I stood beside the truck; I saw the flash and I heard the shots.

Jim Eperjesi is dead and buried and so is Georg Bogovich, and so are the ten Chicago strikers. Hundreds have been wounded and gassed. Here in Youngstown alone, more than 225 are in jail. All of them were caught up in a swirl of issues larger than the strike. This attack on organized labor, with its shabby pretext of being willing to make, but not to sign, a contract such as 258 other steel firms have signed involves far larger issues than the lives of a few thousand steelworkers. It is the looked-for assault of big business on the Roosevelt administration.

The steel strike has emerged in its true colors as a major political offensive against the labor policies of the president. Its object is not merely to crush labor and go back to the despotism that for two generations has ruled the steel towns. The objective is larger. It is to split the Democratic Party over the issue of the CIO.

Throughout the country, there has been a careful portrayal of the CIO as a subversive communistic organization. There has been a premeditated identification of the president with the CIO. He is openly mentioned on all sides as its partner. He is pictured as the defender of the sit-down strike.

It is naive to consider the present impasse in steel as the work of Tom

Girdler and a small group of willful men. Every evidence points to
Girdler's offensive as a planned attack on the administration by big
business, an attack of which the independent steel companies are the
spearhead. Behind them is the force of the United States Chamber of
Commerce, buttressed by the other powerful anti-administration
forces inside and outside Congress.

The building up of the mail case to a national issue from a matter
which the local postal authorities had described as "nothing to worry
about," and the speedy hearing in Washington; the storm of disapproval of Governor Earle's closing of the Johnstown mills—these are all
parts of the antiadministration battle that is splitting the Democrats
from north to south. It is a fight to the death.

Jim Eperjesi was killed Saturday night, June 19. I did not see the
first part of the fighting that night; I had been out in the country and
when I got back, one man had already been killed, many were
wounded and hundreds gassed.

With Scotty O'Hara, I went down Poland Avenue toward Stop Five,
where the trouble had been going on. The street was dark. We walked
through the drifting remnants of a cloud of tear gas, past a sparse line of
pickets. A truckload of deputies went by us and were booed by the
workers. Ahead of us there were a few dark figures—not enough to be
called a crowd. Another truckload of deputies went by and stopped a
little ahead. Suddenly, without the slightest provocation, the deputies
opened fire on the strikers. I was glad that we were protected—as I
thought—because we were behind the truck. Two men ran toward us
and dropped at our feet. Scotty O'Hara also sprawled on the ground,
and I thought he had done so to get out of the way of the bullets. I had
better do the same thing, I thought, and the next I knew, I was lying on
the ground myself near one man who was groaning and another who
lay motionless. . . .

As I left the hospital after having the wound in my forehead closed
and stitched together, other injured persons were pouring in. Automobile loads of them kept arriving. There was a little boy who was shot
in the leg; three persons, two women and a man, sat in a row, all
wounded. A woman lay motionless on a stretcher, staring up at the sky.

It was some time later before I found out just what had happened.
This had been "Women's Day" in the strike, the first thing of the sort
ever seen in the steel-mill country. Two thousand women had assembled at a meeting and had chosen nine "picket captains." Many of
them wore armbands with the words "Woman's Brigade."

"We got tired of standing and someone brought us chairs from a
nearby restaurant, so we could rest our feet," an elderly woman explained to me. The chairs, it seems, were a few feet across the line
marking the limit of the company's property. Captain Richmond, who
has been accused by the strikers from the start of trying to provoke

them, sharply ordered the women to move on. Tired and resentful of his actions, they didn't move fast enough to suit him. Some of them talked back, which is a crime when a steelworker does it to a policeman.

Suddenly, the police fired tear gas point-blank at the women. Among the scores who suffered from it—and tear gas is a much more serious matter than most people suppose, often causing permanent injury to the eyes, nose, and throat—was a four-month-old baby, which one of the women was carrying. In half an hour, 200 gas bombs had been exploded. The scene was like war, including flares hanging in the sky, burning with a blue flame and helping the police to aim their projectiles with the greatest effect. In spite of everything, the workers held their ground.

Monday night, the officials of the Republic and Youngstown companies announced that the mills would open next day. They did this in spite of the gassing and shooting of the night before, and in spite of the fact that the specially appointed Federal Mediation Board was sitting and that both Mediator Charles Taft and Secretary of Labor Perkins had asked that the status quo should be maintained. The air was heavy with approaching disaster. The strikers then sent their famous telegram to the president. Many private citizens sent telegrams of similar import. Ministers offered public prayers that bloodshed might be averted. All day long, people gathered on the street corners discussing what the morrow might bring. Three thousand truck drivers struck in protest against the steel companies' action. Meantime, workers from other cities, sympathetic to the strikers, began seeping into town.

At midnight, word came that the mediation conference had temporarily broken down. Tom Girdler refused to do anything except to reiterate his declaration that he would never sign. The anti-Roosevelt forces chose wisely when they picked him to carry the brunt of the fighting.

Late in the night, the workers were again massed in front of the mill gates, prepared for an all-night vigil. Among them were many who had been hurt the night before, by tear gas or bullets, but were back on the picket line, prepared to face whatever was ahead of them in the struggle for their jobs. At picket headquarters there was a busy scene. News came in by telephone and by messenger from other points throughout the area. Then suddenly we heard that there would be no battle after all. The mills would not seek to reopen next morning. The troops were coming.

Smiley Chatok stood before the dark crowd near Shop Fourteen and told them the news. He said: "Folks, everybody now he can go home quiet."

"Hey, we want to wait and see the troops come in," someone shouted.

"Sure, I know you want to see 'em, but better everybody she go to bed. Captain of police, he come and ask real nice—everybody he get off picket line, right now. Go home."

By morning, the troops were arriving on foot, a long, wavering line like a khaki-colored caterpillar. All through that night, and all the next day, strikers were being ferreted out in their homes and elsewhere and arrested. While they were attending the funerals of those who had been killed, their houses and union headquarters were being searched for dynamite and arms. One of the union offices was raided and the records were confiscated. "A steelworker could be arrested for having a penknife or a toothpick," the strikers said. One man was actually put in jail for possessing a fork. In all, 225 people have been arrested and locked up, with no charges preferred against most of them. The leaders like Smiley Chatok, Robert Burke (former Columbia University student), and John Stevenson, who had worked all night persuading the strikers to go home peacefully, are under arrest "for inciting to riot."

There matters stand as I write these lines. The National Labor Relations Board (NLRB) has a staff of investigators in Youngstown, who are looking into the charges made by the Steel Workers' Organizing Committee (SWOC). The SWOC says that armed thugs and gunmen have been used to interfere with peaceful picketing, and that this has been done through collusion between the Republic company and the local mayor and sheriff. The SWOC further charges that the Republic company has maintained extensive arsenals in its plants in Youngstown, Warren, Niles, Canton, and Cleveland. The extent of the Warren arsenal is already a matter of court record.

After the final breakdown of the mediation conference, Governor Davey announced at midnight that the mills would reopen. During the night, foremen and mill officers phoned and visited workers' houses, telling them to go back to work. All civil rights had been denied the workers; their sound truck had been confiscated. Access to the radio, which all day had reported a return to work, was denied the union. The leaders were in jail. Confused and without communication with their leaders, many believed the strike was over and returned to work. In spite of state troops, county and city police, and deputies used to break the strike, in spite of the radio's and the newspapers' insistence that the strike is lost, there is still a stubborn resistance among the majority of the workers.

Papers throughout the land are screaming about the anarchy of labor. The rule of big business in the mass industries has been the rule of anarchy. The La Follette Committee and the findings of the NLRB have shown over and over again there is literally nothing, including murder, at which big business will stop to prevent labor from organizing. This offensive against steel's labor—and against the president— proposes the resumption of rule by spy, thug, and gunman.

# Workers' Welfare Is War Work

## The Woman's Press, 1943

⚜

*By mid-1942 it was clear that the success of the American war effort was dependent upon the greater use of female workers, especially as replacements in jobs traditionally held by men. Federal and private agencies accordingly began a propaganda campaign to recruit women in areas of labor shortage. Although there was a large quantitative growth in the female labor force during the war, the number of new women workers who would not have entered the labor force except for war conditions was in fact relatively small. The steady upward trend in the number of working women, especially middle-aged, middle-class, and married women, was well established by the 1930s and continued to rise even after the war ended. The societal tension between the urgent need for women war workers and the never-ending fear that after the war women might permanently desert their "natural" place within the home, meant that very few women would be provided with the basic social services necessary to ease the problems they encountered as "temporary" workers during the war years.*

We were sitting in the pleasant club rooms of the YWCA Center in Huntington Park. These club rooms are part of the Y's war expansion program and had recently been opened for the girls working in the war industries in this almost unknown section of Southeast Los Angeles. Here great industries follow one another until their names form a who's who of big business.

The girls were of a dozen different origins: Polish, American, German, Czech, and came from as many parts of the country and worked in as many different industries. The club was their one common meeting ground, the only place where they could talk together about their mutual problems.

Tonight they were discussing a play to be given by the auto workers' union. It was to be a war worker's *My Sister Eileen.*

"The first thing Eileen does is to look for a room," began the girl from Chrysler's, "and won't she have a time—for there just aren't rooms for girls."

"I thought I'd never find a room," said the girl from the Goodrich Rubber Company. "Didn't it give you an awful feeling when you went from one address to another, from one address to another, and they snapped at you, and said, 'Only rooms for men—no girls.' I got to feeling I had the smallpox."

"Sometimes people act as if they hated the girls who come to work here," said another girl, and in this she was right.

The girl from the great aluminum plant of Alcoa said, "I couldn't find a room here at all. I'll never forget how tired I got looking. I come from Burbank every day and it takes me two hours and a half. I never do get to eat a hot meal."

"That would be another of Eileen's troubles," the girl from Goodrich took up. "The trouble she has getting anything to eat. If a girl gets one hot meal a day she's lucky."

"I'll say she is. I get two hot meals a day but I cook them myself and that's some trouble, let me tell you. Try and cook two meals a day, and pack your own lunch and your husband's, and see how much time you've got left over."

"Well, she's not going to have trouble getting to find something to eat before she's got a job. Suppose we find her a job. Do you remember how tired you were the first day that you got your job?" The girls remembered only too vividly.

"I thought that getting a job in a war industry was just like getting a job anywhere. You just talk to the personnel man—if he likes you, you're hired. That's how green I was. I didn't know that in a war job you had all those questionnaires to fill in, and had to bring your birth certificate and be fingerprinted and photographed and get that physical examination."

"And now Eileen's got a room and a job, now what?"

"Now she's got trouble with her foreman, of course," everybody said, and they all laughed.

"Yes, and why do foremen have to act like they do?" asked one of the girls. "I don't remember that my foreman's ever spoken to me except to bawl me out."

"We'd all work a lot better if they'd tell us when we did something good. But it gets you down not to have a man speak to you except to be mean. Especially when you're all tired out, it makes you jumpy."

"They don't seem to think that a girl would last longer if they looked after her. I've got a friend in one of the big airplane plants. She does wiring on final assembly. When they get through with a plane it's going to take an hour and a half before a new plane is set up, but they won't let the girls sit down. They just have to stand there on their feet all that time doing nothing. They say it's because the Army might come through on inspection."

"The UAW is having a campaign for seats for women. They can't have it too soon for me. My feet just about fall off nights."

Parenthetically the Department of Labor is also making a drive for seats for women. It is an odd commentary on the good sense of industry that the unions and a great government agency should have to make a drive for so elementary a thing as conserving workers' strength, which means actually conserving manpower. These girls were part of that vast tide of workers who have flowed into the war industries. Every town that has war contracts is full of them. The powder plants, the shell-loading plants, the machine shops, the shipyards and aircraft plants are full of girls and women, many of whom have never before either been away from home or had a job. Many of them are very young. The sampling of 1,000 girls in one munition plant showed 60 percent under twenty. Hundreds and thousands of these girls who stand in crowded buses an hour or more going to work, whose food is inadequate, who live in crowded conditions, work in dangerous trades. The shell-loading plants, the powder bag plants, the work on detonators, the powder lines, are more and more taken over by girls and women. There are communities where many faces of girls on the street are yellow from "working in the powder."

When explosions occur, as with every precaution they are bound to do, the girls stick to their jobs. "The boys can take it, so can we," they say. They recognize that they are necessary to the fighting force, even if the communities where they live often do not. Old inhabitants only too often look on war workers as an affliction instead of an opportunity to help in the war, and fail to realize that the fate of their boys at the front and the welfare and happiness of these girls are irrevocably enmeshed.

In the midst of sometimes hostile and dangerous surroundings, the workers in war towns find all the simpler problems of existence difficult. Many places charge for laundry privileges or don't allow them at all. How to get heavy oil-soaked dungarees washed, how to find time for a shampoo, is a problem. There is frequently only one bathroom for twenty or thirty girls. How to find time to do the necessary shopping or even get a paycheck cashed are among the difficulties of workers living on a three-shift basis in a one-shift world. The towns are few which have stores that keep open evenings for shopping.

There are thousands of girls who walk a mile or more to get from their rooming places to breakfast, so they eat doughnuts or a bun out of paper bags as they go to work or stand on a street corner waiting for the bus. These buses are as inhumanly crowded as a city bus at rush hour. People stand packed like sardines. There are other thousands of girls who go to work without any breakfast. The soda fountains and restaurants are so crowded that there's no time to eat before they rush to work.

The coordinator of women in one of the big airplane repair plants says that many girls faint away in the late afternoon and that she has found that they have been able neither to get breakfast in the morning nor to get at the lunch counters at noon.

The problem of food for workers is daily becoming more acute. Those who eat at home find the shelves bare of meat and vegetables by the time they can go to the store. Restaurants everywhere are closing, and prices are skyrocketing.

To say that the eating facilities in many plants are unsatisfactory is a wild understatement. Even when there is a cafeteria, the workers on the production line do not have time to go to it. Girls are cracking up every day and going home for the simple reason that they are not eating enough of the right kind of food to sustain them.

A girl I know who works in a big airplane repair plant in a southern city is a typical instance. She works on the swing shift and gets up in time to have her only good meal of the day. A half hour is allowed for lunch around 8:00. There is no way of getting hot food. Lunch wagons with sandwiches, milk, and coffee provide the only chance to eat. She leaves the plant at midnight when the restaurants are all closed, so unless she has provided a snack for herself in her room she eats nothing more. How are girls to build airplanes on such a diet? The answer is they can't for long.

The situation of the professional and clerical workers in war towns is quite as serious as that of the girls on production. Every camp and depot has a group of service workers who live under the most congested conditions and generally with much lower pay.

As far as I know, few communities have adopted the idea that to give girl war workers breakfast and kitchen privileges is war work. For the communities of this country are not yet aware what an opportunity to help with the war the war workers afford them. If they did, the enemies of production—homesickness and loneliness—would not cause the turnover which they do.

Homesickness is the first enemy. The girls come from the warmth of a family circle, from a community where they are known, into anonymity and into the impersonal surroundings of a town where they are outsiders, too often looked on with suspicion and dislike. Too often not a hand is held out to them in friendship. So hundreds go home. Any plant employing girls will tell you that it is in the first two weeks that the great turnover occurs. Thousands of girls with no one to help them through this crucial time give up then and go home. That this is so is from lack of neighborliness, from lack of understanding of the role these girls are playing in the war. They deserve friendliness and hospitality as their right from a community as much as do the servicemen, since it is on their faithful work that victory depends. Anyone who fails to uphold them with welcome and whatever other help is needed is failing to support their boys at the front.

The tougher-minded girl gets through the first attacks of homesick-ness. Loneliness still remains. Any YWCA secretary from the East to the Pacific Coast will testify that girls are driven by sheer loneliness to accepting another set of standards than those they followed at home. A girl needs to have fun, a girl wants to dance, and there is literally no place in many a town where a girl can meet boys except on the street. If there is no YWCA nor United Service Organization (USO) for indus-trial workers, there are seldom recreation rooms open to girls. So they go to jukebox joints and honky-tonks while the townspeople complain about the girls and gossip that they pick up men on the street.

There are some towns where the industrial workers are practically ostracized. A friend of mine lived in a town a few miles from a shipyard in which her husband worked. As she said, "in a very nice part of town. It was so nice no one would speak to me. Literally no one spoke to me at church or when I was out shopping or in the house where I lived, or anywhere. I got so lonely that I went out one day to the park and sat there and said to myself, 'If I don't get to talk to someone today I'm going home.'"

This woman had been a trained nurse before her marriage. She was a beneficent woman and would be a blessing in a sickroom. The little town where she lived had been swarmed over by construction and shipyard workers and the town had closed itself against them.

Even church people often avoid the war workers. A Vacation Church School was opened by a minister in a midwestern town. It was for war workers' children as well as local children. Several teachers were selected from among the war workers. The minister called on all the trailer people asking the children to come. His report of this reads, "They responded well and at the close of school we had a picnic which many mothers attended. Our own people were not kind to them and the trailer folk wondered, 'What do we have that is so catching?' mean-ing a contagious, loathsome disease as if they were of low caste. It hurt them very much and a number never came back." Anyone who has traveled through this country will have found this attitude toward war workers repeated time after time.

In most towns the first animosity toward war workers softens with time. There is a great deal of unorganized goodwill everywhere. It needs a channel through which it can flow. In many cities the YWCA has been the agent which has brought many different groups together and has been able to interpret the needs of the industrial girls and women. In new industrial towns the YWCA through its USO division has often been able to organize the good feeling which is latent everywhere, and has found the community giving full and enthusiastic cooperation with its program. A small town overwhelmed by a new population finds the problems too great to be coped with alone and needs the help of such agencies as the YWCA and the USO.

There are towns where community responsibility has been realized, where people believe that every girl who stays on a job because some women has spoken to her pleasantly and made her feel welcome is another pair of hands saved for war work. One little town of 2,800 took in 1,100 girls. They made their slogan, "Workers' Welfare Is War Work."

# The Pirates' Nest of New York

## Harper's Magazine, 1952

*Almost from its inception in 1894, the racket-ridden International Longshoremen's Association (ILA) in the port of New York was dominated by criminal overlords, aligned closely with union officials, as well as with many employers and politicians. After World War II, demands by returning veteran longshoremen for more effective and honest union leadership led to large wildcat strikes in 1945 and 1951. Several New York investigative bodies publicized the sordid tale of union corruption and criminal influence upon the union, and in 1953 the AFL expelled the ILA, spending close to $1 million in an unsuccessful effort to build a rival longshoremen's union. Under pressure, the ILA did reform somewhat and was readmitted to the AFL in 1959, welcomed back partly because AFL leaders feared that the ILA might otherwise join forces with the Teamsters.*

"When Johnny Cockeye Dunn went to the chair for the murder of Andy Hintz, before he died, they found he'd done at least thirteen murders," said Father Corridan.

"Didn't Johnny Cockeye use the concrete?" asked the longshoreman, an old-timer. He was talking to two Jesuit priests about the New York docks, where the convenient way to get rid of embarrassing corpses is to dump a man in a barrel, fill it with concrete, and drop it down to the twelve-foot ooze at the bottom of the harbor.

"No, no," said Father Corridan. "Johnny Cockeye never used concrete. He used what is called the Chinese method entirely—a quick bullet in the back of the head and the car radio turned up."

"Didn't he put Peter Panto in the concrete, Father?" asked the other priest gently.

"You have it all confused, Father. Peter Panto didn't go in the concrete at all. They found him in the lime and garroted nearly a year after he disappeared. To this day, the police say they don't know who got to him, although the Anastasia mob has been suspected." Father Corridan turned to me. "Peter Panto was a hiring boss who couldn't stand the waterfront rackets, so he protested. He was called in and told the boys didn't like what he was doing. Four days later he disappeared."

We were in the office of Father John M. Corridan, S. J., assistant director of the Xavier Institute of Industrial Relations. His organization offers instruction to New York City laboring men on the techniques of union activity—classes in parliamentary procedure, union organization, labor journalism, public speaking, and the like. In the course of learning to do their own jobs the Jesuits have had to find out a great deal about the city and the ways in which its work is done. Father Corridan has become an authority on the waterfront. He talks of murder in a quiet, matter-of-fact-voice. The two priests might have been discussing a change in their students' schedules instead of sudden death.

The twenty-five-day longshoremen's strike of October–November 1951 had ended spectacularly at 1:00 the night before. A billion dollars' worth of cargo lay on the piers. The strike was estimated to have cost millions in spoilage and demurrage, and $300,000 daily in wages—$40,000,000 in all. The immediate cause of it had been discontent with their contract, which the longshoremen claimed was "a phony" and which they said put back the clock twenty-five years in loading procedure, even though their international union leadership accepted it. They showed their discontent in the most eloquent way they knew—"voting with their feet," which means walking out on a wildcat strike.

"The strike is over," Father Corridan said, "but the disturbance behind it is not." From a nearby room came the voice of another priest, telephoning: "This wasn't a strike. It was a revolt!"

"You heard Father Dobson?" asked Father Corridan. "The causes of the strike were deeper than resentment about a contract. There'll be trouble on the waterfront as long as there are union officials with long criminal records, as long as stevedoring companies use criminals for hiring bosses. The strike was a revolt against mob rule. The men on the docks are living for the day when they'll be out from under it."

There is no concentration of power and might and beauty in any port on earth like that of New York City. Its exports and imports are worth over $7 billion a year. Yet this magnificent harbor, with its shoreline in many cities, is a pirates' nest. Violence and theft are as much taken for granted as they were in Morocco during the boisterous days of the gaudy bandit Raisuli, forty years ago—or as they are today in many ports of the Orient. Murder is common on the waterfront. New York District Attorney Frank S. Hogan says that there are more murders here per square yard than anywhere else in the world. Death comes quickly to men like Andy Hintz or Peter Panto who protest against "the system."

The "system" is an informal, fourfold understanding between certain union officials, businessmen, gangsters, and politicians. During the strike the New York City Anti-Crime Committee, headed by Spruille Braden, sent a telegram to Governor Dewey asking him to end the "cancerous condition on the waterfront" which underlay it. The telegram mentioned by name five unsavory individuals, all but one of them highly placed union officials, who control most of the waterfront—Tony Anastasia, Alex DiBrizzi, Ed Florio, Mike Clementi, and Harold Bowers. Men like these (three of them have substantial criminal records) exercise authority with the full consent of union leadership and the big stevedoring companies, and with the passive consent of shipping companies. Attempts to investigate their activities have never succeeded in removing them from power.

Among the many complex reasons why this port of unsurpassed splendor is the most expensive in the world for shippers, why its business is steadily ebbing away to other cities, is the existence of organized pilferage, a polite word for piracy. It is reflected in the insurance rate—25 percent additional on cargoes consigned to New York. Each year gangsters are believed to rob ships alone (not including the warehouses) of between $65 and $100 million worth of property, maybe more. Loading itself, under the local arrangement called "public loading," is so much a racket that it costs $15 million annually. The overcharges for loading are about 20 percent more than if the same goods were shipped elsewhere on the Atlantic seaboard. Another major source of illegal income is the incredibly profitable smuggling of narcotics; so is extortion, which sent Socks Lanza—until then the waterfront boss on the East Side—to jail. Among the many minor ones which affect the longshoremen are loansharking, kickbacks, "short" gangs, "voluntary" contributions, and gambling rackets.

The conviction of Johnny "Cockeye" Dunn in 1947 together with the killer Andy "Squint" Sheridan is considered a milestone in waterfront history. Andy Hintz broke the rigid code of silence of the waterfront and identified his murderer before he died, but the code still lives. You die if you talk, longshoremen say. Years of living in an environment which makes it almost impossible to get anywhere and remain honest have given them a different moral standard than we have on the "outside." Though, as everywhere, there are honest men on the docks, in the unions, and in the shipping and stevedoring companies, few of them believed that there was any law on the waterfront higher than that of hired thugs, or that a killer as carefully protected as Cockeye Dunn could ever be convicted. His execution in 1949 was a first step against mob rule, and the strike of last fall was another one.

Joseph P. Ryan, president for life of the International Longshoremen's Association (ILA), insists that Communists played an important part in the unauthorized walkout. Father Corridan, who opened a strike meeting with a prayer, denies this. Yet, in spite of the opposition of their union chief, there was a moment when the "insurgents" trembled on the edge of success. "You might say that the men had the ball on the five-yard line," one striker put it. "Anyway, they had walked out on Joe Ryan and the only ones he had with him were the gang-sters."

Joe Ryan has expressed the belief that the method of hiring longshoremen best suited to the port of New York is the shape-up, an archaic system long since abandoned in the great ports of Europe. England abolished the "shape" early in the century, having found that it "led to graft and favoritism." Since that time the West Coast ports of Portland, Seattle (where the shape was abolished in the twenties), and Los Angeles, shortly followed by San Francisco, have regularized the hiring of longshoremen—but not New York. These reforms in hiring practices, whether in England or Portland, have all been accomplished through the cooperation of workers' groups and employers.

"The number of criminals operating on the waterfront," District Attorney Hogan has said, "is a direct result of the shape-up. It is responsible for kickbacks, loansharking, and a large percentage of other crimes on the waterfront. The shape-up is the root of the evil. I think it is a system that spawns criminal activities so regularly that state legislation might legally abolish it."

"The 'shape' is a real experience," one longshoreman told me. "The men stand around and tell dirty jokes and talk about sports and girls. The dock is chilly and it gets in your bones, and all the time everyone is waiting for the 'shape.' At five minutes to eight on any dock in New York a whistle blows, and the men who have been waiting form a circle around the hiring boss. Unless you're on the inside track with him, you don't know until that moment whether you're going to get the brass check, which means you're hired. No matter how long he's worked on the docks, every man is hired fresh every day. There are always more men than they want and many who are not hired wait in a saloon for another 'shape.'"

Under this system the hiring boss has the power of life and death over the longshoremen. He controls their economic life and sometimes their physical life, for many of the hiring bosses have criminal records. Some stevedoring companies prefer such men. "If you squawk you leave the docks, most likely in the fruit wagon," said one longshore-man. (The "fruit wagon" is the ambulance.) "If you don't leave in a barrel of cement," added another.

The shape-up and favoritism are inseparable, and they keep alive the threat of unemployment. I was told the familiar but grim story of a new hiring boss, during the Depression, who saw himself surrounded by five hundred hungry men when there were only a hundred jobs. In despair, he threw the brass checks into the circle and let the men fight for them. "And that," said the old-timer, "was the fairest 'shape' they've had in years."

The disproportion between the numbers of jobs and the number of longshoremen continues to this day. It shows itself in the difference between the distribution of longshoremen's wages for 1949 in New York and on the West Coast, where the shape-up was no longer the method of employment: Comparisons are difficult to make, since the incomes are differently calculated in each instance, but the latest available figures show that in 1948–1949 the average annual earnings of West Coast longshoremen were $3,760. In New York in 1949–1950 only 8.8 percent made over $4,000; 43 percent made under $500.

Other advantages can be cited for the West Coast. From 1949 to 1951 inclusive, 500,000 man-days of work were lost to strikes on the East Coast waterfront, as compared with 75,000 lost days for the West Coast. Companies pay much less compensation per man-hour worked on the West Coast than in the East, because of the lower number of accidents there.

Not only is the longshoreman the victim of perpetual insecurity but his employment itself is hazardous. According to the Bureau of Labor Statistics, a longshoreman has one chance in five hundred of being killed or disabled for life, one in forty of permanent impairment. One man in every four has lost thirty-four days annually because of temporary injury.

The longshoremen themselves can best tell you how the "system" affects their lives. There is not one who has not suffered, not one who has security. Take Tony Mike. (I have changed everything but his name and I have changed the names which follow, together with the unessential details of lives, for on the waterfront the code of silence is still observed.) Recently the Labor Subcommittee, which drafted a report for former Mayor William O'Dwyer of New York, stated that kickbacks are a thing of the past. Tony Mike laughs at the idea.

"They oughta go to Hoboken and Jersey City and watch the toothpick gangs. A man who's ready to kick back sticks a toothpick behind his ear. If there ain't a toothpick behind his ear, he don't get hired. The hiring boss picks out the man who wears the toothpick, for he's going to pay three dollars a day for working."

The New York City Anti-Crime Committee backs up Tony Mike's assertion. It states that a recent grand jury heard accounts of the kickback from people who had just left the shape-up and who told why they hadn't been hired. The records of the number of longshoremen at work tell the same story between the lines. There are 15,000 dues-paying longshoremen, but the Shipping Association records 35,000 longshoremen working.

Tony Mike has been a member of the International Longshoremen's Association for twenty-eight years. He has four children. He lost his job as hiring boss because he protested against "short" gangs. "A gang is supposed to have twenty-three men. They hire a gang three, even five, men short and then they collect the wages of twenty-three men. They make big money that way. Suppose you got five gangs to unload a vessel. On some piers you oughta have 115 men. That'll come up to near $2,000 a week that the hiring boss and the stevedore people can split between them. They just take it out of the hides of those poor devils. And when I don't like that and try and fight for a full gang, I lose my job."

At Harry's they were looking at a fine television set. The little cold-water flat had recently been done over as pretty as a bird's nest. It costs as much to heat as it does to rent and the bath is outside, but the kitchen is a housewife's dream.

Like his father, Harry is a cooper, or cargo repairman, and he has worked eleven years on the waterfront. We were talking about the difficulties for the ordinary worker in the ILA. "Take me," Harry said. "I was overseas twenty-three months, and when I came back they'd let a lot of longshoremen work as coopers who'd never learned the trade, so I was out of work eight months. My wife had to go to work. That's how it is when there's no seniority in a union."

Harry is a man who wants the "paper locals" ended. "What we care about in our local is that we don't have any representation. We don't hold union meetings; we don't elect officers or our delegates to the wage scale committee. See here, this is the sort of thing we're sore about." He showed me Murray Kempton's story in the New York *Post* on the ILA's ratification of last fall's controversial contract on Staten Island. "The men met in a hall only large enough to hold half of them. The business agent sat on the only chair. 'All those in favor of the contract, keep standing,' he said. 'Anyone against it, sit down.' The docker who told the story claimed there was just enough sitting room on the floor for a cat. 'What were we supposed to do,' he asked, 'drop dead?'

"There's a lot of us out to change that. We want a union that represents the men, and we're ready to fight for it." Harry said. "We didn't have anything left when we struck. My wife had to go to work again. We were lucky that my girl's so big she can look after herself and we got relatives where she can visit after school."

Art Delponte is a naturalized Italian who has worked on one of the West Side piers for fifteen years. He has three children, all of school age. Rent doesn't bother him because he's lived a long time in a cold-water flat near enough to the docks to go home between shapes. He's a docker, one of the men who load and unload the cargo. He thinks the waterfront is better than it used to be, bad as it still is.

"Everything we won," he said, "we won by wildcat strikes. We struck in '45, in '47, and '48. We got vacations with pay, a welfare fund, and our pensions. More pay too. If we don't strike we won't get anything." This belief is general among longshoremen.

I asked him what was the worst thing from the worker's point of view in being a longshoreman. "The hiring boss," he said. "If the hiring boss is down on you, you might as well leave the docks. If you're out of luck, you used to be able to go to Pier 53. They called that the 'Foreign Legion' and the 'Last Outpost.'

"One of the worst things is the weekenders. Firemen and even policemen, or any man who stands in with the big ward boss, can get a cut-rate union card. I know a big Jersey official who usta sit in a barber shop in Jersey City and just give out ILA cards. So that means weekenders go and get the longshoremen's jobs. These fellows pick up $30 that we ought to have. Then there's the ship-jumpers. They call them 'geeps.' They jump ship and get jobs as longshoremen.

"Very few lower West Side docks are bothered with kickbacks. It's the Yugoslavs on the East Side, or the Italians, and especially ship-jumpers, who pay kickbacks, some as high as ten dollars a day. The mobsters know who they are and threaten to deport them if they don't kick back. There's other ways a longshoreman's job is took off him. Sometimes there's a bunch of truck loaders hanging around and maybe a hiring boss goes up and hires two or three of them to fill out a gang instead of some of us. I've seen that happen when I was a fill-in. And when I made a beef, I'd find myself on the sidewalk.

"Sure I've been to the Shylocks. Everyone on the dock has. If I was to borrow ten dollars to see me through the week, I'd give my brass check to the Shylock. Then he puts in for my pay, and he pays himself my loan of ten dollars and two dollars more. If you was to borrow fifty, you pay ten dollars for it. But say you can't pay it back this week, then you owe him seventy."

"You're paying him 20 percent a week," I said. "Isn't there any other way you could borrow? Couldn't you go to a bank?" He laughed. "What bank would loan a longshoreman anything? We don't work steady. But you get work if you've got a loan shark on your tail. He sees to it you stay to work as long as you owe him something. He'd haul you out of bed, if he had to, to see you get to work."

When I climbed up the tenement stairs to Andy Dubrow's place, it seemed as though the hand of time had turned back thirty years, when the whole swarming East Side lived in tenements like this one. It smelled of dirt and bad toilets. Mrs. Dubrow let me in.

"Excuse this place," she said. "With all the children, you know how it is." The shades were broken; paper was peeling from the wall; there was a baby in a highchair near the table. Two other children played quietly on the worn and dirty linoleum floor. There were two more children in school, and the Dubrows were worried about their boy of sixteen, who "never seems to work steady."

"One time we lived nice. We had a different sort of place; it was after Andy got a smashed leg we began to have bad luck. He used to work good—always on the same pier. He made fifty and sixty dollars. He stood in with the boss." Mrs. Dubrow pushed back her hair with a hopeless kind of gesture that took in everything, the hopeless way the housework had got beyond control, Andy's bad luck, the boy they were worried about. "When he went back, there didn't seem to be no work for him. The boss had changed. He don't get more than two or three days a week, sometimes not that. We couldn't live without welfare. Oh, how I wish we didn't have to take it."

There's nothing spectacular about Andy Dubrow's story. He made no gesture of defiance. After a bad accident, he was less useful; and he became one of the innumerable "extra men" on the waterfront, one of the thousands that work less than five hundred hours a year and who have to be helped out by one of the social agencies.

It is an hour's journey by bus to Robert Donovan's spick-and-span, four-and-a-half-room flat. Donovan is regular. He thinks Joe Ryan is a great man who does as well for his men as he can. Like Joe Ryan, he points out how wages have risen since he came on the docks twenty-eight years ago. He talks of the recently established vacations with pay and the welfare fund. It doesn't make any difference to him that a recent meeting of his local is the first in years. He's no reformer.

He has known terrible times when there were four babies and almost no work. During the Depression he suffered from kickbacks and loansharking. "I guess we all did." That was when his wife had to work before the new baby was a month old. "We had to go to the Red Cross to get through at all." Donovan had his leg crushed and spent months in the hospital. "Compensation? I didn't get any. Few do."

Now things are going well with him. The Donovans have a new flat, for which they pay eighty-five dollars a month. There are three boys of school age at home and one girl at New York University. The Donovans have one wish, which is to give a good education to all their children. This is made possible by Mrs. Donovan's working. Donovan is sure of $66.75 after his Social Security and union dues are paid. He makes over one hundred dollars in rush times by working overtime and Sunday. He leaves home at 6:30 for the 7:55 shape, and if they want him back at night he has to wait around until seven. It makes a bad day.

"Pilfering? Of course there's pilfering. There's always been pilfering on every dock in the world. It doesn't seem the same as stealing. When I was young I got to taking home a few things myself—not much, a couple of bottles of whiskey for the holidays and a bottle of French perfume. Everybody grabs a bottle of perfume when they can.

"Then one day I thought, what's the matter with me? I wouldn't any more think of taking a bottle of liquor or perfume from a store than I'd think of robbing a bank! I began sort of preaching. I'd say to a buddy, 'You oughtn't to take that gold watch,' and the next thing I knew I was off the docks—and I wisht I'd kept my big mouth shut. But it's funny how natural it seems to take home something when everyone else does." It should be remembered, of course, that "personal" pilfering by individual longshoremen is insignificant alongside the highly organized piracy practiced by the gangsters.

Compared with many longshoremen, Donovan's is a success story, yet he got down to his last five dollars in the 1951 strike. "My son-in-law was just going to help out when the strike ended." Donovan has never forgotten the insecurity of the bad days. The fear of losing his job is always with him.

The port of New York is solidly organized by the International Longshoremen's Association. Long ago, Joseph P. Ryan, the union's president for life, gathered even such independent unions as the tug-boats and the barges into his capacious pocket.

The power of the union is supposed to stem from eighty ILA locals. About thirty of these are actual longshoremen's locals, but only a few vote and elect their own officers. Many of the rest are what are known as "paper locals."

The policies of the union are initiated in the Joseph P. Ryan Association, where no ordinary longshoreman ever sets foot, and carried out by the New York District Council, many of whose members are appointed by Ryan, as are the members of the all-important Wage Scale Committee.

A notable-looking, big, barrel-chested, red-haired man, Joseph P. Ryan has been ruler of his union for twenty-five years. He is an important political figure in New York City; indeed he is as much a politician as a union leader.

In his moments of quiet absorption, he is said to whistle "Danny Deever" under his breath. He boasts that he neither smokes nor swears, and more often than not goes to 8:00 Mass. He is a devoted family man.

Ryan completely denies the existence of corruption or rackets on the waterfront. Whenever there is a wildcat strike (and in the memory of man there has been no other kind) he thinks Communists are at the bottom of it. He was saying that years ago, and he told it to me at the New York State Board of Inquiry hearing after the recent strike. "The Communists started the walkout in Brooklyn and kept the strike alive there." (This same board of inquiry stated in their report that the strike was without Communist influence.) "I welcome an investigation of the waterfront," Ryan told me. "But why do they always investigate the waterfront? Why don't they investigate the garment trades for a change? They're full of racketeers.

"They talk about us giving jobs to men who've gone wrong and have served time. Where are those poor devils to go? Because a man's done wrong once, it don't show he's a criminal. Why, a man can't get paroled unless somebody'll give him a job, and those are the very men who stop other men from stealing. Many times, we've heard of a fellow who's got a record stopping men who are broaching cargo. Lay off, boys, he'll say. That'll go against me."

He brushes aside the fact that the Kefauver committee reported his union to be "infested with hoodlums" and said that "here, after twenty years of repeated effort to correct conditions, there still persists one of the ugliest situations in labor union history." He also seems to ignore the histories of a number of his outstanding officials that are written lengthily into police and Sing Sing records.

The New York waterfront is divided into spheres of influence and control. The farthest uptown piers, where the *Queen Mary* and *Queen Elizabeth* dock, are called the "pistol local," sometimes "the superhomicidal local." Harold Bowers is its international organizer. Though he himself has no criminal record, he works in close harmony with his cousin, Mickey Bowers, who has been convicted as a machine gunner and bank robber. All pier truck loading in the neighborhood is handled by the Allied Stevedoring Company, controlled by the Bowerses and their friends.

On the piers below Fourteenth Street are the remnants of the Dunn gang. Ed McGrath, the brother-in-law of Johnny "Cockeye" Dunn, was long the international organizer here. He is still a union official. He has been in Sing Sing for robbery and assault, and in all he has been arrested twelve times, once on a charge of homicide.

Brooklyn is still the domain of Tony "Bang Bang" Anastasia and his less spectacular brother, Jerry. His influence derives partly from the fact that he is the brother of Albert Anastasia of Murder Inc. Tony Anastasia has many interests. Not only is he a hiring boss, but he has diversified business connections and is known as a skillful strike-breaker. Ryan has commended him as a fine anti-Communist fighter. It is believed, however, that the Anastasias have ceased to be useful to the underworld and are "on the way out."

The overlord of Staten Island is Alex DiBrizzi. Mr. Ryan has referred to him as "a very fine gentleman." He is the head of Local 920 and vice-president of the New York District Council. His nephews, the "Three Dee's"—the D'Alessio brothers—control Staten Island (and its water-front), as a recent New York State Crime Commission hearing showed. He has political power in both parties, and his varied harbor enterprises have made him a millionaire. Mr. DiBrizzi has been arrested twenty times, but only for gambling and bookmaking.

Another prominent waterfront citizen is Edward J. Florio, whose elevation from president of Local 306 in Hoboken to international organizer was signaled by a testimonial dinner, presided over by

Joseph P. Ryan and attended by the mayors of Hoboken and North Bergen. Among the guests were other political bigwigs and Florio's good friend John "Fifi" DiRobertis, then at liberty on a federal narcotics charge. Florio himself has but a meager criminal record. He has only served a year and a day in jail for possession of an illicit still and for tax fraud. He has often been arrested, however, on such charges as felonious assault, fugitive from justice, possession of stolen goods, and so forth. Speaking of his appointment, a longshoreman remarked that "it looks like you have to have served time to be appointed organizer in the ILA." Florio's many relatives are either hiring bosses or enjoy other good union positions. Florio replaced Charlie Yanowsky, an associate of such aristocrats of the underworld as Mickey Cohen, Willie Moretti, and Albert "Ackie" Ackalitis, whose release from Dannemora Prison at the end of April is expected to disturb the balance of power on the waterfront. Yanowsky was found in a field, stabbed with numerous ice-pick wounds, in 1948. As Florio said, the boys get ambitious; they want to better themselves; then they are likely to get hurt.

The lives of these men are complicated. At one and the same time they are union officials, active in politics, engaged in trucking and stevedoring or other businesses; yet they have found time to accumulate criminal records. It was shown in the Kefauver hearings (and has been fully documented elsewhere in official sources) that a link exists between these union organizers and the amorphous and indefinable cartel of criminals that was described by Senator Kefauver as a "national crime syndicate . . . led by Costello, Joe Adonis, and Meyer Lansky on the East Coast." (They have such beautiful names—Anastasia, Florio, Clementi—names as beautiful as aconite and belladonna.) "In all the history of crime," writes Burton Turkus, the former assistant district attorney who prosecuted the leading members of Murder Inc., "there has never been an example of organized lawlessness to equal the Syndicate . . . an association in which every mob of any importance in the United States had membership."

All these organizers of the ILA have appeared at one time or another at the annual dinner given by the Joseph P. Ryan Association for the glory of the old labor leader. At this strange festival, criminals join the highest in the land to honor Ryan. The list of sponsors and guests has included governors, mayors, and churchmen. So respectable is Joe Ryan's front that many of his guests seem to have remained ignorant of the disreputable characters with whom they were mixing. Attending the dinner of 1951 were, among others, John A. Coleman, former chairman of the board of governors of the New York Stock Exchange; Colonel Ivan Annenberg, circulation manager of the *Daily News;* Mayor Vincent Impelliteri of New York; and Mike Clementi, ex-convict, an ILA official who lately succeeded Socks Lanza as overlord of the East Side. (Lanza, a lifelong friend of Lucky Luciano, is now out on probation.) Another guest was Edward Florio, the unfortunate Mr. Yanowsky's successor. The chairman of the arrangements committee was William J. McCormack, waterfront tycoon and boyhood friend of Mr. Ryan.

Until lately, Mr. McCormack was as invisible in waterfront affairs as he was rumored to be omnipotent, but recently a grand jury investigation in New Jersey and several newspaper and magazine articles have penetrated his anonymity. No one has led a fuller life than Mr. McCormack in his translation from West Side boy, driver of a vegetable truck, to his present lofty position. He is a Knight of Malta, a multimillionaire. As Mr. Keating of the New York City Anti-Crime Committee said over the Columbia network, "On the one hand he controls certain key union locals; on the other he owns and operates the very businesses that those key unions serviced. This puts him in a beautiful position to make even more money." Among his many assets are the Transit Mix Corporation (sand and gravel) and the Penn Stevedoring Company. A large proportion of New York's fruit and vegetables arrives in transportation he controls.

It is safe to say that no waterfront reforms could be accomplished without McCormack's nod. His political influence is vast; he is a maker of mayors, and his friends include the highly placed in Washington and the politically prominent of New York and New Jersey as well as many a bizarre waterfront character. Among these friends is another member of the ILA, John "Gene" Sampson, the business agent of Local 791 and leader of the recent wildcat strike.

John "Gene" Sampson occupies an anomalous position, one that is new to me in the labor movement, for experienced analysts of the waterfront call him the "loyal opposition." In late January, at the time of writing, he and three other "insurgents" had been removed from minor appointive positions in the ILA, apparently to indicate that they had incurred Ryan's disapproval. Yet Sampson remains business agent of his local—and a useful man. He is useful to the longshoremen as a bulwark against mobster rule; his brother Frank's position as deputy mayor and chief patronage dispenser of New York shelters him from gangster attack. When the longshoremen became so restive under their many burdens that they were bound to strike, Sampson led them against Ryan. After the men had struck awhile and the time was ripe, Sampson led the strikers back into the fold again. The dramatic one-o'clock-in-the-morning strike agreement in November was preceded (as reported in *Collier's*) by a meeting between Sampson and McCormack. When the new year opened with the threat of a new strike, Mr. J. V. Lyon, president of the New York Shipping Association, condemned the action of Sampson and his fellow insurgents. Reporters who wanted the true story, he said, should get it "from the headquarters of Mr. Ryan."

Even Mr. McCormack and Gene Sampson couldn't have ended the work stoppage without the promise held out to the longshoremen by the New York State Board of Inquiry, appointed by Industrial Commissioner Edward Corsi, at the suggestion of the New York State Board of Mediation headed by Merlyn Pitzele. The board of inquiry's chairman was R. M. Catherwood of Cornell University; Dean Alfange and the Right Reverend John P. Boland, who has grown old mediating labor disputes, were the other two members. So great was the longshoremen's hope and confidence in the board that the promise of a speedy publication of the report stopped a new flash strike (a result of the dismissal by Mr. Ryan of the four members of the insurgent strike committee).

Sampson was on the witness stand when I first went to a hearing of the board—a young sixty-two-year-old who looked as though he were the survivor of many compromises. He was testifying that Ryan had said the strike was a minority strike, that Ryan had said he would be behind it if it were a majority strike. "So we went out and got the majority." Sampson was followed by Eddie Barry, whose unshakable testimony caused Joe Ryan to take rapid notes one after another while Louis Waldman, the union attorney, cried out: "I protest. The witness has only been called for the purpose of giving damaging testimony." Day after day the longshoremen continued their testimony and showed what the report later called "an obvious lack of confidence in union leadership."

The report was released late in January. Embedded in its 144 dignified pages was as deadly an indictment of the New York waterfront as had yet happened. But the longshoremen, and others who have been as deeply concerned with what happens on the docks, felt that its recommendations were not in proportion to the evil it revealed. These consisted chiefly in the appointment of a permanent arbiter to settle disputes, the appointment of an ILA fact-finding board of three public members to sift grievances and make recommendations, and numerous reforms in voting procedure to be carried out by—Joe Ryan. (Ryan subsequently appointed his union lawyers, the law firm of Waldman & Waldman, to investigate "abuses and undemocratic practices" in ILA locals, though he said he thought they would find only minor faults traceable to the longshoremen's "reluctance" to attend meetings.)

On its publication, the report caused bitter disappointment among the insurgent longshoremen. Their attorney, Peter Johnson, said that the board of inquiry had "ignominiously arrived at an invalid conclusion when it upheld the ratification of the contract after detailed, documented evidence of fraud." The board, however, had not found fraud enough in the ballots to warrant a reopening of the contract. It is no wonder Joe Ryan welcomes investigations of the waterfront. In his experience they come and go, and up to now he has endured them all.

In 1916 there was the investigation by Mayor John Purroy Mitchel. In 1941 Governor Dewey, then district attorney, rounded up hundreds of ILA men to question them about loan sharks and the kickback. The last time I saw Mary Simkhovitch of Greenwich House, she discussed with me the Citizens Waterfront Committee of 1946, of which she was a member. This was a committee which included eminent clergymen and representatives of the Russell Sage and the Phelps Stokes foundations. There have been many other investigations, including that of the Kefauver committee. A full-dress investigation with nine subcommittees was set up by Mayor O'Dwyer in 1950, to discover why New York's port traffic had ebbed away. The subcommittee on Labor Conditions on the Docks was headed by W. J. McCormack and Joseph P. Ryan. It makes one think of the old cartoon. Two skunks are talking in the moonlight.

"Have you joined the foundation?" says one. "What foundation?" asks the other. "The foundation to investigate that horrid smell around here," says the first.

The report of this subcommittee was delayed until December 1951. It found there was nothing wrong with labor practices on the waterfront. Of the eleven members, only five signed the report. One who did not, Joseph P. Curran, president of the National Maritime Union, called it a whitewash.

At present no fewer than five investigating groups are fishing in the waters around the docks. The most far-reaching in its program is the New York State Crime Commission, for which, at Governor Dewey's instigation, $500,000 has been pledged to cover the waterfront investigation. The commission is headed by two able men, Judge Joseph M. Proskauer and his counsel, Theodore Kiendl. "This is the first time as far as I know," Judge Proskauer has said, "that there has been an all-out combination of all law-enforcement agencies to attack this problem and try to solve it. . . . We are going into the damnedest investigation we have ever had." Another is the active New York City Anti-Crime Committee mentioned earlier, which has done more to alert public consciousness than any of the rival organizations that are trying to change the incredible situation on the docks. The grand jury in Brooklyn, reporting to Judge Samuel Liebowitz, is also investigating the Brooklyn shoreline of the port. The judge has stated that he aims to catch the "big fish in the slimy waterfront pools, not just the little fish." New York and New Jersey have joined together to make still another inquiry into "racketeering, organized crime, and restrictive practices" in the harbor that borders both states. And there is also New York County District Attorney Frank S. Hogan's port-crime investigation, which has been in progress for some time.

With the public indignant as never before about crime in high places, this may be the psychological moment to clean up the waterfront and to put an end to these monstrous conditions. It will not be an easy task. Over the years a way of life has been established through which ships are loaded fast enough to satisfy their owners, and everyone but the longshoremen becomes rich. Before now, in part because of the code of silence, no complete investigation of the waterfront has ever been made. Perhaps the many grand juries and crime committees between them will at last succeed in making one. Arrests will help, as will the unmasking of those politicians who profit from the waterfront rackets. The partnership of politicians and gangsters can be broken if drastic enough measures are taken—and if they *are* taken, it will be because the public has demanded them.

Yet much more lies within the power of the shipping companies. Ultimately it is they who control the loading of the ships. The New York City Anti-Crime Committee continually emphasizes that the respectable elements behind the port crimes are as guilty as the criminals themselves, that not the conviction of a few hoodlums but a breakup of the system is imperative. As the board of inquiry has pointed out, if the shipping companies continue in their present course they will draw a noose around their own throats. If the grand juries and the crime committees do not bring about a change, if the system continues, we will have broadcast to an attentive world the fact that the city of New York, its greatest port, is powerless to rid itself of gangster control.

Meanwhile the men who suffer most, the thousands of anonymous longshoremen on the docks, are ripe for "revolt against mob rule." They are living, as Father Corridan had said, for the day of liberation from it.

# America's Submerged Class: The Migrants

*Harper's Magazine, 1953*

*Mary Vorse's fervent interest in the condition of farm labor in the United States began with her reports of the desperate struggle of black and white sharecroppers who formed the Southern Tenant Farmers Union in the 1930s. She subsequently supported the left-led United Cannery, Agricultural, Packing and Allied Workers of America organized in 1937. In the New Deal years, Vorse welcomed the establishment of the politically embattled Farm Security Administration, which was specifically concerned with the problems of destitute farmers, tenants, and farm workers. Yet she knew that federal and state intervention to relieve the distress of migratory farm laborers, while in many ways beneficial for farm workers, most often served best the interests of agribusiness. When César Chávez established the National Farm Workers Association in 1962, Vorse enthusiastically sent him a series of small contributions, representing a large proportion of her tiny income. It seems appropriate, then, that Vorse's last publication before her death, written when she was 78 years old, should address the plight of migrant farm laborers.*

Little Walter Giles was crushed by a truck on the farm of Grant Berry in Pemberton, New Jersey, last August. He died at Mount Holly Hospital on the night of August 24.

Walter was a little Negro boy of six who, with his twelve-year-old sister and his ten-year-old cousin, had accompanied their parents on a "day haul" from Philadelphia to pick beans. About a third of this crew of bean-pickers were children, in spite of the fact that New Jersey is one of the few states that have good child-labor laws which cover agriculture and forbid children under twelve from working in the fields.

The little boy became quite famous after he died. The American Federation of Labor (AFL) unions sent out releases about the tragedy, the *CIO News* ran an article about him, and a well-known labor commentator mentioned his death on the radio. For it called attention to the presence in American fields of children who should never have been there.

The U.S. Wage and Hour Regional Office division of the Department of Labor found over 480 children under sixteen at work during school hours in New Jersey fields between the beginning of 1951 and November 1952. And this did not include the children like Walter who did their work out of school hours or on vacation.

Less than a month before Walter's death, old man Tobin was killed by a tractor driven by an eleven-year-old boy on Fred Thomson's farm in St. Lawrence County, New York. Old Tobin was still haying at seventy-five because there's no retirement age for farm workers, nor do they get old-age insurance. The vigilant farmers' lobby had seen to it that the Department of Labor's Hazardous Occupation Order No. 2, which forbids the employment of children in dangerous jobs, didn't apply to farm trucks.

These two deaths illuminate the story of the migrant workers of the United States—an unregarded army of people who, from the cradle to the grave, are "children of misfortune."

"We depend on misfortune to build up our force of migratory workers, and when the supply is low because there are not enough unfortunates at home, we rely on misfortune abroad to replenish the supply," says the report of the President's Commission on Migratory Labor. Yet they are vital to our agriculture. As one farmer put it to me, "We need 'em awful bad when we need 'em, but after they're through we want 'em to get to hell out."

How does it happen that in a nation which prides itself on its enlightened labor legislation, its generally good labor conditions, and its outlawing of child labor, these people are still disregarded?

No Marxian but Father James Vizzard, S.J., of the Catholic Rural Life Council, gives one answer: "We had our industrial revolution in agriculture, which has created its proletariat." For these migrants are mostly employed on the great farm factories and the small captive farms tied to canneries.

In the words of William M. Leiserson, "Our farms are manufacturing plants. Agriculture is not learning from industry how an industrial revolution can be handled. . . . instead of learning from the rotten conditions that we had in our industrial revolution in industry, we are going through all of the same things that we did a hundred years ago."

A peculiarly helpless group of people have as their employers some of the most highly organized and powerful industrial groups in this country. These workers are especially vulnerable, because they are always on the move. They follow the crops, moving from Mexico and Texas to the cotton-picking—moving up to the central and northern states for sugar beets, and on further for fruit and vegetable crops—moving from Mexico and southern California to do the fruit-picking of the Pacific Coast—moving northward from Texas with the combines through the wheatfields of the Great Plains—moving from the Ozarks and the Kentucky and Tennessee mountains to harvest the crops of the central states—moving northward from Florida and other southern states to pick crops along the Atlantic seaboard—and coming out of city slums on day hauls to do the harvesting scores of miles away. Wherever they are, they are nobody's business: "State by state, county by county, township by township, nearly every unit of government seeks to evade responsibility for these migratory workers," says the report of the president's commission.

And so the laws of the land which protect other workers don't apply to migrant farm workers. When Social Security aid was extended to some agricultural workers, migrants were excluded. The migrant gets no unemployment benefits; except in two or three states he gets no advantage from the minimum wage laws. In only a few states has he workmen's compensation. Except for child labor, the amendment to the Fair Employment Practices Act does not apply to him. Only here and there are small groups of migrant workers under union protection; generally speaking, if he tries to organize he can be thrown out. He has not even a Taft-Hartley Act to aid him.

Because he has no settled residence, schools are seldom open to his children. Moreover he is excluded almost everywhere from health and welfare benefits. Too often he is despised by the local community and treated as an outcast. Even most churches don't want him. Being a migrant, he has of course no vote, so it pays nobody politically to help him.

The Department of Agriculture has stringent regulations governing the transportation of cattle and pigs. They must be unloaded at stated intervals for rest, food, and water. But not the migrants, 60 percent of whom travel long distances in trucks to get work.

"Many travel 1,800 miles with no rest stops on three- or four-day trips without stopover for sleep or replenishment of food. . . . There is a desperate need for transit rest camps supplied by the federal government," says Dr. Martha Eliot, chief of the Children's Bureau.

Walter Giles was not the only child crushed by a farm truck last year. The pages of the congressional hearings on migrants are littered with dead children—children run down, babies dying by the roadside because no hospital would receive them—while that faithful yardstick of conditions in an industry, infant mortality, piles up records of babies' deaths wherever there's a migrant camp.

Migrants are largely recruited by crew leaders or labor contractors, some of whom get kickbacks out of the workers' pay, or misrepresent jobs, or run camp stores at high prices; and when they do not supply liquor and women, their work groups are likely to be followed by professional gamblers, prostitutes, and dope peddlers.

The case of Mr. X, told by Mrs. Mabel Hopper of the Consumers' League of New York, could be repeated often wherever migrants work. Mr. X owned a taxicab company and a filling station, and had an interest in a bar and grill in Florida, all financed from his earnings as crew leader. He operated crews from Key West to Canada, and had one of the largest crews in New York State. When he was interviewed by Mrs. Hopper, he had a crew of two hundred recruited from Florida to Maryland who had been waiting for work two weeks, and were already in debt to him $1,500. "A cynical disregard on the part of the company as well as the crew leader was revealed on closer inquiry," says Mrs. Hopper. "In order to secure a labor supply being on hand when needed, the company and Mr. X signed a contract providing a minimum guarantee of $5,000 if Mr. X had a crew of two hundred for a four-week period. . . . Mr. X is a good example of a big-time operator."

Only a few states have housing codes for migrants, and so the men and their families are as likely as not to be housed in squatter camps, trailers, barracks, rickety farm buildings, tents, or even chicken coops—mostly below the standards of decency. And although the going rate of pay for migrant farm work has risen from 16 cents an hour in 1940 to 55 cents an hour in 1950, the average migrant works only 101 days a year, for annual earnings of only $514—about a fifth of what the average industrial worker now gets. American prosperity has passed him by.

Heading the list of states which have done something substantial to aid the migrants is New Jersey—with New York, California, and Wisconsin not far behind. New Jersey is the only state which has a Migrant Bureau, whose responsibilities include housing, child labor, wage claims and payments, health and welfare. Farm workers are covered by workmen's compensation. The schools of New Jersey admit migrant children. And the employment agency law has a new provision encouraging farmers to pay workers directly instead of through the crew leaders, who sometimes make off with the men's pay.

The town of Freehold, New Jersey, offers a fine example of how a community can tackle the migrant problem. On a recent trip through the state, I visited its summer school for migrants' children. It was in a fine modern four-room school building; and Mrs. Dorothy Jackson, who supervised it, had three teachers assisting her. Here sixty-two children from thirteen migrant camps were going to school for six summer weeks, and getting a savory lunch; there was even a nursery school for little children. "We can't take all the children who apply," said Mrs. Jackson.

This was truly a community project, with the local board of education providing the school, the state department of education providing the teachers, the Council of Jewish Women donating the milk, a local dairy supplying the ice, the Catholic Daughters giving paper plates, cups, and so forth, the Red Cross furnishing transportation for the women caterer, and the county library lending the books. As I saw the children running back and forth, saying politely, "Excuse me," as they passed on their way to their physical examination which was being held that day, they looked like anything but children of misfortune. Their clothes were neat, they were confidingly friendly, and the nurse told me they had gained pounds since the beginning of the term.

On Saturdays and Sundays, this school was used as a migrant center. Mothers could leave their children there when they went shopping. There were softball and horseshoe pitching for the active boys and men; books, games, music, television, and radio for the less athletic. The police reported that there had been fewer arrests since the center began to compete with the taverns, where there had been frequent disorders.

While I was at the school, a handsome Negro woman sat at the door with her sick grandchild sleeping on her knees. The baby was diagnosed as having whooping cough and pneumonia. "As soon as school is over I'm going to see that that baby gets to a doctor, if it's the last thing I do." said Mrs. Jackson. A day or two later I saw the grandmother again, and found that the baby was miraculously convalescent; and I reflected that here was one baby who might have died but for the care New Jersey takes of its migrants.

Alas, this school and center must be discontinued. The building is required for administration purposes, and no new one has been found. But there is talk that there will be more schools in other New Jersey counties.

The day after my visit to the Freehold school, I saw one of the better migrant camps. It was a row of thirty cubicles, fourteen by twelve feet, of corrugated cast iron, painted with aluminum paint to refract the sun. It was near a tree-bordered ravine, with decent privies at a distance. Like all the camps except one for Puerto Ricans, it was occupied by southern Negroes. One of the men told me that the owner was there every day inspecting the grounds. There was no litter; garbage and trash were neatly stored in bins. Clotheslines with freshly laundered clothes abounded, as they did in the meagerest camps. The camp leader's wife, a fine-looking woman, was doing her washing; another woman, on the steps of her home, was putting a beautiful baby to sleep; children were playing with tricycles.

Vastly different was another camp which we reached after a drive through the fat New Jersey countryside. It was tucked out of sight up a dirt road. There were two rows of blackened, forlorn shacks. Twenty people lived there. In the front sheds lived married people; the back sheds housed the unmarried men, the unmarried women, and one married couple. The floor of the unmarried men's room was so broken that there was a hole large enough "to break your leg in," as one of the tenants put it. "There's an awful lot of rats around," another remarked.

One handsome young woman in Copenhagen blue shorts had scrubbed her floor and had a clean spread. But the other rooms were dirty and cluttered, and the beds—with sagging mattresses and soiled and flimsy bedclothes—were the only furniture. Down a narrow path, overgrown with poison ivy, was the single privy for men and women, stinking and buzzing with flies.

Up on a small rise was a better four-room shack where the crew leader lived, and his handsome blue car was parked nearby.

It was shocking to come across this place in this opulent countryside. Yet even this was better than many camps had been before the New Jersey migrant law was passed. At least it had electricity; the well was covered; the garbage was in two big receptacles, although there was some dismal litter about. "Formerly garbage covered with flies rotted where it was thrown, the season round," one of our party told me, "and rats sometimes drowned in the open wells."

At another camp which we visited later—a larger one with about fifty people—the crew leader was gambling with the men and women of his crew. Piles of folding money had gravitated to him. At one side a large slot machine stood ready for use. He was a large, fleshy man, brutal and arrogant, who naturally took a dim view of our visit. As we left the gamblers, a drunken woman lurched after us; one of our party recognized her as a camp follower who had come from Trenton.

Life here was roaring. It was the most wide-open place I have ever seen in my travels—part saloon, part gambling joint—but worse, for here also were children, and there was no chance for the respectable crew members to get away from the all-pervading atmosphere of evil.

"I didn't sleep none last night—all them drunks shoutin' and yellin' an' tryin' to break into cabins," one woman complained.

The last camp we saw that day was in an old farmhouse, where there had been a bad fire. A gap in the wall had been filled by a slab of corrugated iron. No one was at home except three little children who showed us their downstairs room; it had a beautiful pillared fireplace, but the walls were blackened by smoke, and there were two double beds and two cots, dirty beyond any I have seen human beings occupy. And upstairs (where the children told us the single men lived) the walls were stuffed with cardboard where the plaster had fallen; there were piles of the insides of decayed mattresses, dirty double beds and a cot, and a small room or closet heaped high with rags and ancient bedding—an invitation to fire. It was as spectral as an Addams cartoon.

The camps we saw later with an inspector from the Migrant Bureau were reassuring. One of these—occupied by Puerto Ricans—was in a farmhouse beside a road. In one clean, well-swept room there were four cots. The mattress of each cot was rolled up neatly. On the bare springs of each cot lay a suitcase next to which was a well-polished pair of shoes. One might have thought that the room housed an army outfit, except that from the pegs on the wall hung workmen's clothes. This was a good example of a change for the better, for an attractive farmer's wife who lived in a big farmhouse nearby pointed to a blackened row of farm sheds that had formerly housed the workers.

In another camp, which housed about forty people, there was an outdoor communal kitchen with bright linoleum and tables under the trees. The crew leader's wife, a notable-looking Negro woman, told us, "My husband don't allow no drinkin' and no funny business here. He bounces 'em right out." The inspector remarked that the crew leader had to be a big, strong man to do that.

One of the largest farm factories of the Eastern states is the Seabrook Farms of New Jersey, which employs thousands of workers. It is among the few agricultural plants whose migratory workers are under union contract. Both the cannery workers and the farm workers have been organized, to the satisfaction of both management and workers, by Local 56 of the Meatcutters and Butchers A F of L. The relationship has been considered such a successful example of collective bargaining that reports of it have been used in various colleges and universities teaching the subject. This is the more noteworthy in that attempts to organize farm workers have been generally resisted, often with violence. Seabrook Farms has cooperated with the Home Missions Council and the state in maintaining clinics, nursery schools, recreation programs, and religious services.

There are some admirable camps in New York State too, for New York—spearheaded, as is New Jersey, by the Consumers' League—has done almost as much as New Jersey to ameliorate its migrant problem. Its interdepartmental Migrant Commission has almost the effect of the New Jersey Migrant Bureau, and it has outstripped New Jersey in its child-care centers and its suppression of child labor. Many communities have been zealous in helping migrants—notably Suffolk County, Long Island, which has a Migrant Farm Labor Committee appointed by the county board of supervisors.

At Cutchogue in Suffolk County I saw a big camp, run by the Potato Growers' Association, which can house four hundred people, though there were only three hundred living there at the time of my visit—in huts built by the Farm Security Administration (FSA). A grove of trees surrounding the settlement made it a pleasant place, and the old FSA huts furnished decent housing.

We went into the day nursery where children were sleeping in cots. At the infants' end a baby was being tended by the colored nurse in charge. Any child, it seemed to me, would have been delighted at the play material. I learned that soon the nursery would be transformed into a school, run by the county; that the place served for recreation in the evenings—radio, television, and so forth, and that divine service was held there on Sundays, with a Home Missions missionary officiating. The Council of Home Missions of the Churches of Christ first started the day nursery, as they have done in many other places.

Yet, even in Suffolk County, as in New Jersey, there are grim enough camps. Gone, as a result of the new laws, are the one-time tent colonies "whose smell would knock you down because people were dying of dysentery"; but even in the states with the best laws, right in the midst of prosperous communities, there remain rural slums which don't get the policing that ordinary slums do.

"The flight of human migrants is not as swift as that of birds, but their pattern of migration is almost as rigid," one observer has said. At present, the human flight would seem to be of less importance than the bird flight; while an appropriation of $6,000,000 for birds was under discussion not long ago, Senator Paul Douglas was ruled out of order when he proposed that $181,000 be diverted to assist the states in providing schooling for migrant children. Like the number of birds, the number of migrants has been only approximated. The nearest figure—including their families—seems to be about 2 million.

Mexico is the biggest reservoir of migrant labor, legal and illegal. Here we have a border 1,600 miles long and only 750 border patrolmen and immigration officers to guard it, who consequently, as they say, are "wallowing in illegal aliens." The "wetbacks," as they are called, pour across to the roughly estimated number of a million annually. "Getting rid of them is like shoveling sand against the tide," immigration officers say.

Surely this is a scandalous situation. While Ellis Island is corked tight as a bottle against anybody who is under suspicion of having a pale pink spot on his past, the Mexican border is a gaping wound in our security. This wide open and relatively unprotected frontier is an open door where Communists may enter unchecked. A short walk or a brief wade or swim when the Border Patrol isn't there, and they're in the United States.

It would profit the staunch congressional protectors of our borders to ponder the testimony of Archbishop Robert E. Lucey of San Antonio, Texas. He points out that while in 1944 there were fewer than 100,000 deportations and voluntary departures of Mexicans who had entered this country illegally, in 1950 there were—believe it or not—565,000. And for every Mexican who was deported, the guess is that from one to ten slipped through the wide-meshed net of the Border Patrol and Immigration Services.

What happens when these Mexicans slip across the border into the United States? They displace, in the labor market, a lot of American citizens, who thereupon migrate northward. In 1950, according to the Texas Employment Service, 90,000 Texas farm workers were counted at various points of exit to other states, and this count did not include their families. They were looking for work farther north, driven from home by the cheap Mexican labor, legal and illegal.

"While we were getting rid of 90,000 U.S. citizens . . . in 1950, we legally imported 51,000 aliens from Mexico, not to mention those who entered illegally," says the archbishop. "It does not make sense."

Incidentally, the Mexicans who entered the United States legally—190,000 of them in all, counting also those who were bound for states other than Texas—did so under legal contract (provided for by treaty) which provided for their wages, health, transportation, and housing; and there were over 500 U.S. Employment Service men working in Mexico, and public health doctors as well, supervising their exit. The cost to the American taxpayer has been estimated at $85 per immigrant—a cost which might be classed as a subsidy to the large employers of cheap labor. Puerto Ricans also come in under contracts which do not exist for workers born in the continental United States.

The illegal immigrants, the half-million or so wetbacks, have of course no protection. They are a wretched lot who must work for anything offered, even for a wage as low as twenty cents an hour, according to the President's Commission. They live anywhere—in the brush, in holes in riverbanks. Their water comes from ditches and canals where others wash clothes and dump waste; their babies die of dysentery, and they of TB and malaria and venereal diseases.

In a scholarly monograph on the wetback of the Lower Rio Grande, Sanders and Leonard have summed up his plight: "Being illegal, he can protest over nothing, small pay, uncertain employment over long hours; so his docility makes him as attractive as his low pay." And what a bonanza to farmers this low pay is! A farmer who produces fifty bales of cotton a year saves $1,000 by employing wetbacks, and the big farm factories which produce over 100,000 bales can really cash in.

No wonder, then, that a strong political bloc has developed to maintain the status quo, and that when the Immigration Service asked for adequate money to protect our borders, it got not one red cent from the House. The Senate granted it $1,000,000, but Public Law No. 78 so multiplied the administrative requirements surrounding the bringing in of legal Mexicans that the service got no good from the appropriation, as far as much-needed personnel were concerned.

For a short time, under the Farm Security Administration, there was a migrant program in the hands of people who really wished to do something and had authority to do it. Government-operated camps with decent housing, and with health and child services, were set up in the nineteen thirties to meet the needs of the Dust Bowl fugitives. The program was expanded in World War II; under the stress of wartime shortages, the FSA recruited, housed, and transported workers in orderly fashion. The number of people employed on some farms was decreased 50 percent through orderly procedure. There were as many as ninety-five labor camps for 75,000 workers. "We made a determined and realistic attack on this many-sided problem, and for the first time challenged the exploitation of agricultural labor," says Robert W. Hudgens, director of the American International Association for Economic and Social Development, and former associate administrator of FSA. "Here was something that was working; and when it got working well, then all at once it stopped."

What happened was that in 1943 the FSA program was turned over to another agency, and Public Law 45 was passed which gave it a $36,000,000 appropriation—under these restrictive terms:

> No funds shall be used directly or indirectly to fix, regulate, or impose minimum wages or housing standards, to regulate hours of work, or to impose or enforce collective bargaining requirements or union membership with regard to any agricultural worker, except with respect to workers imported into the United States from a foreign country, and then only to the extent necessary to comply with the agreements with the government of that foreign country.

The camps, still used during wartime, were then dismantled, the buildings were bought up by individual farmers, and the enormous saving of time and workers that these distribution centers had made possible was wiped out. And—despite the fact that in the opinion of many experts there is enough farm labor in this country—the wholesale importation of foreign labor began.

The situation is not without hope. In the first place, the widespread concern for migrants which culminated in the President's Commission on Migrant Labor, and in the comprehensive hearings of the subcommittee headed by Senator Humphrey, shows that a great many Americans feel guilty about the situation and want something done about it. In the second place, there is a rising interest in many states and localities, represented, for example, in the work of the Texas Good Neighbor Commission; in Wisconsin by the work of the Governor's Committee on Labor, which was preceded by the former Governor's Commission on Human Rights; and in Denver by the work of the Mayor's Commission on Human Relations.

California began employer camp inspection at least forty years ago. Since 1920 it has had migrant schools. Its child-care program is as good as any in the United States; and one should mention, too, the Governor's Committee to Survey the Agricultural Labor Resources of the San Joaquin Valley.

Applause should go in addition to the Consumers' League, especially that of New York and New Jersey, which printed a study of migrants as early as 1905, and has led the battle which has resulted in New Jersey's progressive laws. The Division of Home Missions, National Council of the Churches of Christ, has done signal work over the past twenty-five years. From Texas to Minnesota, from California to Delaware, there are communities that are coping with the problem as Freehold does.

Perhaps the most significant, because the most fundamental, gain is in the fact that associated groups of farm employers are beginning to take an interest in the fortunes of their migrant workers—pooling their alien contract labor to make better use of the available supply, and, here and there, giving guarantees to domestic labor comparable to those given to Mexicans and Puerto Ricans.

This is an important beginning as a sign of recognition that as American agriculture becomes industrialized, the migrant problem is essentially an industrial problem.

Instead of studying the management of labor as industry has done, the farmer industrialist, like his industrial counterpart of many years ago, imports cheap foreign labor without utilizing the pools of labor existing within the country. Many leaders of farm organizations are saying today just what the industrialists were saying in 1923: that American labor won't do the work. If they had their way, the seasonal labor would soon be largely composed of Mexicans, Puerto Ricans, Bahamians, and so forth.

The majority of farm organizations, and the farmers they represent, according to their own testimony before the President's Commission and in congressional hearings, appear to want cheap, docile, unorganized labor, and a big labor surplus. Their point of view is understandable. For the farmer is so harried by the vagaries of the weather and of insects, and the fly-by-night instability of his labor supply, and is so driven by the absolute necessity of getting his fruit and vegetables picked, or his harvesting done, at the optimum moment, that it seems essential to him to have men on hand, ready and waiting for the time when he will need them, without uncertainty and without palaver. The idea that these men might organize is a nightmare to him; he thinks it means dry cows, rotting fruit, spoiled crops, and bankruptcy. And on top of all this it seems outrageous to him to be beset by commissions composed—as one representative of a big farm organization put it—"of people totally ignorant of the subject they are investigating." Yet the fact remains that American agriculture is the most efficient in the world—except in securing its seasonal labor supply. That is why any sign of interest in solving the migrant problem by farmers themselves represents a step forward.

Yet despite these signs of promise and the good work done in a few localities, it would be misleading to say that more than a beginning has been made in solving the national problem of the migration of 2 million men, women, and children. We have hardly begun to face up to what needs to be done. What is needed is a bold plan for concerted action by federal authorities, state governments, and local communities. Such a plan was proposed by the President's Commission on Migratory Labor.

Proposed bills to carry out that plan were blocked in both houses last year. Their passage would have been a start toward improving the shameful condition of the migrants. But no such plan will be put into effect until we, the American people, realize that there is too much blood and disease and dirt on the food we eat and become indignant enough to demand that our migrant farm workers get treated like human beings.

# The Strike at Henderson, North Carolina

## Mary Heaton Vorse Papers, 1959

*After World War II the AFL and CIO launched organizing drives in the South, where in 1946 the textile industry was only about 20 percent organized as compared with about 70 percent in the North. The success of both drives was impeded by the jurisdictional rivalry between the AFL and CIO, and by the AFL's heated charges that the CIO was Communist-led. The concerted employer efforts to counteract unionization of Southern textile workers led to a great deal of violence against unionists and blacklisting of union members. The AFL terminated its southern organizing campaign in 1948 and the CIO gave up its southern drive in 1953. At the time of the 1955 AFL-CIO merger, there were over 1 million textile workers in the United States, with only 300,000 of these organized; over 500,000 of the unorganized were in the South.*

*The November 1958 strike by over 1,000 textile workers against the Harriet-Henderson mills in Henderson, North Carolina, was the largest strike in the twenty-four-year-old history of the Textile Workers' Union of America (TWUA). The TWUA considered the strike crucial to the success of its southern campaign. Violence began in February 1959, after the company hired enough strikebreakers to reopen the mills. The TWUA's southern vice-president was beaten outside his motel room, injured when his car was forced off the road, and finally indicted, along with seven other strike leaders, for conspiracy to destroy company property. All eight were convicted on highly suspect testimony and sentenced to terms from two to seven years. The strike effectively ended in 1960 and the union disappeared from Henderson.*

The shift in the Harriet-Henderson Mills was about to change. The long line of National Guardsmen stood with their backs to the road racing toward what should have been a picket line. There were only eight pickets. A veteran with a row of ribbons on his shirt carried a placard which said: DID WE FIGHT FOR THIS? I made for a bench in front of a small grocery store. Boyd Payton, Textile Workers Union of America (TWUA) Regional Director of the Carolinas, said, "That's inside the seventy-five-yard line. I hope they won't arrest you." For no one was allowed inside the line at change of shift.

There were two benches in front of the grocery store. The grocer's pretty young wife and some friends were sitting there watching the line of National Guardsmen holding their bayonetted guns.

One said, "It don't seem this can be happening to me."

"It seems like a bad dream, don't it?"

"Henderson won't ever be the same again."

I heard that echoed again and again. "Henderson won't seem the same again."

There were 400 National Guardsmen. Almost one for every two of the 900 strikers, 60 percent of whom were women.

The whistle blew. The strikebreakers left the mills in cars escorted by the National Guard, and the second shift went in.

A young mother said, "I suppose all these guards means they'll put the third shift on soon."

"Anytime now," the older woman said.

"What'll we do then?"

"Pray," said the older woman, smiling.

They do pray. They open and close their union meetings with prayer. They lead in prayer in their churches. Two things stand out: the massive power of the state that is used to crush the strike; the military and police forces; the courts, public officials, and the legislature—and the strikers' steadfastness and courage.

There is the flame of the labor movement. The flame ebbs, it fluctuates, it never goes out. In the spontaneous uprising of the textile workers of Lawrence, Massachusetts, it was present. It is this flame which leads forlorn hopes, wins victories against incredible odds—faith, courage, and beauty are its texture. When people are gathered together, when the individual is forgotten for the collective good, there is this quickening. Suddenly, the aspirations of some anonymous, lonely people have come together and formed the flame. The workers in Henderson are deeply religious people. Their devotion to the union has a religious quality. They are all members one of another. An older man expressed it when he said, "When they hurt one of us, they hurt all of us." He had invented again labor's old slogan: "An injury to one is an injury to all."

Without their steadfastness, without the unflinching determination, this could not be the historic struggle that it is.

The prosperous city of Henderson, North Carolina, and its kindly people are being wrecked by the longest and most turbulent textile strike in the history of the South. For twenty-five years, since the ill-fated general strike of 1934, there had been good will between management and workers. When the Textile Workers Union of America organized the Harriet-Henderson Mills in 1944, there was barely a ripple. The contract, with insignificant changes, was always renewed without dispute, always, that is, until last August.

On August 10 the workers voted to renew their contract. They didn't ask for a raise although they are among the lowest paid of industrial workers. They asked nothing. When the company refused to renew, they expected only small changes. Not until a week before the contract expired did the workers learn of the company's amazing about-face.

"Old Cooper came in and threw down the list of what he wanted and said, 'Let me know when you are ready to agree to that.' He didn't want a comma changed," a striker told a local reporter. What did he want? It amounted to wrecking the entire contract. The company proposed to change every clause in the contract—for the worse.

When the company refused to extend the contract on a day-to-day basis, as is usual while negotiations go on, the workers said, "The company's asking for a strike. They are forcing it on us."

So the mills shut down November 17. During the next weeks the company rejected every proposal the union made.

For three months the strikers lived off their own fat and on the groceries the TWUA distributed, lived through a meager Thanksgiving, Christmas, and New Year's. The only bright spots were the union meetings and the occasional mass meeting. The armory was crowded to capacity to hear officers like William Pollock, president of the union. He told them that "Henderson is a powder bag." And he was right.

Around St. Valentine's Day came the well-known "back-to-work" movement that has broken so many strikes. On February 13 an advertisement appeared in the papers inviting the former workers back to work and announcing the mills would open on February 16.

The strikers got a unique valentine from Judge William R. Bickell. It was a court order forbidding them to interfere with exits and entrances of the mill, or to assemble near motor vehicles hauling people going to work. It limited pickets to eight, standing seventy-five feet from the mill. Since then dozens of pickets have been arrested and given severe sentences for contempt of court.

On February 16 the mill opened. Guarded by 150 state police, 58 workers, going past the jeering picket lines, appeared. Most of them were related to the foremen and superintendents. Since then some former workers have gone in and as many have left.

At first, an effort was made to recruit local labor. It proved futile. On March 2, escorted by highway patrolmen, 300 strikebreakers, recruited from Halifax County, Virginia, and places outside of Vance County, entered the mill while the company and the local authorities clamored for the National Guard.

For three more weeks the strike went its tumultuous way. Of course, there was violence. The men and women on the picket lines saw the only thing they owned—their jobs—being taken from them by uncouth strikebreakers from another state.

Lieutenant R. R. Chadwick, the executive officer of Troop B of the state patrol and commandant of a special detail at Henderson, told the *New York Times* that there had been more than forty bombings since the strike began. "However, most took place in open fields or in the yards of workers' homes and caused only minor damage."

Strangely, only strikers were shot or beaten.

On February 23, late at night, Vice-President Boyd E. Payton, the union's Carolina director, was aroused by a knock on his door at the Henderson Hotel. He was left bloody and unconscious in his doorway.

Late in March there was a second attack on Payton. His car was stoned, the window broken and his head cut by occupants of a passing car. Both attacks on Payton bore the marks of a professional job by gangsters.

So did the latest attack in a small strike of 375 textile workers in Fitzgerald, Georgia. The victims of this outrage were TWUA Field Representative Frank Barker, and Frank Chupka, secretary-treasurer of the TWUA. They were dragged from their motel as Payton had been, and were slugged and slashed with knives.

There again the beating of union officials, happening in widely different places, found a pattern.

A local matter was the wounding of James A. Manning. Honorably discharged from the Air Force, Manning returned home to visit his parents—both strikers—and was shot so severely by a supervisor in the mills that he was hospitalized. A little boy was shot in the back. . . .

Thirty of the most outstanding women workers called on Governor Hodges asking him to close the mills as a sure way of keeping order.

Twenty women journeyed to Washington to tell their story to George Meany, president of the American Federation of Labor and Congress of Industrial Organizations (AFL-CIO), and to see their senators.

Suddenly they found they had friends everywhere. Textile workers from other states came making contributions. Other workers showed their solidarity not only in money. For example, a bakers' local baked their bread. There is a happy picture in a union paper of textile workers' daughters graduating from high school being dressed in their graduation dresses made for them by the International Ladies' Garment Workers' Union.

"We never dreamed we had so many friends."

Boyd E. Payton and Julius Gry share the leadership of the strike with the presidents of both locals, Luther Jackson and Charles Ranes. Each local appoints five members to attend strike meetings where the problem of the strike is discussed and the policy decided.

Payton, tall, soft-spoken, and gentle, wanted to be a minister. He makes the important daily broadcast of the strike progress. Both he and

Julius Gry came up from the ranks and are both southerners. Julius Gry has a lawyer's mind and specializes in contract matters. Negotiations take up much time.

Scores of workers were given severe sentences, out of keeping with the charges against them. One of my last memories was of a frightened boy who looked younger than his nineteen years, accompanied by his indignant mother. He had been sentenced to sixty days or *three years* parole for possession of pyrotechnics, in other words, a giant firecracker, illegal in North Carolina, while two strikebreakers whose car was full of guns, which they were about to carry into the mill, received only a suspended sentence.

The TWUA charged the company provoked the strike with malice aforethought and was "using a carefully planned formula to eliminate the union." This the company denied. The union filed charges of unfair labor practices against the company with the National Labor Relations Board (NLRB); the union filed a complaint with the U.S. Attorney in Raleigh, charging violations of the Anti-Strikebreaking Act. This forbids transportations of persons across the state line for the purpose of obstructing peaceful picketing or the right of employees to organize or bargain.

Finally, on March 24, Governor Luther L. Hodges called in representatives of the company and the workers. When the talks broke down, the mayor of Henderson asked for prayers in all the churches. The streets of Henderson were empty in a voluntary curfew. An anonymous citizens' committee watched for suspicious strangers or any suspicious doings, and cars abroad at that time were stopped and their reason for being out asked.

The picket lines continued, and the first word some babies spoke was "scab."

At last, on April 17, the tired governor announced triumphantly, "The company and the union have resolved their differences and have reached an agreement that is mutually satisfactory."

The church bells rang. The horns blew. People cheered. In the mill villages all the churches were open, and the workers streamed in to give thanks. There was dancing in the streets. The long anxious time of waiting was over. Henderson could again be the peaceful, friendly place it had always been.

The rejoicing wasn't for long. When the workers reported back to the mills they found only about thirty jobs available. The second shift had been already engaged and manned with strikebreakers although it had not yet been called in to work. Mr. John D. Cooper, Jr., said that he had engaged these people and felt bound to them.

Governor Hodges stated publicly that he had understood that the second shift was available. He begged Mr. Cooper not to inaugurate the second shift. Mr. Cooper replied that that would be "absolute surrender to force and violence." He agreed to put off the third shift.

The disillusionment of the strikers was complete. Some responded with anger, a few wept openly, but there was no wavering among the union members.

They were unbeaten.

On May 5, President William Pollock announced that the TWUA Executives Council had voted to set up a Harriet-Henderson strike fund and voted $100,000 to begin with.

George Meany, president of the AFL-CIO and the Executive Council, asked the support of the whole labor movement for the Harriet-Henderson strikers.

For this is not a local strike, or even a North Carolina strike. It is not even a textile strike alone. It concerns all organized labor in America. What is really being fought out at Henderson is whether the South can be organized.

On January 25, the Executive Council of the AFL-CIO, meeting in Puerto Rico, voted to underwrite "Operation Dixie." The goal: organization of the 800,000 unorganized factory workers in the South. That included the 500,000 textile workers, of which only 70,000 are now organized.

As Payton told a reporter, "If they break this strike, they've broken the union. And if they can break this union, they can break any union in America."

There are seven other textile companies in widely different parts of the South, belonging to different companies whose managements have demanded contract changes that are almost identical with the changes Cooper wants for the Harriet-Henderson mills.

There is one sure and well-tried method for breaking a strike. It is to call out the National Guard and import strikebreakers.

There is another way, a method being increasingly used, and almost foolproof. And that is to vote the union out, under cover of the law.

The labor-management relations act of 1947, popularly known as the Taft-Hartley Act, provides for what is called a decertification election.

It works like this. The union in the plant calls a strike. The owner replaces the strikers with strikebreakers. Then he goes to the National Labor Relations Board and petitions for an election, alleging that the union no longer represents a majority of his workers. The NLRB obligingly sets up an election to find out if this is so.

It always turns out to be so. For the quirk in the law is this: the strikebreakers can vote, but the strikers may not. In short, the law makes the strikers cut their own throats.

The O'Sullivan Rubber Company used that tactic on October 17, 1957, in Winchester, Virginia. It worked so beautifully that it has since been used successfully elsewhere to nip off locals of such powerful unions as the Steel Workers, Auto Workers, Amalgamated Clothing Workers, and the International Union of Electrical, Radio, and Machine Workers.

The cotton manufacturers evidently plan to eliminate the Textile Workers Union as a devastating blow at Operation Dixie before it can get off the ground.

## The Workers

Sunday, May 17, when the strike was six months old to a day, the president of Local 384, Luther Jackson, and his wife came home for a brief visit. His house had been shot up.

In the afternoon he came for me and drove me to his house. He took us into the bedroom to show us the course of the bullet. "This was done by someone who knew the house," he said. "Looking at this room you would have to get out of your car and fire beyond the the Norway spruce. He shot where the bed was. That slug had my number on it."

There was a continual stream of neighbors coming in to see where the house had been shot up.

The slug, an inch and a half long, had gone through the window frame, the metal bar of the venetian blind, and ricocheted off a hardwood bureau. Anyone lying in the bed might have been killed or wounded.

The talk turned to various shootings from the mill by the strikebreakers. "It seems as if they always use slugs. It was a slug that almost hit Lester Hedgepath's foot standing on the picket line. A shot came from the mill but took the kid off his shoe."

"My backyard's been shot into more than once," Esther Robeson contributed. Another neighbor said, "Blanche Lewis was sitting out on her porch and a slug made a dent in the side of the porch you could lay your finger in."

Mrs. Jackson said, "People in the houses opposite the mill have had to move their children to the back part of the house on account of the strike."

"Charlie Ranes, the president of my local, almost got hit with a slug, it zoomed so near him."

Luther Jackson said, "They are always 'phoning the officials and saying that we better leave town. I give them back as good as they send."

Edith Adams, secretary of Local 584, said, "I hate to answer the 'phone. You don't have a chance to sleep and hardly eat with so many fake telephone calls. They were jeering me—at half-past one they woke me up to jeer."

One of the strikers added: "They just 'phoned that today was my last day on earth."

. . . She is blond and has great distinction, but so worn out and so tired with her extra responsibility of distributing and keeping account of the payment of doctors' bills and utilities she is almost ill.

Equally tired is Esther Johnson, the secretary of local 578, with whom I went to church earlier, where I was made truly welcome as though I were an old friend happily returned. When we left church, Esther asked me to Sunday dinner. Her son was being transferred to the Pacific Coast and he was soon going overseas. He and his wife and their little boy had been here only for two days. This was his last day, and yet his mother cordially asked a stranger to share a few of his last hours with her. I couldn't accept. It was too great a gift. I knew she had been working without let-up in the union hall and had almost no time to spend with him.

I will not soon forget a former mill worker. During a rain I sheltered in her husband's grocery store, the kind of neighborhood store where children swarm after school to buy a nickel's worth of candy and joke with the proprietor.

She and her daughter-in-law, a magnificent brunette, had just come home from fishing in the lake, driven away by the rain.

"Don't you love little girls?" she said, fondly looking at some of the customers. "I like both kinds," I said, "both boys and girls."

"I dote on little girls, especially, for I only had boys—three of them. I did so hope I'd have a grandchild who was a girl but my daughter-in-law gone and has another boy. My boys are wonderful. I never could have kept on working at the mill—and I needed to in those days—but for them. You know those little fellows did all my housework. They cleaned up and they even did the washing."

"Of course we're for the strikers," she said. "My husband and I have both worked in the mill. We remember the long hours and poor pay. We know what the union has done for textile workers. Most everybody in North and South Henderson are for the strikers."

"And many more of the merchants in Henderson are for them," her husband interrupted. "But if you're in business you can't take sides too much. You might be boycotted by one side or the other. But everyone knows the mill workers didn't ask for nothing at all. And everyone can see the patrol carried right out of Henderson by the scabs. What people want to know that aren't strikers is, why did Mr. Cooper do as he did? We all liked him. We figure he must have taken bad advice."

The rain had stopped and I started to 'phone for a taxi, nothing would do but she must drive me herself to the union hall.

There I got into a talk with an elder woman, May Forsythe, at the South Henderson Union Hall. She was tall and straight. Her white hair was parted in the middle and drawn into a soft knot. As a girl she must have been a dazzling beauty, judging by her delicately small features and lovely complexion. As we went down the stairs, she said:

"Won't you visit me? I live right close by—"

Together we walked slowly over a rough path across lots. She said: "Wouldn't it be nice if we could have new bodies. We will some day, but I'd like mine right now, wouldn't you? Just to be able to do some of the things we used to do."

We went into her neat house with its pretty curtains. Like all the workers' houses that I saw, her house was tastefully furnished, and neat gardens surrounded it. People say, "Our homes may not look like right much from outside, but many people who live in the city of Henderson haven't as pretty homes as we have inside."

She introduced a high-school-age boy, "He can go to school—that's more than I could. I started work at the mill when I was nine. I've had eleven children and adopted two grandchildren!"

"When did you stop work?"

"I stopped on the first day of the strike."

She asked me to stay to supper but I had already promised to meet friends. I don't know how the name of the young couple came up who had recently gone back to work to the shame of their parents who were also both of them strikers.

"I couldn't do that, for then I'd be a traitor," she said, "and a traitor is something I hope never to be."

That is the spirit that has kept them together through all of the meager days—all the days of going without—without complaint, for complaints I never did hear. And that makes those workers with their strong spirit of unity an inspiration to all who see them.

Violence is the smallest part of a strike. Though the public never learns of the constructive side. During a strike men and women discover new talents for organizing relief, collecting and distributing food, and running their own finances.

### The Cost

The enigma of the Harriet-Henderson strike is Mr. John D. Cooper, Jr. Here was a man who for years got on well with the union. The workers respected and even loved him. Many are second-generation workers who worked for Mr. Cooper's father, who founded the mills over sixty years ago.

Mr. Cooper was considered a progressive employer. He testified in favor of the minimum wage and made it easy for the workers to buy their own homes, formerly owned by the company. He had classes in the mill teach the workers better methods of work. His yarn was the best on the market, and his workers took pride in their work. Like his father before him, who dropped in unannounced for a meal at the home of a worker, he had close relations with them. Even since the strike started, it is easy for a union secretary to have a talk with him on the phone.

The Harriet-Henderson Mills is a one-man show. Mr. John D. Cooper is it. He has no industrial relations expert to advise him and no public relations man either. He is both himself. He and his family are said to own 82 percent of the stock. The other stockholders are few.

"My people are good people," he says. "They have been misled and deceived by the union."

The workers say, "He's listened to those lawyers. He's old and sick and has taken bad advice." I have heard more than one worker say, "I pray for him every night." Even now he will not admit that he does not wish the workers to belong to a union.

He told Payton, "I know exactly where I'm going and am prepared to take full responsibility for my actions. I will operate with my kind of a contract. If I can't do this, I will operate without a contract. If I can't do either, I will liquidate the mills."

Apparently, this sharp-eyed, pleasant spoken, sixty-year-old man with his dry sense of humor came slowly to his irrevocable resolution to pull the teeth of the union.

He told me that for ten years he had had no quarrel with the union. He said he felt before the last contract was signed that the arbitration clause had been "eroded" and had no meaning, a phrase he has used quite often.

This canny man of Scots ancestry told Richard J. Whelan, associate editor of the conservative *Richmond New Leader,* that the "abuse" of the arbitration clause was the reason he wanted it out of the contract. "The college professors who arbitrate the contracts were steadily eroding the meaning of the contract," he said.

However, of the nearly 200 grievances taken up in the fourteen years of the union's life, only 25 have gone to arbitration, and the company won as many as it lost. So this cannot be the reason for locking out one's trusted workers. It is not strange that the workers think it is the union itself that Mr. Cooper is out to destroy.

Mr. Whelan calls the arbitration clause the "peak of the iceberg as far as the union is concerned." For Mr. Cooper told him: "From the beginning the union has tried to drive a wedge between the workers and management. Anyone reasonable knows that the people who work in a plant are dependent on the plant for their security, not on the promises of the union."

There is the heart of the matter. He feels rejected. His workers have deserted him for the union. Therefore, he is willing to "close the doors of the mill and keep them closed."

But if he feels betrayed, so do the workers. Each side thinks the other was misled by evil counselors.

Mr. Cooper always preserves the amenities. He always shakes Boyd Payton's hand when he leaves and seems unruffled by anything Mr. Payton may have said about him in his daily broadcast about the strike.

Occasionally though, he shows his inner grievance, as when he said: "If the union is so important to these people, let them collect their dues themselves. Let them strike if they want to. But don't let them tell me how to run my mills."

To have the kind of contract he wants, he is ready to pay any price.

The price paid by the town is too great to be measured. The cost to the state is fantastic. And the end is not in sight.

Adjutant General Capus Waynick has said the cost to the state is $42,000 a week. That doesn't count what the U.S. government has spent. The state legislature appropriated $175,000 to keep the National Guard in Henderson until November. Before the guard came, 150 of the state patrol had been added to the normal small force. Their cost was high in money—far more in loss of life. Pressure had been brought on Governor Hodges to return them to their natural duties of patroling North Carolina roads instead of guarding strikebreakers. The total accidents and deaths had risen tremendously; 102 people had been killed on North Carolina's roads where Virginia had suffered the loss of only 6.

There were also expenses to Henderson besides the armed forces of an Office of Special Investigators which was set up. It has been estimated that the community and state have probably spent more than the payroll of the mills, which was $3 million a year. The workers to date have lost more than that.

The mill is now working at full capacity of all shifts, but what the strikebreakers make goes out of the town, most of it out of Vance County, and quite a little to Virginia.

Until recently the workers got only food as strike aid. That cost the union $7,500 a week. On May 2 the Harriet-Henderson Strike Fund was set up. Utilities, medical expenses, and some payments are being made by the union. It is impossible to say what the cost has been to the company in loss of contracts and other leases. These money losses are high.

But other costs are important. These are the imponderables. Newspaper accounts, so often exaggerated, and sometimes false, always speak of Henderson as a strife-torn town. On the surface, a stranger would not notice that anything had happened. However, a very important thing has happened.

The social fabric of the city has been torn to pieces. The population has lost the peaceful feeling that was one of the great attributes of the town. It is not only the strikers who say that Henderson will never be the same.

Mill mothers are now separated from their well-to-do fellow townsmen by a unbridgeable gulf. The latter naturally sympathize with management.

In the mill villages the situation is worse. Parents are ashamed of their children who want to work and become that shameful thing—a scab. The basic quarrel is everywhere. It has penetrated the churches and poisoned the schools. It has sundered old friendships.

Revolution has come to the peaceful, friendly town. The workers felt invaded and despoiled by the strikebreakers who have thieved their jobs. Many are divided between two loyalties, like the police force; almost without exception the police have relatives among the strikers.

Talking one day with a striker I said, "I feel sorry for everyone. I'm sorry for the strikers and for the merchants and for the whole town."

She nodded heavily and replied: "The one I'm sorriest for is Mr. Cooper. He was surrounded by the love and respect of his workers like a garment and he trampled it underfoot. I pray for him every night."

# Women's Lives

# The Quiet Woman
## *The Atlantic Monthly, 1907*

The dusk was wiping out the colors of the world, spreading over the tender greens and pale pinks an indefinite nameless color more beautiful than any we know. The apple trees loomed up, great masses of bloom, and their sweetness drifted to Katherine mingled with the smell of young leaves and spring—it was as if all the souls of the myriad growing things had breathed themselves forth into the night.

The dusk deepened and then grew blonder; the moon was coming up. One could see again that the trees were green, one could see the small flowers in the lawn. The white trees cast deep shadows on the young grass. Everything was very still; Katherine thought that the beating of her own heart was too loud for the miracle of the night. Everything—the trees and sky and hills—gave her the sense that something wonderful was about to happen; surely they were only the setting for some greater miracle. Then there came over her an appalling sense of desolation. It was terrible that on this most lovely night she must be so alone; that there should be no kind hand anywhere to meet hers. Katherine's need of companionship grew more poignant; the beauty of the night weighed on her as too great a burden to be borne alone; but she listened in vain for the sound of a human voice mingled with the voices of the night. The neighboring houses turned blank, unlighted faces to her; Katherine was as solitary as if she had been adrift on some unknown sea.

Then, in the garden on the slope of the hill below a white shadow moved; it flitted about, unsubstantial, unreal, now stopping as if to look at the night, now moving on slowly, then lost to sight among the flower-laden shrubs. At last it stood out in a little open space, attentive, even reverent, in its attitude. Without realizing what she did, Katherine trailed through the wet grass toward the motionless figure, her shawl hanging loose around her; it was as if one white spirit went forth to meet another like itself. She made her way through the loosely planted shrubbery which divided one garden from the other, and was near the other women before she turned her head toward Katherine. She greeted Katherine quietly as if she had been waiting for her. They stood a moment in silence, then the woman said:

"I could not have stayed out here alone—" she stopped shyly and turned toward Katherine to see if she were understood, and Katherine wondered if here was some one as terribly alone as herself, as in need as she of sympathy. They looked at the night together, as silent as old friends who do not need to talk to one another; they did not know each other's names, and yet already they had ceased to be strangers; the fellowship of spring had brought them together.

A voice called from somewhere beyond a screen of white apple trees, a man's voice, gay, mocking, jovial: "Mother! mother! Where are you? Mother, you'll be *moonstruck*."

The woman turned gravely to Katherine.

"My son is calling me," she told her. "Good-night, I am glad you came." Then she added wistfully, "This is the first time in many years that I have had a friend by me as I looked at the night."

With the sound of the man's voice and his gay, chaffing "Mother, you'll be *moonstruck*," the mirage of the night had vanished; the frail, subtle tie that a moment before seemed to bind the two women into friendship had snapped. They hurried their several ways, a little ashamed of themselves—for what, they didn't know exactly.

Next morning, when Katherine came out, there was a woman working in the garden below. Kathering had no doubt that it was her friend of the moonlight and made her way toward her.

"I am your new neighbor, Katherine Paine," she said.

The older woman smiled at her, greeting her in silence; but it was a silence with a more enfolding welcome than any words Katherine had ever heard, and she knew that they had gone on with their friendship begun so oddly the night before, for all they ignored their first meeting as something too apart from the ordinary events of life to be discussed in broad daylight.

They walked several paces through the lovely garden before the older woman said, "I don't know whether you know my name or not— it's Eunice Gaunt." Her voice had none of the New England aggressiveness; it was indeed singularly sweet; it had a shy little note of hesitation very charming to listen to; and she chatted away about her garden as if to an old friend.

From the house there came the same jovial voice of the night before: "Mother, mother! Oh, there you are!" and a man swung down the path. He stared at Katherine in a way that was just short of disconcerting. It was almost as if he had said, "Yes, on the whole, I think you're a very pretty girl." He looked bold, stubborn, domineering; but one forgave him all that—there was a large gaiety about him that went to one's heart. As he put his hand on his mother's shoulder with an air of assured ownership, it flashed over Katherine that all the same this dark bold man was an odd sort of son for the delicate, sweet little lady to have mothered.

She was saying, "This is our new neighbor, Miss Paine—"

"Mr. Gaunt?" Katherine murmured in acknowledgment of his formal greeting.

"His name is Wetherill," Eunice Gaunt corrected tranquilly.

"Why in the world did you think my name was Gaunt?" he demanded. The stand-and-deliver tone of his question and the little lurking amusement in his voice embarrassed Katherine; before she could answer, his mother explained:

"I told her my name was Eunice Gaunt—and so of course—"

He burst out into loud, gay laughter. "Couldn't you," he asked, "for respectability's sake, add a 'Wetherill'?"

Mrs. Wetherill smiled gently at him. She seemed to have abstracted herself from the scene; it was as if she had actually walked away from them and left them together alone, as she replied, "I think of myself, I suppose, as 'Eunice Gaunt.'"

"She's only had forty years to get used to 'Wetherill,' Miss Paine." He turned a humorous eye on his mother, who kneeled down to examine a plant; she had ceased to have any connection with them.

"Well," said Wetherill, "I must go. I'm delighted to have met you, Miss Paine; it's nice you're our near neighbor. I'm especially glad that you and my mother have made friends so soon. Good-bye. Good-bye 'Eunice Gaunt.' Please don't work too hard." He bent over her and drew her toward him. "*Promise* me you won't work too hard.—She does a man's work in this garden every day, Miss Paine.—You'll go in and lie down like a good girl, yes? and you'll call Ezra if you've anything heavy to lift, yes?" He kissed his mother, and with a pleasant nod to Katherine, was off.

"Come," Mrs. Wetherill said, "I want you to see my daffodil border under the hedge." She took up the conversation where her son had broken it, quite as if he had not been there at all. "Do you mind my asking you," she continued, "what wind blew you here?"

"I always took care of my mother," Katherine answered; "she had been ailing for years. She died not long ago—and I wanted a quiet place to rest."

Katherine had told the whole story of her uneventful life. It had left her at twenty-six with the eyes of a young girl.

For a moment Mrs. Wetherill looked at Katherine kindly, sweetly, as a sister might. Then, as if brooding over what she read in the girl's face, "How we eat up one another's lives!" she said.

Katherine had gone out that morning with an empty heart, and she came back with it filled. "Eunice Gaunt" had some way taken her in, opened the door of her heart to her; and Katherine wondered how she had passed by all the boundaries of reserve. She wondered again, as she had the night before, if her friend was perhaps as lonely as she; if, like herself, she needed so greatly the touch of a friendly hand; then she put that from her as absurd; there was a spiritual quality about the older woman, a sweet content that made the idea of her needing anything impossible, and companionship least of all.

Katherine had rented the house for the summer from an old friend of her mother's; so during the first few weeks of her stay a procession of ladies came to call, as they had evidently been asked to do by the owner of the house.

Mrs. Carling was the first to put the inevitable question, "How do you like Thornton?"

"Very much," Katherine answered, and added that she found her neighbor charming.

"Your neighbor?" Mrs. Carling wondered.

"Mrs. Wetherill," Katherine explained.

"Why, has *she* been up here?" asked the other.

"She 'runs in,'" said Katherine; "I think I 'ran in' first"; and Mrs. Carling gave forth an astonished, "Well, well!" To Katherine's look of inquiry, she explained, "She's a very quiet woman and rarely goes anywhere, and when she does—never a word out of her! Not a bit like her son. Henry's sociable enough."

She went way, leaving Katherine with the impression that Mrs. Wetherill's "running in" on her, which she had so taken as a matter of course, was for Mrs. Wetherill something very much out of the common. The other ladies of the village, as they called one after another, made this certain. The news of Mrs. Wetherill's neighborliness had gone forth, had been discussed, it was evident; and Katherine became very well acquainted with two people whom she amused herself by calling Mrs. Wetherill and Eunice Gaunt. One she knew only by hearsay. She was a silent woman, but so kindly that in the hard little New England village she was well beloved. Though she was no recluse and attended club meetings, doing her share of work in the village, she seldom opened her lips; and as for strangers—why, Mrs. Wetherill never went to see *them.* Of Mrs. Wetherill, Katherine was sure that she had never had so much as a glimpse; she couldn't in the least identify her with Eunice Gaunt. Eunice Gaunt, for all her shy, hesitating manner, had plenty to say—to Katherine anyway; companionship with her had a significance far beyond any companionship Katherine ever had. There was a certain freshness to all her words, as if her very silence had kept her mind young. Her thoughts came out clear and shining, minted quite fresh. How different the two, the Mrs. Wetherill of Thornton and her friend Eunice Gaunt were, Katherine could gauge by the curiosity their friendship excited. How alone Eunice Gaunt had been, she saw only too plainly by the subdued, almost tremulous eagerness with which she gave Katherine her friendship.

She couldn't help wondering why her friend was shut so closely in the house of herself—Eunice Gaunt couldn't indeed have been more separated from the world around her had there been question of locks and keys.

"The house of herself," was Eunice Gaunt's own word.

"We all of us keep the real 'me' locked up in the house of ourself," she had said once to Katherine. "Sometimes it is self-consciousness that turns the key, and sometimes shyness, and more often circumstances." Then she added wistfully, "Some happy people come in and out at will." They walked side by side toward the little wood. Then Eunice Gaunt put her hand on the younger woman's with an indescribable gesture of tenderness. "You open the door for me, my dear," she said.

They stood face to face, silent in the contentment of perfect understanding, and Katherine went home, to wonder again why this loving, lovable woman should live so aloof from her fellows. How aloof this was, she found out the first time they went out together; it was a party at Mrs. Carling's, and not only, as Mrs. Carling said, was there "not a word out of Mrs. Wetherill," but no promise of words or anything else. A diffident, smiling little old lady was all she seemed, who, as Mrs. Carling had put it, "wouldn't say 'Boo' to a goose"; one would as soon have expected treasures of companionship and understanding from the tufted chair on which she was sitting. As they left the house Henry Wetherill joined them.

"Well, mother," he chaffed, "did you tell them how to raise strawberries as good as yours?"—and without waiting for an answer, "Mother, you know," he explained, "is forever telling people how to raise things like hers; but *I* always have thought she was like the housekeepers who leave out the important thing when they give away their recipes."

There was a little edge of patronizing sarcasm in his tone, a mere suggestion only, so imperceptible that Katherine thought she must be mistaken. Mrs. Wetherill hadn't noticed it. She smiled absently at her son, and absently she left on Katherine the burden of keeping up a conversation—which she did not unwillingly. She liked Henry Wetherill, even if his abrupt way of asking questions disconcerted her to dumbness.

Mrs. Wetherill turned in at her own gate, saying good-bye to Katherine with the same gentle formality she had shown in taking leave of the other ladies.

"I'll walk over with Miss Paine," Henry announced; and Mrs. Wetherill replied with a smiling, aloof, "Very well, dear," and "Good-bye, Katherine."

Once at Katherine's gate, "I think I'll come up and sit on your piazza," he said, "if you'll let me, I mean." He might have been asking permission smilingly of a child of twelve. He arranged himself comfortably in a big piazza chair, and from his attitude a passer-by would have gathered that he was a daily visitor, so much at home he seemed.

He stared at Katherine in his embarrassing way; and when she felt herself flushing and caught a twinkle of a smile in his eyes, she had an unreasoning impulse to run away and lock the door in the face of this man, who stared one into self-consciousness and then smiled tolerantly over one's confusion.

There was, however, no hint of the smile in his voice as he said, "You don't know how glad I am that you and mother are such friends. I'm like my father; I hate a gadding, gossiping woman; but I think mother goes too far the other way."

Katherine warmed to him over his concern for his mother, and for a while they chatted together. To Katherine's shy invitation to come again, "As often as you like," he answered warmly.

When he left, Katherine felt that her house was empty, his large radiant personality had so filled it. This was not to be the last she saw of him that day. Later, as she made her way through the shrubbery in search of his mother, she heard Wetherill's voice saying, "Why don't you put them where Mrs. Wetherill told you to?"

His voice was not raised beyond his usual tone, but it cut like a knife. One couldn't call it bullying; it was a finer and more wounding way of getting what one wanted. "Why"—he continued in exactly the same pitch—"don't you answer me?"

Katherine knew he could continue indefinitely on the same insulting key. Through the bushes she could see the old gardener grubbing away at a flowerbed, Wetherill standing over him. While the old man did not answer or pause in his work, every outline of his old, bent figure expressed indignant protest. Mrs. Wetherill stood a few paces distant, trowel in hand; she was gazing off at the distant horizon, calm-browed, apparently unconscious of everything around her.

"*Why* didn't you put them where you were told? You think you know everything about a garden—but you're here, aren't you, to do what Mrs. Wetherill says?"

Katherine had gained the open lawn and was only a few steps away from her friends.

"Why—" Henry began again.

The old man jumped to his feet, his brown face red under the tan.

"I *be* doin' what she told me," he cried angrily. Then, appealing to Mrs. Wetherill, "Ain't I settin' them plants where you said?"

It seemed to Katherine that Mrs. Wetherill brought herself back as from a distance, and that it was an effort for her to realize what was going on.

"Why of course you are, Ezra," she answered, "why not?" She

looked with surprise at the angry faces of the two men; then she saw Katherine. "Why, my dear child," she cried joyously, and stopped herself abruptly.

"Do you mind telling me," Henry asked his mother politely, "why in the world you let me sail into Ezra as I've been doing on your behalf, when after all he was doing what you said?"

She looked at him mildly. "I didn't hear what you were saying, Henry," she replied. Henry threw out his hands despairingly.

"Did you ever see such a pair, Miss Paine? I was perfectly sure Ezra was planting those roses where I heard mother tell him not to. I go for him loud enough to be heard across the street, and there she stands and, perfectly unruffled, lets me maul him. Actually she hasn't heard a word!"

He turned to his mother. "Where were you anyway? I never saw such an absent-minded woman! I talk and talk to her and I might as well be at the other side of a plate-glass window. Ezra, you old fool, why didn't you tell me sooner?"

Henry was entirely restored to good humor now, and his question to Ezra was almost an apology; but the old man did not answer or take any notice of him beyond hunching an offish shoulder.

"Look at them, Miss Paine," Henry exclaimed. "They never speak! Sometimes I think I'll buy a parrot for company!" He had put a large arm around his mother's neck and lifted her face up toward him like a child's. "Why don't you listen when I talk to you?" he demanded with savage affection.

"You're so like your father, dear," she replied irrelevantly.

Henry Wetherill hastened to fulfill his promise of coming often to see Katherine. Indeed he formed a pleasant habit of "dropping in" for a few moments' chat, and while he was there he would not take his eyes from her. She resented this at first; in the end she liked it, in much the fearsome way she liked Henry Wetherill. She was filled with a sense of excitement when she was with him. Conversation with him was an adventure. She could never tell when he would swoop down on her and extinguish her. What he did to give her this impression she could not for the life of her have told; but with him she felt she had to fight for her life or cease to be; the irritating part of it was that he was largely and serenely unaware of the effect he produced, and it is a humiliating thing to be fighting for life with a force which doesn't even realize that there is a fight.

So, between her companionship with the mother and her friendship with the son—for that, in spite of everything, was what it was coming to be—Katherine found her life very full. She turned her face resolutely from that blank time when she would have to go away—after her tenancy had finished there was really no good excuse to keep her in a snowbound New England village—and when one day Henry Wetherill abruptly asked her what her plans for the winter were, she told him promptly, "Oh, I'll go south, I suppose."

At that moment Mrs. Carling came in, and when, in a few minutes, Henry Wetherill left, Mrs. Carling hardly waited for his broad shoulders to be turned before she raised significant eyebrows at Katherine, and followed it up with a surprised, "Well, you *have* done it—to be sure!"

"Done it!" Katherine wondered.

"Mother and son both! Well I declare," her visitor pursued with relish.

Evenly, but with inward annoyance, Katherine turned the subject. Mrs. Carling, however, had given her a clue to something that had mystified her. For the past few weeks Henry's mother, in some indescribable fashion, had seemed to slip away from her. There had been nothing one could put one's finger on; one could only say in the good old phrase that "things were different." There had been a mute appeal in her friend's eyes that Katherine now thought she understood.

"I must stop his coming here so much," Katherine decided; but in the bottom of her heart she knew how powerless she was to stop Henry Wetherill in anything that he wanted to do.

As he came up the path next day Katherine noticed that his brows were drawn in a somber line. But as he saw her on the piazza waiting for him, he smiled at her brilliantly, and Katherine felt as if the sun had come out in the midst of a thunderstorm.

"Do you know," he began without preamble, his eyes looking directly into hers, "what I was thinking about when I came up the walk? I was wondering what would become of us all when you went. You don't know, I suppose, what you mean to me—I'm as lonely in a way as mother. Until you came I didn't know there was any other way to be—" He faltered a moment; and there was something very appealing in his hesitation: after all, he needed companionship and affection as do the weaker people of the world, and this touched Katherine to the quick. They stood facing each other, troubled and embarrassed, Katherine's heart beating fast. Now she knew: yesterday's absurdity had become the reality of today.

"You see how it is—you can't go away; you mustn't. I've *got* to have you." Then, as Katherine would have spoken, for it seemed to her that for all his tone of eager pleading she was being swept down the swiftflowing stream of his desire, and she wanted very much to tell him the truth, which was that she didn't love him in the very least, he stopped her.

"I know what you want to say. You want to tell me you don't care for me. I know that. But you don't hate me—you like me even, and after we're married I'd be a poor sort of a fellow if I couldn't make you care."

*He* cared; that was the principal thing after all, his manner seemed to say.

"It's all so right, don't you see," he pleaded eagerly. "You so belong to us."

The "It's all so right" was what won her. What if she didn't love him? It *was* all so right. The "us" touched her too. His constant thought for his mother was one of the things that drew her most to him.

"How would your mother feel about it?" Katherine asked shyly.

His mother's attitude in the matter had evidently never occurred to him. He looked at her blankly. "Why shouldn't she like it?" he demanded with a touch of anger. It was as if he had said, "Let her not like it and she'll see what she'll get"; and the little vague terror that he had given her from the first came over her; but it vanished as he laughed his loud boyish laugh.

"What an idea!" he shouted; "why, I can't remember mother's not liking anything I've done since I was grown up. She likes *everything* I do," he repeated with serene assurance. "What made you think she wouldn't like it, my marrying you?" he persisted.

"Why, it's seemed to me that the more I saw of you the less I saw of her; the better I got to know you the more she withdrew herself," Katherine faltered.

He looked at her, a tender glow in his eyes. "Don't worry about that," he assured her lightly. "Mother's only part there most of the time; she's the most absent-minded woman in the world—always in the clouds."

And Katherine forbore telling him how much "Eunice Gaunt" was "there" when her son wasn't. He evidently was not aware of her curious smiling aloofness. Katherine longed to ask him if he never got behind it, never saw the other side; but she only insisted, "I don't think she'll like it."

"What a funny girl you are," he said, smiling. "We'll find mother and ask her, and then—"

"And then," Katherine interrupted, "if she doesn't like it—I love her so dearly I couldn't for the world—"

"You'll see," Henry Wetherill repeated. There was not a shadow of doubt in him; if there was anything he was sure of, it was his mother.

They found Mrs. Wetherill in the garden. "Mother," he called to her joyously, "this foolish girl thinks you wouldn't like me to marry her." His tone was gay, happy, assured. There was a certain finality in it also, as if she already belonged to him, as he added, "Tell her you think she'll be a good wife to me."

For a fraction of a second, Mrs. Wetherill stared at them wide-eyed. Then, "She would make the best wife in the world for anyone," she cried warmly, and kissed Katherine.

"You see," Henry triumphed, and Katherine wondered if he actually had not noticed that his mother had turned white at his words; if he could not see how her hands trembled as she smiled her little vague smile at him.

"I'll leave you to talk things over," he told them. Mrs. Wetherill stood watching him until he disappeared beyond the tawny lilies into the house.

"Now tell me the truth," Katherine said gently, taking both her friend's hands in her own.

Mrs. Wetherill raised her troubled, somber face to hers; her mouth quivered pitifully; slow tears gathered in her eyes.

"You don't need to say anything," Katherine went on still more tenderly, "I can understand. He's your only son—"

But as Henry Wetherill's mother whispered under her breath, "Oh, I can't live it all over again," Katherine understood that here was more than a mother who finds it hard to give up her dear son.

"You're so near me," Mrs. Wetherill went on, so low that it was as if she were afraid to hear her own words, "that I can't let you suffer what you would have to. You're so near me that you seem to me like my own child—"

In this moment they passed beyond the door of friendship. They stood for the moment closer than it is often possible for one human being to come to another. They were at the very threshold of Eunice Gaunt's hidden life. For Katherine's sake she had opened a door that such women keep closed even against themselves.

"I hoped," she went on, "that you would see for yourself—you see so many things other people don't—"

"You don't think I'd be happy with Henry," Katherine suggested gently. She was beginning to read the riddle of her friend's life—her curious relation with her son, her attitude toward the world began to have a new meaning.

"Men like Henry don't know how they hurt women like us," Henry's mother said gently. It was an apology, not an accusation. "Henry's like his father," she went on in the same gentle tone. "All the Wetherill men are alike. They crush the weaker people around them out of existence; they don't mean to; they don't even know they do it." While she told what her son was, she had to cry out in the same breath, "It's not his fault." With a gesture of unfathomable motherliness, as if Katherine was really her daughter, she put her hand on the girl's head and gazed long into her eyes.

"My dear," she asked, "do you *love* Henry? Your face is the face of a little girl, as it was when I first saw you—"

"He said," Katherine faltered, "that it didn't matter, that he would make me like him."

"Poor Henry," said his mother; "if you had loved him—there

wouldn't have been anything to say. I should have lived over through
you all that has been hard in my life. It would have been like having my
own at war with my own. I should have had to know that no day of
yours went by without its humiliation, without its bruise. I should have
known that it was my son's fault. He couldn't help doing it, and you
couldn't help him. You would try and try, and then you would see that
neither patience nor submission nor love could change him."

All the things Katherine had failed to understand fitted in together
like parts of a puzzle. Now she knew why her friend was as she was.
Henry's father and Henry had shut her into the "house of herself" with
their noisy wounding anger, with their wounding laughter. She had a
sharp vision of Henry's bullying tenderness, of his mocking laugh, of
the glimpse she had had of his insatiable irritation; and a fear of him
came over her, the fear of the weaker animal for the stronger. She
meditated over what she saw, and Eunice brooded over her own past;
at last she cried out—it was her only moment of bitterness—

"They are the men with no woman in them. They are the ones who
first created our meannesses and weaknesses and then laughed and
scolded and sneered at us for being as they made us." Her voice
softened. "They can't help themselves for their unconscious abuse of
power," she said.

This was her final judgment of the two men who had made up her
life—her husband and her son. It was her only revolt, her only outward sign of discontent. Now she stood upright, as immovable as a
figure of justice, and in her Katherine saw more than a woman telling
the long tragedy of her life. It was as if through the voice of her friend
she heard the immemorial cry of all the weaker creatures who have
suffered through the strong. Without passion or anger she put in words
woman's world-old quarrel with man. Bits of it would come to
Katherine long afterward.

"They are the sort of men who make cowards and liars of women,"
was one.

"I understood the meannesses of women when I had been married a
few years."

"Often I have seen on a woman's face a look of anger or fear or
cunning, and I knew that here was another of me. There are more of us
than you think, and we use in self-defense guile, or flattery, or affection, or submission, according to our natures."

"There are few women who haven't been sneered at and reproached
for being women."

She told her story, a few sentences at a time; and unconsciously she
showed Katherine her final victory, her acceptance of life as it was, the
conquest of her own inward peace. She told how she had borne their
unconscious brutality, first with tears, then with smiling aloofness; her

road to escape had been a withdrawal from them and from everyone, for she had left no point where they could hurt her.

"How did you bear it all?" Katherine asked at last.

Her friend looked at her in gentle surprise. "I loved both of them dearly always," she said. "And I knew they loved me even more dearly. Love goes deeper than understanding. We've lived our lives, Henry and Henry's father and I, talking different languages; but I have always been upheld by their love for me and, curiously enough, by their dependence on me. If you—had cared—" she did not finish, but smiled at Katherine, all tenderness in her eyes. Then Katherine knew that the secret of her inner content was more than self-mastery; she had always had them, whatever else had been lacking; mysteriously they had made up to her for all the pain they had all unconsciously given her.

She had no time to answer, for Henry was bearing down on them, gay and confident. At the two women's serious aspect, "Well?" he asked, raising his eyebrows in question.

"I have been telling Katherine not to marry you," his mother said steadily.

He stared aghast. "You have been telling her *what?*" he repeated; his tone was low, there was in every word the concentration of anger. "What does she mean?" he demanded of Katherine. "Answer me."

"There's no use asking her," Mrs. Wetherill told him simply. "I'm sorry, Henry, I had to do it. You could never have made Katherine happy."

She had told him everything he could understand.

"Let her speak for herself," Wetherill commanded sternly. "Katherine, will you marry me?" The entreaty in his voice, his anger, his very lack of understanding, went to Katherine's heart. She was nearer loving him that moment than she had ever been. Had they been alone she realized that she must have promised whatever he wished— and then run away. With her friend's protecting arm around her she managed to falter forth,

"No, oh no!"

He turned on his mother.

"You've made mischief between us!" Anger vibrated in his low voice. "You've dared, *you, you,* to judge whether I could make her happy! *You* know whether this means anything to me! *You* know whether I've ever cared for any one else. The first woman I care for—Oh!"—he was white with the rage and despair of it. The creature on earth he loved most had turned on him, treacherously. His world had gone to pieces under his feet, and he raged at it. It was the man's side of it, old as time; and like the first man betrayed by his faithful servant, he raged against the faithlessness of women.

There was nothing mean in his anger; it didn't occur to him to try and control it because of Katherine; such as he was he showed himself. He resorted to no trick of gentleness to win her. Like his kind, he had got everything through the brute force of his will, as his ancestors had got everything by might of arm. If all the protest of women from all time against the unconscious abuse of power had been his mother's story, all man's rancor against woman was in his denunciation. As his anger spent itself, he stood before the two women in very despair at his impotence. He didn't understand them; he didn't understand anything. There was not one of the many questions he put himself that he could answer. His own had turned on him. Why? He couldn't tell. The woman he loved had all but given herself to him, and then turned from him. Why? He didn't know. All he knew was the common knowledge of the men of his kind, that women were the enemies of men, creatures one couldn't understand, moved by irrational impulse, untrustworthy and fickle. And as his mother watched him she understood, she trembled for him in a very anguish of pity. He stood before them, a tragic, lonely figure, suffering as a child suffers without knowing why; then he turned from them abruptly and left them. Katherine threw her arms around her friend.

"You shan't stand it," she cried. "Come away with me. You mustn't live with him any longer."

But Eunice Gaunt did not hear her. She watched Henry out of sight while slow tears gathered in her eyes. She breathed so low that Katherine barely heard her, "Oh, my poor son!" and again "My poor son!" and then, "Oh, how could I hurt you so much?"

# The Women at Armageddon

## *Metropolitan, 1913*

*The International Woman Suffrage Alliance meeting which met at Budapest in June 1913 was the seventh of its kind, drawing delegates from twenty-six countries and an audience of 3,000.*

When one is all through with a great convention; when one has for days listened to speeches, for days watched the temper of a crowd, and finally lost one's personality in the crowd emotion, and has had one's heart beat as the big overheart of the crowd will, there is in the end one great composite impression that is made up from all one's warring and diverse impressions. And in the seventh biennial convention of the International Woman Suffrage Alliance at Budapest in June the impression left on me was one of romance—the high romance of great enterprises.

It seemed as if I had been present at something at once deeply touching and deeply thrilling; as though I had watched a young and hopeful army getting ready to march on to victories of peace such as no other army had dreamed of attempting; as though I had watched, too, one of the most impressive things in the world—the loosing of long-pent-up and hitherto unused forces.

As I felt, so did hundreds of others, for my impression was theirs, since it was the result of the crowd spirit. I wonder if my surprise was theirs also, for one comes with peculiar interest to a big suffrage convention; one comes to it with curiosity; one looks forward to the possibilities to be met with, but one hardly expects to be stirred and thrilled to the depths.

Perhaps it was stupid not to have expected this, for with a little more imagination I might have guessed how profoundly moving would be a great congregation of women, gathered from all the countries of the earth in this most distant capital of Budapest to bear witness to the faith that is in them; to speak together of the things nearest their hearts and to echo and reecho the cry, "Women of the World, Unite!"

## In the Shadow of the Bastion

The Fisher-Bastion sits high on a hill in the old town of Budapest. Its walls and ramparts commemorate the victory of the fishermen of the Danube over some ancient foe. One may walk around these walls and look down across the Danube on all of Budapest. Behind the great court of the Bastion, on one side rises up the beautiful Gothic spire of the church of St. Mathias, and on the other the ministry buildings. Church and state, lofty, spacious, stately, sit magnificently side by side, while in front of them, shielding and protecting them, is the bastion of victorious armed force—that church and that state who from all times have said to all women, "You may not speak in our assemblies nor may you preach from our pulpits," and lately when women have been bold enough to ask for reasons, they have made that feeblest of all answers, which goes, "Because you cannot stand on that rampart in front of us to protect us."

And there in the open air Court of Honor, with Church, State and Army symbolized by the buildings, were met the women of all lands and all creeds and all classes, whose national and social and religious differences have all been swallowed up in this common cause. There were high-colored Scandinavian women; women who stand squarely on both feet; women of solid frames, wide hips, full of good sense, and determination as indomitable as it was temperate; Polish women, tense with the quality of slender drawn swords; women who have lived so long under such oppression that one feels in some of them a spiritual quality that is like that of a high explosive; groups of *hausfraulich* German women, whose looks now and then made one think irreverently of the pages of *Fliegende Blaetter.*

Here and there was a woman wearing her national costume; the bright dress of a Finnish delegate would flash through the crowd, and especially one noticed the graceful headdresses of the two Asmundssons, mother and daughter, from Iceland, Miss Asmundsson the picture of a northern heroine under her white veil. She is a very young girl, who looks like those fragile, intrepid flowers which bloom at the edge of winter.

This mother and daughter were sent by their government as an act of good faith, to tell the women of the world that it was only through certain political complications that this most northern country has not given women the franchise during the last year. Proud and democratic Iceland does not wish to be classed among certain faithless governments who have deceived their women with false promises.

There were women here from all the nations of deferred hopes except China, and their accounts of why they have not the vote in their various lands is a poignant lesson in the trickeries of what is known as "practical politics." No woman who has been engaged in this fight for franchise can ever have the reproach put upon her that she "does not understand what politics means." There is no shifty trick or turn with which she will be unfamiliar, since all have been used against her. There were women from both the suffrage and nonsuffrage states of our Union to give account of the fight of the last few years; women from the states and countries where they have been victorious; who had come from the remotest parts of South Africa, from Australia, from New Zealand. There were small, dark, swift-gestured women from the troubled Balkan states talking with long-legged blonde English girls, while all through the crowd, bringing to it its highest element of beauty, were the Hungarian girl pages—gleaming, lovely creatures of a peculiarly noble type of beauty.

## The Women from the Fields

No one could look at this assembly, gathered here in this so pictur-esque a setting, without a moment of emotion. We women have sat solitary in our separate little houses so long; so long in secret dreamed of many sorts of freedom—often for the mere freedom of speech; so long wished for the great adventure of life, and many of us, alas, have so long remained indifferent to all the world if we had our own happiness; so long have said, "I am well off, so all must be well with the world!"

Such an assembly as this makes one remember that it is only within the last few years in the history of all the ages that we have been able to move freely up and down the earth in large numbers. It is hardly more than a decade since women have assembled from distant countries together to discuss the common interests of women; and here there were over three thousand from the earth's ends, of all types, all classes and all ages.

In this vast crowd there were two wonderfully touching elements. One the group of gallant old women who have fought the long and courageous battle against superstition, and who have lived to see the realization of that for which they dreamed and fought—the coming together of the women of the world in a common cause. Accompanying each one of these older women are the shadows of their former companions: Women now dead who fought when no victory was in sight; who fought in the face of all opposition; leaders of forlorn hopes, infinitely lonely in their struggle. Women who for years unflinchingly faced the bitterest of all foes, the ridicule and misunderstanding of those whom one loves.

The other affecting element was to be found in the delegations of peasant women from Balmazayvaros, Hungary. Over their heads were tied the cotton handkerchiefs that Hungarian peasant women wear. Their short skirts measured yards about. In their hands, tanned like old leather, they carried the yellow and white banner that has become so familiar to us, with the familiar VOTES FOR WOMEN inscribed in unfamiliar Hungarian. They had heard Miss Rosika Schwimmer, who is one of the most ardent workers in the Hungarian movement, lecture some years ago, and their ardor has never died since that day. So they saved up, penny by penny, that they might come to this convention. Railroad fares cost too much, so they had planned to walk the trifling 150 miles, but the committee of Hungarian women heard of them and sent them money to come by train. It would have been hard to find a dozen shrewder faces in the assembly. In some way these peasant women were a measure of the zeal of the crowd. They told in concrete facts the sacrifices that had been made by no one can tell how many other women.

One thing became more certain the more one looked at the shifting groups: that every person of this throng meant the death of a prejudice. The presence of every woman, from the national delegates to the humblest visitor, meant a victorious battle with age-old misunderstanding. The individual woman might not have had to fight it herself, but somewhere, whether in an obscure, hide-bound community or whether in wide-flung battle line for the franchise of a country, there had been a conflict, and the sum of these conflicts and victories had made possible this congress.

Only a few years ago this movement was one of no political significance. It was only a matter of personal faith to a handful of devoted women and a matter of indifference or ridicule to the world. Now all of Budapest, from the burgomeister down, turned out to do honor to the convention, which for a moment occupied the town. There must have been a large outside population that didn't know anything about it, but even in a great city like Budapest a gathering of three thousand foreign women makes an impression, especially when they fill up the principal streets, when they swarm in the cafés and hotels and overflow the great halls where their meetings are held. And especially as each individual citizen of Budapest seemed to feel responsible for the entertainment of as large a number of the three thousand as he or she possibly could. No one wearing a convention badge could wander from the main thoroughfare without having delightful Hungarians swoop down upon her in cab or motor car to take her where she wanted to go. Indefatigable girl-guides haunted the hotels to see if the visitors were comfortable; got them as if by magic anything on earth they required for their comfort, and seemed to feel badly only that the requests were not more numerous. Inside the headquarters of the congress a band of earnest Boy Scouts was ever in attendance. Their glances eagerly entreated you to send them off with letters or telegrams.

The note of the whole convention was struck at the first meeting in the Academy of Music when the president, Mrs. Carrie Chapman Catt, of New York, read her opening address. From almost her opening words one was compelled to think in terms of vast distances and great numbers; one had to realize that this women's movement concerned no little corner of the earth, but was something as universal as it was deep. She gave the impression of recounting the progress of some past onrushing force when she said: "When the organization of the Alliance was completed in 1904 only eight nations had woman suffrage associations. Now, nine years later, with the exception of the Spanish-American republics, there are in the entire world only seven constitutionally organized nations without an organized woman suffrage movement. Only three of these are in Europe: Greece, Spain, and the Grand Duchy of Luxemburg. The remaining four are the Negro republic of Liberia in West Africa, Turkey, and Persia, which are not well-established, self-governing nations, and Japan, which is still more autocratic than democratic. Organized groups also exist on many islands of the sea, among them being Java, Sumatra, the Philippines, and Hawaii."

### A Message from China

During the past two years Mrs. Catt and Dr. Alletta Jacobs, president of the Holland Woman Suffrage Association, went around the world with the object of trying to ascertain as far as possible the position of the women of the Oriental countries, and it is significant of the breadth and universality of this women's movement that a large part of Mrs. Catt's opening address to the women of the West concerned the condition of the women of the East. She called attention to the fact that within the old religious sects new sects have arisen also which boldly espouse equality of rights for men and women. She told of the Chinese women of the revolution, many of whom enlisted as soldiers, and of their demands for a share in the liberty which they helped to earn.

So it was brought home that it is not alone with us that women are uniting to fight world-old prejudice—and there has never been any one widespread, concerted movement that makes so surely for the breaking down of superstition and prejudice as does this wide-flung women's movement—but the women of Asia, patient and long-suffering, are also stirring restlessly and behind their curtains, whispering to each other of freedom, and those who can uniting themselves in sympathy with the more fortunate women of the West.

It would have been a person with a small heart and smaller imagination who would not have been thrilled at the presentation of the great scarlet and white banner sent by the Chinese Women's Suffrage Alliance. On this was embroidered in Chinese characters, THE MUTUAL HELP SOCIETY: TO THE INTERNATIONAL ALLIANCE. HELPING EACH OTHER; ALL OF ONE MIND. Hardly less strong as an appeal to the imagination was the telegram sent by the women of Teheran, Persia, to the Alliance: "What Hath God Wrought?"

It is a measure of the sweep of this movement when in a matter-of-fact tone the admission of China into the International Alliance was proposed by Hungary and seconded by South Africa.

During the business of the first day Madame de Schlumberger, president of the French Alliance, in the name of the presidents of all countries, begged Mrs. Catt to remain international president. There has never been a public officer more universally beloved than this sweet-faced American woman, whose judgment is so keen and so far-seeing, whose tact is so unfailing; the fire of whose deep indignation against oppression burns so deep.

The way in which Madame de Schlumberger presented this appeal was characteristic of the entire congress. It was done simply, without flourish, without a hint of that murder of all joy, the "frockcoat gesture." Throughout the whole convention there was much eloquence, but no oratory. There was preserved a certain quality of informality; there was seriousness, but no solemnity, and there was much wit and humor. Perhaps the entrance of women into public will put an end to the quivering voice, the chest thumping, the owllike solemnity and the other oratorical tricks that have so long made the public utterances of the average man so difficult for sensible persons to listen to.

As one watched the women of so many nations working together for a common cause; as their speeches betrayed what the feeling toward the feminist movement is in their various countries, one realized that such a convention is profoundly significant because in a condensed and almost terribly concentrated form it gives one the woman question almost as it has existed down the ages.

With the great widening of the movement, the interests of the women engaged in fighting for suffrage have broadened in equal proportion. It is interesting to observe that the women who already have the vote are the ones who most cheerfully acknowledge the cheerful paradox that the vote has done more for women than women have done for the vote. Mrs. Frederick Spencer from Australia and Miss Maud Younger from California both insisted on this point, even at the moment when they were giving their satisfactory reports concerning the activity of women in civic life in their enfranchised communities.

The practical reforms that women have accomplished with the ballot are all excellent; but far above the enactment of wise laws, far more important than any of these outward signs of victory, is the spirit of solidarity that has been bred among women. This and its accompanying democracy are precious things which cannot be overrated. The wisest women see the limitations of the power of the ballot, but there is almost no limit to the force of a burning public opinion. Such public opinion is what has changed the maps of the world. It has been behind the wars that have stricken off age-old tyrannies, and it is against the worst of all tyrannies that the highest forces and the deepest feeling of this congress of women was directed.

### In Arms Against Vice

This whole women's movement is not a battle for a mere ballot. These women were here not only to demand political recognition, but to protest against all unjust conditions under which the women of all ages have labored. When you think of the women's movement, therefore, do not let your mind dwell on the question of mere franchise, but loose your imagination until it beholds the women of the whole world engaged in a battle with world-old injustice; until you see that this movement is already, for one thing, a flaming, on-marching battle against commercialized vice.

When Mrs. Catt offered her resolution concerning the white-slave traffic there was evident in the audience an intense and unquenchable desire to right this old wrong. There was pity and more pity, and indignation that such things could be, and tenderness toward the victim of the ages. The resolutions presented to the congress read:

> 1. "We send from this Congress of the International Woman Suffrage Alliance a request to the governments of all countries here represented that they institute an international inquiry into the extent and causes of commercialized vice.
> 2. "Be it resolved that the woman suffrage organization of each country ask its own government to institute a national inquiry on the same lines and that women be included in the commission."

Mrs. Catt's speech in presenting the resolution was eloquent of woman's uncompromising attitude toward the ancient evil. "Down all the centuries." she said,

> we have considered that commercialized vice was a necessity. It was believed that certain women, because of degenerate nature or owing to

conditions over which nobody could possibly have any control, were driven into this life.

I believe that commercialized vice is not a necessity. I believe that it is the greatest crime that was ever committed in the entire history of the world.

When you take away from a class all its privileges, the right to earn money, the right of education, of free speech, of free publication, if you take away these rights from any class of human beings, you have made of them, if not slaves, economic dependents. You have placed them in a position where they may be commercialized, and it is because of this fact that we have a condition of commercialized vice.

Here is this imaginary demand on the part of men, and here is this commercialized vice to feed that demand. And under this system of commercialized vice hundreds and thousands of women are annually delivered to disease and certain death to supply that demand.

Who is going to take their places, those slaves that are gathered from all parts of the world? The white-slave traffic is going to continue no matter how many white-slave traffic laws you make in your country. The bottom of the problem is that the whole of this commercialized vice is wrong, is unspeakably abominable, and it has got to go, root and branch.

If our question of the vote is international, infinitely greater is this question of vice. It lies at the bottom of our worldwide subjection, and we will never rest until we have conquered it.

You and I may be educated. We may even have the vote; but so long as down there at the bottom there are other women, you and I are cheapened; we have not yet been emancipated.

I once believed the vote would be the means of emancipating us. I still believe that it is the weapon we need with which to accomplish these greater ends. But the women of the world will never be emancipated until this abominable evil has been removed.

There was little or no public discussion in the convention of "militancy," and it was not an issue. But there is a militancy of another kind arising within the ranks of the nonmilitant suffragists. There is a militancy which cries: "Away with my ease, my peace of mind. I cannot live while horror waits so many women. I cannot be happy while they are segregated to perform this service for mankind. I must leave everything I love to protest against this crime against us. This traffic in women shall cease."


## Woman's Inhumanity to Woman

Again and again in the congress this spirit sprang forth like a white aspiring flame. It sprang out at Mrs. Charlotte Perkins Gilman's protest against the sacredness of undesired motherhood. It sprang out at Miss Maud Royden's protest against one set of virtues for the governing class and one set of virtues for the governed. Miss Royden said that to teach a woman

> that she may be indifferent to the sufferings of the world if she be devoted to her home and her family is to corrupt the whole moral standard.
>
> We hold that virtue is one as truth and beauty are one, and that to divide it is not to lessen it, but to *destroy* it. We point in proof of this to the fact that women have been expected to specialize in the virtues, among others, of chastity and gentleness, but not in courage. As if any one could dare to be merciful who is not brave. What has been the result? That you will find women, merciful women, women whose whole lives are one long act of devotion to those they love, who will nevertheless consent to the great social sore of prostitution, because they say, "If it were not for these outcasts we ourselves would not be safe." Will future ages believe that such cruelty has been possible? Will you ladies who have heard at this congress, perhaps, some harsh things said about men, ask yourselves whether there is any cruelty more unspeakable than this, by which a woman consents to be safe at the expense of another's eternal loss? What do we mean by safety? What do we mean by purity? Do we really suppose it can be bought at such a price? Do we think that when we have kept our safety at the expense of another's shame we are, in the sight of God, pure? We do not consent to the sacrifice. We repudiate altogether the standard of morality which has created this supposed necessity. And we reject the idea—inherent in any society which has one great class in absolute subjection to another—that any human beings have a right to use other human beings to exploit them as a supreme immorality.

As one listened to the applause which followed this it seemed as if one saw the old and shameful reticences, the smug and immoral virtues, burn up in the fire of a high indignation. Especially was this spirit abroad in the audience that listened to Madame Marie Verone's speech. This fiery and able French lawyer won one of those heart-moving successes when a whole audience arises unexpectedly to its feet to applaud and throw flowers. And Madame Verone's high moment of triumph was when, after tracing the existence of certain unjust laws against women and prostitutes, she protested against the slighting term of "girl-mothers," and said: *"There are no girl-mothers—there are only mothers."*

Consider what this applause meant. Only a little while ago good women had no sympathy for the girl-mother, nor might her shadow fall across the threshold of decent doors. But in this applause it was as if on the faces of this great mass of women from all over the earth one could see the sacred fire of indignation. Not only for this, but for all these wrongs from commercialized vice on to industrial injustice, and that here at last fire had been added to fire, until one had at last something like the sacred and imperishable fire that in former times has broken through the superstition of ages and freed slaves. And for a moment the audience would be transformed and one was in the presence of a splendid fighting army to whom all things are possible. In the face of the white-hot intensity of this emotion it seemed impossible to believe that in the history of the world men and women had never before banded themselves together to say to the slavery of prostitution, as to other slaveries, "You shall not be."

It seemed incredible that the only answer that the state has made to the question which prostitution put to it was the punishment of the delinquent woman. In the light of the flaming indignation of these women one seemed to have advanced centuries along the road of civilization, and for a moment to be looking back at some old horror of another age.

At one of the last sessions of the congress Mrs. Crystal Benedict reminded her audience that they must face the fact that the battle is not yet won, "that, politically speaking, we have less voice with our governments than the small boys who today are playing ball in the streets. In many places it is going to be a long fight—a fight against "tradition and prejudice, a fight against organized interest and, most discouraging of all, a fight against the colossal weight of woman's own indifference."

Now that is the appeal that this convention makes to every man and woman. It is for every man and woman to consider on which side he or she stands. Are you a part of that dead weight of indifference which checks progress? Do you care whether things go on in the old way? Do you care if men continue to traffic in little girls and subnormal children, who in turn take their sinister revenge on innocent and guilty alike, if any can be counted innocent in a community that tolerates such a condition without protest? The convention asks its own members such searching questions. And to the spectators it asks: "Are you of those who are forging a chain of indifference which will hamper this so splendid and glowing desire for freedom? For, besides the inertia, besides the smug and cruel and terrible indifference of good men and women, the supporters themselves of commercialized vice are a small enemy. These "good," but indifferent, men and women are the outworks behind which the evil lies safely entrenched.

The appeal which this seventh convention made to its members, it is going to make to the separate governments, and to the people of the nations; and in the next few years everyone will have to answer as to where he stands.

# The Woman Who Was

*Good Housekeeping, 1914*

As I think of the life of Sarah Adamson, it stretches out before me like a wide, far-reaching landscape. The first part of it is a flowering land with poetic vistas, bits of enchanted woods, valleys and mountains, and the sound of running water. Then gradually this changes into long, unending, dusty plains. And so I think it will go on until she dies, perhaps of thirst, for the sight of some green, growing thing.

I suppose she thinks: "Tomorrow I may strike the woodland stretch. Yesterday I thought I smelled spring coming in the winds that had blown over a garden," for, of course, she did not arrive at once at the gray limbo in which she now lives. Now life would be sweet, and then there would be a barren place: Such things may happen to any one. There are a great many women of Sarah Adamson's age traveling in this same country, and they meet and stop and compare notes, and generally make believe, because they are too proud to tell the truth about themselves; because to tell the truth means to tell the story of an utter defeat. Sarah Adamson did not tell the truth, for it meant confessing that, having done the very best she knew how in this world, having spent herself unceasingly and kept no bit of herself that she could give—the last third of her life had very little in it besides hunger and thirst—unless, in the future, it may hold that doubtful reward which good Christians call "resignation." And for an old-age pension of the emotions that is not much to live on.

I saw Sarah Adamson first when she took the place next door to ours when I was a little girl. I used to go down and eat cookies that she made, and go out with her to feed the chickens. In some ways she seemed to me different from other grown-up people, for she gave me no feeling of grown-upness. Certainly she must have been a shining thing, to have affected me as she did. I don't know now if it was herself or her happiness. Housework in my home seemed a dull-enough affair, full of tiresome routine; housework at Sarah's had a magic quality. With what satisfaction we used to roll out corn bread together in golden sheets! How meticulously everything was made sweet and clean! I know now why this was so. Housework was a religious rite; every little thing that she did was done in the service of her husband. She washed his clothes for glory of him; she adorned his house with a heart brimming with love. She was a woman of great energy, and used to work in a garden besides, and raise chickens. She made little economies and sacrifices to make life better and easier for the best person in the world. He was her profession; he was her religion; she felt, indeed, as we have been told an ideal woman should feel.

It was not until I was grown up that I understood the significance of all her toil, or the rushing joy of her when she went to meet him when he came home of an evening. It was such a poignant thing, so vivid with life and with love, so deeply touching, that the picture remained engraved upon my little plastic mind until I was old enough to understand what it meant. Adamson was a fine, big, good-looking fellow, and very much in love when he married. I remember my sisters saying so, for they used to talk about them, and so did my aunts.

"That's no way," I remember one of them saying, "to keep a man's love—always throwing yourself at his head."

"Even a married woman ought to have more reserve," another aunt agreed.

"He's beginning to be patronizing in his manner already," said one of my older sisters.

I did not know what that word meant exactly, but it made me very angry.

"He doesn't do it," I cried out loud, "he doesn't patronize her." I clenched my fists. They all laughed and went on with their miserly philosophy, which really means this: a man has only so much affection for a woman, just as there is so much butter in a pound—and how, dear sisters, shall we spread it over our bread? They, of course, were all doing just what Sarah was doing! Their woe and weal were as bound up in their men as were hers. If their men failed them, they were failures. If, after a time, that fund of the affections was used up, or the stream of love chose to run in another direction, little was left for them; but they were wise plotters, and Sarah was a spendthrift. One might as well have asked any one of the forces of things to be restrained, cautious, and penny wise.

I pondered on that word "patronizing." I knew by my sister's tone it meant something that wasn't kind. I knew this, that there were times when the shining atmosphere of pure happiness that had drawn me into it, in these days had clouds. Sadness had no attractions for me. I wanted stories to have happy endings, and I hated to see people cross, and I had afternoons of keen disquiet. Now I know that these were the times when she had offended her man in some way, or thought she had. Now I know, too, that it is hard on anybody to be someone else's profession and religion.

There comes to me a picture of singular intensity, of a moment when I was to share prematurely in an anguish so poignant that for a moment it forced me to become a woman. It was as if the dark curtain of the future had been drawn away from before my eyes, and I saw the fate that awaited women who love too much.

One night the sweet smell of evening and damp growing things brought me out of doors, and I moved through the dusk as furtive and shy as any of the little nocturnal creatures that were stirring about. When out of earshot of my house I fled, fleet of foot, down the hill until I came to a hole in the fence between our place and the Adamsons'; and then I stopped, for from the little grape-arbor at the back of their house came a feeble lamentation, as though of some mortally wounded thing. I crept toward it. The little noise was so helpless; it spoke of such abandoned despair that the mother in me awoke in my hard little girl's heart. It was Sarah. She sat there in the grape-arbor, all humped up like something infinitely old and infinitely broken; it seemed as though she was the embodiment of the broken heart of woman, as she sat there stifling her sobs, the bitter stream of unquenched tears flowing from her eyes. I clasped her knees with my little arms and pressed my face close to hers, whispering, "Don't, don't!" and asking anxiously: "What is it? What's happened?" And still she cried as though some secret and terrible force of nature was crying through her, and I stayed with her, shaken to the very core of me, tears running down my own cheeks as though I had become part of this grieving thing, for she did not seem to me to be like Sarah then. I did not put it into words, but now it seems to me that she was like the other side of love. I had seen her so triumphant, and so beautiful, and so glorified, that the least act of life for her had its precious and hidden meaning; and this was the price she paid—in common with all women of her kind. At last she spoke, and each word was like a sob of pain, bitter, hopeless.

"He—doesn't—love—me," she said, "he—doesn't—know what—it—means." And then, as if a dry, hot wind from the future was blowing upon her, and she had a glimpse of the land that was ahead of her, "and—less—and—less—he—will—care—and—I—I can—never—change."

It was grief beyond the grief of death. At last she said, "Go, it's late." So I left her, and the sound of her suppressed sobbing followed me.

We never spoke of this again, but from that time there was a curious bond between us. As I grew older, the meaning of this cataclysmal grief became clear to me, though even at that time it stirred some curious rebellion deep in my heart. Later, I formulated this in the resolve that I would never in my life give myself so completely to anyone. But afterward I understood that it wasn't the complete gift of oneself that mattered, but that Sarah had left herself nothing else in life; she had no interest apart from his concerns, her work drew its meaning because it pleased him: she wanted him and him alone and nothing else, and she had no anodyne of any kind with which to still the intolerable ache, ache, of her heart if he were away.

There was just one other episode that I remember at this time. I watched Adamson and had been very much astonished to observe no change in him at all. I had romantic thoughts about some deep unhappiness between them; instead of this he seemed very fond of Sarah. I remember one Saturday afternoon when she asked me to stay until he came. She expected him by two, and at half-past two the air was tense with her waiting. Her eyes were always seeking the window through which she could see the road; suspense grew until it was something that suffocated me. I wanted to run, I wanted to get away. We were picking over some berries for preserving, and my little fingers were red with the juice of the ripe fruit, but she worked without zest and always her eyes were on the road. Every little while she said, "It's funny, he's so late." Moment by moment the intolerable feeling of suspense grew until my nerves were strained and racked with it.

At last he came striding down the road, head up. She opened the door, and he stood there laughing and boyish. She sprang to him.

"You're so late," she cried. "I was frightened." There were tears in her eyes. He patted her shoulder and kissed her.

"There," he said, "there, you know I have to be late sometimes, and you know I was later today"—he threw back his head and laughed his boyish laugh—"I was later today just because I was tired, and I knew you would make a fuss, and I kept putting off coming home. Now, you have it!" he flung at her, still with his boyish smile.

"You *knew* I would be suffering and waiting, and—let—me?" she answered, the words coming in little gasps. He pinched her arm and nodded toward me as if to tell her to command herself. Then she told me very sweetly that we would work no more that afternoon, and I ran off glad enough to go. Now I know that this was the prelude to some storm.

I told this scene to a friend once. "The woman was a fool," she answered. But that's where she was wrong. There is scarcely a woman who is not living her own individual existence as well as loving her husband who does not through her demands destroy or at least wound his love.

My intimacy with Sarah continued. Perhaps there was some deep instinct in me that made me watch the intimate spectacle of marriage that she showed me. At any rate, the memories of various pictures I have of her are among the most vivid of those early days. I remember how it clutched at my heart when at some little word of Adamson's she would wither up. Love, for Sarah, had opened the door of her nature to a thousand doubts and fears and hesitations, which day by day took from her the very things that he had loved—her radiant air, her joy of

life, her upstanding independence. As I watched her, the unformed
thought came to me, more and more definitely, that one is nothing in
life if one is not oneself. As I grew older this desire to belong to myself
through life and love, and through marriage, became part of my inner-
most essence. I wanted love, and the things that love brings with it—
husband, home, children—but I desired with a still greater intensity to
have my own life besides.

An older woman who once heard me say things like that said to me,
"Remember, you can't eat your cake and have it, too, my dear." This
was the old-time view of such things: This would have been Sarah's
view. When I found myself getting slack about my work, a vision would
come to me of that strained look on Sarah's face when she waited for
Adamson's return—the world having become a vacuum for her, a place
of nothingness, as if all her life were suspended until he came.

When I was a long-legged girl already beginning to think about boys,
we moved away. I often wondered what had become of Sarah, and it
was a very long time before I found out; so long that the picture of her
had ceased to be associated with my resolve to be myself.

Years afterward, a full-fledged young lady, I was spending a little
time in a seaside place when one day I witnessed a scene that cramped
my heart. I heard a young woman say to her husband: "Why, is *that*
Adamson's wife?" That was all. She went away hanging on his arm with
the triumphant air of the well-beloved, that radiant air about her that
some women have in the first days of their marriage. The words had
carried some distance to me and to a woman near me. She sat there
like some meager-plumaged bird frozen to a tree. Her mouth sagged
open, her face turned gray. There was mingled with her look of horror
an expression of ludicrous incredulity as of one who had heard something so monstrous that he can't believe the evidence of his senses. She
was lost to every other outside impression, her eyes on the beautiful,
careless, confident woman, the words, "Is that Adamson's wife?" vibrating throughout her whole consciousness. Under the shock it was as
if the grayness of her spirit was revealed indecorously. I continued to
look at her as she kept her petrified gaze on the retreating figure of her
judge and executioner. No human being, I felt sure, had ever more
lightly passed a crueler sentence upon a fellow being.

During the few seconds that I watched her, shame mounted in me,
for I had listened at the door of a human soul in a moment of extreme
anguish. All this occurred very swiftly. It was one of those poignant
dramas that happens while one might open and close the lens of a
camera. Before I had sorted out my impressions, a man came swinging
down the piazza toward the stricken woman with a casual "Hello,
dear," on his lips. While it hadn't occurred to me that I had seen the
woman before, I recognized him easily enough. It was Adamson. He

didn't notice that anything was wrong; he didn't notice her at all; he was good-tempered and confident, and from him radiated an air of success and prosperity which had been foreshadowed by his bearing in the earlier days. In a moment I had sprung forward to greet them, instinct telling me that any diversion would be a relief from her anguish. She held me in her arms and kissed me tenderly, very glad to see me, as though I were some little fragment of her own youth returned to her. She proclaimed she would have known me anywhere—I had the same head, only perched on a bigger body, and longer legs. I told them both they hadn't changed at all.

Sarah seemed to be comforted by this word of mine. "I'm not looking very well now," she told me. "I haven't been very well since my last baby was born." There had been one baby before I left, and now there were two others, and the youngest, six. This was the first of the series of little pathetic lies she told me, trying to hide her heart and what the condition of her life was. Adamson, in the literal sense of the word, had no use for his wife whatever; he wanted life, and enjoyed the companionship of men; he liked dancing, he was enjoying the holiday, and while he tried his best to be kind to her, it was perfectly evident that he enjoyed himself far better when she was not with him.

He was kind, as I said, and good, too. Sometimes I think Sarah might have suffered less if there had been some "other woman," though that seems a strange thing to say. But if you lose your husband to another woman there is always the thought that perhaps he will come back to you: You can comfort yourself with a number of theories, or you may get angry. Sarah's case is the commonest in the world, the case of a woman who has her husband, and who yet has lost him.

She had nothing with which to reproach him. He was one of those men who can say with truth, "I give her everything in the world she wants," meaning thereby, all the tangible things in life. He was without vices. His only fault was a too-ready impatience, a too-great emphasis on that patronizing quality of which my relatives had spoken so long before. For him life was full, and if his emotional life was not very rich, he made it up with friends, with work, with his own life, in short. He liked new people, too, and took an innocent vanity in the popularity which his good looks and easy laughter gave him.

But as for Sarah, she had poured out her youth, and her vitality, and all her interest in life for Adamson and for the children, and there was nothing he wanted less than this outpouring. Life has very few purgatories that are darker or more devastating to live in than the constant refusal of the beloved to accept the gift of oneself.

That was why life had changed to Sarah. From being a series of acts full of meaning, small acts performed in the same joyful spirit of devotion in which the truly religious live and draw breath for the glory of

God, it had changed to a life where no act had any meaning. There were, of course, the children, but their affection was not enough for her. Only the two oldest were with them, for Sarah was "run down," or at least that was what the doctors called her malady. Starved, was what she really was. Adamson's love alone could have saved her soul alive, and love was just what he did not have to give her.

Starvation changes the nature of all things. Under starvation gentle animals become ferocious, shy things become bold, and simple things, crafty and cunning. In the end the strong become weak, and finally, weak and strong alike die.

Under the stress of her spiritual starvation, Sarah had altered. Life and its interests had diminished to one thing, and that was, how to get the food her heart needed. The words that she had heard the woman speak had aroused in her a panic for fear she would never get it, and that was how I witnessed the curious and terrible game of blind-man's buff that went on between them. You might say that Sarah stalked Adamson and Adamson evaded her with almost the unconsciousness of an animal. First, she tried the little superficial things, like a new dress, to make him notice her. She called me in to help her, and as I hooked it up and patted it into place, it seemed to me I saw a whole army of women uselessly dressing themselves, sometimes making themselves fair and beautiful, sometimes accentuating their age, and all of it making no difference, since they were dressing themselves for sightless eyes, as was Sarah.

I could imagine her waiting for his approval, for some little sign that he noticed her. God knows, when such women do these things, it is not flattery they want; they do it in the same spirit that a neglected dog tries to call attention to himself. I could imagine her finally making him notice her, asking him, how did he like her new dress, and his deadly and indifferent kindness as he answered absently, "Oh, very pretty, very nice, my dear." And then her feeling of total defeat, the desire for darkness, and for tears.

But with such trivial wounds of the spirit one must carry one's head high. A man has to be very much in love indeed not to be alienated and bored by tears on occasions like this, but when a man is very much in love indeed, occasions like this do not arise.

I think the words that she had overheard must have effected some curious change in Sarah. I think they crystallized the situation for her. They aroused in her a deep need of reassurance. She wanted to prove to herself and to the world that she *was* Adamson's wife, and not just somebody he had happened to marry a long time ago. She planned three or four different little excursions with him alone, or with other people, and each time he evaded her. She was always pursuing him, gently, yet tensely and remorselessly, and he was always slipping through her fingers.

One afternoon, I remember, she planned a walk, and put in the party one or two people he liked. I was standing talking with Adamson when she came up and put the proposition to him. I saw a swift look of relief cross his face. He was glad to have her provided for of an afternoon.

"I am sorry I cannot go," he said, "but I am going sailing at four with Lorimer."

"Oh!" she cried eagerly, "can't I go, too? We can take our walk early, or perhaps I could get out of it. There is nothing formal about it."

"I'll fix it for another time," he said, with a curious little air of evasiveness; "there are no women going this afternoon, and so, you see—"

She *did* see, just as she always saw. A woman does not need to be clairvoyant to know when the beloved really wants her and is regretful that she cannot come, and when he is deeply relieved.

We went out on our walk, Sarah absent-minded, as she often had been, when I was a little girl and she was waiting for Adamson's return. Then when we came home, she sat down to watch the incoming boats. When Lorimer's boat came in the men got out, and with them one of the wives, a young, pretty creature in a saucy sailor frock.

Sarah saw her and had a short struggle with herself. Her common sense told her to stay where she was, but every fiber in her body urged her to go down to meet her husband. She could not help herself, and as I saw her go I contrasted her manner now with the onrushing Sarah of long ago. I saw her greet him and draw him aside, and I knew that what was in her heart had had to find expression. I knew she had said, "But other women did go," and I knew by his half-impatient, half-deprecating manner that he was saying: "But I didn't know she was going, my dear. She hopped in at the last moment."

She was hanging on his arm, and he was arguing with her with restrained impatience. She had evidently let drop some incautious remark, and through it had won an empty victory, since for the next few days he stayed more with her. He was restless and listless at once, forever tugging, it seemed, at an invisible leash that held him; and she suffered as a woman must suffer whose thought for days had been, "If he could only be more with me, I could make him care again," and finds that once she has her desire she is worse off than before, since she has the letter of the dream fulfilled but none of its inner significance.

As I watched them together and saw her ineffectual attempts to interest him, now playing cards, now reading, or taking walk together, a deep pity for both of them seized me, and I saw that forever and ever there must be this strife between them, his indifference and need of outside things, against her gnawing need of him.

Life might have jogged itself on in this gray monotony except that one day Sarah swam out too far. I watched her, swimming along listlessly, quite a distance from the other bathers. Then all of a sudden I saw a hand go up in the air, waggling helplessly above the surface of the water. Nothing was less spectacular than the way she almost drowned, and the way that she was saved. The tragedy and the drama of it did not lie to me in the danger she had run. Adamson went for her so quickly that there was not any doubt that her life hung in the balance. The drama lay in the look that she gave him when she opened her eyes and found him bending over her with deep solicitude. It was as if she had gone through the bitter waters of death to find herself in some long wished-for paradise. All the hunger and thirst in the world were in her look. He leaned over her, calling her little affectionate names that, perhaps, she had not heard for years, telling her not to be afraid, telling her that he was looking after her.

I saw them going around together during the next few days; she was hanging on his arm with a look of ineffable peace upon her face. During that week she seemed to come back to life. People noticed it. "One would think that being almost drowned had done her good," they said. Happiness shone through her, like light through glass.

Then one day the moment came when his shield of kindly indifference broke. We had gone on a picnic, and Adamson and I, and one or two others, had wandered away from the rest. Adamson threw himself down on the grass, like a weary man, and I idled off a little distance. Then through the trees came Sarah, and sat down beside him. He sprang to his feet, said something, and walked away. Sarah sat there and presently beckoned to me. When I came she put her hand out, and I laid mine in it and so we sat in silence. Then she spoke, her words dripping out slowly from a depth of grief that left no place for tears. She looked at me while she talked, with the expression of a hurt animal which asks why it should suffer so.

"What is there wrong with me?" she began, the words torn from the very depths of her. "Why should he not care for me? I'm not different from other women, am I? He shouldn't hate me, should he, because I've aged more than he? I have had children. Sometimes there are days when I feel repulsive to myself, days like this. Do you know what he said when I sat down here? His face darkened at the sight of me, and he said, '*I wish you wouldn't always tag after me, Sarah.*' What *is* wrong with me?"

What could I tell her? What was wrong with her couldn't be altered: I could only comfort and pet her, humor her. I told her she was too sensitive, scolded her for minding such little things.

"He must care a little, don't you think?" she said. "He never looks at other women really, you know." I could do nothing but agree with her.

"I have become so deep a part of his life," she went on, "that he does not know how much I am in it. He is only just a little impatient, and I am foolish. I am like the air he breathes," was the conclusion she came to. "Don't think I would stay if I thought he did not want me; that would not be decent."

But I knew, and in the depths of her she did too, that she was to him only a necessary encumbrance to life, and that he was happy in spite of her, never because of her.

"I have always lived for him," she went on with a little air of pride. There one had it! She had lived for him, and very few men could have stood their wives living for them as well as Robert Adamson had stood it. I was glad when it was time for me to leave, for more and more I had to walk around the dreary treadmill of Sarah's thoughts and her contemplation of her life. I could not bear watching her go through her cycle of alternate hope and despair. I did not want to see the slow process by which she would join irrevocably the hundreds and thousands of women who make themselves no place in the world; but busy themselves in meaningless activities, and sit and wait for some little sign of affection from their husbands, for the careless visits of their children. There are those in this band of women who are faded and hopeless; there are those who are apologetic for being alive; there are those who still demand clamorously of life more life, although they themselves have nothing left to give to life.

For there you have the answer to Sarah's tragedy: She had nothing left to give. In the beginning she gave splendidly to life, but she took nothing from life. She despoiled herself of everything, even of her own personality, to serve those whom she loved. She gave up her days to service, but it is spiritual service that counts with older children and with man. She expected others to feed her, and this in life does not happen: Forever and ever one must feed oneself and replenish one's own forces. These spiritual laws are as inevitable and as cruel as the laws of nature, and that is why Sarah Adamson now has no place in the world, and why, at a moment of her life when men are in the fullness of their powers, she who was so radiant, so instinct with life when I first knew her, is a failure today, something that "was." This is the reason why she has no deeper place in the life of her children. To have a place in anyone's life one must be something oneself.

# Emily Henshaw
## *Mary Heaton Vorse Papers, c.1915*

At the time this story begins the two most salient facts in Emily Henshaw's life were first, that she was thirty-seven years old, and second, that she lived in Warwick, Connecticut. Warwick is the kind of little Connecticut town whose principal output is ancestors. A prodigious number of progenitors of people living in other states seems, somehow or other, to have come from Warwick. Most of their progeny apparently moved away, for Warwick today is a little sleepy, overgrown with elm-shaded streets, and a beautiful, dignified old church, Congregationalist, and a new, squat, smart-looking church, Unitarian. It is untainted by any outside influence. There is no business in Warwick, to be called business. But there is a library. There were also what Warwick people call "our New England traditions." Warwick is decorous, respects itself and the past, and laments the present. As you walk down its elm-shaded streets you feel that at any moment you might bump into a blue law that has whisked suddenly around the corner from out of the past. On the other hand Warwick is not negligible. As the local papers have it, a number of prominent men make their summer homes here. They live without ostentation, with that adherence to the old traditions of New England upon which Warwick prides itself.

You can see for yourself that for a woman to be thirty-seven years old in Warwick meant that she was thirty-seven years old. She wasn't as old as she seemed or as old as she looked. She was thirty-seven, and everybody knew she was thirty-seven. And the only thing approaching society and gaiety was engendered in Warwick by young ladies considerably under twenty, Emily's own nieces, Lois and Margery, for instance. It was with them, or rather with her brother, that Emily lived.

When Emery Henshaw married, his invalid mother lived with them; so did Emily to take care of her mother. Her mother died and she stayed on to take care of Lois and Lois' mother, who was frail after Lois was born. Then she stayed on to take care of Margery, and Lois, and Lois' mother. And then she stayed on to take care of Emery, and Margery, and Lois, and their mother, and so on. She kept house, and oversaw, and did mending, and first made baby clothes, and then hand-embroidered the girls' clothes when handwork came in so much, and helped the girls with their lessons, and the spring and fall cleaning, and stayed with the children so that poor, tired Mrs. Henshaw could get off a vacation with Emery, and filled in the kitchen at the frequent interregnums of the hired girl, and did the preserving and pickling, and even made a little pin money by making extra jellies, though she didn't need to, having a tiny income of her own of which she was glad because it kept her from feeling that she was a burden on her brother.

This is the way that Emily Henshaw had lived for eighteen years. In the fullness of it she had been asked to join the Thursday Club. Women of proper social standing, when they were about thirty and there was a vacancy, were asked to join the Thursday Club. This club was the chief pride of the Warwick ladies.

The Thursday Club jogged along in its intellectual way, talking about Mme. Curie and Metchnikoff and the principles of aviation very much to its own satisfaction until about three years ago when it suddenly woke up to modern issues. It woke up with a bang to see that the sacredness of the home was being menaced, that a dread hysteria was assailing woman—the homemaker—and, in fact, things were "going to pot" generally, though it never would have used so vulgar a phrase as this. And it felt its duty to be up and to fight this modern Apollyon. For this purpose it organized a vigorous antisuffrage league, affiliated with the state league.

Mrs. Henshaw, for all her frail health, joined it.

"You will join, of course, Emily," she said, with that definiteness with which she was used to address her sister-in-law.

"I'll think about it," Emily replied, with the indefiniteness with which it was her custom to meet her relative's assertions. "I'll see about it later. There's going to be an awful lot of quinces to put down this year, and I have never seen so many barberries."

"You're too domestic, Emily," said Mrs. Henshaw. "You ought to have married."

To this Emily made no reply but went on tranquilly scalloping a piqué collar for Alice. Romance had once smiled upon her. An artist, from the artists' settlement two towns away, had strayed down to Warwick. They had met and talked. He had come to see her one evening. It seemed to her that it was the first time she had ever communicated with another human soul in her life. For three days she walked as if she had the stars for play-fellows. Then he walked home with her and, as he stood by the gate, he kissed her. Alas, Mrs. Henshaw happened to come out at that moment. She did not, of course, mention this occurrence to Emily. She looked up at her as Emily came in the house, her face aflame, shame and joy in her heart. Mrs. Henshaw was a small, round woman and wore glasses, and Emily was tall and slender. Mrs. Henshaw remarked, with a naturalness of diction so perfect that the insult was hidden, "Why, is that you Emily? I thought it was Freda," Freda being the name of the Swedish maid. At the moment the silver chord was loosed, the golden bow was broken. Emily's pink face changed to fiery red. Her actions had been those of a servant girl! Her romance was turned to disgust.

This may seem an irrelevant incident, but it had a strangely molding effect upon Emily's character. For some reason it always made her furious, not at Mrs. Henshaw but at all of Warwick, whenever she thought of it. What right had Warwick to criticize her in such a way for kissing anyone she chose? she had hotly demanded, having grown old enough to see Warwick in perspective. It made her angry even now when she thought of it after all these years; and curiously enough it was to this episode that Emily's mind always reverted when anyone spoke to her of marriage and not to the one most advantageous if unromantic offer of marriage that Emily had received.

"I think," Emily's sister-in-law went on, "it's the duty of all of us to protest against this hysteria about the vote. Women don't need the vote and they don't want the vote," she pursued with rare originality. Emily said nothing.

"It's the expression," Emily's sister-in-law went on, "of a group of idle women, driven by their love of excitement. Surely, Emily, you see that it's your duty to join." Emily drew her embroidery cotton neatly through the piqué.

"I have so much to do," she demurred.

"You'd better come," Mrs. Henshaw persisted.

Emily followed the line of least resistance. They had a speaker from out of town—a sweet-faced woman with a cultivated accent.

"It has been the memorial mission of woman," she said, "to be the conserver in the midst of war, through the vicissitudes that have as-sailed the home; she has to be the conserver of the pure, the good, the beautiful. Woe to her if she forsakes her trust to wrangle in the market-place! It does a woman more good," she persisted further, "to hear a beautiful concert of stringed instruments than to constitute herself the guardian of garbage. The beauty of a woman's soul who has contem-plated in her life only beauty, shines like a star. Such stars are the lodestars of men. If this light be put out in what darkness shall we find the earth? If every women in the world would but turn her mind to beautiful thoughts, look upon beautiful things, make her life a series of beautiful acts, all that is bad, sordid, vile, or unhappy in life will disappear. That is all that is needed to regenerate the earth. I would be very glad to answer any questions," she said with sweetness. There was silence. Emily arose to her feet.

"Would a concert of wood instruments," she inquired, "serve the purpose of a concert of stringed instruments?"

Everybody in the room turned to stare at Emily. Mrs. Henshaw flushed deeply and looked at her program. She glanced covertly at Emily to see whatever she was up to. It was curiously shattering to the meeting for some reason, this question of Emily's which drifted out a trifle hesitatingly, nor was there any mockery in Emily's steady grey eyes. But still the possible irony lurking behind this question served as a disintegrator for the harmony of the afternoon. The papers "Ballet and Motherhood," "Woman's Place, the Home," and so forth, dragged. The question uppermost in the minds of all the spectators was that Mrs. Henshaw asked the moment she got outdoors. It was: "What on earth, Emily, ever made you ask that question?"

"I suppose I wanted to," replied Emily in that baffling and unsatisfactory way of hers.

"What did you think of the meeting?" Mrs. Henshaw demanded.

"I thought it was bosh," Emily replied mildly.

Mrs. Henshaw made no reply; her mouth shut with that definiteness that made one gather that she was afraid of what she would say if she let herself say anything.

That evening she told her husband: "Emily is the strangest girl! I sometimes feel as I don't know her at all." At this, Emery Henshaw peered over his glasses at his wife.

"Don't know Emily?" he queried. "Why, Emily has one of the least complicated dispositions that I have ever seen."

It was a few months after that that a new Congregational minister took charge. His wife had hardly returned her parochial calls before she started a suffrage league. The town was aghast. It had not been so shaken since the last Indian raid. Its membership was Mrs. Elder herself—and when I tell you that she was over thirty and, though a minister's wife, dressed fashionably and looked young and blithe, you will agree that Warwick had had a good deal to bear from her already; five young girls whose youth made them feel the need of committing the daring acts; and old Mrs. Houghton, who walked like a grenadier and who had a perfectly distinct gray moustache. She brought with her Minnie Hogan, a servant whom she had had for twenty years and with whom she had quarrels daily. At this the antis laughed loud and long. They stopped, however, and opened their mouths and eyes in wide amazement when it was learned that there was another member and that this member was Emily Henshaw.

The Henshaw household was threatened to its foundations.

"I told you," Mrs. Henshaw said with a shade of sad triumph to her husband, "that Emily was a queer girl."

"I think for our sake," cried Lois, "you might have kept out of this, Aunt Emily." Here Emily, with a curious expression in her face and with extreme gentleness of manner said, "Why, Lois, should I keep from doing anything I want to on your account?"

"I suppose you'd like if you were in my place, to have little boys calling after you on the street, 'Your aunt's a suffragette. Your aunt's a suffragette!'" said Lois with the bitterness of seventeen.

"There are worse things than that happening to one," Emily responded, and there was a certain metallic edge to her gentle tone that ended the discussion.

It was just three months after this that a campaigning party stopped at Warwick. Feeling ran high. The little boys who usually distributed the rare posters of Warwick struck.

"We ain't goin' to carry posters for them wicked women," they announced. The minister's little son, William Elder, together with Emily was forced to distribute the announcements. William came back dirty, with a scratched face, and though one eye was rather discolored, he had tested life, one could see.

"I licked 'em all down the street," he told his mother. "They went for me first, an' I licked the tar out of 'em. Johnnie Davis dared me to bust the plate glass window out of his father's store like a real London suffragette. 'I'll bust yer lamp,' I said, an' I did." There was a parishioner calling on Mrs. Elder at the moment of this frank revelation and she went away shocked to report that Mrs. Elder had not chided her son. It was hard in Warwick to find windows in which one might put up posters. Emily nailed one to the elm tree in the front yard.

"Look," Lois and Margery dashed into their mother's room. "Look," they said, "what's outside."

"However did that get there?" Mrs. Henshaw cried, going out to inspect the incriminating announcement that there was to be a meeting in the Town Hall that night.

"I put it there," said Emily, still at her mildest.

"She hasn't any right to put it there, has she?" asked Lois. "Isn't that tree father's? Would he like it?"

"I'll take it down," said Emily, the gentle. "I'll take it down and just stand there holding it." There was an aimless obstinacy about her gentle voice as she confronted her two nieces and her sister-in-law.

"I think," faltered Mrs. Henshaw, "your father wouldn't mind. It's outside the gate. All sorts of posters get nailed up there."

"I think Aunt Emily's gone dippy," Emily heard Lois saying when she thought herself out of hearing.

"Oh," said Margery, "old maids most always get queer."

Emily went up to her room, her cheeks flushed. She wasn't used to the controversy. Besides, she had caught Margery's verdict. Was this all that her life of service amounted to, then? Would these two girls, to whom she had been a second mother, be so ready to turn her out of house and home with their insistence that the tree was theirs, so ready to put to naught all the years of patient service that she had given them and their household? After all these years had she no deeper place than that? she wondered. Here she was, sound and healthful and thirty-seven. She looked at herself. The glass gave back a serene brow—a purposeful, adequate-looking woman. There was a certain expression to her face not unlike that of people who have lived under orders—calm, and strength, and youthfulness. For many years Emily had looked in the glass almost solely for the purpose of seeing if her hair was neat and her collar tidy. She had also those moments which occur in the life of every normal woman who isn't too plain, of giving herself an approving nod that meant that she was really a pleasant sight to look upon that day.

This time Emily surveyed herself differently—she looked at herself as an outsider might, an outsider who knew all about her. There she stood, a human being unexploited by life. She had too sound nerves to fret herself with small discontents. In a calm way, less colorless than one would suppose, she had enjoyed life; she had enjoyed the children when they were little; she had loved to work with her hands. But the work she had done had only touched the outer fringe of her energy, and meanwhile, in that half-acknowledged background of thought that almost all human beings have, there had blossomed an ambition; and now Emily knew that that ambition had thrust its roots into her very soul—that it was a part and parcel of her life; that she could not pull it out without pulling out life itself; that to deny it would be to deny life. It made no difference that this ambition had come to her under a thousand guises and with a thousand names, and that for the present it had no name. Its essence had been the same. It had shown itself to her under so many forms as did some of the gods of old, for the inner heart of this ambition was to enlarge her circle of endeavor. She wanted to go on serving as she had all her life only to the full limit of her powers, with all the latent and enriched energy within her, with all the un-touched strength of her mind and body. This ambition had come tenta-tively and vaguely when she was a young girl with a desire to go to college.

She stood there and reviewed the four different times in her life when ambition had come to the point of flowering, to the point of her leaving home to go out into the world to study or to work, to lead her own life, and each time the family had stood up and said, "Stay here, Emily." There had been a sickness. Once they had laughed her out of her quixotic ideas. This was when a Warwick girl had wanted Emily to be a matron in a fresh-air colony. Once her brother had needed money badly and she had given him all of her savings. They had made her think that she was of importance; they had made her pity them until she spent herself, and her time, and her energy like water upon them. They had made her part of them, too. Mrs. Henshaw was six years older than Emily. Her eyes peered through her round glasses like those of a critical bird. Her brother had the trick of speaking to her with authority. He treated her now as he had at fifteen, with the indulgent criticism that a male relative has for an unformed female. And, after all, this wasn't her home. No home is one's home that one doesn't build for oneself. They stood together in an appealing solidarity, and she stood apart in an equally appealing loneliness. She had never spoken to one of them a syllable concerning the things that gave life its meaning to her. This did not mean that they did not love her and that she did not love them profoundly; it only meant that they were that curious and intimate and warm thing that one calls the family. She was an outsider, someone who had served the family, sewed for the family, cooked for the family, waited on the family in sickness, but forever and ever on the outside just as they were forever and ever on the inside. And Emily realized at the same time that this again was no one's fault; that this was inevitable with any grown person who lives someone else's life. During this reflection Emily had been dressing herself at her prettiest. She had a natural gift for clothes, which gift had blossomed mostly for Lois and Margery and for putting her own clothes on with that delicate precision that Warwick expected of a gentlewoman of her years. This half-hour of revelation had left more than a casual trace on her. Her color was high; her eyes were bright; her face had lost its habitually gentle vagueness of expression. There was nothing in the world less negative than Emily Henshaw. She met her sister-in-law in the hall. Emily's bearing and expression made her stop abruptly on some errand to the kitchen.

"Where are you going, Emily?" she asked presently.

"To meet the suffrage speakers at the train," replied Emily in the most matter-of-fact tones. Indeed, at this moment it seemed the most everyday thing in the world for her to be doing. Mrs. Henshaw lifted her hand in a sort of helpless gesture which seemed to say: "Well, then, go on to your own destruction," but she made no comment. The first question that the group of suffrage workers put to Emily and Mrs. Elder was: "Have you been able to get any local speaker? You see, Miss Towers has been overdoing her voice and now she's got a bad cold and can't speak above a whisper. Is there no one you can get?" they asked.

"Mr. Elder will speak," Mrs. Elder volunteered with calm certainty, at one with her husband. Then from Emily's lips came the most amazing words that she had ever spoken.

"I'll speak, too," said she.

"Why, Emily," cried Mrs. Elder, "I didn't know you spoke."

"I've often spoken without notes at the Thursday Club," said Emily with calm assurance.

What Emily said that night is of comparatively little consequence. After all, there are just two kinds of speeches—those that hold their audiences, and those that don't. Emily's held. It was the first time that she had ever had a chance to voice openly her convictions with intensity. It seemed to her that it was the first time that she had ever escaped from herself, the first time in years that her real self had held communion with any human being. Now she talked the way she had looked to herself in the mirror, forceful and direct and simple yet persuasive. Almost, she felt as if another person were talking, so little was she accustomed to seeing her real self in public; all she did indeed was to be acquiescent and useful. She had no stage fright. It made no difference to her that this audience was composed of curiosity seekers, of hostile people, many of whom had come to see her make a fool of herself. In her mind it was Warwick, the town that she was going now to leave, and as she spoke she saw the miracle happen that fortunate speakers see. She saw the hostile elements listening with attention; she saw the town weld itself together to listen to her; she saw her audience following her. For that moment she led them and then she stopped, leaving them to wonder about her. After they had all congratulated Emily, Mrs. Tennant, the principal speaker, said to Emily, "You know that Mary Tower won't be able to speak for a week yet. Why can't you come on with us?" For that moment all that that would mean took Emily's breath away. Then, "Why, I'd love to," she said as if she was accepting the most everyday offer in the world. When she went home she found her brother walking the floor restlessly.

"Did you speak?" he asked shortly.

"Yes," replied Emily, looking at him squarely. Someway, her attitude toward him had changed. It didn't make any difference to her what he thought of her any more than her sister-in-law's flushed glances through the round eyeglasses would ever again make any difference to her.

"Well, thank goodness," said he, "they'll go tomorrow, and this tomfoolery is over."

"I'm going with them to speak for a week," Emily let fall. He looked at her like one bereft of wits.

"You're going to do no such foolish thing," he retorted. "No sister of mine is going to make a fool of herself, speaking on soap boxes and cart tails."

Here it was that Emily made her second suffrage speech; it was brief.

# Women's Peace Conference, 1915

## A Footnote to Folly, 1935

*When the International Woman Suffrage Alliance's biennial confer-
ence, scheduled to meet in Berlin in 1915, was canceled due to the war,
an international women's committee issued a call for a woman's peace
congress to meet at The Hague, Netherlands, from April 28 to May 1.
Jane Addams was invited to preside over the meeting at Amsterdam.
The women's peace congress would show that women, unlike the socialists in the warring nations, could maintain international solidarity in
rejection of state-based madness. The congress drew over 1,000 visitors
and 1,136 delegates from twelve countries. Vorse was the delegate of
the Women's Suffrage Party of New York City, representing 151,000
women of greater New York.*

*The congress drafted a set of resolutions which set the conditions for
a just peace; many of these propositions were later to be embedded in
Woodrow Wilson's Fourteen Points. In its most hotly debated decision,
the Congress of Women voted to send peace delegations to urge a plan
for continuous mediation prior to armistice upon the belligerent and
neutral countries. The delegation to the war capitals was headed by
Addams. The second delegation of women made visits to Denmark,
Norway, Sweden, the Netherlands, and Russia. These excursions by a
handful of women seeking peace were treated by the international
press with scorn and ridicule. In the end the women's proposal for
continuous mediation by a conference of neutrals came to nothing.*

The one small green leaf left on the withered tree of internationalism
by the spring of 1915 was the women's movement. The women of the
world did not stop communicating with each other. The women of
England had sent greetings at Christmastime to the women of Germany, and the women of Germany had replied. Letters of protest and
of sympathy for women of other nations appeared in the international
women's magazine, *Jus Suffragii*. Letters came from Frenchwomen
and from Russians. Fräulein von Heymann's open letter, *"Women of
Europe, when will your cry ring out,"* found women in every country
ready to receive it.

In part she said:

Millions of men have been left on the battlefield. They will never see home again. Others have returned broken and sick in body and soul. Europe's soil reeks in blood.

Shall this war of extermination go on?

Women of Europe, where is your voice?

Are you great only in patience and suffering? Come together in the North and South of Europe and protest with all your might against this war, which is murdering the nations, and perform your duty as wives and mothers, as protectors of true civilization and humanity.

The women's rising tide of protest against the war came to a point on February 12, 1915. On that date a great peace meeting was held in Washington by the women of America. On the same date, in Holland, an International Congress of Women, to be held in Amsterdam, was called by Dr. Aletta Jacobs, a famous Dutch suffragist.

Joe O'Brien felt that I should report this conference. I never had a decision so hard to make. I had never been away from the children for a longer time than a few days. Joe pointed out that he could take care of them as well as I and that his health seemed reestablished. With frightful reluctance and an indescribable feeling of homesickness, I made preparations to go.

I was made delegate for the Suffrage Organization of New York State, representing 150,000 women. I got assignments from *McClure's*, then edited by Charles Hanson Towne, to cover the conference, and assignments from *Century* and other magazines to do articles on the civil population in wartime.

I finally sailed, very heavyhearted. Nor was I to forget my homesickness for one moment, for it was only intensified by the crushing experience of seeing war face to face.

The American delegation, the largest which attended the congress, was headed by Jane Addams. It included such people as Grace Abbott, Julia Lathrop, Sophonisba Breckinridge, Dr. Alice Hamilton, Miss Kittredge, Mrs. W. I. Thomas, who, with her husband, was so bitterly persecuted during the war for her pacifism, Fannie Fern Andrews, Mary Chamberlain, from the *Survey*, and Marian Cothren. At my table were Mary Chamberlain and the Pethwick Lawrences.

Besides many of the most forward-looking women of America, the group also included cranks, women with nostrums for ending war, and women who had come for the ride. New Thought cranks with Christian Science smiles and blue ribbons in their hair, hard-working Hull House women, little half-baked enthusiasts, elderly war-horses of peace, riding furious hobbies.

As a background was Jane Addams, unassertive, contemplative, and sensitive. All the way over we discussed our program. All the way over, that great woman, Miss Addams, listened with as much patience to the suggestions of the worst crank among us as she did to such trained minds as Miss Breckinridge. I have never known anyone who had a greater intellectual hospitality or courtesy. When I spoke of this to her one day, she said quietly, "I have never met anyone from whom I could not learn." We were held up for four days in the English Channel, off Dover, and arrived late, just in time for the opening meeting on April 27.

The women who attended this congress were for the most part well-to-do women of the middle class. It was an everyday audience, plain people, just folks, the kind you see walking out to church any Sunday morning. Labor was unrepresented except for Leonora O'Reilly, of the Woman's Trade Union League, and Annie Molloy, the president of the Telephone Operators Union. It was an audience composed of women full of inhibitions, not of a radical habit of thought, unaccustomed for the most part to self-expression, women who had walked decorously all their days, hedged in by the "thou shalt nots" of middle-class life. This meeting of these women seemed all the more remarkable on that account, much more significant than the famous Ford Peace Ship.

The congress was held in a great hall, called the "Dierentuin," in the Zoological Gardens. In front of the gardens on a wide field, soldiers were perpetually drilling. One saw them move off more like automata than men. One saw them go through various maneuvers. They were perpetually there, a living example of the awful madness of war. A Dutchwoman said to me, as we walked past them: "It is only since the war that I have realized that they do this to learn how to kill other men and to offer themselves to be killed. My head has always known this, but my heart only since the war!"

Counting visitors, there were between 1,200 and 1,500 in the audience. There were delegates from twelve countries. But no delegates from France, Serbia, or Russia. Not even the Socialist women would send a delegate while the enemy was on French soil.

On the proscenium sat some of the most famous women in Europe, almost all internationally known; Miss Jane Addams and Miss Fannie Fern Andrews, from America; Dr. Aletta Jacobs and Dr. Boissevain, from Holland; Miss MacMillan and Miss Courtenay, from Great Britain. One wonders where those old feminists are now, Dr. Augsburg and Fräulein von Heymann of Germany, Frau Kruthgar or Frau Hofrath von Lecher of Austria. What has become of those able fighters of twenty years ago from Central Europe?

Of the two hundred English who had planned to come, only two had been allowed visas. And only one Italian delegate had got through, but there were delegates from Poland, from South Africa, and from Canada.

For the first time in all the history of the world, women of warring nations and women of neutral nations had come together to lift up their voices in protest against war, through which the women and the workers gain nothing and lose all.

Usually when many people gather together there is soon developed some dominant rhythm to which the feet of the audience keep time. But here the emotion was smothered, it found no easy outlet. There was something more powerful here than the will to protest. At last I understood what the inner meaning of this assembly was and what was the preoccupation of these women.

What I saw was grief and fear.

I had, I suppose, expected a noisier protest and a more revolutionary spirit in a group of women whose very presence there was a revolutionary act and who were enacting one resolution after another of a revolutionary nature—resolutions which, if they could have been carried out, would have reorganized the planet. Instead of that spirit, there was a spirit of terrible endurance such as is bred by grief and fear and suspense. A spirit with which I was familiar, for I had lived in a fishing village and I knew the granite calm of women during a storm when their men were at sea. As they grow old, the faces of such women take on a sort of iron repose, terrible to look at when you know its reason. It was this resisting quiet that held the women at The Hague.

There was not one woman from the belligerent nations near whom death had not walked. There was no man left at home in all Hungary. The Boy Scouts who had so joyfully posted our letters two years before at the suffrage convention in Budapest were all in the trenches. Two years ago they had been long-legged little boys.

All the women of Germany and Austria and Hungary had seen men, who had gone out singing, return wounded and wrecked. The women of Belgium had seen worse. Four of them had seen Antwerp fall and its miserable, hopeless, and homeless population stream forth. They had seen little girls, too young to know their own names, wandering around strayed from their families. They had found old women who had dropped from exhaustion. The wide and fertile plains of Belgium had been trampled into a bloody battlefield.

A new set of war statistics, concerning the morality of noncombatants, especially of children and women, had trickled in from the women who had not stopped writing to each other.

From Serbia and Montenegro, Miss Durham wrote: "Bad as the lot of sick and wounded may be, I consider it child's play, to the sufferings of the wholly innocent victims of the war, the burnt-out women and children who wander miserably and starve slowly; mothers trying to feed their children on boiled grass and crouching in the rain against the blackened walls of their ruined homes."

News had come from Poland of a suffering so vast that we could not measure it. All America had helped feed famished Belgium.

From Bulgaria came the word: "One of the cruelest results of war that men wage upon each other is the sufferings of women and children. In dispatches no mention is made of the heroism shown and the tortures endured by women, by mothers for their starving children. Wars will never cease until women at whatever cost to themselves are admitted behind the curtains."

"In the Boer War I *was* behind the curtains." Miss Emily Hobhouse wrote in reply: "It seems futile to turn to statesmen, governments or prelates for aid. They are tied and bound by position, custom and mutual fear. They await propitious moments. Famine, disease, and death do not wait. The women have this advantage: they are still unfettered by custom and expediency; they need consult only the dictates of humanity."

All this was known through interchange of letters. Now, on this platform the women of the warring countries and the neutral countries told their stories. The stories of the women followed each other relentlessly, until it seemed as if all the grief of Europe were concentrated here in this hall.

The Polish delegate told how her country was the battlefield of the eastern armies. Thousands of villages had been laid waste and the dwellers of these villages were starving in the forests.

There was one woman whose family owned estates in the Masurian Lakes, into whose swamps the Germans drove the Russians and the Russians then drove the Germans and the Germans and Russians drowned slowly together. The horror of it could not leave this woman, her mind constantly came back to it. She could talk only of that.

From Italy came the story of a state not yet at war but living in nameless suspense. "Our people are starving," the Italian delegate said, "and some say: 'Let us make a revolution' and others, 'Let us go to war, then at least our women and children will be given something to eat.'"

The women of Bavaria repeated over and over again, "There will be no Bavarians left if this war continues," for at that time it was the Bavarian troops who had suffered most.

The woman who, even after all these years, stands out most completely in my mind is Frau Hofrath von Lecher, delegate from Austria. Simple, an aristocrat, so naive that her original speech, which was shown beforehand to the press committee, had to be deleted, for in it she told too much. Already in April 1915, food was lacking in Austria, dressings were lacking, anesthetics and supplies of all kinds were lacking. It was not possible to let her make public the things she told so innocently. Until the war she had lived a quiet private life. Now she had an important position in an Austrian hospital which cared for five hundred wounded.

She made the most moving speech of all the congress. It was so simple that it was as though through her all the women of Europe were speaking. She said:

> I am not a strong and militant woman accustomed to speaking as most of these who have spoken before me. I have never before stood on a platform. All my life, like most of the women whom I know, I have been dependent on my men. But I have seen our men dependent on us weak ones. I have seen their strength wrecked. What are we women of Europe to do? We cannot live without our men, so we dependent women for whom I speak must join ourselves to you strong women and protest against a civilization that under pretension of protecting us, takes our men from us, and so I have come here to cry out: "Give us back our men!"

I talked with her afterward and she told me: "I ask as they lie there wounded, 'What are you fighting for?' and they all answer, 'We do not know—we were told to fight.' When I told them of this congress, they begged me to come and, in the name of their wives and children, implore the nations of the earth to make peace."

Everyone there knew that peace is a militant thing, that any peace movement must have behind it a higher passion than the desire for war. No one can be a pacifist without being ready to fight for peace and die for peace. Perhaps some day a fanatic will arrive and put into action some of the talk of the more militant groups, for there was a glimpse of this militancy. The league for antiwar action, for instance, which appealed in a circular printed in four languages to the women of the congress, urging them to join this militant group. The circular read:

*To Women!*                                           *Know Your Power!*
You who abhor war, and want Peace, what have you done?
You work for the Red Cross and Committees for War Relief, you work to soften war and you ought to work for Peace.
Where are your multitudes, who will kneel before the Powers for hours, days, weeks! not giving way, before the swords are put back in the sheaths and the guns are at rest?
Where are you—innumerable—who will lie down on the roads so that men, horses and cannon must pass over you to reach the battlefields?
Where are you, who refuse to give up husband and sons for war?
Up, you Women, who know the price of Peace;
To princes and people
To battlefield and fortresses
To prisons and executions
Through mockery and scorn
Up to Peace!
The arms *shall* be put down, it is the *will of women.*

The spirit found its expression in the wife of a Dutch officer who from the platform urged the Dutchwomen to throw themselves before the horses of the regiment, should Holland be called to war. It found its expression in a resolution which was not voted on, but which came from a group of Austrians:

> This International Congress of Women, believing that a future war becomes almost impossible if the women of all countries refuse their help, urges the necessity of uniting the women in a Band, every member of which promises to refuse any personal or financial help in case of war.
>
> That means: that we openly declare that women refuse to do the work men cannot do because they are busy murdering other men—that women refuse to repair the damages brought about by men when they wantonly burn and destroy houses and property, that we refuse our help to mitigate poverty and misery caused by the war.

The congress found its most open expression of this militant feeling through Rosika Schwimmer. In the midst of her speech, she paused and requested the audience to rise to its feet, and standing, spend a minute of silent thought on the dead of all Europe and on Europe's stricken women. So this great audience of women rose to its feet and with bowed heads thought of their dead.

I do not know how long we stood there in that terrible quiet. I stood looking into their stricken faces. Tears streamed down the faces of the women. An iron-faced old man opposite me held his head up, while tears slid unchecked down his face. Behind me I could hear the stifled sobs of Wilma Glucklich, for whose family in Hungary I had not dared to ask. An awful, silent, hopeless, frozen grief swept over this audience which, throughout the congress, had been so contained.

Grief was in the air, one stifled in it. The dumb sorrow of that audience crushed one; and when, after what seemed a long time, we sat down at last, it rushed over me: These stricken women *were not the women who had suffered most*. They were neutral, for the most part: and those who had come from the warring countries were not, and could never be, the most deeply affected. The women in this meeting would never lose everything as could the stricken women of the people. Hunger and want and slow starvation would not follow in the wake of irreparable loss. In that hall there was only a faint shadow of the grief and despair of the women of Europe.

These women could only suffer. They hated war, but could not make a significant, arresting protest against it. The meeting was only a gesture. It could be no more than that.

They made a final protest, as brave as it was futile. A resolution brought in by Rosika Schwimmer had been passed providing for committees of women to see the heads of the governments of the warring nations requesting them to stop the war. Miss Jane Addams headed the American delegation which plodded on its useless errand from one chancellor of Europe to another.

I had hoped to get into Belgium from Holland through England. It was possible; permits were later given to one or two of Miss Addams' party. But it was also difficult. Belgium was cut off from the world, except that a few went in and a few came out. Down near the terrible Yser district a thin trickle of German deserters came over the border. Four Belgian women had been allowed to come from Antwerp. They had come by automobile, by trolley, on foot, finally by train. At the border, in spite of military passports and papers of all kinds, they had been searched to the skin. These women had seen the fall of Antwerp and had nursed the wounded ever since the beginning of the war.

One day the kind Dutchwoman, by way of distraction and diversion, took us through the tulip and hyacinth beds of Haarlem. I am sure no such strange, harassed band of women ever walked through these peaceful ways before. That day I talked a great deal with Belgian women. I noticed that they never smiled.

Through Juliette Rublee I met the wife of the mayor of Aerschot. She had managed somehow to escape across the border. She had been made to stand by while her sons and her husband and the other men of her village were shot before her eyes.

Paxton Hibben, whom I met then for the first time and whom I saw a great deal, advised me not to try to get into Belgium. Like most of the other correspondents, he had no patience with the Peace Conference. He felt that the reason the German, Austrian, and Hungarian women had been allowed to come was because it was a peace movement by the Central Powers to undermine the morale of the Allies. At this time he hated Germany with a terrible bitterness and blamed Germany for the war. Later he came to hate war itself as he hated Germany and to place the blame for war on the underlying social system.

He was interested in my assignment to write articles on the civil population, and gave me letters to Ponsot, head of the French government's Publicity Bureau. Together we did some strange sightseeing. We went to a place near the Zuyder Zee to a concentration camp where the German soldiers who had been forced over the Dutch border were interned. In the barracks the bored soldiers were living that peculiar, limbolike existence of the interned: bored, useless, impatient, but after all safe.

The chauffeur who drove us from the concentration camp to the refugees' camp still limped from a wound in his leg. His mother, father, and sisters had been killed before his eyes as they hid together during the bombardment of Antwerp.

We came to a town of neat wooden sheds on an implacable sandy plain on the edge of the Zuyder Zee. There was a church, a school, a hospital, a theater, and an assembly hall. The wide spaces between buildings had been planted with formal gardens and ornate designs of white stone and ground pine. It had everything but life. Over the place hung the air of a perpetual Sunday. There were twelve hundred children, but they were not playing in the broad streets. Everyone seemed eternally waiting.

The refugees divided off little spaces for privacy with blankets or cloth given to them by the kind women of Holland. There they were, old people and young, men, women, and children, in small calico cubicles, small storekeepers, working people, peasants, all leading this strange, limbolike existence. There were woods nearby. The refugees were starting to plant small gardens.

One of the women with me was an American who had been living in a little Dutch town. She had been helping care for the flood of miserable refugees who came over the border from Belgium. And there was no end to her stories of disaster. One landscape remains with me as though I had seen it yesterday. Near the refugees' camp was a cemetery. There were hundreds and hundreds of tiny white crosses. Smallpox had broken out, and the children had died.

# The *Sinistrées* of France
## *Century, 1917*

It is a smiling, fruitful country over the surface of which graves are everywhere scattered; men died fast along this country lane; in the grain are crosses, in the dooryards of what once were peasants' houses are more crosses. Here and there in the pleasant wood trees have been mown down as by a scythe, and when the road leds to a town, heaps of brick, tortured ironwork, and shapeless mounds of stone confront one, and in strange contrast to the general desolation, scattered seemingly at random, are occasional wooden houses, temporary dwellings which the English Quakers in cooperation with the French government have been building in what is aptly named "the devastated areas."

In these districts, over which the full fury of war passed, they will tell one, as they do in Paris, that "things are more normal now." In these areas of destroyed towns and grave-strewn fields live the *sinistrées*, a sinister name for those war victims. These, again, are divided into three classes: the refugees, the burned, and the pillaged.

It is strange and terrible to visit Paris—and no one can be happy—but to one who has loved France it is far worse to visit the lovely northern country. There is here a sense of emptiness, as if terror still hushed the normal cheerful noises of mankind. The people of these regions have lost everything: their houses are burned; their animals, even the rabbits, are gone; their farm implements are shapeless pieces of grotesquely melted iron. They live in temporary, patched shelters and in the houses built by the Society of Friends, or mass themselves in some nearby village that escaped destruction at the hands of the crown prince's retreating army. After a time in this silent country one gets the sense that destruction is normal, and tears start to one's eyes at the sight of an undestroyed French village smiling in the sun. So changed are all values that I could feel nothing strange in the words of the woman who told me, "Fortunately, my husband is a hunchback."

Then through the empty countryside come a few soldiers, or a band of wounded men stagger and grope their way on their first walk forth from the hospital gates; and the thought comes to one that in the world there are always devastated areas and men wounded in battle.

It is in the devastated areas, from the *sinistrées* themselves, that one will learn how simple women feel toward war. It is there one will hear more fully expressed the thought that I had already heard in different languages and in different countries.

"We do not live in the world in which we believed that we were living. None of us thought that it could happen to us, in our time, to the lands we knew, to our husbands and our sons. No one could believe that the world was like this and continue to bear children. And all the time, like some hideous growing plant, war was preparing; it was there waiting for us a few years away, a few months away, a few days away, and no woman believed it could be.

"Then came the horror that we refused to believe in: war came."

War held up a hand and said, "Stop!" Civilization stood still. Suddenly men and women went separate ways; common life was cleft in two by war.

When war called all the able-bodied men to the bloodstained ditches and burrows that rend France from the channel to Alsace and gave the command, "Destroy!" it also said to the women: "Go your fruitful way, bear more children, bind up your men's wounds, bind up the wounds of the country. See, beside your own work of children and home, I give into your hands the families of a million refugees. Bind up the wounds of their spirits, put hope into the hearts of the old, save the lives of the little children, put together those countless families that have been torn apart; then the work that your man has left I give to you to do, and later I may come and destroy the fruitful fields you have planted, and in a day undo the work of careful centuries. I will kill your men and your old people and little children, and when I have done this, you must again rise up and again bear children and again repair the ruin I have wrought."

A well-known writer who has had unusual opportunities for observation has searched almost in vain among the wounded and among those men who have suffered most in war for men who hated it, and has found discouragingly few. Had the search been among women, he would have had a different story.

The simple man accepts war as he accepts birth and death. It does not show its face to him as a monstrous and bleeding horror. Among the many wounded men I talked with, the emotion I found often was a naive self-congratulation that they had been through so much. They, too, when they were old, could tell of their adventures in the great war.

No woman in France could speak this way, but the women of the devastated districts, educated or simple, have a special loathing of war and a bitter and intelligent hatred of the conditions which make war possible. As they talk about it, one feels that there has surged into their fruitful, painstaking lives a hideous monster having no connection with the civilization of which they were a part, a terrible and indecent anachronism, as though from some hidden place of slimy ooze some primeval creature had reared its head and come forth to ravage a countryside.

It is in the quiet of the devastated areas, where from one week's end to another you will see no young man, that you will find the sharpest contrasts between women's and men's parts of the world's work in wartime. In the foremost ranks of what one might call mobilized women have been the schoolmistresses. In one little village, which is recorded as totally destroyed, one house has been rebuilt. This one house serves as schoolhouse and *mairie*. The schoolmistress was a youngish woman, frail and delicate, with lines of sorrow and overwork on her intelligent face. She and an assistant teacher instructed eighty children. It was her energy and resourcefulness that caused the reconstruction of this one house.

She also acts as mayor of the village. The mayor himself is of course mobilized; so is the curé. This means that she takes upon herself much of the relief work that the curé would naturally have performed. The acting mayor is an old man who comes from a village at some distance as infrequently as possible, only to sign the papers necessary for giving receipts for money from the government, and so forth; for the French government gives to all *sinistrées* twenty-five cents a day for every grown person and ten cents for all children under sixteen years of age. The distribution of this fund, as well as the private charities, falls, therefore, into her hands. She sat there in her little office and talked about the various sides of her work, and said in a tone of apology:

"You see, there is really more to do than I can do well. There are eighty children to care for, and their families, and I have an immense correspondence." She motioned to some vast portfolios. "Two thousand French soldiers fell on the battlefield over there"—she nodded out of the open window—"and I am of course still answering the inquiries of their families."

She was of course still answering the inquiries of their families, and she was of course teaching eighty children; she was of course doing all manner of relief work; she was of course giving all sorts of comfort and kindness, making a circle of light in the desolation in which she lived. And as I looked at her, I realized that there were hundreds of women like her who were of course doing the same thing through all the vast, desolated country of the north of France, merely standing by their posts as the telephone and telegraph girls had done during the invasion, unwitting heroines performing their tasks of incredible difficulty. This woman did not mention that she was merely doing her duty; there comes a pressure in human affairs where one ceases to think in terms of duty for one's self, where one works to the limit of endurance and then beyond that limit.

During the war there have been thrown to the surface extraordinary

women like the "Mayor of Soissons," but even more characteristic of
the spirit of the people are the unusual qualities that have been called
up in those who are merely the nation's ordinary women.

I looked out of the window. Here indeed was the biblical word
fulfilled, "There shall not be left one stone upon another." What had
been an orderly and sweet French village was a nameless heap of
stones and rubble, only rearing their heads, gaunt and fireless amid the
general destruction, were the chimneys and the hearthstones, as
though the *foyer,* the hearth, of France, refused to be destroyed. Pom-
peii, beside it, was habitable. It looked as if some great natural calamity, known as an act of God, had passed over it. So it seemed.

Then came to me the intolerable thought: man did this thing. No
incredible cataclysm of nature, but man, more relentless than the sea
in his hideous self-destruction.

I looked from this work of man to the toil-burdened schoolmistress
who in the midst of this desolation had assembled her children together, and contrasted her work with that for which the men of Europe
had been preparing, and one nation so supremely well and with such
loving care. The careful Germans had brought with them petroleum
cans, solid and German, with which to burn the villages through which
they passed. An old man, standing in his flowering garden, showed me
a can that had escaped in the general conflagration; he called it his
"little souvenir which the Prussians had left him." They even brought
with them paraffin with which to burn the manure heaps, so that, in
case they should not hold the land, the civil population might suffer to
the utmost, as they have indeed suffered, but with what unshakable
gallantry it is impossible to express.

This unquenchable spirit was forever being interpreted to me by
some person like an old woman whom I found working in her flower
garden. No dwelling of man was now near that garden, only the
shapeless ruins of what had once been houses. All about was the quiet
of the country and fields, fields studded with graves—graves and ruins,
and there was that garden, bright with peonies and other flowering
things, and the old woman working it. She looked up from her weeding
to offer me flowers.

"Of course my garden is not what it may be another year," she told
me, "for I have walked eight miles to get here, and I cannot always
come; but I cannot bear the thought of losing them altogether. Flowers, you know, require cultivation."

This blooming garden in the midst of the unspeakable desolation of a
ruined village was a part of this old woman's contribution toward rees-
tablishing order. Whether there has been war or not, the education of
the little children must go on, and flower gardens must go on, and all
the blooming, graceful things of French life must go on, as much as
they can.

Among all the *sinistrées,* only once did I come across the suggestion from any woman that there was no use in going on. This woman had lost all her sons in battle, and her husband had been ill all the winter as the result of exposure. She sat with hands folded in her lap; when a woman from the Society of Friends asked her if she did not wish to put in an application for a temporary house, she said: "There is no use in it for us."

Her husband, beaten by illness and the loss of his sons, sat there as though still stunned by the immensity of his misfortunes. These two people were so apathetic, so detached from life, that they seemed to be only waiting for death; and it came to me that they were the first I had seen whom the Germans had beaten. But I had reckoned without their eight-year-old daughter, Rose.

"Madame," she said as we were leaving, "they want this house." She came forward, her face flushed. She stood there before us, her little head erect, her eyes shining, the embodiment of the courage of the women of France. "I will go with you," she said, "to the *mairie,* and we will put in our application."

She knew what she wanted; she knew the cost of the house; she knew the business details connected with it. "For I can read," she said; "I have been reading about these houses upon the posters."

She had sat there amidst her mother's tears, her father's dumb despair; she had watched them relax their hold on life, and, baby though she was, there had come into her heart the resolve of a woman: She would have their little house; she would reestablish their family.

And now, at this writing, Rose's house will already have been built, and her parents will again be reawakening to life. For such a heroic child they can do nothing else.

I left the country of the *sinistrées* with the words of a friend of mine echoing in my heart: "I have seen so much beauty, so much mutual aid, so much self-sacrifice since the beginning of this war that I can never distrust human nature again."

But above this thought is another one. Must heroic and great qualities of men and women be organized forever only for war and for repairing the destruction that war causes?

There is an office which passes a procession of dark-clothed men and women, where all day long the words "We regret there is as yet no news" are heard. Once this had been a language school; today it houses the Bureau de Renseignements pour les Familles Dispersées. This is one of the thousands of familiar places in Paris that war has changed to its uses.

The red cross floats over the place where there had been a club for girl students; a favorite restaurant houses a workshop. The reception rooms of hotels are turned into *vestiaires;* schools house the most miserable of all *sinistrées,* the refugees. The altered use of public and private buildings is the outward sign which tells you that all through France the thought of anything except war has ceased. Life in its ordinary course has ceased. People get up and go to bed, pursue their various businesses, as in a vacuum. The ordinary business of life has no longer any meaning; nothing has meaning except that unnatural and ghastly work of killing; nothing counts that is not connected with this work of destruction. The complete spiritual isolation of a whole nation from all subjects that do not concern killing and being killed, or the contemplation of the destruction attendant on war, is another of war's least negligible by-products.

In the strange and nightmare country of the trenches where the men of France live, the real lives of the women of France are passed.

There is not a single little family on the remote border of France whose eyes are not fixed on that long, narrow strip of bloodstained country, that tormented and tortured country of barbed wire, of mitrailleuses, of shells, of great guns and trenches. The state of soul of a nation which has subordinated the fruitful industries of life to the subject of killing and being killed is a strange thing. The spirit of a nation which sees its young manhood and its youth surge up to the country of death and then ebb back wounded and dead is strange and grave; so strange and so grave that, if you had lived there before, the unfamiliarity of its familiar aspect is a terrifying thing.

As I went about among my friends, I became aware of the overpowering sense of something that was almost more poignant than grief; a nerve-racking spiritual discomfort overwhelmed me, outsider though I was; and presently the meaning of this discomfort translated itself into words: suspense was what brooded over all the men and women whom I met. They were waiting; they gave the effect of a whole nation listening to invisible voices; and while the surface of conversation was as normal as it could be, since it dealt with such abnormal things as war and the lamentable by-products of war, they were all of them waiting, waiting, for news from the front, waiting to learn if sons and husbands were still alive, waiting for the end of the war.

Suspense was everywhere, but it brooded more closely in that office, where once people went to learn languages and where they now go to wait for tidings of their mothers, of their children, lost years ago, in the time when the German army overran France and created the army of the *sinistrées.*

In the vast confusion that occurred when the German army swept down upon Paris—a confusion which affected a civil population of millions of people—members of families lost one another. In the vast card catalogues of the Bureau de Renseignement les Familles Dispersées is concentrated the suspense and anguish of a nation.

Of this vast suspense, this anguished searching of mothers for children, of daughters for mothers, of fathers, of sons for all their families, nothing is heard in the outside world. This calamity of the tearing asunder of thousands upon thousands of families, which, had it come at another time, as the result of some cataclysm of nature, would have caused the pity of the whole civilized world to stream forth, is now only a little incident for the world at large, an incident for everyone except those concerned in its hideous tragedy.

There are many little children in France, tiny youngsters, babies so young that they cannot speak, who have strayed on the roads, and of whose parents no trace has yet been heard.

The newspapers in France also contain advertisements of fathers searching for their children, and wives for their husbands, and soldiers for their families.

So today when I think of France, I cannot think merely in the terms of a country invaded. Another great, shadowy army fills my mind—the army of mothers searching for their children, of daughters searching for their old parents, waiting day by day for news of those whom they love, wondering among what strangers they are living, and then, perhaps mercifully and perhaps sadly, after months, again united. My mind reverts to this group of women searching continuously for the lost, and helping to reunite the members of those families.

War, which had welded the men of the country into an engine of destruction, had sent its women forth on countless works of mercy and reconstruction, and this work I had come to France to witness. As I went about on this strange and heartbreaking sight-seeing, as I visited barracks in which not wounded soldiers, but wounded families, lived and ate, saw workshops, hospitals, there came to me a vision of what a total disorganization war meant to the civil population.

Day by day among the *sinistrées* I heard stories of flight from burning villages, until such a flight seemed a usual experience. I heard tales of lost relatives. I saw families cut in half by war. I saw women searching for old mothers. I saw refugees who had lost little children. I listened to the dreadful prattle of children who talked of killing. I saw listless, sad-eyed young girls who had witnessed the death of all dear to them. I saw women sitting with folded hands, their means of livelihood gone, their husbands gone, their reason for living gone.

I saw little children below the age of speech, who had been found wandering on the roads by soldiers, and two Belgian children who had been found in the very trenches where they had fled terrified during the bombardment. No one can ever know who they are; their mothers will never see them again.

I saw women, in deepest grief over the loss of their sons, stay by their posts unflinching, never stopping in their work, and everywhere I saw beauty and unquenchable courage, even though many walked with the weary air of those whose illusions have been killed and with them their inner reason for living. High and low worked with the desperate activity of ants whose anthill had been stepped on. I looked and listened until I was drowned by what I saw, until I could see no more and hear no more.

And as I saw these things, all the vast, restless stirring of women, which, when it is self-conscious, we call feminism, seemed to me to have supremely gained in significance; it seemed that its very roots lay in women's age-old mute protest against war.

I had, in the weeks that preceded my journey into France, heard a great deal of talk concerning the basic racial and economic causes of war. Here is the contribution to these reasons of a very simple woman, and it seems to me that in it there is a very profound truth.

The name of this woman is Mme. Etienne, and she was once my concierge. I always go to see her when I am in Paris, for I love her homely wit and her gaiety. Her three boys had been almost young men when I had last seen her, and I wondered if she had joined the women in mourning. She met me dry-eyed. She seemed, indeed, as if turned to stone, for she told me in a hard and steady voice:

"They are all dead, all. All three died within six weeks. Since then I have read no papers. There is no victory for me. There can be no victory for those whose sons are dead."

From the streets came the sound of singing, cabs rattled by decorated with Italian flags. War had called to something deep in the hearts of these men, and found there a response. We watched them in silence a moment. Then Mme. Etienne stretched out her hand toward them and cried:

"As long as men love war like that, there will be war, and when they hate it as we hate it, there will be no more war."

And at her words the oppression that had followed me since the beginning of the war found its meaning. She had said the thing that I had seen since I had realized to the full the terrific cleavage war had brought between men's affairs and our affairs, but had not wished to put into words.

Since the war, even the men at home had turned to me the faces of strangers. They thought negligible what women thought important. The things we asked one another as we talked about the war held no interest for them. The sense of men's strangeness has bred a fear in me that had no name and no face. Now at last I saw the reason with terrible clearness.

Now I knew why even the men of my own country had seemed so alien to me, and the reason is that the difference between men and women is the difference between birth and death. I had thought that the profound differences between men and women became trivial in the face of their still profounder similarity. But now it seems to me that our deepest experience is giving life and their intensest moment is when they are called on by war to go out and destroy the lives for which we have risked our own.

Man plays a very small part in the supreme adventure of birth. When a woman goes down to death to give life she goes alone. Man is nothing to her then. Her husband, the father of the child to be born, cannot share in her pain. Her intensest moment she lives by herself. The great miracle of birth is no concern of his, and he can only shrink back, a frightened witness, and wait and wait interminably and pray that all is well. The great experience for her, and for him only the permission to wait.

When men go out to fight they, too, go alone. We cannot go with them; we only wait while they risk their lives that other men may die. Men and women go alone to their supreme adventures.

# The Pink Fence

### *McCalls Magazine, 1920*

Mary Davis walked up the back street looking for a cheap room. She was a teacher away on her holiday and had failed to find anything she could afford on the front street.

The back street was high above the town, on what had been the crest of an ancient dune; from it you could look down on the tops of trees and the shingles of the gray, weather-beaten roofs, and the whole town was spread like a panorama before you.

It was very hot—how hot you could tell by the color of the bay, which was stretched out like a sheet of sapphire. The street was as pale as a pastel. Its houses, where the Portuguese crowded out the New Englanders, were painted pink and pale green, and even robin's-egg blue. Handsome dark-skinned children played in the streets. Opulent women moved about their work slowly, and lazy dogs lolled at ease in the white dust in the middle of the road.

The low, light houses were shaded, now by wide-spreading willows, and now by silver maples. In all the yards flowers bloomed; the golden disks of sunflowers stood out against the pale houses; golden-glow, abundant and disheveled, grew in clumps by gray fences; dahlias nodded heavy heads and hollyhocks spired in rows against the barns, and everywhere were pale phloxes.

At the top of the hill a garden beckoned Mary Davis. This garden was so cherished and of such luxuriance that it seemed as though the other abundant flowers all had flowed from it, as though this garden had been as infectious as happiness.

Lila Bent, the owner of the garden, stood among the flowers staking up a dahlia, shining like a flower herself. Her hair was silver and her face pink, and, in spite of her white hair, an air of almost girlish loveliness still clung about her. A long apron with a small gray figure in it covered her from top to toe. The face of a dryad she must have had, Mary reflected; the sort of face that comes peering out at you behind a tangled web of green leaves. A small boy with hair the color of marigolds was working gravely beside her.

She heard Mary Davis' footsteps, and looked up. Their eyes met and held each other as if they were old friends slowly recognizing each other, though they had never met before, though both of them were

320

timid women brought up in the atmosphere of reticence. So arresting
was Lila's personality, so lovely the garden, that it seemed natural for
Mary to exclaim: "How beautiful your flowers are!"

Lila Bent's color, which came and went like that of a shy girl, height-
ened. "Won't you have a posy?" she asked. She began constructing "a
posy" of sweet peas surrounded with candytuft. The two women
chatted a moment about the flowers, for even the roadways were bordered by a tangle of bouncing-betties and Queen Anne's lace.

"Sort of queer combination, ain't they?" said Lila Bent. "Such a
down-at-the-heels tramp, the bouncing-bet, and the Queen Anne's
lace such a lady. Always together in spite of themselves—somethin'
like being married to a stranger."

As she said this a shadow passed over her, as definite a thing as a
fleck of blue on the dunes cast by a scudding cloud. The women
chatted over the fence, of gardening, of what makes flowers grow, and
of the conflict of the gardener with the hostile forces of nature forever
marshaled against him.

"Seems like mean things is always trying to get the better of one,"
said Lila. Her eyes smiled at Mary. "Just like in oneself, you got to get
up bright and early or they get ahead of you, and your flowers is et or
withered."

Mary moved at last. "I've got to go look for a room," she said. "You
don't know any place I could get where there's a view, do you?"

Lila Bent paused, and it was as though a pool of silence had spread
itself around them. A ripple of excitement passed over her face, and
then, with an animation that held in it a sense of adventure, "Why
don't you stop with me? I got a spare room. You could get meals real
handy—down to Whorf's. Come and see if the room suits you."

She led the way up the brick walk and into a gloomy impersonal
house. It might have belonged to someone else, and that Lila Bent
moved in only yesterday. It had plenty of space but it had been cut into
a multiplicity of small rooms for some former numerous family, and
now it cried out to have partitions removed. The furnishings were
formal and ugly, nor had one adornment of a personal nature been
added.

With Mary and the little boy following, Mrs. Bent led the way up
the narrow stairs built, as in so many Cape houses, like the companion-
way of a boat. She opened the door of the spare room. It was hung in
bright faded chintzes, pink as the flowers in the garden. It was a lovely
gay room, waiting as though ready for a welcome guest, and so at
variance with the rest of the niggardly house that Mary stared. And
Mrs. Bent, as if she sensed her guest's astonishment, explained:

"I fixed this room up for my folks when they'd come to visit me, but
lately not many of them have come along. What with them moving

away, and all . . ." She let her voice trail off, and gazed out of the dormer window which gave over the bay.

The harbor was formed by a frail scimitar of sand, and around from the outside came winged vessels in stately flight. Lila Bent fixed her gaze on these, and her face darkened.

"The fishin' fleet's in early," she said. "I wasn't expectin' it until tomorrow." A look flashed between the child and Lila Bent, an uncomfortable look of understanding.

Later, after Mary Davis had gotten her bags up, she heard a man's voice below.

"Who's that moving around upstairs?"

"That's the roomer."

"The roomer?" repeated the voice. "The *roomer!* Why Lila, I thought you was dead set against roomers! I thought you wouldn't stand no strangers in this house!"

"Well, with prices going up so," came Lila's voice. "You know you was talking about it th' other day—the prices. Anyhow, she don't seem no way like a stranger," she finished. He grunted his approval.

"Ef you'd 'a' taken my advice years ago," he opined, "there'd be a tidy little pile of money in the bank today. What ails wimmin? You kep the spare room empty. Always one excuse after another—one excuse after another! The spare room had to be ready for your folks, an' now . . ."

Lila's voice cut in, even and detached from all that had gone before: "Supper's ready."

When Mary Davis saw Lila again, her personality was as though washed from her; dimmed, was what she seemed. And as for Ed Bent himself, he was a weather-beaten nondescript man; such distinguishing marks as he had, had been put on him by the sea. An insignificant man who thought well of himself. He had once been handsome, it was evident, and he still fancied his looks and considered his black eyebrows jutting out over his blue eyes striking. The two appeared to belong together as little as Lila and the house—remote and chance-met was what they seemed, instead of man and wife.

One night, soon after, the women sat in the arbor and watched the saffron clouds roll up from the west and the sea darken itself and throw out into relief the sails of fishing boats. They were absorbed in its beauty, which had in it a savage menace of storm. The silence of suspense brooded over the town; Lila Bent's voice drifted as if from a distance.

"Seem's if you can feel what the sky was thinkin' when you look on the face of the bay—"

And now from the front of the house came a voice. "How pretty Lila's flowers are in the evening light, Ed."

"Take up an awful lot of space," Ed Bent answered. "Next year I don't think I'm a-goin' to have 'em! I'm a-goin' to plant vegetables!"

Mary Davis shot a look at Lila Bent, who sat poised on the edge of her chair. Nothing in the world existed except the sound of her husband's voice. Everything else in life was excluded. There was such a still violence in her pose that it startled Mary. She wanted Lila to cry out at him, to contradict him, to do anything except sit there rigid and listening.

"You're goin' to do *what?*" came the woman's voice. "You're goin' to tear up Lila's garden?"

"Folks is gettin' too much for vegetables to waste all that space," he answered.

"But, *Lila!*" cried the woman, "What' *she* goin' to say? Why, the store she sets by that garden! The comfort she takes givin' flowers away!"

"That's just it, she *gives* 'em away!"

"But what'll she *say?*" the woman persisted.

"She won't say," he asserted. "What should she say? She won't say nothin'." He brought it out with the truculency of the weak. "I spoke to her about it—she never said a word. She's a real good wife, Lila is—not unreasonable like some folks."

He was leaning against a tree, a nondescript grizzled man, proclaiming with complacency to a horrified world that his spirit was so bankrupt that he could destroy the work of Lila's hands for the matter of a few dollars. You had only to watch her in the garden to know that, in her life, it had taken the place of children. It was her career. Her love of the world and of beauty flowed out through these flowers, and Ed Bent was talking of uprooting the work of years as one would dispose of a row of withered beans. And he thought she wouldn't mind!

The neighbor's voice rang out sharply. "It's a shame for you to talk so, Ed Bent—you making good money, fishing like you do!"

The listening women heard her feet tapping indignantly down the road. While Lila Bent sat there like one frozen with the cold grief of sudden bereavement, her eyes on her garden, Mary could find no consoling word. What can you say to a woman whose husband casually announces that he intends to kill what makes life valuable and beautiful to her?

At last they arose as if by common consent. "I think I'll go for a walk; won't you come with me?" said Lila. She went into the house and Mary stood there looking with aversion at Ed Bent still leaning against the tree.

"Where you goin', Lila?" he called as they started out.

"For a walk," she answered.

"But where's my supper?" he wailed. "What am I goin' to *eat?*"

"I left it for you on the table."

"But what if I *wanted* somethin'," he protested. He stood there staring after the two women as though trying to figure out what unaccustomed thing had entered into his ordered scheme of life.

The abiding kindness of the back country enfolded them; they walked along a sandy trail bordered with sweet-smelling bay. A path gleamed white in the shining darkness of the wild-cranberry carpet. The trail led them through a rolling country, down a silent glen where the leaves of the bull-briar, already touched by autumn, shone like little plates of gold. After an abrupt climb up a sandy path the dunes lay spread before them, savage, untamable, their cups already swimming with lilac shadows.

"What I can't bear," Lila at last let drift out, her eyes seeking the place where the dark ribbon of sea met the yellow of the dunes, "is for him to say 'You've always been a good wife.' *A stranger can't be a good wife, can she?*"

Mary Davis didn't understand. "A stranger?" she repeated automatically.

Lila Bent's face was silhouetted against the sand's deep yellow in the evening light. She seemed part of the impassioned strangeness of the dunes.

"Could anybody but a *stranger* have talked like he did? I never said it before out loud. I've never said it to a soul. I felt I owed him a lot—not feelin' toward him like a wife. But someways I always wanted to say it out loud. Hundreds of times I wanted to say out loud to folks: 'He ain't no kin of mine; he's a stranger to me! We've been married thirty years but he's a stranger to me,' 's what I wanted to say. I've been waitin' to tell everybody ever since I found out. I've been waitin' to tell *him*—"

"Why haven't you?" Mary Davis asked.

"Because I've been afraid of him," she answered somberly. "I've been a coward but I've been less afraid of him since I had a fight with him the other day. He never knew it—he never knew that I had a fight, for I didn't speak out loud. He said to me, 'How much room your garden takes! It costs us a pretty penny. I guess I'll grow vegetables next year.' I stood there feelin' just like I did when I first knew I was marryin' a stranger; the same frozen feelin' like I had a lump of ice in me instead of a heart. I couldn't believe his word. Then I quarreled with him.

"'Who's goin' to take care of your vegetables?' I thought inside myself. 'I won't plant 'em, and if you plant 'em I'll tear 'em up!' But I didn't say nothin'. I didn't speak a word. And he bein' a stranger as he is, he never noticed. He kep' right on talkin' about how much money we'd make out o' vegetables, but by and by my heart began to melt

inside me. I knew I wasn't afraid no more. I felt like I got to show him
how I wasn't afraid. You know Dicky Souza, the little boy with the red
head. I leaned over my fence and I called right out to him:

"'Dicky, you want a flower? Come over and see Mis' Bent,' and
Dicky, he came runnin', keepin' a weather-eye out for Ed—for Ed
can't stand children, they make him nervous.'"

She paused. In all this recital she never lifted her voice. She had the
tense quiet of violence, the vibrating revolt of a peaceful women whose
peace has been deeply disturbed. Her tranquility was as disturbing as
the pause before a storm.

"Did you know he was a stranger before you married him?" Mary
Davis threw into the silence.

"I knew it the night before I was married. You know how girls are—
in love with love. Ed was a good-lookin' fellow, and smart. What did I
know about him? What do young people know about life and love?
They want the sweets of life—sweet things, sweet cakes, sweet girls,
sweet kisses. That was all I knew up to the night of my weddin'. I was
sittin' on the porch and the smell of syringas came up sweet. It was a
sort of a silver night and I felt as if I was swimmin' out into it. I was
dreamin' those kind of dreams girls dream—they had children's voices
in 'em and flowers. And while I seemed part of the night, I was listenin'. I was listenin' to hear if I wouldn't hear his footsteps pass the
house. I'd hear people ever so far in the stillness. Old man Bickers
came down, I could tell his lame walk as far as I could hear it; then a
girl and a man walkin' slow under the elms—sweethearts. Then, I
heard *him;* there was someone with him, and the other fellow was
jokin' him—the kind of joke that men make when a fellow is goin' to be
married. I couldn't hear the words, I could just hear the way they
laughed, and my cheeks grew hot. It was somethin' about children.

"'Children!' I heard Ed's voice snap out. 'You said "children." I don't
want none. I'm gettin' *married*. I ain't goin' to have none botherin'
around me and turnin' out God knows how, spendin' my money.'

"My heart turned right to ice just like it did today. I thought, '*Why,
I'm marryin' a stranger. Who's this man I'm marryin'?*' I thought. I
didn't know him. He was a stranger and I knew he'd always be a
stranger. In spite of his laugh I knew he meant what he said—you can
say that for Ed, he's consistent. He was young and bonny, but I'd
looked behind all that an' seen *him*. I'd just done, before I was married, what hundreds of men and women do afterward—I'd seen clear
beyond.

"I didn't sleep all night. By mornin' I knew one thing more and that
was—I wouldn't never want a child by that strange man."

Mary Davis started to speak.

"I know what you're goin' to ask. 'Why didn't you get out of it?' Why don't you get off the train if it's goin' where you don't want to go? Why don't folks commit suicide? I hadn't the courage. I told my mother. What she said only made it worse. 'All girls feel panicky the day they're gettin' married.' And then when I cried so, she said, 'Why, how you take on. It ain't like you. What's Ed been sayin' to you?' How could I tell her? I knew right then that she would think it was awful for one to be thinkin' about children at all; and still worse, that I didn't want 'em—not his children, not the children of a stranger.

"And yet, why didn't I go? Sometimes lookin' back I don't understand myself why I didn't run. But you don't run when the place you lived in is burnt down, or when a flood has swept your garden away. You just stay there starin' at where it used to be. I was like that—I was dazed.

"My aunt came to my room. I can think just how she looked. I can remember everythin' that happened that night and my weddin'-day more clear than anything since—like in a way life had stopped right then. My aunt was a handsome, high-busted woman, and she looked down on skinny girls. She fancied women who favored her. She was dressed for the weddin', her plump arms was in wine-colored sleeves as tight as skin. She had on the biggest bustle that I ever saw. Even on my weddin'-day I admired that bustle.

"'What ails you, Lila?' she said. 'What's this your mother tells me?' And I knew even if her sleeves were skin-tight, she understood more than my mother did.

"'I'm marryin' a stranger,' said I.

"'We all marry strangers,' said she. 'All men are strangers to all women. Lila,' she said, 'if really you don't want to be married, stop now—but *don't you get married and come back to your folks!* There's never been any woman in our family who came back to her folks!' She said that and she closed the door.

"Well, the hours went on. I couldn't stop 'em any more than I could stop the weddin'. I was a coward. I was afraid of them; I was afraid of him. I'd always been a biddable girl. My thoughts ran round like a squirrel inside a cage. But by the time I was dressin', my thoughts came clear and straight. I suppose no girl dressin' for her weddin' ever had funnier thoughts than me! I'd be no worse off, I figured, than many a woman who hasn't married. Not all women had children. I made my bargain with him just as if I'd talked to him. I knew what his answer would 'a' been if he'd known—and yet, I always felt because I hadn't talked to him I owed him lots.

"'I'll keep house for you,' I thought, 'I'll marry you though you are a stranger and you'll always be a stranger.' I've done it all these years—and he never noticed."

She paused again. "It's not been a bad life, but it's been a lonely one.

It's always a lonely life for a woman that has the voices of children whisperin' at her, and the want of children tuggin' at her heart. It's got to end now! He's got to know what I think. He's got to know that he's got no right to tear my life up."

The next day was Sunday and Lila came down before church time. She wore a sunbonnet and carried a basket in her hand. Ed Bent stared at her.

"Ain't you goin' to church, Lila?"

"No," she said in the unassertive tone in which she always spoke to him, "I'm goin' out beach-plummin'. I'm goin' to take a day off. I'm not comin' back for dinner."

"You're not *what?*" he cried. "Have you took leave of your senses, Lila?"

"I haven't taken a day off I don't remember when. I never had a Sunday off since I been married," she said in her tone of invincible mildness.

"Who's goin' to get my dinner?" he cried.

"I baked pies yesterday and there's meat in the ice-box."

She walked with the gait of a young girl, swinging down the dusty street bound for the limitless freedom of the dunes.

Mary Davis, coming into the kitchen, heard Ed Bent mumbling to himself.

"Lila's gone off," he exploded. Then, hesitatingly, "You noticed any-thin' queer about her lately? She ain't touched, is she?" He was angry and baffled. "A man's got a right to a hot Sunday dinner," he protested. "I'd like to know what ails her."

He had no chance to find out. The *Constellation*, the vessel on which he fished, sailed in the morning for George's Banks.

Next day, when Mary Davis came out, Lila was at work, painting the fence. She had a bucket of whitewash stained with a light saffron pink.

"Ain't that a pretty color?" she asked. "Just flushed, like some of these flowers. I always wanted a pink fence. Oh," she cried, "there have been so many things I always wanted." Suddenly, "I'm goin' to do it!"

"Do what?" asked Mary.

"Bargain with him!" she cried. "I was only workin' to keep my gar-den. Now I'm goin' to bargain with him for Dicky. I won't stay without Dicky—he's an orphan, you know."

She was no longer fighting for the right to exist or for a little shelving foothold on the happiness of life, but to fill up the unsatisfied and empty spaces in her heart. It was a sudden and late and reckless flowering into the daring of happiness. If she couldn't have Dicky, she was ready to pay her price by doing violence to pride and tradition by "goin' back to her folks."

Later the fog closed in and passed its simplifying hand over all the
world. Trees loomed up ghostly, and what one could see of the town
had a shimmering loveliness. As Mary Davis came up the hill, the
flowers glowed at her like a sort of witchfire. Lila's toiling figure
seemed, through the fog, to have some symbolic significance; and the
tender pink of the fence unrolled before Mary's eyes like a flag of
freedom.

All next day the fog continued. The long booming horn from Paint-
er's Rip answered the slow tolling bell of Land-End's Light. Outside,
the vessels hooted and bellowed at one another like marine monsters.
The world was shrunken; mystery enshrouded it.

With a feeling of unwarranted suspense, Mary sat with Lila. When a
knock came on the door, both women jumped. Two women and a man
were there. Lila ushered them into the forbidding chill of the living
room. They stood a moment with the awkwardness of those who have
bad tidings. Finally, one woman blurted out:

"You ain't heard yet? The *Constellation's* been run down in the fog!"

"Don't take on, Mis' Bent," the man said gently. "'Tisn't as if you was
like some of the women, with a lot of children and maybe your husband's life not insured."

"Yes, poor things. They've got something to cry for, some of the
women in this crew. You can thank God you're well fixed, Lila."

When they had gone, Lila turned to Mary Davis and there delivered
her judgment on Ed Bent's life. "Now I can have Dicky to live with me
without fightin' for him."

She busied herself in fixing black clothes. "I wouldn't in any way
shame him," she explained. "Ed was a good man in his way." She
listened with reticence to the women who came to comfort her.

"It'll be lonely for you, but now you can fix the house over to suit
yourself, Lila. You remember the time you said how you hankered to
make the inside match the garden with some bright chintzes and a new
bay window cut, and a porch with ramblers climbin' over it?"

So they prattled, unabashed, until Mary Davis had the uneasy sense
that if destiny should have taken their husbands away from them, they
all knew exactly what small compensations they would have had.

Happy thoughts went streaming through Lila Bent's head as she sat
stitching her black clothes—thoughts of children and flowers, and a
bright cheerful house—but she said nothing of them, even to Mary,
not wishing to shame the name of Ed Bent who had nothing wrong
with him except himself.

Three days passed when more news came from the *Constellation*.
She had been hit squarely in the fog by a big freighter, and she had
gone down with all hands.

At dusk, on the fourth day, Mary Davis walked down the street with

Lila Bent in her black clothes. Beside her ran Dicky, with his marigold hair. An atmosphere of still content shone about Lila. From now on Dicky was to be her boy. She saw the little house blossoming like the garden, lighted with the sunlight of Dicky's presence and the bright color of his shining hair.

Suddenly, Lila stood as if rooted.

"Look!" she said, grasping Dicky's hand.

Coming toward them was Ed Bent and his dory mate, Uncle Joe Silva.

They both walked like men desperately tired. Ed came up to Lila crossly. "What ails you?" he said. "What ails you, gapin' at me like that? What you dressed in black for? Who's died?"

"Why, haven't you *heard?*" she said.

"How'd I hear anythin', me rowin' in from George's Banks? Went off and left me, the *Constellation.* Went off in the fog and left me adrift. I won't ship with her no more, nor will Uncle Joe."

A woman passing by gave a loud scream and ran into the house.

"Well, of all things!"

"She thinks you're a ghost," said Lila gently. "The *Constellation* went down that night with all hands, that's why you couldn't find her when the fog lifted."

At that the two men stared at each other, and then Ed Bent rent the quiet with a shrill cackle of laughter. It was like a knife ripping through sailcloth.

"O-ho," he laughed. "And we've been cussin' our luck, eh, Uncle Joe? And look at my woman here in mournin' for me."

Gradually a small crowd gathered around Ed Bent and Uncle Joe Silva. They were the heroes of the hour. The evening light struck the creamy pink of the fence. It showed out deeper than in the day.

"What's all this?" cried Ed Bent. "What's this fence of ours doin', painted up like a circus?"

A flush mounted to Lila's face. "That's the first thing I ever done of my own will in all these thirty years."

Anger flamed up in him and then died down again. "I don't know what ails you lately," he appealed as though to the universe. "You've always been a good wife."

"Good wife!" she cried in a still fury. "I've never been a good wife. I've treated you as I would a stranger, you and your things, and you treated me like your housekeeper. You wouldn't let me keep a dog; and the children that loved me you chased out of the house. You stood between me and life, Ed Bent. You stood between me and little children to love. And then when I made my own life, you talked about rootin' it up—but you can't root it up—not even now you've come back!"

The little crowd drew away as though retreating before the still, intense flame of her anger, and left Ed Bent isolated.

"Until I thought you wasn't comin' back any more, I didn't know how sweet life could be. But I know now and I'm goin'. I'm a-goin', and I'll take Dicky with me, and that's all I'll take from out your house."

"If it's the flowers, Lila, don't worry—"

She cut him short by a slight, imperious gesture.

"But what am *I* goin' to *do?*" he cried. He stood there, a little bankrupt man, lost in his anger and confusion, gaping after her as she swept by him, Dicky's hand still in hers, on her way back to her folks.

# Milorad

## Harper's Magazine, 1920

*In all the murderous havoc created by World War I, there was no place, not even Russia, where the results were more tragic than in Serbia, where the war began. In 1915 the country was overrun by invading armies. The Serbian soldiers, accompanied by thousands of civilians, retreated to the sea over the snow-covered mountains of Montenegro and Albania. Of the 250,000 Serbian soldiers in retreat, less than half survived the march. Much of Serbia's population fled their homes.*

*In addition to the destruction of Serbia's transportation and communications systems, buildings, hospitals, food animals, and crops, one out of every five Serbians died during the war, from starvation, disease, exposure, or battle. In early 1919, 150,000 Serbian children were in desperate need of food; clothing was so scarce that newborn children were wrapped in paper. There were over 71,000 abandoned or orphaned children in Serbia in 1919.*

The rain fell in Mitrovitza and thinned the streets of women and little girls, and it was as though it washed the color from the world, for the women of Mitrovitza wear trousers of orange and vests of green, while their headdresses are saffron and pale yellow. No women in all Serbia are as brilliantly dressed as the Jewish women of Mitrovitza. They look equivocally at the men from their long eyes, for the town is a sink where the races and tribes of the Balkans meet. Here they eddy and swirl about one another; then they stream out over the roads through Albania to Montenegro. They go south to Uskub and north over the mountainous paths of the Great Retreat. Here come the Albanians from the hills in their white homespun clothes, braided boldly in black with the slash of their red sashes around their waists, while the soldiers of France and England meet those of Serbia in all the streets. Some come to Mitrovitza and see in it a great and wicked city and drink of its wickedness; and some see in it a lost and vicious little hole, a town part Turkish, part Albanian, and part Serb. For here begins the welter of the irreconcilable hates of Macedonia.

I walked past the shop where the Albanians were weaving rugs; past the bazaars, outside of which hung kerchiefs of scarlet and green and white and lemon and orange; and over the bridge, looking for bread for my journey. Turkish women, black even to their veils, hurried past me in hasty stealth. A cart drawn by water buffalo waggled by. I stopped at the bread shop, where the old Turk, in a well-wound turban, white stockings on his feet, sat cross-legged beside his piles of round, flat loaves.

A coal-black "madagash"—a French colonial—his red fez on his black head, asked, in Serbian, "How much the bread, Turko?"

At a little distance a little boy stood watching me. He was dressed in rags, but so is half of Serbia. His gaze, uninsistent, speculative, and suffering, did not leave me, so I went to him and asked him if he were hungry, at which he shook his head, settled himself closer within his rags, and slopped off, the mud clinging to his big *opankas*.

I passed him again as I turned my back on the town, its strolling soldiers, its swarming boys, its tortuous byways ankle-deep in mud, and its white minarets.

The station, like all those of Turkish towns, was distant from the city and isolated as a pesthouse, for the Turk feared and mistrusted the railway and kept the abomination as far away as he could.

No train was ready; no engine was in sight; nothing indicated the departure of the Uskub train but the groups of soldiers standing patiently in the ruin by the track, which stopped with finality near some ruins. Some were in ragged overcoats laden with equipment packs holding out their overcoats like bustles. Some were in mustard khaki—cloth bought from the English. Some in horizon blue, bought from the French—a nondescript, ragtag army, bronzed, lean, formidable, and composed of gentle, innocent men.

Time passed; the slate-colored rain fell as the little engine puffed up noisily, as though to look at us, and puffed away. Groups of people laden with bundles and boxes came down the hill. They were wet and forlorn, and gradually they filled up the station agent's room. I sat on my duffel bag; the woman from Mladnavo sat on her valise, her head in her hands, and the Turk from Mitrovitza huddled in the doorway.

The soldiers began to talk to pass the time.

"Where do you come from?"

"From Belgrade."

"On foot?"

"How else?"

"I go to Nish—"

"I have not seen my family for eight years—"

"I go to Salonique—"

A light feeling of friendship moved among us—a fresh breeze that cleansed the air, stagnant with waiting. They began to laugh. A soldier in horizon blue came up to me.

"Have you any one to carry your bags, *sestra?* No? Then I charge myself with them."

The Turk from Mitrovitza sat on his bundle and sang. The air smelled of wet clothes, of garlic, of packages of food.

The engine puffed up again; some of the soldiers climbed into the wagons. We still waited. The ragged boy I had seen in town stood on the platform. Presently he began to cry. He cried without violence, but as though the hopelessness of life had made his tears well over. The soldiers gathered around him, kind in their curiosity. "Why do you cry, *mali?*" they asked. He cried on disconsolately, without answering.

Then his story dripped out slowly, like rain falling. He raised his head and looked at the soldiers and talked without emphasis, with the manner of recounting the inevitable. There was no protest and no hope in his voice.

"He is an orphan. He has no one—he has no one at all," they reported.

The women clucked sympathetically: "Poor *mali*, poor boy!"

"He was going to Uskub to look for work, and now he has not money enough, he finds. He can get nothing to do, no place to stay in Mitrovitza."

The women rested kind eyes on him, hands went to pockets, soldiers brought out money.

"Here, *mali*—"

The boy stood looking out over the railway. He was twelve or thirteen; his grotesque rags once had been men's clothes. On his head was a battered cap. His face was brown and sharpened with hunger. His eyes were like a dog's, wistful and frightened and set far apart. The rags of his homespun coat dripped about him—his torn socks were pulled over his trousers, Serbian fashion—and on his feet were *opankas*, a sort of moccasin tied on with thongs, these, too, man's size.

He seemed so lost and so forlorn that a chill crept over us. He stood there unconscious, his gaze lost in the distance, isolated by his dirt, unattached, humble, standing a little bent, as though the weight of life were too heavy for him to bear. All at once the day was more cheerless, the station seemed the remotest place in the world. We shivered a little and moved restlessly about. We could not forget him, though he made no demands on us, did not even notice us. He did not ask our friendship or our attention, but stood there in the fading light, waiting humbly. He seemed not like a child, but a symbol of the lost children, crawling miserably over the roadways of the world, sleeping, as he had recently done, in the mud of ditches.

Our chatter flared up and died, for always our eyes went back to him and to his somber significance. I went up to him with a soldier in horizon blue who spoke French with me.

"Ask him where he comes from."

"He come from Stenia," the soldier translated. "His father fell in the first offensive. His mother died of typhus. Then he worked for a farmer for nearly three years. He was a poor man. When his son came back he could keep the boy no longer. He paid him and told him to find work in some other place. That was soon after New Year's. He has been looking for work for nearly two and a half months—they do not want such little boys."

He told his story monotonously, without emphasis, without protest, with very faint gestures of his grimy hands. He told it with a deadly air of indifferent matter-of-factness. A common tale.

I could not bear his isolation. I suffered from his loneliness.

"Please ask his name," I said, for I felt if I knew that it would save me from his seeming to be a symbol of the desolate company of children disinherited by war.

At the soldier's question, the boy turned to me.

"Milorad Bachinin," he told me.

We straggled slowly to the train. The troops entrained in the carriage. We got into a boxcar—the little group of soldiers and civilians who had made of one another the friends of an hour. We disposed ourselves on the floor; we pulled our blankets over us.

"*Sestra*, sit here. So you shall be out of the draft."

"*Sestra*, let me arrange your things. Are you comfortable so?"

"Gospodja Draga, draw up, draw up. Do not leave us for strangers!"

Laughter and talk. The bleak boxcar became an encampment and its cold walls were warmed by friendship. The boy sat down on a bale of goods; delicacy made him withdraw himself. He was so dirty that in any other country he would be a pariah, but here no one made him feel this.

The conductor came among us encamped on the floor, perched on bales, done up in Pirot rugs, or sitting on our bags.

"Who are you traveling with?" he asked Milorad.

"With the American *sestra*," he answered, without hesitation, pointing at me.

The conductor nodded. The soldier in horizon blue smiled.

"A quick lad—children are not supposed to travel alone," he explained.

We undid valises; we opened musettes and packages and began to eat our supper. Every one remembered Milorad.

"An egg, *mali?*"

"Bread, *mali?*"

"A bit of meat, *mali?*"

He ate hungrily, smiling at me across the others, searching my eyes at each gift of food, as though to say, "I have an egg, *sestra*—bread." He must share these happinesses with me.

The night wore on. We had long since lighted our candles, and they made long shadows.

Milorad sat always on the bale of goods, isolated by misfortune. He sat relaxed, his dark eyes fixed on nothing, a forlorn picture of the fatherless. I turned away my head, and then I was conscious that he was looking at me, and we smiled across the others' heads.

"What will become of him?" asked Gospodja Draga. She asked it impersonally of the world of Serbia, of America. "What will become of Milorad Bachinin? If he were a little older—but twelve and not strong—there is little enough work now." He sat disturbingly quiet and mutely asked all of us, "What will become of Milorad Bachinin?" Will he go on from town to town, asking for work at doorways, cold, hungry, more and more beaten, more and more despairing? The train rattled on in its slow progress.

"What—will—become—of—Milorad Bachinin?"

"If I had him in Mladnova," said the soldier in horizon blue, "I would give him a home." He was dark and swift of motion, eager toward life, eager to help, eager to talk. Love of life and of laughter shone from him. "I have a little commerce in Mladnova. A store—that boy would help."

"A great help—a good thing for you," they answered.

"But how to get him back from Uskub?"

"Yes, how?" they agreed, with resignation.

"I may have to walk from Metrovitza—two hundred kilometers. He could never walk so far, poor boy!"

The night wore on. Some slept in abandoned attitudes at the other end of the car. Some soldiers drank too much and sang monotonously and noisily.

Milorad sat there, a hunched, grotesque figure, bobbing with fatigue; his shadow waggled about with monstrous levity in the candlelight. Suddenly I had to know what would become of Milorad Bachinin.

"Is it true?" I asked the soldier, softly, for Gospodja Draga slept. "Will you really take him?"

"If I could bring him back," he assured me. From Mitrovita there is no railway. The back of Serbia is broken and no railway joins the north and south, so those going to Belgrade must walk or get taken by chance camions.

"I'll see you get taken by camion, the Red Cross or the English," I promised.

"Then it's settled. I take the lad." He smiled at him.

"Will you go with him?" I asked Milorad. He looked at the soldier gravely.

"I will go," he answered, but without a smile, his eyes on me.

The floor of the car became littered with people lying in the awkward abandon of sleep, as though slain on the battlefield of fatigue. The hoarse shouting of the guards brought us startled to our feet. We had arrived. We reeled out under our burdens on our unsteady feet, walking along like people hypnotized, sleepwalkers. My soldier in horizon blue carried my things.

"How shall the boy find you?" I asked.

"We'll find each other," he said, with his easy assurance. "We'll meet on the streets. Every one goes up and down the main street in Uskub."

"And does he understand where to find me?" I asked him.

He turned to Milorad. The boy looked at me very earnestly, a long look, as though he were trying to make up for his lack of words, and made his reply with his grave eyes always fixed on me. And then the station which had sucked us into its dim interior spewed us forth onto the dark streets.

I expected that he would be there waiting for me the next morning, but the street was empty of him. I thought somehow that he would find me and that he would be anxious about himself, about his clothes, for I had promised him new ones, and as to whether I had gotten transportation for him. Then I went out, down through the main street of Uskub.

There were shops where Albanians sold curded milk; shops with round Turkish bread, Greeks selling sweets that looked like poison—candy of bright green, candy of cerise. Yet the Turkish children eat them without dying. And farther, threading the crowd, are the closely veiled Turkish women, swathed in black robes; red-fezed bootblacks clamored impudently; donkeys and buffalo carts, and the Yugoslav soldiers—volunteers from America—in their neat blue uniforms. Through the shifting pattern of Turk and Christian, of Serb and Albanian, through all the multicolored rags that clad them, I searched for Milorad.

He had disappeared, and so had all the company of the night before. The soldier had gone and the woman from Mladnavo; they had gone, nor could I find one of them, although all day my eyes sought through the shifting tide of people which eddies and breaks perpetually over the bridge.

The town was empty to me and full of fear. What would become of Milorad Bachinin was my business, nor would the thought of him leave me as I went about my work in storehouse and hospital. Always my eyes sought through the crowds for his dumpy figure clad in unclean rags, and vague fears hunted through my mind. I looked for him perpetually in that little shuffling group of misery that waited, wanly hopeful, before the Red Cross headquarters.

Next morning my eyes sought for the thousandth time the group of faithful little boys perpetually waiting against the high yellow wall opposite. He was standing there, drawn apart from them, leaning against the wall, which was something adversity had taught him when it taught him that boys are cruel to misfortune. His somber eyes were fixed on the door.

I saw him before he saw me, as he stood there in an attitude of terrible patience; his arms were crossed on his breast. One could see how weary he was. He had perhaps slept all night outside the station gate and got up to wait when the first ox cart creaked up with its load. Then he saw me and came flashing toward me; his clumsy coverings could not hide his swift beauty. The joy he felt, the darting swiftness of his lithe young body triumphed. His flight to me was like a leaping, happy animal.

"*Sestra!*"

"Where did you sleep, Milorad?"

"In a *cafana.*"

"Have you eaten?"

He nodded, his eyes still on me.

"Your soldier—have you found him?"

He shook his head and spread out his hands. He had never trusted this promise; now he relinquished it with the fatality of the abandoned. My Serbian had run its short course. I called to one of our English-speaking soldiers.

"Explain this paper to him," I said. "There is a letter to the English military at Mitrovitza and one to the Americans. He is to go in the first camion of ours that comes through with his *voynik.*"

Milorad nodded, folded the paper, and hid it carefully among his rags.

"He is to watch continually for his soldier." He nodded again. "This afternoon he is to come here and go with me for fresh clothes, to the Red Cross storehouse, and he is to go with me now to town."

I was leaving before light next day for Salonika, and I wished him to have something for the journey.

"*Sestra,* he says he would like to know your name," the soldier told me. Milorad repeated it carefully, as though committing to memory something precious.

He looked up at me. "My sister—*moya sestra!*" he said, and then my name. What love there was in that voice! Then we went along, Milorad repeating to himself, over and over my first name, which was all he could remember, and then, "*Sestra—sestra—sestra,*" like a song, the most caressing song in the world. It came from the center of the heart of love. He was singing it to me, so unconscious that he didn't even know that his happy lips were busy with this song of his. Some time I listened to him, while the spectacle of Uskub—its soldiers, its beggars, its Albanians, and Turks—flowed before my eyes, as though hastening to some incredible masquerade.

I changed my French money in the shop of an old Jew who had in his window gold from every land; rubles and sovereigns, Turkish coins I didn't know, and golden louis. And when I would have given Milorad this money, he held his hand up in a gesture faint, imploring, deprecating.

"Not money—not from you, my sister—only love—forget I am a beggar," the little gesture said; it was faint, protesting, lovely. He who needed all things could bear to take from me only the things of the spirit. He wished me not to think that he was a beggar.

We had a wordless battle of coaxings, of smiles, and since he could not say no to something I wished, he took it, still with his deprecating protest, and then gently, almost as with reverence, he took my hand in his and pressed it to his brown cheek.

He looked up at me and love streamed from his eyes, and the radiance of it transfigured him. He was so happy that he walked along in a sort of quiet ecstasy. He was so happy that it hurt me to look at him.

He had never wanted, he had never suffered, he had never hungered, he had never been unhappy. We exchanged swift looks full of mutual understanding. We laughed together over the droll things in the street, and wondered over the width of the river and the vastness of the town, the height of the minarets pointing their white fingers to heaven, for Milorad had never been happy before.

What had happened? Why were we so happy in walking down together through the harlequin crowd in Uskub streets?

I had not the answer; it came to me only with tears. Now I was happy, and my happiness had no name and no reason. I was happy with a deep content; drinking in the warmth and loveliness of the moment, not looking forward with the fear of tomorrow, with even knowledge of tomorrow cast out.

I record this as the high moment, higher even than when we got his clothes at the Red Cross storeroom, walking proudly ahead of the crowd waiting for distribution.

I was so happy that I forgot during all that afternoon that I must say good-bye to him that night. And then, as I called a soldier to interpret for me, it came to me as a frightful and unbelievable fact.

"Tell him that I am to go tomorrow to Salonika," I said, "and he must look for his soldier. If his soldier doesn't come, he shall stay here with the American mission."

In answer to this he had something to say. Putting his hand upon the soldier's arm, he talked to him with eager confidence. I saw pity growing in the soldier's face.

"He says it is better that he shall go with you. He says he is sure his *voynik* with not come. He says he wishes to go with his *sestra*."

A numbness came over me. What could I say to him? How could I explain? What use to tell him that I was reporting at Salonika for orders, that I might be sent to Rumania or Greece, that all this was out of my hands. I knew he would not understand, for all places were equally near and equally distant to him. He knew nothing about orders, or passports, or the thousand restrictions. He was talking again eagerly.

"He says many boys like himself have been sent to foreign countries. He says let him go with you. He will work for you. He says it is better for *you* that he goes with you!"

And I—I could do nothing but take him by the shoulders and speak to him in English and kiss him and explain again through my soldier that he must try to find the man who might take him to his home, and that the people in the Red Cross would look out for him if he did not go.

I was still stupefied with sleep when I left my home next morning. The city wore the livid face of dawn, when coming life and the approach of death have so close a resemblance. The same damp wind cut our faces that had greeted us when we arrived. The weary men and women who trickled down the street walked like somnambulists. Some drove animals which staggered as though laden with fatigue. Rain fell in a light drizzle.

We drew up to the station, and from the dusk came Milorad's swift figure. Had he waited all night? I do not know. I only know that my heart expected him. He ran to me smiling, and yet tense with anxiety. I knew what was in his mind. I knew that he thought I could not leave him since he could not leave me.

"Ask him if he has looked for his *voynik*," I asked the officer with me.

Again Milorad made that faint gesture of his—of relinquishment, of negation. He had never expected his *voynik*. He had always known that this home was illusion. He began helping the soldiers with my bags and bundles, plodding ahead, the drizzle of rain crusting his new coat in minute drops.

He clasped my hand and put it to his cheek with that lovely gesture of his as he said to me, "*Sestra, sestra!*" but I knew that my name meant, "Take me with you; I cannot leave you." He turned to the officer with me and spoke in a low voice rapidly, insistently.

"He says to let him go. He says it is better so. Do not go without him."

"Explain to him—make him understand how it is. Make him see that I'm not deserting him."

The officer talked to him earnestly, but Milorad looked only at me. Then, as our eyes held each other's, suddenly I understood both our joy and our pain. Suddenly I knew what miracle had happened to us.

I knew when he had looked at me first he had accepted me for his mother. He did not know this. He had no name for it. He had loved me when he first met me. All his being had gone out to me. Now I knew why I was so happy when we walked down Uskub streets together. We had recognized each other in the wide spaces of the world.

"Mother!" his heart had cried.

"Son!" mine had answered.

"Mother! Mother! Mother!" he had sung.

I had listened with the silent shining happiness that can never come from the song of a lover.

"I have needed you so, mother."

"I have loved you so, son."

"Mother, I looked for you in every face."

"Son, disguised in your rags, I knew you, and my heart leaped at sight of you."

We were strangers, and we did not speak each other's language, but the spiritual bond of mother and son was ours. Not a very good mother—not watchful enough, not patient enough; Milorad a boy on whom adversity had put its cramping hand, with no high courage, nor with the promise of much high endeavor—but to him the love of my heart flowed out, and in my heart were the things Milorad had found in none of the compassionate women of his own land. I loved him not for his goodness, but for his need of me, and because I must.

Now there came to him slowly the bitter knowledge that I, his mother, was leaving him to loneliness and misery. His pain welled over in tears, his sobs racked him and left him gasping. I have never seen a child feel such grief as that which bankrupted Milorad of hope. He had not believed I could go. He came to me and pleaded with me, his words rushing out in the torrent of his tears.

I did not need to know what he said; he was emptying his heart. He threw the treasure of his love before me, and his belief and his pain. People came up to comfort him. Then among the crowd came the woman from Mladnavo.

"Has his soldier not come?" she asked. "Then as I come up next week from Salonika he may come with me. Will you come with me, *mali?*"

He did not hear her; his eyes sought mine in the agony of his loss which shut out all other things. Slow tears came to the woman's eyes.

"I will be kind to him, *sestra*," she promised.

"Listen, Milorad," I said. "Gospodja Draga will come for you next week."

He only knew I spoke to him. He only answered: "Take me with you."

The train moved. I could no longer see his face for my own tears.

He is safe; he does not walk the highways of the earth, nor sleep in ditches. He is not chased, hungry, from door to door. The woman from Mladnavo is good to him—but she is not his mother. Once by chance he encountered her; he knew her, he loved her; and for a happy moment our love flowed together. But when I look out over the implacable silence that divides us, I wonder if it would not have been better if we had not met. At night when I tuck my children in—my children, so safe, so secure—my children who have never had to weep for me, I wonder where you are, Milorad. I bless you, and I imagine you saying *"Sestra"* in your sleep.

# Why I Have Failed as a Mother
## *Cosmopolitan, 1924*

A friend of mine summed up my life. He said:

"You have failed in the two main objects for which you've lived. You have failed in bringing up your children. You've failed in your work."

"What's the matter with my children? They love me, don't they?" I challenged.

"You've no discipline. You can't even keep them out of your room when you're working. Do you suppose there's a man who would stand for that? You're blind if you can't see they hate your work."

This brought me up short. It threw a searchlight on what had been happening between my children and me. I realized with what intensity one of my children hated my work. All her life nurses and relatives had said to her: "You can't see your mother, she's working!" Now she was old enough to assume some household authority she had an excuse for interrupting me for everything and nothing. Nor could anything I said or did stop her.

I hadn't understood it. I hadn't seen she was revenging herself on the past when she wanted her mother.

It was her profound unconscious revolt against the hated writing which had kept her from me when she needed me all her life and I hadn't understood. She had come into her own and showed her fierce resentment against the thwarting of her inalienable right to bring her hurts and troubles to her mother.

Because I was so hurt, I threw defiantly at my friend: "I've earned their living anyway."

"Oh yes, you've earned their living!" my friend agreed, "but you've never done the best work of which you were capable, as a man would have insisted on doing."

I could agree with him about my work. The world could have Swagged along without my books.

My story wouldn't be important if it were the story of one woman. My failure is that of almost every working woman who has children and a home to keep up, whether she scrubs floors, or works in mills, or is a high-priced professional woman. It's nearly impossible to do both jobs well. So most women fail in either or both. Their energy and thoughts are divided.

Behind the great men whose names have starred history there is almost always a mother who gave herself without stint to educating her son. Not in "book learning," but in drawing out from him the genius that was there. Such women never have for their unwritten epitaphs "Failure." I couldn't give myself without stint to my children. I was an absentee mother, away long hours behind closed doors.

My ten-year-old showed how much he felt this by saying: "Wouldn't it be fine if you didn't have to work! I wish you could do the cooking like the other mothers around here and we kids could help you."

He felt shut out too. He missed something the other children he knew were getting. His mother wasn't accessible, sure to be around the house ready to do anything from tying up a cut finger to answering a question.

My oldest son has a different attitude toward my work—I thought. I remember how he use to come into a room where I was writing, put his finger on his lips and tiptoe out. He seemed to accept writing as a matter of course. He never interrupted me. It was not until he was a big boy that I found out there was a hole in his life I could never repair. He had always wanted what he called "a regular ma." He too had looked with passionate envy on boys whose mothers heard their lessons and shook them out of their lazy spells. He wanted a mother who was *there*, while I was often gutted by fatigue, my thoughts forever on my work.

These things flashed through my mind with terrible corroboration when my friend said: "*You've failed as a mother!*"

I knew far more than he did how much my failure was my own fault. He thought that a woman couldn't do two jobs and that I and the children were caught in a net of circumstance, since I had to support them. I had other guilty knowledge.

I've always told myself that I began writing because I wanted to earn money so my husband would have more time for his own stories. Later, life said to me, "Earn your children's living." Life says to some women "Scrub!" "Go to the factory!" To others life dictates "Take an office job!" "Go into business if you want your children to be educated." And women flock out of their homes. They have to. Most of us are failures as mothers, so this is no "back to the home" story. There would too often be no home if women didn't go out to work.

There is another phase to my writing that no one knows but myself. I grew ambitious. Writing "got" me.

I wanted to do good work for its own sake.

From that moment I was lost. I had fallen in love. I had surrendered myself to something outside of myself. There could be no more comfortable days when I could think that I was writing only because this was an honorable way of supporting my children. *From that time I wouldn't have stopped if I could.*

Maybe my failure began then. I know very well from that moment I found plausible reasons for leaving home to do work. The truth was I lusted for new experiences and new forms of work. Now, instead of merely being absent behind closed doors, I was really away. And I liked being away. The relentless details which all women must meet if they would see their houses run well slipped from me like a burden.

Since then I have kept on finding excuses which made me leave the children and which would give me the most material and the best chance to write. We can always find noble reasons for what we want to do. Yet I am a woman who likes the affairs of the house. I am never at war with it, except when it interferes with my work and so interferes with its own existence, since without money I could have no house.

I know I needed to go away as much as I know my children needed me home. It sounds like a paradox to say I found peace in constant traveling which I hadn't known in my quiet house because at home there was a never-ending conflict between my two jobs.

I had been faithful to my house and its demands so many years. Don't housewives deserve a sabbatical year? I am sure that all women with imagination, however much they care for their families, however content they are with their work, turn longing eyes to the road that leads to new places. They crave the experience of adventure as much as men.

I remember a woman I knew very well. She had spent the greater part of her life on a farm four miles from the village. For years she had superintended the work on the farm herself. No one ever heard a complaint from her lips. Yet when she died her private desk was found full of cuttings. There were reproductions of pictures she never could hope to see, cuts of strange foreign cities she could never hope to visit, newspaper accounts of great foreign demonstrations, and of first nights and operas which she never could have hoped to have attended.

While she walked across her fields looking for the nests of turkeys which had strayed from the barnyard, while she was arranging for the planting of winter wheat, the eyes of her spirit had been turning to foreign lands. Her eyes and her ears had searched for beauty which forever was to be denied her. This is no unusual case. What one person wants, hundreds and thousands of others want also.

I am not satisfied with my sabbatical year. I am deeply impatient, almost for the first time, at the interruptions which my children naturally make. I am as indignant at an interruption, now that I have known what it is to be uninterrupted, as a man would be if his work were held in light esteem. I have felt as men must feel when they know that their wives are sitting waiting to welcome them affectionately. I don't even want the affection of my children when I'm through work. All I want is to be let alone. I often dread to leave my workroom to meet their never-ceasing demands. They seem to me like a nestful of birds, their yellow beaks forever agape for me to fill.

Is there any mother who wouldn't escape from the relentless persistence of her children for a while if she could?

One thing all women want—love, a home, children. They may find a terrible conflict between this basic need and the passionate desire for independence. Who will make the adjustment? Women are going to go on working. They have to. They want to. I know I would go on working whether I needed to or not. I have never wanted to write as much as I do now.

On the other hand I have never realized my children's needs so clearly and have never wanted so much to fill them. Are the two things possible? Must there always be a double failure?

## DUE DATE

Printed
in USA